The Dynamics of Industrial Conflict

LESSONS FROM FORD

HENRY FRIEDMAN
and SANDER MEREDEEN

CROOM HELM LONDON

British Library Cataloguing in Publication Data

Friedman, Henry
    The dynamics of industrial conflict.
    1. Strikes and lockouts — Automobile industry —
    England — Dagenham 2. Ford Motor Company — History
    I. Title II. Meredeen, Sander
    331.89'282'9206542175 HD5366.A82 1968.D3

    ISBN 0-85664-982-1
    ISBN 0-7099-0374-X Pbk

For Esther, my mother — and in memory of
Abraham David, my father.

Sander Meredeen

For my friends, the rank-and-file
activists at Ford and in the labour movement.

Henry Friedman

Printed and bound in Great Britain

CONTENTS

ABBREVIATIONS

ACAS	Advisory Conciliation and Arbitration Service
AEF	Amalgamated Union of Engineering and Foundryworkers
AEU	Amalgamated Engineering Union
AUEW	Amalgamated Union of Engineering Workers
BALPA	British Air Line Pilots Association
CBI	Confederation of British Industry
CIR	Commission on Industrial Relations
CP	Communist Party
CPRS	Central Policy Review Staff
CSEU	Confederation of Shipbuilding and Engineering Unions (Confed.)
DE(P)	Department of Employment (and Productivity)
EETPU	Electrical Electronic Telecommunication and Plumbing Union
EOC	Equal Opportunities Commission
ETU	Electrical Trades Union
FMC Ltd	Ford Motor Company Limited
FOB	Ford of Britain
FOE	Ford of Europe
GMWU	General and Municipal Workers Union
IMF	International Metalworkers' Federation
ILO	International Labour Organisation
IR	Industrial Relations
JNC	Joint Negotiating Committee
JWC	Joint Works Committee
MIIRP	Motor Industry Industrial Relations Panel
MIJLC	Motor Industry Joint Labour Council
NBPI	National Board for Prices and Incomes
NJACCWER	National Joint Action Campaign Committee for Women's Equal Rights
NJNC	National Joint Negotiating Committee
NUVB	National Union of Vehicle Builders
PRC	Profile Review Committee
PTA	Paint, Trim and Assembly Plant
TGWU	Transport and General Workers Union
TUC	Trades Union Congress
UAW	United Auto Workers Union (of US)
UOP	Urwick Orr and Partners

ACKNOWLEDGEMENTS

This book owes its origin to the fact that the authors were once both employed by the Ford Motor Company Limited. It was through their experience of working for Ford and their personal involvement in its industrial relations over many years that they felt able to embark upon writing the book. Their first debt is, therefore, to former comrades and friends with whom they worked and suffered and amongst whom they both learned some of the more important lessons of managing industrial conflict and co-operation. Henry Friedman is particularly indebted to Fred Blake, Rosie Boland, Lil O'Callaghan, Bernie Passingham and Les Moore; Sander Meredeen, for his part, to Bob Ramsey, Paul Roots, Oscar DeVille, Ron Webster and Barry Welch.

The writing of this, their first book, preoccupied the authors for more than two years — during which time they inflicted a disproportionate share of their creative frustrations on the members of their respective households. They here express inadequate thanks for the tolerance and good humour shown by Alma Friedman and by Sue, Jon, Adam and Rachel Baynes.

Because of the structure of the book and the unusual way it was written, the text passed through a number of critical transformations. For their skilful transcription of sometimes inaudible tapes and often messy manuscripts — and for their coolness under stress — our thanks are due to Beryl Willis, Carol Snape and Noelle Finney.

Finally, we must express our sincere thanks and appreciation to our academic colleagues — to Professor John T. Dunlop who, in October 1968, first invited Sander Meredeen to talk to his graduate students at Harvard about the Ford Sewing Machinists' strike; to Professors Ben Roberts and Basil Yamey at LSE who, in May 1976, encouraged him to write about the experience of Ford's industrial relations; to our students from whom, as always, we continue to learn as much as we ever teach them; and, in particular, to those of our colleagues and friends who kindly read the typescript and who offered so much encouragement and constructive advice — Stanley Alderson, Ted Benton, Michael Mann, Daniel Vulliamy and David Winchester.

For the views we express — and for any errors of fact which may have escaped our detection — we alone are responsible.

INTRODUCTION

Why do workers go on strike? What does it feel like to take part in your first stoppage of work? What can a foreman or manager do to prevent that strike from taking place? And, once it has begun, what steps can management take to contain the conflict and stop the strike from spreading? How do Shop Stewards organise a major strike? When does it reach its climax, and who makes the first moves to secure a return to work? When should management stand firm on a matter of principle and when should it make concessions? Why do some companies enjoy good industrial relations whilst others have an international reputation for militancy and strike-proneness? What lessons do workers and Shop Stewards, foremen and managers, learn from their own experience of victory and defeat in industrial conflict? How far can those lessons be learned, without cost, from the bitter experience of others? And when should the state step in to protect 'the national interest'?

To provide some of the answers to these questions the authors of this study focus on the dynamics of industrial conflict in the British motor industry. They have each drawn on some thirty years' experience of industrial relations, to describe, analyse and explain the unique structure and character of industrial conflict in British industry. They are concerned, above all, to provide an insight into the concealed 'learning process' which goes on continuously below the surface of every system of industrial relations. For, like history itself, industrial relations are part of the mainstream of human endeavour, now checked by conflict, now impelled by co-operation, not just in Britain but in every advanced and emerging industrial society in the world. It is the 'learning process' in industrial conflict and co-operation which helps to shape the system of industrial relations within a factory, an organisation, an industry or a nation. That 'learning process' is itself shaped by certain key events of special significance — and it was such an event which provides the point of departure for this study.

On the afternoon of Tuesday 28 May 1968, all 187 women employed as Sewing Machinists at the Ford Motor Company's River Plant at Dagenham in Essex stopped work in protest against their job grading and pay. On the following morning they failed to report for work and instead spent the day — Derby Day — at the races. History does not record whether they placed any bets or won any money on Epsom Downs that afternoon. But one thing is certain: by their simple protest strike on 29 May 1968 and their determined action over the weeks that followed, these few women won themselves an honoured place in labour history by securing equal pay for the women of Britain. More than that – they helped to shape the future course of British industrial relations.

The Ford Sewing Machinists' strike was a landmark in the evolution of industrial relations at Ford and in the history of industrial conflict in Britain. From small beginnings, it became the biggest and most important strike by a group of British women since the Bryant and May Matchgirls' strike in 1888.

The *internal* consequences of the dispute for management and unions at Ford were both immediate and long lasting: after a decade of setbacks and defeats, the rank-and-file leadership drew inspiration and renewed strength from a successful campaign, waged against the combined forces of Ford management and most of the Ford Unions. Within ten years of the dispute, many of those rank-and-file leaders were sitting as full members of the NJNC – the joint negotiating body whose decisions they fought throughout the dispute. Management, in turn, was forced to take steps to meet a powerful threat: the novel combination of shop-floor militants and the newly elected left-wing leadership of two major Unions. The dispute compelled the Company finally to come to terms with the shop floor.

The *external* consequences of the dispute were no less far reaching. *First,* the strike led directly to the passing of the Equal Pay Act 1970 and so contributed indirectly to the Sex Discrimination Act 1975 and the Employment Protection Act 1975. *Second,* the strike coincided with the publication of the Report of the Donovan Commission, set up to inquire into trade unions and employers' associations. It thus effectively focused public attention on the need to 'do something about Britain's industrial relations'. Following the Sewing Machinists' dispute, Barbara Castle, Secretary of State for Employment, and Prime Minister Harold Wilson produced their controversial White Paper *In Place of Strife* and then the Labour Relations Bill 1969 – acts of political ineptitude which sealed the fate of the first Wilson Government and prepared the way for the Conservative Government's Industrial Relations Act 1971. *Third* – and arguably the most important outcome – the strike exerted a major influence on the development of the women's movement in Britain – an influence the full effects of which may not be felt until the 1980s.

The present study, based on the Ford Sewing Machinist's strike, derives from the conjunction of a long-standing need and an unexpected opportunity. The *need* arises from the general lack of detailed documentation and critical analysis of industrial conflict in Britain in the postwar period. The assertion that industrial relations are the Achilles heel of the British economy and the chief threat to its industrial survival has become a self-fulfilled prophecy. But when serious students of British industrial relations – Members of Parliament and Ministers, their political advisers and civil servants, social and political commentators, editors and journalists, students and teachers, as well as mere laymen and women – seek to subject that Achilles heel to closer examination, they discover a dearth of informed and critical writing which deals with the more important strikes, lock-outs, factory occupations and pickets which together make up so much of the reported texture of British industrial relations.

This dearth of useful analysis is not difficult to explain: for who is there qualified to produce it? Who has direct access to the relevant information? Who knows enough about the background of a particular dispute and its complex development and is still able to distance himself sufficiently from it to provide a coherent and balanced account? Those professionally engaged in industrial relations – both managers and union officials – are for the most part preoccupied with 'fire fighting'. Journalists and editors are more concerned to capture the dramatic than the analytic aspects of an important dispute. Academic writers on industrial relations are too often desk-bound analysts or hardened ideologues, strong on theory but lacking direct experience of industrial conflict, of what it feels like to be on the inside of a major dispute – of the competing pressures which constrain the actors as they seek to resolve their differences. Experience is clearly a necessary condition but not sufficient by itself for critical but constructive analysis – otherwise, in Frederick of Prussia's immortal words, an army mule might well be promoted to Field Marshal. A general medical practitioner, for example, need not have suffered a heart attack or experienced clinical depression in order to diagnose the symptoms or effectively prescribe for them. On the other hand, it is difficult to imagine a useful textbook on these conditions by a physician who lacked extensive first-hand experience of treating them.

In the field of industrial relations, the situation is quite different. There is now a substantial body of literature by authors with no practical experience of coping with the day-to-day realities of industrial conflict in Britain. Many academic social scientists feel a profound distaste towards engaging in anything but the most vicarious form of wealth creation – as if industrial or commercial work denatured a candidate for academic work rather than offering one of the best qualifications for it. The parenthetical plea made here is for more students of industrial relations, and aspiring academics in particular, to go down and work on the shop floor, to become Shop Stewards or Personnel Officers, or simply to work at the machines or on the assembly lines – in short, to gain some first-hand experience of industrial work before plunging into print on the strength of some limited participant observation or, more phoney still, on the effervescent strength derived from drinking too much beer with an unrepresentative sample of activists at a pub too distant from the workplace.

Through thirty post-war years, a succession of private and official reports have caricatured British industrial relations, attacking workers and Shop Stewards, trade unions and employers' associations, castigating the TUC, then the CBI and finally the government itself for failing to 'do something' to control the unions and reform our system of industrial relations. In all these reports, lip service is invariably paid to the need for more industrial relations training. To be fair, some important and influential courses have been provided – notably by Ruskin College, Oxford, by a few university Departments of Industrial Relations, by the Regional Management Centres of the major polytechnics, by the Open University, the Workers' Education Association and the BBC. But the achievement continues to lag far behind the need.

As recently as 1975, the National Economic Development Office published a Report on Industrial Relations Management Training,[1] which recommended the establishment of a national Industrial Relations Training Resource Centre – to help identify management's industrial relations training needs on the one hand and to evaluate and improve the quality of management training courses on the other. The new Centre, based at Ashridge Management College, has made a promising start but, like other training centres, it has to overcome many problems. One of the principal deficiencies in any industrial relations training is the lack of first-class teaching materials. Another is the lack of seasoned managers and Trade Union Officials, able and willing to work as teachers in a field in which first-hand experience is essential. As already suggested, those engaged as practitioners in industrial relations are rarely qualified or motivated to write about or teach the subject which they practise.

What needs to be done depends, *first,* on one's perception of the discrete events which go to make up British industrial relations; *second,* on one's interpretation of those events within the long-term pattern of industrial conflict; and *finally,* on one's vision of the kind of society one would like to build. So what needs to be done first? In the authors' view there is an immediate need for a more carefully researched and detailed retrospective analysis of major outbreaks of industrial conflict in Britain. Such critical analysis is an essential prerequisite for those who seek to understand the past, to cope with the present and to prepare for the future of our industrial society. That analysis would yield material from which we should be able to develop better courses for the education and training of Industrial Relations Managers, Trade Union Officials, policy makers and administrators, teachers and students. In short, it would make a positive contribution to the training of all those who are called upon to make decisions and exercise judgement in industrial relations, as well as all those who cast their votes to secure the more productive and equitable democracy we all profess to want. This study is offered as a modest contribution towards meeting the need for such critical analysis.

It is intended, however, as something more than just another case study of conflict within the British system of industrial relations. The Sewing Machinists' strike is placed, *first,* in the specific context of an evolving system of corporate industrial relations and, *second*, in the wider context of a fast-changing industrial society, of which the motor manufacturing industry represents one of the most conflict-ridden sectors. The study examines the causes and character of conflict in that industry and seeks to explain that conflict within the peculiar structure of the British system of industrial relations.

The study focuses on the 'learning process' which takes place amongst the actors who engage in the conflicting and co-operative exchanges of one company's industrial relations system. It seeks to show how a previously deferential group of women workers experience an 'explosion of collective consciousness', throwing themselves into a militant ideological struggle; how the more experienced Shop Stewards harness that militancy and use it for both instrumental and political ends; how the top management of a multinational corporation develops its strategies and adapts its tactics to cope with shop-floor pressures in an attempt to contain the 'perpetual chaos' of industrial relations in the British motor industry; and how the state intervenes to secure the 'neutral' settlement of a major dispute, seeking to safeguard 'the national interest' between the entrenched forces of advanced capitalism and organised labour. By concentrating on the *dynamic* processes of industrial conflict, the authors seek to show how far the different groups of actors make sense of their experience of conflict, extracting and utilising the relevant lessons in their subsequent conduct of industrial relations.

The *opportunity* to undertake this study arose from a chance meeting, after an interval of several years, between two of the principal actors in the Sewing Machinists' strike – the former Convener of the Dagenham River Plant, who led the women out on strike and who was responsible for the conduct of the dispute on the union side; and the former Manager, Hourly Personnel Policies, a member of Ford's Central Industrial Relations Staff, whose initial refusal to meet the women's demand for up-grading triggered the one-day protest strike on 29 May 1968 and led to the subsequent three-week stoppage of work. The authors of this study are those two principal actors in the dispute, both now engaged in university teaching and research in industrial relations. They met in the summer of 1977 and agreed to collaborate in producing what is believed to be the first joint retrospective analysis of a major British strike, written from the inside by two of the chief protagonists involved. The events and the emotions of the dispute are recollected and discussed in academic tranquillity, far removed from the fret and strife of Dagenham and the passion for equality which originally inspired and finally obsessed both sides engaged in the dispute.

In view of the unusual structure of the book, some explanation may be useful about the methodological assumptions underlying the study. It soon became clear, in the early days of their collaboration, that the authors could not hope to produce a jointly written account of events which are essentially political. As John Dunlop, the father of the academic study of industrial relations, has observed, the entire subject matter of industrial relations stands at the crossroads of many disciplines: history, law, economics, psychology, sociology and so on – all of which are inevitably value-laden. How were the authors to bring together their contrasted perceptions and interpretations of events they supposedly experienced in common? At this point the distinctive pattern of the book began to emerge: *first,* to present two separate accounts of the dispute, as perceived by each of the authors, adopting the now familiar social action approach – that is, accounts of events as seen through the different frames of reference of the actors themselves; *second,* to confront these two accounts in a way which would offer a deeper analysis than either of the authors could provide on his own. It was therefore agreed that, like two retired Generals, the authors would meet again on the field of battle, to relive the conflict, without the sound of gunfire, in the hope of achieving a better understanding of the events portrayed in the two narratives.

But no industrial dispute stands in isolation of the events that precede and follow it. However faithfully and dramatically the events of one dispute are presented, its real significance can only be understood in terms of a set of evolving relationships, the complexities of which must be honoured. This was particularly true of the Sewing Machinists' strike, which occupies a special place in the evolution of industrial relations at Ford. It was therefore necessary to provide an outline of that evolution, before dealing with the dispute itself, and then to show the consequences that flowed from it.

Part I sets the scene for the dispute. It provides two contrasting accounts of *The Evolution of Industrial Relations at Ford* — from the arrival of the first Model T on the roads of Britain, just after the turn of the century, down to the Wage Structure Review of 1966 which indirectly precipitated the strike. Chapter 1 presents *A Management View* of those events as seen from Ford Central Office and Chapter 2 *A Shop-Floor View* as seen from Dagenham.

Part II offers two accounts of *The Dispute* itself. Chapter 3 describes *The Dispute Seen Through Management's Eyes.* Chapter 4 offers a very different view of *The Dispute Seen Through Shop Steward's Eyes.*

Parts I and II were planned and drafted independently, without much prior consultation between the authors. Once the first two parts had been drafted, it was decided to confront the two accounts of the dispute, to identify the more important areas of disagreement and to seek to resolve them wherever possible.

Part III takes the form of a *First Dialogue* between the authors, in which they discuss their respective accounts of the strike. The material contained in Chapter 5 — *The Dispute Analysed* — was recorded soon after the authors had exchanged the first drafts of their early chapters. It attempts to elucidate some of the lessons of hindsight which emerge from Parts I and II.

Part IV picks up the narrative thread with two separate accounts of *The Internal Consequences of the Dispute* as they influenced the future conduct of industrial relations at Ford. Chapter 6 presents *A Management View* and Chapter 7 *A Shop-Floor View.*

Part V seeks to show the more important *External Consequences of the Dispute,* its effect on the women's movement and its influence on legislation in the field of sex discrimination in Britain. Since the external consequences are less open to partisan interpretation, the authors decided to present *A Joint View* of them in Chapter 8.

By September 1978, when Parts I to V of this study had already been drafted, Ford once more became the focus of an intense national debate about Britain's industrial relations. Nobody can be left in any doubt, after the nine-week strike at Ford over 'free collective bargaining' and the subsequent battle with the government over its attempts to impose economic sanctions against the Company for breaching the 5 per cent pay guidelines, that frequently, in the evolution of Britain's industrial relations, 'Ford leads the way'. Some commentators have argued that the Ford strike and its repercussions led directly to the widespread industrial dislocations during the winter of 1978/9 and so contributed to the fall of the Labour Government in the General Election of 3 May 1979 and the Conservative Government's decision to introduce fresh industrial relations legislation. Be that as it may, the authors decided that the 1978 Ford strike was sufficiently important to justify its inclusion as the concluding episode of the study.

Part VI takes the form of a *Second Dialogue*, in which the 1978 strike is considered within the context of the more theoretical themes of the study, in order to bring out *The Learning Process in Industrial Conflict*, discussed in Chapter 9. This dialogue prepares the way for the jointly written *Conclusions*.

In the course of this study the authors have referred to the passion for equality which inspired both sides during the Sewing Machinists' strike. But in setting out to write their study, the authors have put aside that other passion which seems to obsess so many students and teachers of history and the other social sciences. We make no ritual genuflections at the altar of that elusive and abstract goddess, Objectivity. On the contrary: we freely acknowledge our respective prejudices and bias. In undertaking the research and writing for this book, we have been conscious of both the explicit and the implied conflict between our respective frames of reference in recording and interpreting events and the parts we played in them. Nor are we surprised at our inability to eliminate those prejudices — even after the passage of ten years. For in the field of industrial conflict — as in all other fields of human conflict — whoever seeks the truth must first declare his own truth. That is what we have tried to do here. Our readers will decide how far we have been successful.

Note

1. National Economic Development Council, *Management Training in Industrial Relations* (NEDO, London, 1975).

Part I

THE EVOLUTION OF
INDUSTRIAL RELATIONS AT FORD

1   A MANAGEMENT VIEW

When the turbulent history of Britain's post-war industrial relations comes to be written, the Ford Motor Company will occupy a special place and present a powerful paradox. Over the past thirty years, the name of Ford has become a synonym for bloody-minded industrial conflict. The very mention of Dagenham or Halewood in the news headlines conjures up images of industrial chaos and confusion: wave upon wave of aggressive confrontation; the forest of raised hands and clenched fists at factory gate meetings; the crude banners and the cruder slogans; lost production, lost wages, lost exports and lost profits. Ford, in short, has become the commonplace symbol of an industrial society at war.

The news media must carry some of the responsibility for the reputation which Ford has developed. Dramatic newspaper headlines, selective and inaccurate news reporting, the instant punditry of radio and television commentators — such impressionistic evidence may be grossly misleading. But the more reliable evidence of official statistics and reports cannot be so easily dismissed, though this, too, may conceal more than it purports to reveal: spontaneous walk-outs over sectional grievances; solidarity strikes over major wage demands; selective overtime bans and working-to-rule; the conspicuous waste of men's lives and men's labour; and some of the world's most advanced technology standing ludicrously idle. To judge by its reported industrial relations, Ford now stands in the frontline of the battle between the forces of advanced capitalism and the forces of organised labour.

The paradox — which comforts whilst it mocks — is that, by any objective standard, Ford is today amongst the most productive, the most profitable and the best-managed companies in Britain. In 1975, when the volume of foreign car sales reached critical proportions and the government was forced to rescue both British Leyland and Chrysler from imminent bankruptcy, the British motor industry was subjected to intense scrutiny by three independent bodies. From the published reports of the Ryder Committee, [1] the Central Policy Review Staff[2] and the Expenditure Committee of the House of Commons,[3] as well as the government's own 1976 White Paper on the industry,[4] Ford has emerged with by far the best record of industrial performance. Whether measured in terms of investment per head or output per worker, of return on capital employed, of the degree of rationalisation of product

19

range, or of the integration of production facilities, Ford came closest to its continental European competitors in meeting its cost, quality and production targets. The unions with whom Ford negotiated were not slow to appreciate this dramatic improvement in the Company's fortunes. In presenting their 1978 wage claim, they adopted the Company's favourite advertising slogan to show that 'Ford leads the way' — a highly profitable and aggressively expanding company, well able to meet the cost of improved wages and fringe benefits, far in excess of the government's 5 per cent guidelines — 'without increasing prices or harming profitability in an already highly profitable Company'.[5]

How is this paradox to be explained? How can Ford stand in the front line of industrial conflict and still represent efficient capitalist enterprise? This chapter explores that paradox by analysing the evolution of the Company's industrial relations over the past thirty years from a management viewpoint. For despite Henry Ford's insistence that 'History is bunk', a clear line of development can be traced in Ford's industrial relations strategies, showing the major shifts that have resulted from crucial decisions taken in specific historical contexts. It will be argued that, so long as Ford management accepted Henry Ford's dictum and ignored the lessons of history, its industrial relations strategies failed. In so far as it has been willing to learn the lessons of its own experience, those strategies have been largely successful.

The Ford Industrial Creed

'For many years' wrote Robert Heller, 'Ford was less famous for its management strengths than infamous for its labour relations'.[6] That early reputation for aggressive management and bad labour relations stemmed directly from a corporate industrial relations philosophy which reflects to this day the dominant influence of the Company's eccentric founding genius. More than forty years ago, Ford set out the basis of its policy towards its British workers and customers:

> Mr. Henry Ford never believed from his earliest days as a motor manufacturer that any benefit could derive from the artificial division of the factory into separate and hostile camps. Instead, he sought to promote the novel conception of management and workers as partners in the mutual task of giving the best possible service to the community; and he further conceived the management as having clearly defined responsibilities in seeing that every operative was

relieved of cares and worries which might tend to reduce his efficiency in the partnership...

It is part of the Ford industrial creed that the right of a man to proper leisure is inescapably bound up with his right to a wage which will enable him to live a full and useful life and make good use of that leisure. This end cannot be achieved by a business policy of paying a worker merely on Trade Union standards or according to the state of the labour market. It involves the determination on the part of the management to maintain a standard which they consider fair and equitable.[7]

This extract conveys more than many pages of analysis the essence of the original 'Ford industrial creed'. Its paternalistic and authoritarian character were to be found not only in high wage rates but also in shorter hours, paid holidays, pensions and savings schemes, sports clubs and allotment gardens, trade schools and scholarship plans, subsidised canteen meals and a factory medical service – in short, Ford presented itself as an industrial welfare society, the provisions of which fell short of the comprehensive ideal only through lack of a maternity and funeral service.[8]

The 'Ford industrial creed' found its clearest expression in an obstinate refusal to come to terms with trade unions or employers' associations and a determination on the part of Ford management to fix wages and conditions according to some mystical standard considered by them to be equitable – namely 'a fair day's pay for a fair day's work'. Henry Ford and his managers took a special pride in going their own way, based on an unclouded belief that management alone was competent by training and by instinct to know what was in the best interests of the Company and its workers. Ford's implacable hostility to trade unions was reflected in a corporate policy applied throughout the Company's world-wide operations. By the mid-1930s, the United Auto Workers had succeeded in organising the US plants of General Motors and Chrysler, but Ford successfully resisted recognition by a policy that relied largely on sheer physical force. The early history of worker resistance to management autocracy and the struggle for union recognition in the 1930s bequeathed a legacy of bitterness and mutual distrust, not only in Detroit but in Ford's subsidiaries throughout the world.[9]

The Early History of Ford in Britain

The first Ford cars seen on the roads of Britain, shortly after the turn of
the century, were American-built models, assembled in Britain under
licence from Detroit. By 1909, with the world-wide demand for Ford
cars fast approaching half a million per annum, the Company found it
could no longer supply all its overseas markets from the Rouge Plant in
Detroit and therefore invested in a new manufacturing plant at Trafford
Park, Manchester.

In 1911, when the Ford Motor Company (England) Limited was
registered and the Manchester Works opened, Ford sold less than 1,500
cars on the British market. But, according to Allan Nevins, that total
doubled annually, from 3,000 in 1912 to over 6,000 in 1913.[10] By the
outbreak of war in 1914, Ford had built up a network of almost 1,000
dealers who were expected to sell up to 10,000 Model T's in that year.
The successful transplantation into Ford (England) of mass production
techniques, inspired by the 'scientific management' movement and perfected by Ford in Detroit, is demonstrated by the fact that the
Manchester Works, producing 150 cars per day, outstripped the entire
production of the next five largest British car firms taken together. But
there also appears to have been something of a free exchange of ideas
which helped the Company on both sides of the Atlantic.

> It was in no sense a one-way traffic and in this respect it is worth not-
> ing that two years before Mr. Ford astounded America with his five
> dollars a day wage rate (in 1914), at Manchester the policy had al-
> ready been proved by the payment of a minimum wage of 1/3d. an
> hour compared with the industrial average of 7d. per hour.[11]

In 1928, the Ford Motor Company Limited was inaugurated as a
British Company with 60 per cent of its shareholding retained in the
hands of the American Company. A spectacular new manufacturing
facility began to arise on the banks of the River Thames at Dagenham in
Essex. With a planned production capacity of 200,000 units per annum,
it was the biggest vehicle manufacturing plant in the world outside the
United States. Although the world-wide slump kept unemployment between 10 and 20 per cent in Britain throughout the 1930s, the new
Dagenham factory provided jobs for over 6,000 men when it opened in
1931 and for over 12,000 men by 1939.

By the late 1930s, workers in motor manufacture were amongst the
highest-paid wage earners in the country.[12] The average hourly rate at

Dagenham was over two shillings, time-served craftsmen earning much more. Ford's combination of high rates, a 40-hour week and good conditions were by no means general and were certainly not enjoyed by workers at the two other American-owned factories on the Dagenham Estate, Briggs Motor Bodies Ltd, Ford's main supplier of body panels, and Kelsey Hayes Limited, which manufactured wheels and other components. In November 1937, a group of Briggs workers addressed a moving letter to Ernest Bevin, General Secretary of TGWU, castigating the unions for their failure to organise workers on the Dagenham Estate. The writers described themselves as:

> ...the victims of low wages and high speed production. The work is such that we are becoming mere appendages of the machine, the machine setting the speed, every one in these works is panicky and nervous, accidents occur by the dozen, the first aid is, in the nature of things, also working at top speeds... The normal day work here is from seven (morning) until seven thirty (evening) at straight time, no overtime money is allowed, the wages average about one shilling and fourpence per hour. Some children are paid fourpence halfpenny. We work fifty to sixty hours per week, it is a terrible strain, as workers we plead that you use your power in order to make these conditions public property, as we have to be very careful owing to the well oiled espionage system in force here. We are approaching your organisation first, if this plea fails, desperation will make us look around for others who make us bring our grievances to the fore, for reasons that are obvious, we are very sorry, but we can only sign ourselves, *Twelve Briggs Workers.* [13]

Alerted by Bevin, the young Vic Feather, then working in the Organisation Department of the TUC, persuaded Sir Walter Citrine, General Secretary, to convene a conference of 'Unions interested in Messrs. Fords, Briggs Bodies, Kelsey Hayes, etc. with a view to seeing if anything can be done regarding recruitment of Trade Unionists in these works'. [14] But nothing came of the initiative because Ford refused to have any dealings with the unions. [15]

In 1941, however, an apparently minor dispute occurred at Briggs which was to transform that situation. It proved to be an early landmark in the history of industrial relations at Dagenham. The dispute followed the dismissal of a Shop Steward for his alleged defiance of a foreman's authority and his resort to 'hasty words'. Ernest Bevin, now Minister of Labour in Churchill's wartime government, set up a Court of Inquiry under Sir Charles Doughty. The resulting Report noted that Briggs management had agreed 'to permit engineering division employees to elect from their number their own representatives to negotiate on their behalf with the Management... and to define the position and responsibilities of elected representatives'. The Doughty Report explicitly endorsed that agreement before making its final recommendations:

> In large works, misunderstandings and sometimes even injustices may occur, and we recommend that this Company should adopt the normal procedure for discussing and settling disputes which necessarily involves the recognition of those Unions to fairly and largely represent their work people.[16]

The 'normal procedure' for settling disputes in the British motor industry was set out in the 1922 Engineering Industry Procedure Agreement. But since neither Briggs nor Ford were parties to that Agreement, it was left to the workers and managements of both firms to continue to argue about the form which such recognition might take. Briggs workers had clearly established their right to organise and negotiate directly with management, without the interference of outside officials. Briggs management felt obliged to comply with the recommendations of the Doughty Report for fear of the penalties which might otherwise ensue under wartime regulations. For Ford management, too, the writing was on the factory wall: in that same month, the National Labor Relations Board, set up under the Wagner Act 1935 as part of Roosevelt's New Deal, granted exclusive and legally enforceable bargaining rights to the UAW in all Ford plants in the United States. The first Ford-UAW Agreement was signed on 20 June 1941. This historic victory by the American Union gave fresh hope to Ford workers at Dagenham who continued to press vigorously for recognition. But the British management stood firm, under strict orders from Detroit.[17]

The Seeds of Immanent Conflict

The breakthrough at Dagenham came in 1944, following a sit-down strike which disrupted essential war production. Seizing this opportunity, Bevin put pressure on Sir Percival Perry, now Ford's British Chairman, to recognise the Trade Unions which represented Ford's highly skilled workforce, in the interest of maintaining good relationships. Perry was finally persuaded. He was nothing if not a realist. In

Detroit, the UAW had succeeded in tying management's hands. At Briggs, 'management function' had been eroded by a strong local bargaining agreement. Perry was determined that if the time had come for union recognition of any sort, he must form an alliance with such responsible officials as Citrine and Deakin, General Secretary, TGWU, by offering them a legitimate role as 'partners in control' of Ford's highly politicised and potentially disruptive workforce. That strategy was embodied in the 1944 Agreement. To avoid a monolithic industrial union on American lines, Ford agreed to recognise a multiplicity of British unions, provided they would bargain together in one joint national body. A rudimentary Procedure was established for channelling shop-floor grievances to a Joint National Committee (JNC) — a Procedure which has survived, albeit in modified form, for almost forty years. Of crucial importance was the fact that this JNC *alone* was empowered to negotiate wages and all other major conditions of employment. In 1946, the Agreement was amended to provide a limited role for Shop Stewards as members of a Joint Works Committee (JWC) established at each Ford factory to deal with immediate day-to-day problems. The distinction between negotiation at JNC and consultation at JWC was firmly institutionalised.

Turner and his colleagues have noted of this first Agreement that, unlike the system operated by the car firms in membership of the Engineering Employers' Federation, it provided no role for stewards or local officials in workplace bargaining, treated workload as exclusively a matter for managerial determination and thus involved the stewards' organisation in

> an attempt to establish standards for the use of labour informally, on a custom and practice basis... The result was necessarily a situation of immanent conflict, combined with a general frustration of the steward organisation which provided the basis for the militants to assume the leadership.[18]

But Ford was not slow in responding to 'the challenge from below' or in devising a legitimate role for Shop Stewards. Unlike its federated counterparts, Ford recognised the right of its employees to 'an adequate number of representatives appointed on a craft, departmental or geographical basis to act on their behalf'.[19] Each representative or steward was elected by all the union members in his constituency and not just by those members of his particular union. This unusual provision enabled Ford to limit the number of stewards with whom it had to deal but it simultaneously reduced the effectiveness of official union control and discipline by fostering rank-and-file collaboration across union lines. As the Report of a later Court of Inquiry points out, the distinctive Ford pattern of representation 'makes it easier for a highly organised militant element among the employees to exercise a dominating and disturbing influence over the conduct of affairs in the plant'.[20]

Turner also observed that, since the Company was forced to concede recognition under pressure from government and TUC, it was committed to 'a singularly clumsy bargaining and conciliation arrangement in the first place, and to a system of workplace representation which was exceptionally divorced from union control and guidance'.[21] Rank-and-file activists at Ford have always been ready to exploit that independence. They have 'frequently argued that their direct action forced the firm to recognise the unions and have often returned to this point in justification of unofficial and unconstitutional action'.[22]

That propensity for direct action was actively fostered by the militant stewards' sincerely held belief, born of experience, that 'If you do nothing, you get nothing'.[23] Whatever the basis of that belief, it serves as a guiding thread throughout thirty years of recurrent conflict at Ford: 'You can talk and argue as much as you like. Detroit does not believe in the finesse of negotiations. They only believe in one thing, that's if you stop their plants and their source of profit.'[24]

The procedural issue was finally brought to a head after 1953, when Ford acquired Briggs Bodies Limited and was forced to reconcile two different systems of bargaining and two sets of wages and conditions of employment. In 1954, Ford put forward its first proposals for standardisation.[25] Several drafts were discussed; all were opposed by Briggs stewards, seeking to preserve their traditional independence. In May 1955, the Ford JNC was enlarged to include representatives of Briggs employees and, by August 1955, the newly designated Ford National Joint Negotiating Committee (NJNC) had thrashed out a revised Recognition and Procedure Agreement.

Management Prerogative and the Achievement of Efficiency

When they sat down with Smith and Hennessy to negotiate the terms of the first collective Agreement in 1944, Citrine and Feather were presented with a draft the opening clause of which imported a distinct transatlantic flavour:

1. The Trade Unions and the Company agree on the need:-
   (a) to achieve efficient production by all reasonable means, and
   (b) for the introduction of labour saving machines and methods.

It is not part of the duty of any Shop Representatives, whose constitution and duties are defined hereafter, to deal with such matters
in the Shop, but he may refer them for consideration by the Works
Committee, as hereinafter appears.[26]

Clause 2 removed any residual doubts that 'the rights and responsibilities of management rest in the Company'. It spelled out that 'The
Company, having in mind continuity of employment and flow of production, may transfer employees from one job to another as may be
desirable' and that 'Deliberate action by an employee to retard or
restrict production or refusal to accept the Company's established
methods for achieving efficiency shall be grounds for dismissal'.[27]

The wording of these opening clauses, which epitomises Ford's
approach to the efficient utilisation of manpower, has been retained,
virtually unchanged, in every subsequent Agreement under the heading
'The Achievement of Efficiency of Operations'. Ford's continued assertion of managerial prerogative in the achievement of efficiency through
the unilateral right to determine manning levels and workloads has long
been a prime source of employee discontent and of unconstitutional
action.

The Cameron Court of Inquiry, 1957

The subject of disputed work standards[28] forms the background to
several of Ford's most publicised strikes. In January 1957, the Company
dismissed a former Briggs steward, Johnny McLoughlin, for calling an
unauthorised meeting on Company premises during working hours.
During the protest strike which followed, involving more than half the
Body Plant's 10,000 workers, the Company wrote to the NJNC, denying
the unions' allegation that it was attacking the principles of shop representation and showing bias against trade unions. It reaffirmed its acceptance of the Procedure Agreement as the proper means for settling any
disputes and said that the Agreement was being disregarded by 'those
very Trade Union officials who are most vociferous in accusing the
Company'.[29]

To help resolve the dispute, an official Court of Inquiry was set up in

February 1957, under Lord Cameron, which centred on the failure of
the 1955 Procedure Agreement to curb what the Cameron Report itself
described as 'the disease of unofficial stoppages which had become
endemic'.[30] In his evidence to the Court, Leslie Blakeman, Ford's
Labour Relations Manager, described the Company as facing 'a continuous challenge' to its authority. He conceded that a certain amount of
constructive conflict might be conducive to progress and development
but alleged that Ford was dealing with:

> one of the most highly organised Shop Steward movements in the
> country, a powerful and financially strong group whose objective was
> destructive conflict and whose persistent activities made impossible
> the normal give and take of factory life.[31]

The Unions, for their part, attributed many of the stoppages at
Briggs to the imposition of Ford's 'management policy' on work standards, alleging that the Company had introduced a 'speed-up' and a complete re-timing of operations, refusing to negotiate on the difficulties
which consequently arose. They contended that Ford supervisors
handled legitimate grievances in such a ham-fisted, unsympathetic, dila-
tory and unyielding manner that 'a widespread view had taken root in the
minds of the workpeople that the management would take action only
when faced with the pressure exerted by means of stoppages of work'.[32]

The Cameron Report found that the Company had been justified in
dismissing McLoughlin and placed the major responsibility for the many
unofficial stoppages on the militant group of Briggs stewards whom it
characterised as 'a private Union within a Union enjoying immediate and
continuous contact with the men in the shop, answerable to no superiors
and in no way officially or constitutionally linked with the Union
hierarchy'.[33] Lord Cameron found no difficulty in identifying the 'Ford
industrial creed'. The Report noted the Company's 'general emphasis on
discipline and obedience (which) suggests an attitude of mind tending
towards regimentation' and 'a desire to impose rather than agree by
negotiation terms and conditions of pay and work'.[34] Of the Unions'
complaints that the JWC was an ineffective body, the Report remarked
that 'time and patience spent in the handling of this committee, an
important purpose of which is the easing of industrial tensions, might
pay the Company handsomely'. The Report noted that there was 'room
for modification of the terms of the (Procedure) Agreement to improve
its efficiency and speed up its operation'[35] and recommended the
parties to work closely together to make it more effective. Prime res-

ponsibility for securing these reforms was placed squarely on the Company.

The Motor Industry in Cumulative Disorder

The adverse publicity surrounding the 1957 strike and the Cameron Inquiry was a source of considerable embarrassment to Ford management both in Britain and in Detroit. For five years, from 1957 to 1962, the Company persisted in its attempts to involve the national leadership of the Unions in implementing the Cameron recommendations but no positive response was forthcoming. These years were marked by recurring disputes of increasing bitterness, with mounting losses in man-hours and profitability.

Ford was by no means alone in facing this trend of disruption and its record must be seen in the context of an industry in the throes of cumulatives disorder. Writing in 1967, Turner and his colleagues noted that:

> the strike incidence of the car firms has risen from about twice the national average in the early post-war years to about six times the national average during the 1960s — thus contributing substantially to the rise in the national incidence itself. The car worker, in fact, had become at least as dispute-liable as such traditionally strike-prone groups as the miners, shipbuilders and dockers — a phenomenon which led the Minister of Labour to pick out the motor industry from early in 1961 as appropriate for a series of special joint meetings of employers' and Union representatives to reform the industry's labour relations.[36]

Having examined the official evidence, these representatives published a Joint Statement on 20 February 1961, expressing their confidence 'that the various Procedures for handling disputes... are generally adequate if operated in the right spirit'. The Statement offered various suggestions for reducing the causes of friction but was chiefly concerned to stress that grievances must be correctly channelled:

> We have attached paramount importance to the adherence by all parties to the letter and spirit of these Procedures which provide solid foundations for good relations in our industry. Without the observance of the Procedures, the other efforts now being made will be largely nullified and unofficial strikes doubtless continue.[37]

Although the National Trade Union Officials put their signatures to this Statement, it is not difficult to detect the hand of the employers in its drafting. Moral indignation at 'the dishonouring of agreements' runs like a managerial motto through a succession of statements, speeches, fact-finding reports and the employers' evidence to Inquiries and Commissions. Whenever the opportunity presented itself, management has invoked the theme of the moral obligation on both parties to honour agreements freely entered into.[38] The policy of emphasising the sanctity of Procedure was evolved by a small unofficial group of Labour Relations Managers in the motor industry who met throughout the 1950s and 1960s to develop concerted policies. Ford played a major role in sustaining that group. Blakeman became its leading member in the mid-sixties, undertaking such key tasks as the preparation of the Motor Industry Employers' Evidence to the Donovan Commission on Trade Unions.[39]

In December 1961, the signatories of the Joint Statement met again to review progress. Despite the implementation of various measures aimed at reducing the level of conflict, the industry had recorded no less than 256 strikes with the loss of 5 million man-hours in the six months following the publication of the Joint Statement.[40] In January 1963, following further meetings with the Minister of Labour, a more permanent but still informal body, the Motor Industry Industrial Relations Panel (MIIRP) was set up to discuss further ideas for improving labour relations and to provide a Fact-Finding Commission — an emergency fire-fighting force to undertake immediate on-the-spot inquiries.

The Fact-Finding Commission did some useful work,[41] but it soon became clear, however, that the Commissioners and workers in the industry were engaged in a 'dialogue of the deaf'. The number of stoppages and of man-hours lost continued to increase each year in the early sixties. In the first half of 1965, over six million working hours were lost in the industry, excluding consequential lay-offs at supplier firms. In response to a growing clamour from the press, the public and Parliament that 'something should be done' about British industrial relations, the government appointed the Royal Commission on Trade Unions and Employers' Associations under the Chairmanship of Lord Donovan in April 1965. But the number of motor industry disputes continued to rise, reaching their highest monthly post-war level in August of that year. Prime Minister Wilson judged their damaging effect on the country's balance of payments too serious to await the outcome of Lord Donovan's investigations and called both sides of the industry to Downing Street on 3 September 1965, to discuss more immediate

remedies. When the talks resumed in October, the employers reiterated
the familiar theme that the central problem was to ensure that
employees adhered to agreements signed on their behalf by the unions
but this time proposed 'the disciplining of unofficial strikers by the
Trade Unions (e.g. by expulsion either from membership or from working in the motor industry) in return for the Employers' agreement on
100 per cent Trade Unionism'.[42] They pursued this idea in a
Memorandum to the Minister of Labour, proposing legislation against
unofficial strikers and the setting up of a Motor Industry Joint Labour
Council (MIJLC) under an independent Chairman. The Unions supported the idea of a Council but rejected the proposed legislation. The
Minister considered the legislation to be premature, pending the findings
of the Donovan Commission.

By November 1965, the MIJLC was established under the
Chairmanship of Mr (later Sir) Jack Scamp, with the following terms of
reference:[43]

1. to keep the general state of relations in the industry under review and
   to examine matters of general significance for relations in the
   industry;
2. to review the state of industrial relations in individual firms;
3. to inquire into particular disputes leading to serious unofficial strikes
   or lock-outs in breach of procedure.

In that same month, the employers submitted written evidence to the
Donovan Commission, expressing their frustration in the face of both
union and government inaction:

> Much of our industrial legislation was devised in the era when it was
> necessary to protect the servant from the acts of the master. The
> question may now be posed whether in the present day it is necessary
> to protect the master from the acts of the servant.[44]

Having condemned 'the indiscipline which arises from unofficial stoppages by some elements of irresponsible membership', the employers
concluded that:

> Whilst industrial discipline by voluntary means is always preferable,
> experience of the last few years would suggest that this is not suffi-
> cient... It is not suggested that Trade Unions should be deprived of
> the ultimate right to strike... [but] there should be a clear-cut distinc-

tion between unconstitutional and constitutional strikes respectively and the Trade Unions should in future only enjoy an unfettered right to strike where the negotiating Procedure has been exhausted... Our primary concern [is] the need to restore acceptance of the Procedure as the proper vehicle for the settlement of claims and disputes.[45]

From this brief account of the motor industry in cumulative disorder, four significant strands emerge. First, there existed amongst the industry's employers and Trade Union National Officials an apparently genuine belief that its industrial relations problems were fully capable of resolution if workers with legitimate grievances would follow Procedure. Second, it had become clear by the mid-sixties that a protracted campaign of exhortation, cajolery, lobbying and pressurisation of the Unions by the employers to secure their members' adherence to Procedure under threat of discipline had been totally unsuccessful. Third, there was an inexplicable failure on both sides to come to terms with the 'irreversible devolution of bargaining power to the shop floor'. Fourth, and above all, there was a general failure on the part of the industry's employers to recognise the need for a comprehensive review and joint modernisation of collective bargaining which the Donovan Commission would later declare to be the prime and urgent need of the motor industry and of British industry as a whole.[46]

The Jack Court of Inquiry, 1963

Given the Trade Unions' unwillingness to share the responsibility for removing some of the root causes of unconstitutional action, Ford took what steps it could to meet the growing criticism of the parent Company. Detroit made it clear to British management that, unless it took a firm grip on its labour problems, it would not only forfeit any further substantial investment but suffer the indignity of American managers being sent to Britain to fill top management jobs, a prospect that seemed increasingly real after 1961, when the American Company bought the minority shareholding in the British Company.

In January 1962, as an indication of its reforming intentions, Ford in Britain announced the appointment of its respected Director of Manufacture, Bert Jeffries, to the new post of Director of Industrial Relations.[47] Since Jeffries was approaching retirement, his appointment was that of a care-taker, unlikely to initiate radical changes, but he took steps to strengthen the industrial relations function by appointing

specialist IR Managers in each of the main manufacturing areas.[48] Prior
to Jeffries' appointment, the Ford IR function operated as two separate
but unequal entities: the first, headed by Phil Mayhew, Personnel and
Organisation Manager, was principally concerned with all salaried staff
matters, including the powerful offices responsible for management
development, organisation planning and staff grading; the second,
headed by Leslie Blakeman, Labour Relations Manager, was primarily
concerned with hourly-paid employees, including responsibility for all
NJNC claims and the conduct of both hourly-paid and staff negotiations.
The appointment of Jeffries, a non-professional, as first IR Director in
1962 was a double blow to the two senior IR professionals at Ford. Not
only were Mayhew and Blakeman passed over for promotion — they
were now required to work in double-harness for the first time. The
experiment was not a conspicuous success.

By the middle of 1962, it became clear that Ford was taking a much
tougher line in the handling of its labour relations. Not until September
1962 however, when the Company refused otherwise to negotiate an
outstanding wage claim, was agreement reached on steps needed to improve the working of Procedure. In a Joint Statement dated 12 October
1962 — incorporated in all subsequent editions of the Ford Blue
Book[49] — both sides of the NJNC expressed their joint determination 'to
do all possible to achieve harmonious and cordial relationships'. The
Trade Unions recognised the right of the Company to discipline
employees who took unconstitutional action — provided they were not
required to share the responsibility for such discipline or its consequences. More positively, four specific steps were agreed upon 'to assist
in the more expeditious operation of procedural matters'. First, District
Officials were to visit Dagenham on a weekly basis to deal with matters
arising through Procedure. Second, the Trade Union Side of the NJNC
was to meet all JWC representatives once or twice yearly. Third, top
management were to meet Conveners and Deputies at similar intervals.
Fourth, an NJNC Sub-Committee was to be set up to discuss further
ways of improving labour relations.

Within days of the Joint Statement being signed, a major strike began
at Dagenham. It followed the dismissal of another Shop Steward, Bill
Francis, again for calling an unauthorised meeting, this time in the new
Dagenham Assembly Plant. But underlying the more immediate cause of
the dispute was a fundamental conflict of principle: that is, whether the
Company's managerial prerogative included the right to dismiss
employees whom it judged to be unsatisfactory, disloyal or disruptive.

A second Court of Inquiry was established, under Mr D.A. Jack,

Professor of Economics in the University of Durham, its first meeting on 4 March 1963 coming six years to the day after the opening of the Cameron Inquiry. The burden of the Company's evidence was that, despite its repeated efforts to implement the Cameron recommendations, the Unions had failed to join them in securing respect for agreements and obtaining freedom from stoppages of work. After a long and carefully documented submission, Blakeman ended his opening address to the Court as follows:

> The Company's case is based upon the need to operate efficiently... It is based on the need of any organisation to operate to a system of rules... [It] rests upon a determination to manage our establishments. We are very conscious of how our control was being undermined by the skilful and ruthless exploitation of some Shop Stewards of the consultative machinery established by agreement. We do not intend to tolerate any further the malpractices which existed, and which those who practised them defended on the basis of custom and practice. Within the limits which are determined by the observance of a 'fair day's work', we intend to achieve the level of efficiency to which we are not only entitled but which is essential if we are to continue our contribution to the country's export programme, and if we are going to meet our responsibilities to our customers, our suppliers, our employees and the community... At the end of the day it is the management who are left responsible. This is not only their prerogative, it is their obligation. This is the question of principle upon which we take our stand and from which we cannot abdicate.[50]

In their counter-submissions, the Unions reiterated their evidence to Cameron, emphasising the fact that, in their view, most of the Company's problems were of its own making through its determination to preserve a 'sacred garden of prerogatives'. In the words of Les Kealey, National Organiser, TGWU, 'one of the biggest problems at the Company was that nearly every matter which was likely to become a dispute was within the field in which Shop Stewards were not allowed to negotiate' — namely wage rates, premium payments, conditions allowances, merit money, line speeds, labour content, work standards and movement of labour. The JWC was 'a working body with very limited scope, dealing solely with matters in the Plant concerned'.[51]

The Jack Report found that the Company had taken advantage of the opportunity presented by a redundancy to dispense with the services of 17 men whom it regarded as persistent trouble makers. The Report welcomed the belated recognition by the Unions that they must finally deal with the activities of the unofficial Joint Shop Stewards' Committee but said that the Unions

> must carry a heavy responsibility for the poor state of industrial relations at Dagenham. If they fail on this occasion to re-establish their authority among their members they need not be surprised if the Company are obliged to pursue a tougher policy in the future.

Having resurrected most of the Cameron recommendations, the Jack Report arrived at the familiar but lame conclusion that 'on the whole the existing machinery is adequate provided it is properly and loyally used'.[52]

Towards a New Strategy in Industrial Relations

The 'Ford industrial creed' prescribed a strategy of tight labour management, spelled out in a detailed set of administrative procedures. Effective labour utilisation, like other forms of resource management, was the responsibility of line management. But there had been no consistent attempt to re-examine the underlying assumptions of the Company's IR strategy in the rapidly changing social and political climate of the sixties.[53]

Despite the enormous expansion in Company size, complexity and geographical dispersal in the fifties, the IR function failed to establish its identity in the organisational struggle for resources, power and status. Every other major function operated under the control of a Board Director — a factor which inhibited the emergence of a strong and independent IR voice at meetings of the key Policy Committee, which approved Company strategy. The lack of strong effective control of IR must reflect in part on the personalities involved. More remarkable, however, is the parent Company's tolerance of the high level of disruption in the fifties, without insisting on the reorganisation, restaffing and general upgrading of the IR function to match its importance. The most credible explanation appears to be that, despite its strike losses, the British Company enjoyed some of its most profitable years in the sellers' market of the late fifties and early sixties. This fact would have enabled the Managing Director to resist Detroit's pressure for reform.

After the second Court of Inquiry in six years, that pressure became irresistible. With Jeffries' retirement, a second IR Director, Laurie

Beeson, was appointed in 1963, with even fewer claims to professional IR expertise. His appointment was a bitter blow to Blakeman, now passed over twice for the Directorship.[54]

The most significant development to take place during the Beeson Directorship was the setting up of a small Forward Planning Team 'to give undivided and continuing attention to the formulation of a body of enduring industrial relations policy'. This decision, inspired by the parent Company's criticism, voiced during his periodic visits by Robert Copp, Overseas Liaison Manager, Labor Policy Planning, Ford US, was the first real attempt to integrate a professional IR strategy into the Company's wider business strategy. The creation of the European Economic Community presented Ford with its most profitable sales opportunity of the century – an opportunity not to be missed through labour disruption in the British Company. Blakeman was regarded as a shrewd and patient negotiator but, by nature and experience, he was happier in a tactical rather than a strategic role. In terms of its staffing and expertise, his Department was better organised for fire fighting than fire prevention.

Forward Planning set out to change the mistaken emphasis. Its principal objective was to steer the Company away from its preoccupation with current conflict towards future policy formulation. That objective may now seem banal but it was less obvious at the time and by no means easily met. Forward Planning designed a new IR strategy which required all major IR policies to be kept under continuous review by means of a two-year rolling programme with a five-year policy horizon. Short-term problems should be resolved by reference to the Company's longer-term objectives and not settled on grounds of expediency. The grudging recognition of trade unions must be transformed into full acceptance of their legitimate role, first, as a competing centre of loyalty within the Company and, second, as an authoritative bargaining partner. This would only be achieved by replacing the traditional 'arm's length' relationship between the Company and its rank-and-file leaders with a clear, positive and business-like relationship. The Company's aim must be to produce IR policies to a purposeful pattern, ahead of the bargaining pressures. It must capture and retain the initiative rather than react to each crisis as it arose.

Forward Planning's enduring achievement was its demonstration of the value of a permanent planning staff within the IR function, providing invaluable experience for its subsequent dealings with Ford of Europe, established in 1967. By that year, the management of Ford of Britain, as it then became known, had enthusiastically adopted the

Forward Planning strategy for transforming its industrial relations. The arrival of Ford of Europe provided the catalyst to ensure its successful implementation.

The Arrival of Ford of Europe

Questions about the degree of control exercised by American multi-nationals over their European subsidiaries have long fascinated students of industrial relations. Where, exactly, is the locus of management power? Who takes the key strategic decisions? When a major dispute occurs at Ford, how far is Ford of Britain free to resolve the matter alone, and how far must it consult and defer to the wishes of Ford US? Before 1967, the Policy Committee of the British Company authorised all major industrial relations policy changes, keeping Ford US closely informed of its forward plans and intentions. The parent Company rarely intervened *directly* in current problems and disputes. But, like Walter Bagehot's constitutional monarch, Ford US reserved three important rights: to be consulted, to encourage and to warn. As Bagehot remarked:

> a king of great sense and sagacity would want no others. He would find that his having no others would enable him to use these with singular effect. He would say to his minister: 'The responsibility of these measures is upon you. Whatever you think best shall have my full and effectual support. *But* you will observe that for this reason and that reason what you propose to do is bad; for this reason and for that reason what you do not propose is better. I do not oppose it, it is my duty not to oppose; but observe that I warn.'[55]

Through its experience of dealing with its subsidiaries over the years, Ford US had perfected its use of those three reserved rights and used them 'with singular effect'. Throughout the sixties, Bob Copp, Overseas Liaison Manager, would make two or three annual visitations to Ford in Britain, when he closely questioned members of Blakeman's staff about their past conduct of affairs and their future intentions. In most respects, the British Company was free to determine its own policies in the field of IR, as in other fields, subject always to overriding budgetary con-straints and the normal reporting requirements of Company policy. On particularly difficult or contentious issues,[56] it generally paid to seek the parent Company's advice; but if that advice seemed likely to be discouraging, it might be necessary to risk implementing the change and to face the subsequent criticism.

The clearest and most authoritative exposition of Ford US thinking on the freedom of action enjoyed by its national subsidiaries in the labour relations field has been provided by Copp himself. In a 1974 Conference Paper, he argued that:

> local management in the subsidiaries have, and indeed exercise, the authority to develop and to administer industrial relations policies appropriate to the national settings in which the subsidiaries operate. The role of the corporate staffs involves . . . (1) supporting the provision, in each subsidiary, of a competent, professional industrial relations organisation which fully comprehends the needs and problems of our particular business; (2) assuring that thorough study of industrial relations questions supports prudent decisions of managements in the subsidiaries; and (3) reporting and interpreting those decisions to corporate management.[57]

Copp went on to explain that it was the national company industrial relations organisation, along with the Managing Director and the Board of the subsidiary, which was the principal management decision-making activity in industrial relations matters, the corporate staffs acting as consultants and catalysts in employee relations matters:

> Local national managements, faced with a novel question, frequently seek the assistance of the corporate staffs in identifying where, elsewhere within the Ford organisation, there might be the experience and expertise to deal with that question . . . the corporate staffs have by now dealt with enough national company proposals that they themselves have developed an expertise of their own. National company managements, considering new or revised plans, prudently consult with the corporate staffs to exploit that expertise.[58]

In the day-to-day running of industrial relations disputes in the national companies, the role of the corporate staffs was limited to understanding the issues of the strike and to reporting and interpreting these issues to corporate management.

Although that is an entirely accurate account of the formal reporting relationship, Copp's own version is much less forthcoming about the informal reality behind the formal networks than that which he supplied to Duane Kujawa, in his researches into the same area. Kujawa attributes to Copp a much fuller and more frank account of the position:

> The Ford-US overseas liaison manager reported that he and senior
> line management at the home office are advised immediately when a
> strike occurs at any foreign subsidiary and are kept informed on
> strike settlement activities. This is an unwritten policy, except in the
> case of Ford-England (sic), where a written memorandum covers an
> agreement between Ford-England and Ford-US regarding strike re-
> ports. This memorandum defines a strike as any work stoppage likely
> to be reported in the US press or a significant interruption of produc-
> tion. The overseas liaison manager noted that he may participate in
> activities to settle strikes if local management requests that he do so.
> Usually these requests are made by Ford's smaller overseas affiliates.
> The US labor relations staff does not specifically approve local
> management's positions on strike issues, nor does it require reports
> covering strike settlements.[59]

Even that account tends to play down the all-important role of line
management in the plant, group and central staffs when production
schedules are hit by disruptive action. It totally ignores the crucial
position of Ford of Europe, located in the same Central Office building
as Ford of Britain, which not only serves as a 'listening post' for Ford
US but which can and does actively intervene in the day-to-day conduct
of disputes by Ford of Britain. Kujawa himself hints at this active intervention in his concluding comments:

> When viewing the apparent lack of any significant Ford-US involve-
> ment in settlement of strikes at the European subsidiaries, it should
> be remembered that the senior line management at Dearborn
> certainly keeps abreast of all important developments, including labor
> relations problems, at the foreign subsidiaries. When a strike occurs
> at an overseas plant, Dearborn is surely advised of the event and of the
> reasons for it. As progress is made in resolving a strike, a forecast of
> its anticipated impact on the subsidiary's profit plan is developed and
> relayed to the senior line executive at the home office. In a sense, this
> executive approves the settlement forecast, but in a very real sense he
> has no alternative. In addition, the evidence gathered in this study
> indicates that he does not seek to construct or to dictate any other
> alternatives.[60]

Ford of Europe in strictly legal terms is a separate organisation which

assists the national Ford companies throughout Europe to integrate their
functions and make the best use of their resources. In theory, it offers
advice on how they may increase their operational effectiveness but does
not control their day-to-day decision making. Ford organisation charts
feature this elaborate 'double-harness', distinguishing the continuous
lines of national accountability from the dotted lines which signify the
advisory role of Ford of Europe. In practice, Ford of Europe is a legal
fiction the relationship of which with the national companies is both
subtle and complex. Lines of European authority run across national
frontiers so that the senior managers of one Company are frequently
called upon to implement policies made by the senior managers of another Company. The Chairman and Managing Director of Ford of
Britain, for example, is both nominally and legally responsible for all
Ford activities in Britain – design, manufacture, sales, public relations,
legal affairs, industrial relations and so on. But he is regarded by Ford of
Europe as the organisational head of a *Sales Company,* Ford Motor
Company Limited, with no line responsibility for manufacturing the
products to be sold. Ford of Britain's Director of IR, who reports to
him, is part of that sales organisation although the IR problems with
which he is concerned are principally those of the British *manufacturing*
plants.

No senior executive in Ford of Britain or Ford of Germany would
consider implementing a major policy change without first seeking
policy review and concurrence by Ford of Europe. Although its staff is
comparatively small, Ford of Europe is constantly at hand with the sort
of advice which carries all the force of a binding instruction and the
sanctions to back it up. Ford of Europe must therefore be seen as an
important constraint on the development of an independent IR policy
in Ford of Britain after 1967. It operates both as a stimulus and a curb
on national policy makers, requiring new policies to be developed in response to national needs which are also consistent with Ford of Europe
policy guidelines. References to Ford management in the pages which
follow usually signify Ford of Britain. But, in all essential developments
after 1967, the influence of Ford of Europe must be regarded as implicitly present.

Implementation of the New Industrial Relations Strategy

Despite earlier warnings, most of Ford's senior managers in Britain were
shocked by the appointment of an American, Stanley Gillen, as

Managing Director of Ford Motor Company Limited in 1965. The message was clear: none of the senior British managers was considered tough enough for the job. As a result, several top British managers resigned at the prospect of an increasing Americanisation of the British Company. Ford's loss was British Leyland's and Chrysler's gain.[61]

Gillen's brief was to improve the Company's over-all performance in readiness for the coming of Ford of Europe. His appointment coincided with the first stages of implementation of the new industrial relations strategy and matched the prevailing economic and political climate in Britain. The first Wilson Government, elected in October 1964, had embarked on a campaign of modernisation and rationalisation of the British economy, setting out to do for Britain as a whole what Gillen was dedicated to achieve within Ford of Britain. In December 1964, representatives of the TUC, the major employers' organisations and the government put their signatures to a Declaration of Intent on Productivity, Prices and Incomes, which aimed at maintaining 'a rapid increase in output and real incomes combined with full employment'.[62] The signatories undertook 'to encourage and lead a sustained attack on the obstacles to efficiency, whether on the part of management or of workers, and to strive for the adoption of more rigorous standards of performance' on the clear understanding that 'the benefits of faster growth are distributed in a way that satisfies the claim of social need and justice'. Conferences on this theme reverberated with echoes and paraphrases of Harold Wilson's rhetoric about Britain's 'second white-hot technological revolution'. But when the bargainers at the negotiating tables turned from the rhetoric of productivity to the practical problems of how to increase and share its benefits, the atmosphere was less hopeful.

It was a dispute over productivity which gave Gillen his first taste of industrial conflict in Britain. He had barely had time to warm his Managing Director's chair when, in March 1965, he was caught up in a complex dispute amongst Paint Sprayers at Dagenham who demanded an increase in their 'abnormal conditions allowance', which had been fixed at 2d per hour over 15 years previously. Foundry Workers at Dagenham and Leamington soon followed with a similar claim of their own. To avoid the risks of a series of piecemeal concessions, the Company referred both claims to the NJNC where, in December 1965, it offered a general wage increase, subject to union co-operation in achieving greater over-all efficiency. When the unions rejected the offer, the Company agreed to increase the allowances, provided the Paint Sprayers accepted a reduction in 'excessive relief times' — that is, periods of paid recuperation outside the spray booths. After the rejection of this second offer and repeated attempts to negotiate a solution, the Company took the unilateral decision to reduce the relief times and to pay the increased allowances as from 24 January 1966. The Sprayers walked out, Dagenham production was halted in consequence and the TGWU made the strike official. When asked why the Union had backed its members in this unusual way, Kealey told Blakeman: 'We have never had a victory against Ford – this is our chance to get one.'[63] Eventually, after a two-week stoppage, Blakeman persuaded Gillen that, since the Procedure Agreement had been flouted by the action of the TGWU in making the strike retrospectively official, there was no alternative to a domestic investigation by the Motor Industry Joint Labour Council, under Jack Scamp – or a third Court of Inquiry. Since Blakeman was a leading member of the MIJLC, Gillen reluctantly agreed to the Scamp investigation. It was a decision he lived bitterly to regret.

The dispute turned on the number of minutes of relief time to which the Sprayers were entitled. The Company claimed that improved working conditions justified a reduction in relief times. The Sprayers denied the improvement and sought to maintain the existing relief times, long established by custom and practice. Behind the technical argument was a question of principle: whether or not management had the right to negotiate or – failing agreement and in the last resort – unilaterally to implement changes in working practices as technology allowed and as investment justified. Blakeman argued that there was

an increasing obligation on the Company, the motor industry generally, and indeed throughout British industry, to increase efficiency . . . Whilst the trade unions are prepared to enthusiastically support the Government in their appeals for more productivity . . . when it comes to taking more positive action to persuade their members accordingly, there is no evidence of any enthusiasm at all.[64]

Kealey, for the TGWU, made the Union's position very clear:

We are not prepared to co-operate with the Ford Motor Company or any other company in putting a heavier load on our people without some benefit. It is normal practice throughout British industry, except in American firms, that when you make changes and there is increased productivity, it is negotiable and there is something to come for our people. We will co-operate with the Ford Motor Company . . . in getting increased productivity but . . . if there is to be any change whatsoever that gives a financial return to the Company, by the endeavours of our people, then we will want a share of it.[65]

In the view of Ford management, it did not require the wisdom of
Solomon to grasp the fundamental issue underlying the dispute. In his
Report,[66] Scamp left that issue untouched and concentrated his attention on the simple arithmetical differences between the parties. Without
offering any explanation or rationale for his decision, he split the difference, leaving neither side satisfied. Gillen was incensed that Scamp,
Chairman of the industry's own Joint Labour Council, could walk away
from the fundamental principle without regard for its consequences.
Those consequences led indirectly to the Sewing Machinists' dispute.

The New Wage Structure of 1967

Citing the Scamp judgement as precedent, Ford's Foundrymen and
others immediately submitted their own leapfrogging claims for higher
conditions allowances, culminating in a threat by the Company's
Toolmakers to withdraw their personal tool-kits unless they, too, were
granted a special allowance. For two days the Company prevaricated. It
was a moment of anguish for Gillen: if he conceded the Toolmakers'
claim, there would be similar claims from all other craftsmen. If he
resisted the claim, he faced another Scamp investigation or, worse still,
another Court of Inquiry. Gillen had read the Forward Planning Team's
Report on the need for a critical review of the entire hourly-paid wage
structure and decided the time had come when the kissing had to stop.
The Company announced that it would meet the Toolmakers' claim
with a special 'merit money' payment of 3d an hour — but that was the
end of the road. The Unions were invited to join the Company in a
comprehensive review of the wage structure by means of an urgent job
evaluation programme, with the help of Management Consultants
Urwick, Orr and Partners, working under the over-all guidance of the
NJNC.

The Unions' first reactions were predictably cool: with all its faults,
the Ford wage structure still looked better than those in the rest of the
industry. The MIJLC, for example, spoke in its first Report of

the need for most companies to take a serious look at their methods
of payment. In particular, any review of the wage structure demands
a careful and comprehensive approach rather than the continued
application of the present piecemeal and often inflationary

solutions.[67]

The Donovan Report would, in due course, fasten on to that quotation, which it incorporated into its own analysis of the principal causes of strikes in the motor industry. The Donovan Report found that 'the failure to devise adequate wage structures and to agree them in comprehensive negotiations with representatives of all the workers concerned, is responsible to a large extent for the industry's industrial relations problems'.[68] It pin-pointed the adverse effects on industrial relations of fragmented and decaying payment systems which gave rise to 'the erratic and rising piecework earnings, notorious in the car industry'.[69]

For more than sixteen years, Ford had enjoyed the benefit of a coherent, company-wide wage structure, agreed with all the Unions represented at NJNC. It had never adopted incentive payments and claimed to be free from such inflationary piecemeal concessions, a claim which it had substantiated before the National Incomes Commission, five years before the Donovan Report was published.[70]

The virtues of the old wage structure were threefold: it was simple to understand; it was easy to administer; and it was free from internal wage drift. It comprised four grades of labour – skilled, semi-skilled, unskilled and women – each with its own hourly rate, negotiated at NJNC. Some 80 per cent of all workers at Ford were classified as 'semi-skilled',[71] which allowed mobility between different jobs in that grade without loss of pay. Since there were no incentive payments, the only variations in weekly earnings were due to the number of hours worked, plus the premium additions for overtime, shift and weekend working. A relatively small number of production workers (Lead Discers, Paraffin Honers, Paint Sprayers and Foundrymen) enjoyed an abnormal conditions allowance for working in particularly uncongenial conditions. In essence, the Ford structure carried over from the nineteenth century the classic trinity of craft aristocrats, machine minders and general labourers, plus women – a system of job classification which advancing technology had rendered more and more irrelevant. Non-negotiable merit money helped to 'lubricate' an otherwise tight and inflexible grading structure but had degenerated over the years from a genuine reward into just another means of boosting earnings.[72]

The problems facing Ford in conducting its wage structure review were formidable: over 40,000 hourly-paid workers, spread across 24 separate plants, occupying over 700 different job titles – all needing to be identified, described and evaluated before any attempt could be made to decide the number of new grades needed and their differentials.

The review was divided into three distinct stages:

1. The fact-finding stage — in which trained Assessors prepared job pro-files after shop-floor observation and discussion of the job with the employee, the Supervisor and the Shop Steward. Each profile was then double-checked for completeness, internal consistency and value against representative benchmark jobs, first by one of eight Divisional Review Committees, representing management and Shop Stewards in that Division and then by a Central Review Committee, composed of senior managers and a full-time official, appointed by the Trade Union Side of the NJNC. Any profile not acceptable to the Central Review Committee was referred to the Consultants for adjudication.
2. The proposal stage — in which the Company examined the facts revealed by job evaluation and formulated its proposals on the changes it wished to introduce in the old structure.
3. The negotiation stage — in which the Company and the Trade Unions at NJNC attempted to reach agreement on the Company's proposals.

At the end of the fact-finding stage, over 1,800 job profiles were completed, providing an up-to-date and definitive catalogue of all signi-ficantly different hourly-paid jobs in the Company, allowing a consis-tent evaluation to be made of the total work content of each job, with a final over-all rank order of all the jobs covered by evaluation. Throughout this stage, Shop Stewards were actively involved in helping Assessors to complete the job descriptions and Conveners sat as equal partners with management representatives on the various Review Committees. At the NJNC, the Unions were kept closely informed of progress at every stage and their agreement secured to each major step during the job evaluation programme.

The facts which emerged from the evaluation clearly showed the extent to which technological development in motor manufacture had blurred the traditional distinction between 'skilled' and 'semi-skilled' work in the engineering industry. The Ford evaluation had concentrated on bringing out the total 'job value' in terms of four main factors:[73] physical demands, mental demands, responsibility and working condi-tions. These main factors were, in turn, divided into 28 sub-factors, or 'job characteristics'. The resultant ranking by job evaluation showed that familiar craft occupations, like Carpenters, Fitters, Millwrights and Electricians, were not one conventionally homogeneous group, concen-trated into one grade, as in the old wage structure, but were spread across a much wider range of 'job values'. Conversely, jobs which had formerly been regarded as 'semi-skilled' production work divided themselves into three distinct groups, only one of which included the more demanding production jobs, like that of Production Welder, Torch Solderer, Paint Sprayer and Metal Finisher.

Using the results of the evaluation, a management team sat down to consider what changes, if any, it wished to propose in a new wage structure.

In due course, the team recommended:

1. that the old four-grade structure should be replaced by five new grades;
2. that women's jobs should fall into appropriate grades, as determined by evaluation, without sex discrimination;
3. that conditions allowances should be discontinued because working conditions were now fully covered by job evaluation;
4. that merit money should be replaced by a more equitable scale of service increments.

The Company proposed these radical changes to the Unions at NJNC in April 1967, thus setting in train a complex set of pay and productivity negotiations, required to ensure formal government approval under the terms of the existing prices and incomes policy, which extended over the following five months. The Company was determined to secure agreement on its new wage structure proposals and anxious to recoup some part of the additional £5 million annual labour cost. It was not enamoured with the popular vogue for productivity bargaining and would have been satisfied with some token concessions towards increased efficiency. But from July 1966 to the end of 1967, income policy prescribed a 'zero norm' and no settlement could be implemented without prior government approval. Ford of Britain therefore reluctantly embarked on its first and only experiment with plant productivity bargaining.

Despite the time constraints, the contentious nature of management's objectives and the novelty of the exercise, the resultant bargains were seen by the Company as a considerable achievement at the time. There was a systematic discussion of all plant operating problems; agreement or reaffirmation of general efficiency principles, some agreed nationally but not previously accepted locally; the codification of existing undertakings together with some additional improvements. At every plant, a number of traditional practices were changed, including: greater flexibility amongst craftsmen and their acceptance of additional duties;

some traditional craft work to be undertaken in future by non-craftsmen; improved personal efficiency of production workers through acceptance of revised manning standards, different shift patterns and a better overtime response.

All these separate productivity bargains were eventually brought together at the NJNC for ratification and inclusion in a Two-Year Agreement — the first North American-style period contract ever signed by Ford of Britain, containing a crucially important and explicit clause providing for 'no economic claims' during the life of the contract. The complete package deal was finally agreed by the Unions, vetted and approved by the Department of Employment and Productivity and put into effect in September 1967, with retrospective effect from March 1967. It was the first of the Ford 'new model' Agreements — the prototype on which successive Ford Agreements have been modelled over the following decade.

At the end of 1967, the management of Ford of Britain heaved a collective sigh of relief. It had lived through two years of suspense, during the course of its first major programme of joint participative industrial relations reform. At last, the signatures of the National Trade Union Officials were on the Agreement. Ford management had paid a high price before it learned the lessons of its past mistakes. Now, with the Two-Year Agreement and the New Wage Structure behind it, Ford management had taken the first vital steps in the implementation of its new industrial relations strategy and the prospects for 1968 seemed good.

Notes

1. *British Leyland — The Next Decade* (The Ryder Report) (HMSO, London, 1975).
2. Central Policy Review Staff Report, *The Future of the British Car Industry* (House of Commons Paper 342, Session 1974/5).
3. *14th Report from the Expenditure Committee of the House of Commons* (The Duffy Report) (House of Commons Paper 617, Session 1974/5).
4. *The British Motor Vehicle Industry*, Cmnd. 6377 (HMSO, London, 1976).
5. Ron Todd and Reg Birch, 'Introduction' to *Ford Wage Claim* (1978), p.2.
6. Robert Heller, 'Ford Motor's Managing Machine', *Management Today* (London, February 1968).
7. Ford Motor Company Limited, *A Study of Practical Sociology* (Dagenham, 1937), p.7 *et seq.*
8. For a French recipient's comments on the comprehensive ideal in the motor industry, see Jacques Chapuis, 'Je fais du social', *Chefs*, no.4 (April 1945): 'I was born into Michelin baby-linen and fed with a Michelin bottle in a Michelin house. Of course, I played in a Michelin nursery, then as a Michelin apprentice and

operative I had my meals in the canteen and went to the Michelin cinema and Michelin entertainments. If I don't get out of this joint directly, I shall soon be buried in a Michelin coffin.'

9. For an independent account of the state of labour relations at this time, see Allan Nevins and Frank Ernest Hill, *Ford — Decline and Rebirth: 1933 —1962* (Charles Scribner's Sons, New York, 1962), Chs I-VI.

10. Allan Nevins, *Henry Ford: The Man, The Life, The Company* (Charles Scribner's Sons, New York, 1954), p.5.

11. Sir Patrick Hennessy, Paper no. 159, Seminar on Problems in Industrial Administration, London School of Economics and Political Science, 30 November 1954.

12. A Ministry of Labour inquiry in October 1938 showed that men over 21 in motor and aircraft manufacture, together with those in printing, paper and book-binding, averaged 83 shillings per week compared with 60-70 shillings for all employed men. Women over 21 in motor manufacture averaged 40 shillings per week compared with 33-34 shillings for all employed women. See G. D. H. Cole and Raymond Postgate, *The Common People* (Methuen, London, 1938), pp. 642-4.

13. TUC, Organisation Department files, letter dated 6 November 1937.

14. Sir Walter Citrine, letter dated 18 November 1937, TUC, Organisation Department files.

15. For a detailed and lucid exposition of the unitary perception of work relationships amongst employers at the time, see Alan Fox, *Beyond Contract: Work, Power and Trust Relations* (Faber, London, 1973). See also note 31, p.28 below for Fox's paradigm of 'Continuous Challenge'.

16. *Report of a Court of Inquiry* (The Doughty Report), Cmd. 6284 (HMSO, London, 1941), p.12.

17. A quite different position obtained at Ford's wartime factory outside Manchester. Of the workforce of 17,000, over 7,000 were women. Scheduled production of 400 engines a month was reached early in 1942 but by 1943 had risen to 900. Altogether, more than 30,000 Merlin engines were assembled at Ford, mostly by women. Because the Merlin-Manchester factory came under the super-vision of Bevin's Ministry of Labour, workers were guaranteed the right to organise and bargain with their employers. Ford therefore had to recognise the Unions at Manchester although there were apparently no wartime labour problems. See Wilkins and Hill, *American Business Abroad — Ford on Six Continents* (Wayne State University Press, Detroit, 1964), pp.328-9 and 332-3.

18. H.A. Turner, G. Clack and G. Roberts, *Labour Relations in the Motor Industry* (Allen and Unwin, London, 1967), p.215.

19. Ford Motor Company Limited, *Agreements and Conditions of Employment* (The Blue Book), Procedure Agreement dated 25 July 1969; Clause 5(i)(a) repro-duces the equivalent Clause in the 1946 Agreement.

20. *Report of a Court of Inquiry into a Dispute at Dagenham* (Jack Inquiry), Cmnd. 1999 (HMSO, London, 1963), para. 130.

21. Turner, Clack and Roberts, *Labour Relations in the Motor Industry*, p.346.

22. Ibid., p.194.

23. See, for example, the Cameron Report, paragraph 36, quoted in note 32, p. 28 below.

24. Bernie Passingham in B. Passingham and D. Connor, *Ford Shop Stewards on Industrial Democracy* (Institute for Workers' Control, 1977), p.1.

25. The task of standardising conditions and of absorbing Briggs into Ford was immense — but much more successful than, for example, the Austin-Morris and Leyland mergers. The fact that the Briggs-Ford merger was that of supplier and customer made it all the more difficult.

26. Procedure Agreement dated 26 May 1944, Clause 1.

27. Procedure Agreement dated 26 May 1944, Clause 2. For an expression of management's fears of union encroachment in the motor industry, see comments by the Chairman of General Motors Corporation, Ford's main competitor: 'What made the prospects grim in those early years was the persistent Union attempt to invade basic management prerogatives. Our right to determine production schedules, to set work standards and to discipline our workers were all suddenly called into question.' Alfred P. Sloan, Jr, *My Years with General Motors* (Sidgwick and Jackson, London, 1963), p.406.

28. See note 50, p.34 below and reference to new Work Standards Agreement, Chapter 6, p. 244 below.

29. *The Times,* London, 30 January 1957.

30. *Report of a Court of Inquiry* (The Cameron Report), Cmnd. 131 (HMSO, London, 1957), para. 54.

31. *The Times,* London, 30 January 1957.

32. Cameron Report, para. 36. cf. note 23, p. 26 above.

33. Ibid., para. 91.

34. Ibid., paras. 101-4.

35. Ibid., para. 102.

36. Turner, Clack and Roberts, *Labour Relations in the Motor Industry,* p.24.

37. Joint Study Group on Industrial Relations in the Motor Industry, *Joint Statement,* London, 20 February 1961, included as Appendix 1 of Motor Industry Employers' Evidence to Royal Commission on Trade Unions etc.

38. Cf. Ford Evidence to Bullock Committee, para. 26: ' . . . the Trade Union movement with which we deal is so much more fragmented and so much less dedicated to the creation of wealth for the community, and has a tradition of leaving the honouring of agreements to the discretion of individual members rather than establishing some form of control over them to ensure compliance. The result is a far less predictable situation with a greater opportunity for dissidents to ignore the official viewpoint of the Trade Union movement at any give time.'

The same theme was brought out in a long letter from Ford's Director of Industrial Relations, published in *The Times* on 17 March 1977: 'The vast majority of disputes which have thrown men out of work, lost Britain customers and damaged our trading position in the last 30 years have been the result of employees ignoring the agreed procedure for handling problems and doing so with impunity, knowing their Unions do not possess, or would not use, their authority to make them adhere to such agreements.'

Compare the same author's remarks in 'British strikes: why managers can't sleep at night', *Financial Times* 10 January 1979: 'What is virtually unique to Britain is not these [contract renewal] strikes but the incessant daily unofficial strikes, in breach of procedures, which make the jobs of both management and shop-floor employees a misery . . . Interminable unofficial disputes and threats of unofficial disputes make the planning of production a nightmare, concentrate the energies of management and Trade Unions on firefighting instead of building constructive relationships and create never-ending attitudes of antagonism.'

39. See notes 44 and 45 on p. 31 below.

40. A.J. Scamp (later Sir Jack Scamp), Paper no.376, Seminar on Problems in Industrial Administration, London School of Economics and Political Science, 26 November 1966.

41. Motor Industry Industrial Relations Panel, *Report of Fact-Finding Commision,* Cowley Works, Morris Motors, November 1964, included as Appendix 2 of Motor Industry Employers' Evidence to Royal Commission on Trade Unions etc.

42. Motor Industry Employers' Evidence, p.22.

43. Motor Industry Joint Labour Council, *Report on Activities of the Council* (1966), p.5.

44. Motor Industry Employers' Evidence, para. 24, p.7.

45. Ibid.

46. See Chapter 6, note 5, p. 223 below.

47. Nomenclature in all Ford subsidiaries follows that of Ford US. The 'IR function' is a generic term covering all aspects of labour relations, staff and personnel relations, training, welfare, security, medical health and safety, etc.

48. Amongst this group was Robert J. Ramsey, later to become Director of Industrial Relations, Ford of Britain.

49. Ford Motor Company Limited, *Agreements and Conditions of Employment* (December 1978 edn), p.21.

50. 'Transcript of Company Evidence' (4 March 1963, unpublished), pp.27-9.

51. 'Transcript of Union Evidence' (4 March 1963, unpublished), p.43. Note the marked difference, however, between the formal rules and informal practice. Kealey told the Jack Inquiry that 'it was to be expected that the workers wanted to make representations if they felt that unreasonable targets were being demanded. Discussions on work standards and line speeds did occasionally take place because of the very high feeling.' *Report of a Court of Inquiry* (The Jack Report), para. 79.

52. *Report of a Court of Inquiry* (The Jack Report), Cmnd. 1999 (HMSO, London, 1963), para. 136.

53. Top-level succession problems, after the retirement of Sir Rowland Smith and Sir Patrick Hennessy, may have contributed to this failure. Ford US did not immediately send over the best men they could find, raising problems which had also been found earlier at Briggs.

54. Blakeman was not only denied the full personnel responsibility: he was really given full rein only at the time of Courts of Inquiry.

55. Walter Bagehot, *The English Constitution* (Oxford University Press, 1952), p.67 (first published 1867).

56. See, for example, Ford of Britain's consultations with Ford US on the setting up of the Lay-Off and Holiday Bonus Fund in 1968-69. Cf. Ch. 6, p.225 below.

57. Robert C. Copp, 'Locus of Management Decisions in Industrial Relations in Multinationals', Conference on Industrial Relations Problems raised by Multinationals in Advanced Industrial Societies, Michigan State University, East Lansing, 10-13 November 1974.

58. Ibid.

59. Duane Kujawa, *International Labor Relations Management in the Automotive Industry* (Praeger Publications, New York, 1971), p.116.

60. Ibid., p.118.

61. Amongst other 'high flyers' who 'migrated' from Ford of Britain at this time were John Barber, Bert Walling, Gordon Kennedy, 'Oscar' DeVille, Alan Bradley — all of whom filled senior positions elsewhere with distinction.

62. Department of Economic Affairs, *Declaration of Intent on Productivity, Prices and Incomes* (HMSO, London, December 1964).

63. 'Company Evidence to Paint Sprayers' Inquiry' (1966, unpublished).

64. Ibid.

65. 'Union Evidence to the Paint Sprayers' Inquiry' (1966, unpublished).

66. Motor Industry Joint Labour Council, *Report of an Inquiry into Paint Sprayers' Dispute* (HMSO, London, 1966).

67. Motor Industry Joint Labour Council, *Report on the Activities of the Council* (HMSO, London 1966), para. 30, p.11.

68. *Report of the Royal Commission on Trade Unions etc.* (The Donovan

Report), Cmnd. 3268 (HMSO, London, 1968), para.386.

69. Ibid., para.89.

70. National Incomes Commission, para. 122. The Commission found that 'The Company's methods of controlling their wage structure are particularly worthy of note . . . The entire absence of any provision for piecework or payment by results means that any negotiated increase in rates is the increase in actual earnings and the Company are free, at any rate internally, from the complication of wage drift.' (Para. 32.) NIC, Report No.4 (Final), Cmnd. 2583 (HMSO, London, 1965).

71. This categorisation is clearly meaningless. A worker may possess one or more developed skills, or none, but he cannot possess 'semi-skills'.

72. Ford's simple pay structure had served the Company well. It depended on high-quality Superintendents and Foremen, and Ford had both. The old Briggs structure, where money did some of the managing, produced a weaker quality of supervision which was clearly revealed in the vast programme of joint training which took place after standardisation.

73. For an account of the profiling method of job evaluation developed by Urwick, Orr & Partners, see A.L.T. Taylor (ed.), *Job Evaluation* (British Institute of Management, London, 1970). For a more comprehensive treatment, see Brian Livy, *Job Evaluation* (Allen and Unwin, London, 1975).

A recent discussion of the problems of 'whole job' *v.* 'factor comparison' schemes is contained in Hugh Clegg's *Standing Committee on Pay Comparability Reports,* Cmnd. 7640/7641 (HMSO, London, 1979).

For an acutely sardonic account of job hierarchies and pay differentials in an earlier road transport industry, see E.J. Hobsbawm, 'Custom, Wages and Work-Load in Nineteenth Century Industry' in Asa Briggs and John Saville (eds.), *Essays in Labour History* (Macmillan, London, 1960). Explaining how a skilled man would fix his wage standard in relation to other skilled men, Hobsbawm notes that calculations, though tacit and unconscious, were rather complex. Each worker would regard himself as belonging to a particular stratum − say of craftsmen as distinct from labourers − within which was a well-defined hierarchy, 'though it is not always clear whether this represented earning capacity or whether earnings reflected it. Thus the coachmakers in 1839 . . . "are not an equal body, but are composed of classes taking rank one after the other . . . the body-makers are first on the list; then follow the carriage-makers; then the trimmers; then the smiths; then the spring-makers; then the wheelwrights, painters, platers, bracemakers and so on. The body-makers are the wealthiest of all and compose among themselves a species of aristocracy to which the other workmen look up with feelings half of respect, half of jealousy. They feel their importance and treat others with various consideration: carriage-makers are entitled to a species of condescending familiarity; trimmers are considered too good to be despised; a foreman of painters they may treat with respect, but working painters can at most be favoured with a nod".' (W.B. Adams, *English Pleasure Carriages,* London, 1837).

2 A SHOP-FLOOR VIEW

The Ford Motor Company, perhaps more than any other, typifies modern industrial capitalism. Henry Ford was the first to adopt Frederick Taylor's ideas of scientific management and then went on to apply the concepts of 'Taylorism' in practice. He developed the continuously moving conveyor belt and other assembly line processes to manufacture motor cars. These mass production techniques require the maximum utilisation of labour. This can only be achieved by subordinating the operator to the machine process at the most intense level. However, the development of these productive processes enabled Ford, from a small beginning in 1903, to produce sixteen million model 'T' cars – Tin Lizzies – by the year 1927.

Henry Ford was aware of the alienating and dehumanising effect of repetitive and monotonous work tasks which had to be performed at conveyor line speeds.

> Repetitive labour, the doing of one thing over and over again, and always in the same way, is a terrifying prospect to a certain kind of mind. It is terrifying to me, I could not possibly do the same thing day in and day out . . . [1]

A labour process which condemns operators to a pointless work existence, however, did not trouble Henry Ford's conscience too much, because he believed that,

> . . . to other minds perhaps I might say to the majority of minds, repetitive operations hold no terrors. The average worker, I am sorry to say, wants a job in which he does not have to put forth much physical exertion – above all, he wants a job in which he does not have to think.[2]

Allied to this philosophy was his passion for autocratic and total control. It led first of all to the famous Dodge Brothers versus Ford law suit in 1917. This enabled him to become the exclusive owner of the Company. To avoid constraint of any kind he even refused to become a member of the National Automobile Chamber of Commerce, the USA Automobile Manufacturers' 'Trade Union'. This tradition has been con-

52

tinued in Britain. To date, Ford has refused to become a member of any Employers' Association.

Inevitably, this desire for absolute personal control made him implacably hostile to trade unions. Thus, in order to understand the emergence of trade unions and their development at Ford in Britain, it is necessary to look very briefly at what happened in the USA, particularly before World War II.

To prevent unionisation in the 1920s and 1930s Ford employed a private army of 3,500 security men under the command of Harry Bennett, Ford's Personnel Director. It included such notorious characters as Joe Adonis of Murder Inc., and Chester La Mare, the Al Capone of Detroit. These security men continually spied on workers and ensured that the prescribed work pace was maintained. No talking, smoking or eating was allowed. Anyone suspected of union sympathies was instantly fired, and United Auto Workers Union (UAW) organisers were physically beaten up outside the factory gates at Detroit, Dallas and in Kansas City. Walter Reuther, the late President of the UAW, among others, experienced this treatment. In May 1937, during the 'Battle of the Overpass' – a footbridge leading to the River Rouge Plant – UAW organisers intended to distribute leaflets outside 'the Rouge' gates, but were severely roughed up in the process by Harry Bennett's men.

The approach road to the River Rouge Plant was also the scene of the tragic events of 1932 when Dearborn police and Ford security men machine-gunned marching unemployed workers, killing four and wounding over twenty others. Indeed, so effective were Harry Bennett's men that the Union did not win recognition until 1941 – that is, four years after the Union had won recognition from General Motors.

To compensate for this regime, Henry Ford introduced the five-dollar day, and he also preached the virtues of God, of clean living, and of no drinking, smoking or gambling.[3] Henry Ford's belief in God, however, did not save Greeks or Russians from the sack when they took a day off in order to observe orthodox church holidays, nor did it prevent Henry Ford from engaging in a prolonged anti-Semitic campaign in the 1920s in his newspaper *The Dearborn Independent*. His fascist image was further reinforced when he put Dudley Pelley, leader of the 'Silver Shirts', and US Nazi no. 1, Fritz Kuhn, the leader of the German American Bund, on the Ford payroll.

Hitler, too, was greatly impressed with Henry Ford's anti-Labour and anti-Semitic ideology. In 1938, after opening a Truck Assembly Plant in Germany, Hitler's government bestowed the Nazi German Eagle (First

Class) on Henry Ford — an honour he readily accepted.

But politics and ideology apart, Henry Ford did pioneer new engineering concepts, particularly in relation to volume output. However, large national and international markets are required to justify economically the scale of investment in plant and machinery which is necessary for the operation of complex mass production techniques. Therefore, when we examine the historical growth of companies like Ford, we are looking at one of the most advanced models of the 'multi-nationals' in terms of concentration of capital, centralised management control, and the increasing integration and internationalisation of product development (e.g. the Fiesta). We also learn how trade unions emerge and develop in this kind of environment and endeavour to look after the workers' interests.

Ford in Britain — the Battle for Union Recognition

The need to secure international markets for automotive products brought Ford to Britain in 1911. He bought and converted an existing coach-building works at Trafford Park, Manchester, and established the first Ford UK plant there. At first, knock-down parts sent over from the United States were used for car assembly, but by 1914 a conveyor-belt had been installed, and the 'Tin Lizzies' began rolling off the line. Next, Ford established a plant at Cork, in Ireland, after obtaining very favourable leasing terms from the City Council. However, a clash soon occurred with the Cork City Council, who threatened to cancel the lease, because the number employed was smaller than originally promised. Henry Ford, in response, immediately laid off over 500 workers and said he would close down the plant altogether unless the threat was withdrawn. The Cork City Council duly climbed down.

In 1921 the London County Council commenced its slum-clearance programme of the Inner London Boroughs, and chose the Essex village of Dagenham as one of its major development sites. Between 1921 and 1931, 20,000 council houses were built and the population of Dagenham increased from 9,000 to 90,000. During this period, the Unemployment Grants Committee provided two-thirds of the infrastructure costs.[4]

Ford realised the potential of this area, including the availability of a huge pool of unskilled and unemployed labour. Thus, in 1924, the Ford Motor Company purchased, for £150,000, 294 acres of land at Dagenham, along the Thames waterfront, and shortly afterwards doubled the size of its acquisition. Site development started in earnest in

1928, and by 1931 sufficient plant had been completed for car production to commence. At the same time, two associated Detroit Companies, Briggs Motor Body Manufacturers and Kelsey Hayes Wheels and Car Component Manufacturers, also developed sites in the same area.

The workers engaged in these plants were mainly the tenants of the new London County Council's Dagenham Estate. They had comparatively high rents to pay, despite widespread unemployment in the area. By 1933, the workforce totalled 7,000. Another 3,000 workers were employed at the nearby Briggs Motor Bodies Plant. As in the United States, the Ford workers would often be employed only for one or two hours daily and then remain off the payroll for the rest of the day on standby or be sent home. Safety precautions were virtually non-existent. Men worked at break-neck speed and under open and covert surveillance by a large number of security police. To be caught smoking in the toilet, for example, meant instant dismissal. There was also a system of 'Star Men'. They were Supervisors whose main task was to keep an eye on Chargehands and Foremen and other Supervisors.

In March 1933, 7,000 Ford workers went on strike against proposed wage cuts. The strike lasted three days and was partly successful. During this strike, Briggs Motor Bodies operated a lock-out. When the Company recalled the workers at the end of the Ford strike, both the day and night shift decided to stay out for better wages and conditions. The Briggs strike lasted ten days, and, after a meeting of management and Strike Committee, some small improvements in pay rates, mainly for juveniles under 18 years of age, were agreed. Mess rooms for meals and some small pay increases to other grades of workers were also part of this Agreement.

However, these actions were not really union-led, but represented a spontaneous revolt of unorganised workers against the prevailing conditions. There appears to have been little liaison during the crucial stages of this battle with the trade union movement in the Dagenham area, and hardly any developed in the following three years. Bob Lovell, the AEU District Secretary (1943-55), never tired of telling Shop Stewards about those terrible days, and never failed to point out that in the early 1930s the AEU had barely 30 members in the Ford establishments.

In 1937, the Dagenham Trades Council organised a conference for the purpose of trade union recruitment. A campaign committee was formed, and careful preparations were made, but the recruitment drive was largely a failure. In December 1937, an anonymous letter[5] from twelve Briggs workers was read out at the General Council meeting of the TUC. The letter described, in great detail, the intolerable conditions under which men, women and children had to work, and the frequency of industrial injuries and fatal accidents. The letter requested that the TUC publicise these facts and help with the unionisation of Ford. After the letter had been read out, the TUC agreed to convene a national conference for the purpose of unionising Ford. Following this conference, some headway in union recruitment was made. The Ford and Briggs Companies, however, firmly refused union recognition, and had no difficulty in continuing to satisfy their labour requirements, despite bad working conditions and harsh discipline, because their rates of pay were somewhat higher than those generally prevailing in the Dagenham area.

The first breakthrough occurred during the war, and came as a result of a Court of Inquiry into the sacking of John MacDougall, the Toolroom Shop Steward at Briggs Motor Bodies, in 1941. The government set up a Court of Inquiry which was presided over by Sir Charles Doughty. The outcome was that, although MacDougall was not reinstated, the Company reluctantly agreed to accord union recognition to the skilled workers in the Toolroom, but not to any other workers.[6] But Briggs management refused to have any dealings with full-time Trade Union Officials, and it was only after a three-year period of strikes and agitation that the Toolroom Agreement was extended to the whole of the Briggs workforce. General union recognition was not achieved at Ford until 1944, when, with Ernie Bevin at the Ministry of Labour, and against the wishes of the Shop Stewards and local Trade Union Officials, an Agreement was signed by eleven Trade Unions with the Ford Motor Company. Among the signatories were Victor (later Lord) Feather, Jack Tanner, the AEU President, and Arthur Deakin, the TGWU General Secretary.

This Agreement denied the right of shop-floor representation and gave the Company the right, in return for union recognition, to negotiate all problems with the General Secretaries of the various signatory Unions concerned. This Agreement was bitterly contested by the rank and file and by District Officials, and was, in part, amended in 1946 to give limited shop-floor representation, but the overwhelming weight of authority remained with the National Trade Union Officials.

At Briggs, however, trade unionism developed on the basis of the 1941 Toolroom Agreement. This meant that all matters, wages, working conditions, welfare, etc., were negotiated by the Shop Stewards in the plant. Eventually, full-time Trade Union Officials were allowed to assist with the solution of problems, but this outside intrusion was confined to the district level. Thus, there were two plants, barely one mile apart, securing trade union recognition based on two fundamentally different

Agreements: one specifically designed to inhibit rank-and-file development (Ford) and the other (Briggs) promoting it. These initial structural
differences had a profound effect on subsequent trade union development at Ford. The consequences of this divergent development first became noticeable during the 1947 fuel crisis. Both Companies used this
event as a pretext for dismissing hundreds of known or suspected trade
union activists, including most members of the Communist Party, which
had grown in size and influence during the war years. At Briggs, thanks
to the negotiating structure, trade union consciousness was quickly rebuilt, but at Ford, the adverse effects were much longer lasting.

This showed itself in July 1952. Briggs and Ford workers came out
solidly on strike for a 9d an hour wage increase and against proposed re-
dundancies. The strike, however, was conducted locally by two separate
Shop Stewards' Committees who liaised only perfunctorily, and the mass
meetings for the union membership in these two plants were also held
separately. At this time, the 'cold war' was at its height and some
national trade union leaders, Arthur Deakin for example, saw 'Reds'
under every Shop Stewards' Committee's bed. Consequently, for political reasons, and also in order to maintain the existing authority of
National Trade Union Officials, Harry Nicholas, the Assistant General
Secretary of the TGWU, representing all the National Trade Union
Officials of the NJNC, went to Dagenham in the second week of the
strike and spoke to a mass meeting of Ford workers. Addressing the
workers as 'Comrades', he promptly condemned the unofficial action,
and ordered a return to work. He succeeded to such an extent that many
Ford workers literally ran down the road towards the Ford works,
wrongly believing that they could start work immediately. Briggs
workers held a mass meeting on the same site two hours later and voted
overwhelmingly to stay on strike for another week. In fact, they only
returned to work after exacting a commitment from the Company to
pay a wage increase in two months' time.

Standardisation

Following the 1952 strike, Ford in Detroit decided to take over Briggs,
and the Ford Motor Company in fact acquired Briggs Motor Bodies
Limited, employing about 10,000 workers in March 1953. Previously,
Ford had bought up the Kelsey Hayes Wheel Plant, employing about
1,000 workers in 1947.

Thus Ford now owned plants with widely differing Procedure

Agreements and wage structures but above all, Ford, through their acquisition of Briggs, now faced a rank-and-file movement within their plants, which in the early 1950s was probably the most advanced in the country. The Briggs Shop Stewards' Committee was highly politicised, it had its own offices, raised its own finance, employed a full-time secretary, issued its own propaganda and published its own newspaper – *The Voice of Ford Workers.* It was based on a workshop democracy which is not generally prevalent even today. The Joint Shop Stewards' Committee met weekly on Wednesdays (sometimes more frequently), formulated policy and decided on all matters appertaining to wages and working conditions. On the following day, Thursday, all departments would hold lunch-hour shop meetings where matters raised at the Joint Shop Stewards' meeting were discussed, and either ratified or rejected. Whatever view a department came to, the common denominator was that every one in the plant knew in great detail what the Union was doing. This close and intense membership involvement created a loyalty to the Joint Shop Stewards' Committee, and amongst the Shop Stewards within that Committee, which transcended all other craft and union loyalties. In terms of structure, function and commitment, this rank-and-file movement was the most advanced model of genuine industrial unionism at the plant level in Britain at that time.

This close involvement also politicised the membership, for example, when in 1952 the Bata Shoe Company at Tilbury sacked a number of workers and subsequently attempted to evict them from their homes on the nearby company housing estate, Ford workers voted to defend the Bata workers and to resist their evictions. Large numbers of workers travelled daily from Dagenham to Tilbury to man the defences and keep the bailiffs out. They were later joined by dockers from Tilbury. Pressure on the Bata management was so intense as a result of this solidarity action, that they were forced to give way and negotiate a settlement with the Dagenham workers' *Briggs Motor Bodies Shops Stewards' Committee.* This victory established a lasting tradition, so that when, about 15 years later the Ilford Borough Council attempted to evict squatters by hiring Barry Quatermaines' private army, Ford workers once again played a crucial part in foiling this.[7]

Faced with this situation, Ford was naturally anxious to bring Briggs into line with the prevailing Ford national agreement. This policy had the wholehearted support of most National Trade Union Officials, such as, for example, the AEU President, Bill Carron, and Frank Cousins, the General Secretary of the TGWU. Ford rightly assumed that standardisation would wrest control from the rank-and-file movement and render it ineffective. The Briggs Shop Stewards' Committee came to a similar conclusion and in consequence 1953 saw the commencement of a bitter five-year struggle around this issue. At the half-way stage in this battle, a Procedure Agreement was signed in August 1955 which standardised negotiating arrangements at plant, district and national level. But this proved to be only a temporary truce document, and did nothing to lessen the day-to-day conflict, or reduce the number of stoppages: '289 strikes occurred at Briggs in the period immediately preceding the agreement (February 1954 – August 1955) and 234 stoppages occurred over a similar period after the 1955 agreement was signed.'[8]

At that time, the Company was greatly assisted by an intense press, radio and television campaign against the rank-and-file movement at Briggs and Ford. Special television programmes were screened, such as 'The Reds at Fords', starring, among others, Labour MP Woodrow Wyatt. In fact, Woodrow Wyatt led a sustained anti-red crusade in the mid-fifties on this issue, and on one occasion accepted the challenge of Briggs Motor Bodies Convener, Jack Mitchell, to debate the issue publicly. When the debate took place the meeting hall was crowded. Significantly, Woodrow Wyatt concentrated, not on Ford, but on the electoral malpractices in the ETU.[9]

The climactic point of the 'standardisation' struggle – essentially a conflict about negotiating rights – was reached in January 1957, when Johnny McLoughlin, a River Plant AEU Deputy Shop Steward in the Jig and Fixture Department, was sacked. This was during the period of the fuel shortage which resulted from the Suez Canal crisis of November 1956 and which presented Ford with the opportunity to sack 1,729 workers.[10] As in 1947, the Company utilised a national crisis to attack and to decimate the rank-and-file movement. In January 1957, known or suspected trade union activists were picked out and sacked by the hundreds, including some Shop Stewards. When Plant Conveners went to London to consult with their National Trade Union Officials about this situation, they were suspended for being absent from work without permission. On hearing this news, McLoughlin convened a shop meeting during working hours by ringing a large hand bell. This hand bell had been used for many years in the River Plant Jig Shop to signify the commencement of lunch-hour union meetings. When McLoughlin's

Foreman — Ted Martin — heard the bell ring, he

> 'was absolutely raving and spoke to him (McLoughlin) in incensed
> terms'. In order to pacify him McLoughlin said 'leave it alone Ted,
> give yourself a rest'. But the foreman swiftly returned to the charge,
> now 'quivering like a jelly', in company with Mr. Smith, the General
> Foreman, . . . McLoughlin was suspended and thereafter has remained
> 'outside the gate'.[11]

The Ford factory branch of the Communist Party had about 50
members in those days. The Company firmly believed it was the root
cause of most, if not all, of its labour problems. However, to put this
matter into some kind of perspective, it is perhaps worth recording that
the overwhelming majority of Ford and Briggs Shop Stewards supported
the Labour Party and that the fifty or so CP members were spread out
throughout a workforce of about 30,000. None the less, because management was convinced that McLoughlin was a member of the
Communist Party, the Company decided that this was as good an issue
as any for 'Fords to challenge the Briggs Shop Stewards'.[12]

In order to secure McLoughlin's reinstatement, all the Briggs workers
went on strike. In the second week of the strike the AEU Executive
Council decided to hold a secret ballot, ostensibly for the purpose of
ascertaining the AEU membership's willingness to engage in a prolonged
strike to get McLoughlin reinstated. The Executive pledged itself to
abide by the result. It was a device to secure a resumption of work, but,
perhaps more importantly, it seemed a convenient way to dispose of the
issue. Under AEU Union Rules, a two-thirds majority was required
before the Union could sanction strike action. To Union President Bill
Carron and some Executive Council members such as John Boyd, it
seemed a fairly safe bet, that, after a couple of weeks back at work, the
requisite majority for strike action would not be obtained. To the consternation of the Company, the AEU Executive Council and also, of
course, the press, which had been frantically clamouring for a secret
ballot, the result was 1,118 for strike action, 429 against, 7 spoilt
papers.[13]

The AEU Executive Council met on 18 February 1957 to consider
the ballot result; it kept its promise and called a strike against Ford
which was to begin on 27 February 1957. The government thereafter
intervened, and the Minister of Labour, Ian McLeod, set up a Court of
Inquiry under a Scottish judge, Lord Cameron. This provided a convenient way out for the AEU Executive, who promptly suspended the pro-

posed strike pending the outcome of this Inquiry. During the Court of Inquiry, Lord Cameron restated the Company's view, 'that it had upon its hands at Briggs one of the most highly organised shop steward movements in the country, a powerful and financially strong group whose objective was destructive conflict'.[14] And in summing up, his Lordship expressed the view, 'that it was a private Union within a Union enjoying immediate and continuous touch with the men in the shop, answerable to no superiors and in no way officially or constitutionally linked with the union hierarchy'.[15]

Thus Lord Cameron, perhaps not surprisingly, found in favour of the Company, and recommended that 'the dismissal of Mr. McLoughlin should stand and that the requirement of his immediate reinstatement should not be further pursued by the unions'.[16]

Subsequent to the Court hearings, all the seven members of the AEU Executive Council, led by Union President Bill (later Lord) Carron, came to Dagenham to meet the membership. It was an unprecedented event. They explained the difficulties of the situation in view of the Court of Inquiry's findings, and invited those present to express their views. Bill Carron lectured the membership about militant action and advised them to confine their activities to 'mental militancy'. Thereafter, they went away and decided to take no further action. Consequently, McLoughlin stayed sacked.

This defeat greatly demoralised the rank-and-file movement and paved the way for the signing of the 1958 Standardisation Agreement. Thus Briggs' workers now had to accept the wages and working conditions which prevailed at Ford. More importantly, from now on all negotiating rights would be vested in the NJNC – a Committee exclusively composed of Company and full-time Trade Union Officials.

However, the Shop Stewards slowly rebuilt the union organisation over the course of the next five years. Organisational structures were improved, as well as the liaison between Conveners and Shop Stewards' Committees in different plants. During the same period, the Company expanded its operations at Dagenham and built a new Paint, Trim and Assembly Plant (PTA) and a new Foundry.

In 1961, notwithstanding previous assurances, Ford bought out the whole 45 per cent of the British Ford shareholding, thus embarrassing the government to such an extent that even Selwyn Lloyd, then Chancellor of the Exchequer, invited the Dagenham Conveners to meet him. The meeting, however, never took place because Selwyn Lloyd stipulated that he was merely prepared to give information and not willing to discuss or listen to arguments.

Conflict over Line Speeds

Amongst other things, the Standardisation Agreement had the effect of removing wage negotiations from the plant level. Therefore, the energies of the newly 'standardised' Shop Stewards' Committees and workers were increasingly concentrated on control issues at the point of production, such as manning levels, line speeds, time and motion study, shift working and, of course, merit money. These became the focal point of conflict with the Company and, more indirectly, because technical breaches of signed agreements were frequently involved, with the National Trade Union Officials.

Events came to a head in the autumn of 1962 in the new Assembly Plant, which by then was employing about 5,000 workers drawn roughly in equal numbers from the original Briggs and Ford plants. The Paint, Trim and Assembly Plant became operational in 1959 and from then on the intensity of conflict increased. It was a battle about control of the assembly line. Senior management members were flown to Detroit and shown how to raise output. Conversely, the PTA Shop Stewards' Committee operated an 'anti-speed-up' plant policy, which meant resistance to new lay-outs and to the implementation of stop-watch timings. The central objective was the maintenance of the status quo.

The intensity of conflict which this issue generated in 1962 can be gauged from the following figures: 'Output lost through strikes in Company plants outside Dagenham was a half-hour per man, at Dagenham (excluding the PTA), 15 hours per man, in the PTA plant 78 hours per man.'[17]

In the autumn of 1962, the government's taxation policies, i.e. 45 per cent Purchase Tax on new cars, caused a very serious trade recession throughout the motor industry. The Company used this situation to launch an all-out onslaught on the Shop Stewards' Committees in the Body and Assembly Plants with the intention of smashing the rank-and-file leadership once and for all. According to a Dagenham District Union Officials' pamphlet, Ford Vice-President, J.S. Bugas, former head of the FBI in Detroit, masterminded this operation. He was given the task because he successfully imposed a 25 per cent speed-up on an unwilling workforce at the Ford River Rouge Plant at Detroit in 1949, firing hundreds of workers in the process.[18]

Based on information culled from personal dossiers and supplemented from reports by Supervisors, 'seventy trouble makers' were identified and fired. They were mostly Shop Stewards, including the PTA Convener, Kevin Halpin, who, at that time, was also the Communist

Party's parliamentary candidate for Dagenham. There was a spontaneous walk-out in the Body and Assembly Plants and the strike lasted one week. As in 1957, the National Trade Union Officials requested a resumption of work, pledging themselves to secure the reinstatement of *all* those sacked. Frank Cousins, General Secretary of the TGWU, was particularly vocal and insistent on this point. After lengthy and tortuous negotiations, including misconstrued telephone conversations, reminiscent of a Marx Brothers film, the original number of seventy was eventually reduced by stages to seventeen. To preclude official strike action by some unions in support of 'the seventeen', the government set up another Court of Inquiry in February 1963, this time under Economics Professor D.T. Jack, CBE. The Cameron Court of Inquiry files were dusted down, and the Company and trade union submissions amounted basically to a re-statement of their 1957 positions.

Since the Cameron Court of Inquiry, the Company complained, 'the joint Shop Stewards' Committees had not been proscribed by any of the unions, and the Company knew of no efforts by any union to destroy . . . this canker in the trade union movement'.[19]

Les Kealey, the National Engineering Officer of the TGWU and the Union's chief negotiator at Ford, however, obligingly responded. He said:

Unfortunately a number of stewards of certain unions in Dagenham, have got into the habit of trying to solve their own problems. Even more serious are the activities of the Joint Shop Stewards' Committee who have their own offices, and churn out anti-Company literature daily. Their actions make it impossible to build up the sort of relationships with the Ford Motor Company which will enable the unions to obtain for their members, the best wages and working conditions possible, and have brought us to the position where we are forced to declare war on the Company to protect the victimised workers. As soon as this dispute is finalised, it will be necessary, in the interest of the membership of the union, to jointly take action to seriously deal with the problems of union machinery at Dagenham.[20]

This close identity of views made the outcome of the Court of Inquiry a foregone conclusion. The 'seventeen trouble makers', like McLoughlin, stayed sacked. It was another severe defeat for the rank-and-file movement, it enabled the Company to impose a 30 per cent speed-up in the PTA and no further stoppages of work of any significance occurred in this plant until 1965. The outcome considerably strengthened the Company's and the National Trade Union Officials' position for the next five years.[21]

The Wage Structure

Standardisation brought in its wake the application of the Ford wage structure to all other plants. It comprised three grades for men – skilled, semi-skilled and unskilled – and a separate lower grade for women. Grafted onto this, however, was one other important element – merit money. Merit money as conceived and applied in the original Ford establishment – mainly the Engine and Foundry Plants – was a facility and a device to enable a Supervisor to reward a particularly 'good' employee with a penny once every two or three years. This was added to his hourly rate. 'Good' employees with twelve or more years' service thus managed, on average, to accumulate about four or five pence by 1958. Merit money had never been an issue of any interest to Ford workers, and Shop Stewards treated it with a certain amount of disdain. When this aspect of the standardisation package, however, was applied in the plants which had traditionally conducted and controlled their own pay negotiations – i.e. Briggs Motor Bodies – and which, by virtue of the new Agreement, were now precluded from doing so, it was hardly surprising that the workers in those plants seized upon merit money as a means for topping up nationally agreed wage settlements. What used to be an occasional individual award soon became transformed into an annual collective departmental across-the-board award. Further, the practice of one penny at a time was gradually changed to two and three pence at a time. For example, in 1966, Toolmakers in all Ford plants secured a three pence across-the-board merit increase, and it was, indeed, this pressure by the skilled section which eventually persuaded the Company to engage in a review of the existing wage structure.

By 1965, as a result of continuous pressure on the merit pay front, a wage gap of 4 shillings per hour had opened up between the lowest-paid new starter and the highest-paid worker with seven or more years' service. Consequently, what was intended to be a simple three-grade structure, had in reality been transformed, and was spread over more than 40 different individual pay rates. It was the chief topic of daily discussion and a basic cause of conflict.

The situation became increasingly untenable for the Company because of their new plant at Halewood. Assisted by very generous government grants and subsidies, Ford decided to build a major car plant on Merseyside, then as now, an economically distressed area. The Halewood Plant at Liverpool became operational in 1963.[22] Based on a local Agreement with the AEU and the GMWU, the standard pay rates at Halewood were over one shilling per hour less than those at Dagenham. After two years of strikes and overtime bans, the Company finally conceded parity of basic pay with Dagenham. But, since the workers at Halewood were all new starters, they continued, because of merit pay, to receive, on average, about one shilling per hour less than workers at Dagenham. However, to have handed out bigger 'chunks' of merit pay at Halewood to bring the all-in pay rates in line with Dagenham would, of course, have created a demand for similar 'chunks' to be paid out at Dagenham. Conversely, by not bringing merit pay into line, the Company experienced continuous problems and pressures at Halewood.

The defeats, particularly those of 1957 and 1962, made it much easier for the Company to conclude annual 'sweetheart' pay Agreements with the predominantly right-wing national trade union leadership. The size of annual increases were 2d/3d per hour. This practice, however, eventually proved to be self-defeating. The Ford starting rates, as distinct from personal rates 'distorted' by merit pay, became increasingly unattractive, and the Company found it difficult to recruit labour, particularly skilled labour.

The year 1966/67 witnessed the Labour Government's great wage freeze, which precluded the possibility of a straightforward increase in starting rates as a means of attracting the skilled labour the Company so badly needed. It caused Leslie Blakeman, Director of Labour Relations, to write a letter to the NJNC proposing a Dilution Agreement. This, however, was rejected by the AEU.

The introduction of a new wage structure thus became an increasingly attractive proposition, almost irresistible. It held out the prospect of (1) circumventing the wage freeze, (2) eliminating the merit pay jungle and (3) further enhancing the authority of the NJNC at the expense of the Shop Stewards. The Company therefore proposed to the Trade Unions that the existing wage structure be reviewed, and an exercise be undertaken to see what changes, if any, were required.

At Shop Steward level, the attitude towards the possible introduction of a new wage structure was mixed. The old Ford establishment, particularly the Engine and Foundry Plants which had been accustomed to the three-grade structure for years, prior to standardisation, were strongly opposed to any change. They argued, with some justification, that the introduction of a new wage structure would prove divisive, set worker against worker, plant against plant and union against union. The Shop Stewards' Committees of the newly 'standardised' plants which were used to multi-grade structures, Briggs Motor Bodies for example, favoured the introduction of a new wage structure on the grounds that it would create more scope for upward movement, in other words up-gradings. Also, the transformation of long-established and rigid pay and grading patterns would most likely activate workers, who in recent years had shown little desire to fight for improved wages.

The Halewood Plants were generally in favour, because they wanted to achieve real pay parity with Dagenham. The National Trade Union Officials, by and large, were in favour, although for conflicting reasons. The majority of them genuinely wanted to be helpful, and supported all the Company's reasons for instituting a review of the existing wages structure. The few Trade Union Officials who were traditionally less well disposed towards the Ford Motor Company, none the less, supported the idea, because they too saw it as a means of circumventing the pay freeze. Thus the Company received the go-ahead at NJNC level and lost no time in engaging a firm of Management Consultants – Urwick, Orr and Partners – at a fee reputed to be in excess of £150,000, to advise and assist with this project. The original Urwick Orr Management Consultancy was established in the United States at the time of Frederick Taylor, shortly after Henry Ford had begun to base his pro-duction methods on 'Taylorism'. It is perhaps ironic that the Ford Motor Company found the problems fifty years of 'scientific management' had created so insoluble, that it had to enlist the services of a firm of Consultants.

A large and elaborate machinery was constructed for the purpose of reviewing the existing wage structure. The whole exercise was launched by a slick and extensive public relations programme. Messages from the Chairman of Ford Europe, the Director of Labour Relations and the Chairman of the Trade Union Side of the NJNC, extolling the virtue of the Wage Structure Review, were solemnly relayed at specially convened Joint Works' Committee meetings in all plants.

Over 2,000 jobs were evaluated and analysed by a score of Assessment Teams and subsequently processed by Divisional Review Committees consisting of an equal number of Shop Stewards and Company represent-atives. Their reviews, in turn, were finally vetted by a Central Review Committee consisting of four Company members and a trade union observer from AEF Head Offices in London. The method employed was the profiling and ranking technique. It should, however, be emphasised that the job hierarchy and the rank order merely reflected the

Company's view about the relative importance of jobs to their productive needs. Similarly, the original benchmarks and the 28 job characteristics – the standard against which all jobs had to be measured – were pre-selected by the Company and the Consultants.

The detailed and complex methods and statistical processes, linked to a sophisticated computer programme, served to create the illusion that job evaluation was a scientific process and, therefore, objective. However, the initial selection of the 28 characteristics, and the subsequent weightings attached to some of these, ensured that the outcome would indeed correspond to and meet the productive needs of the Company. This is, of course, true of all job evaluation schemes, i.e. the initial standards selected determine the outcome.

At that point in time, the Company needed a revision acceptable to the Trade Unions which would give the largest slices of any improvement to the skilled occupations, and least benefit to workers engaged on routine production operations, a process on which over half the workforce was employed. For about six months, the Company, and the Trade Unions, were totally absorbed by the task of analysing and evaluating jobs. Personnel Managers and Conveners alike remarked 'whatever did we have to talk about prior to the job evaluation scheme?' It was a classic example of how trade union representatives can become fascinated with the routines of management and absorbed by them.

In order to reinforce the 'objectivity image', part of the public relations exercise consisted of telling workers to 'sell' the value and importance of their jobs to the Assessors and the Review Committees to the best of their ability. This experience taught workers the art of selling the value of their job with expertise and ingenuity. They acquired, also, a belief in the importance of their particular job and thus developed a desire to have this importance recognised in terms of rewards on a scale which the Company could not hope to satisfy. In fact, Ford paid a heavy price over a period of four years for generating these kinds of expectations. So much so that Bob Ramsey, the current Director of Industrial Relations, remarked in 1971 that he would rather 'go to the stake' than through another grading grievance exercise.

In order to clinch the deal and as a means of overcoming the remaining pockets of trade union resistance, the Company offered to incorporate a Grading Grievance Procedure into the proposed Agreement, arguing that this would enable any section of workers, who were dissatisfied, to have their jobs reviewed.

This was done and the new Wage Structure Agreement was signed with the Trade Unions in August 1967. The existing three-grade structure was expanded into five grades — A, B, C, D, E. The most highly skilled craftsmen, such as Toolmakers, were placed into the highest grade — E. The women's rate was set at 85 per cent of the appropriate male rate. The basic starting rate for skilled workers was raised by one shilling and sixpence per hour. This was three times more than the amount which the general run of production workers received. The outcome had been a foregone conclusion and indeed met, as has previously been pointed out, the economic requirements of the Company. The number of workers in each new grade in May 1968 was as follows:

Males			Females		
	E	3,985		E	—
	D	3,301		D	—
	C	11,288		C	16
	B	21,761		B	719
	A	859		A	183
	Total	41,194		Total	918 [23]

The job evaluation exercise as a whole encouraged sectionalism and deepened divisions amongst the workforce, without significantly altering the rank order of the occupational structure. The statistical table shows, for example, that virtually all women workers were placed into the two lowest grades, thus causing a good deal of resentment and eventually leading to the dispute which is described in Part II.

Notes

1. Henry Ford, *My Life and Work* (New York, 1922), p. 103.
2. Ibid., p. 103. Contrast with Harry Braverman, *Labour and Monopoly Capital* (1974).
3. For a Marxist analysis of this aspect, see Antonio Gramsci, 'Americanism and Fordism' in *Prison Notebooks* (Lawrence and Wishart, 1971).
4. See J.G. O'Leary, *The Book of Dagenham* (Borough of Dagenham, (1963), and T. Young, *Beacontree and Dagenham,* Report to the Pilgrims Trust (1934).
5. TUC General Council meeting, 8 December 1937. See Ch. 1, note 13, p. 23, above.
6. For more detailed account of this event, see *Report of a Court of Inquiry* (The Doughty Report), Cmd. 6384 (HMSO, London, 1941).
7. Henry Friedman, 'Multi-Plant Working and Trade Union Organisation', *Studies for Trade Unionists,* vol. II, no. 8, WEA (December 1976).
8. Report of a *Court of Inquiry,* (The Cameron Report) Cmnd. 131 (HMSO, London, April 1957), para. 74, p. 21.
9. The meeting turned hilarious when Mitchell started to quote long passages from Wyatt's books on 'haute cuisine' and 'gracious living'.
10. Cameron Report, para. 42, p. 13.
11. Ibid., para. 48, pp. 14, 15.

12. *Daily Express* headline, 30 January 1957.

13. Cameron Report, para. 52, p. 13.

14. Ibid., para. 38, p. 12.

15. Ibid., para. 91, p. 26.

16. Ibid., para. 106, p. 31.

17. *Report of a Court of Inquiry* (The Jack Report), Cmnd. 1999 (HMSO, London, April 1963), para. 29, p. 11.

18. Dagenham District Officials' Panel, 'Years of Struggle against Injustice' (unpublished), p. 14.

19. Jack Report, para. 61, p.23.

20. Ibid., Para. 128, p. 51.

21. For a more detailed account of these events, see Jack Report. For a far left-wing view, Solidarity pamphlet, no. 26, *What happened at Fords* (1967).

22. The Company has continued its policy of building new plants in distressed areas, i.e. Valencia in Spain, Bordeaux in France, Genk in Belgium, Saarlouis in Germany, and Bridgend in Wales.

23. Company submission to the Scamp Court of Inquiry – Table III.

Part II

THE SEWING MACHINISTS' DISPUTE

3 THE DISPUTE SEEN THROUGH MANAGEMENT'S EYES

The Setting

Your first sight of Ford Central Office may surprise and even delight you. Ford's management control centre for the whole of its British and European Operations is housed in a six-storey building of pleasing proportions, clean-faced in Portland stone. Its functional facade is supported by a series of slender curving fins which carry your eye, in one seductive sweep, from the blue and white Ford logo, set amongst shimmering silver birch trees on the front lawn, up the 30-foot flag mast (with its flamboyant Union Jack which reminds you that this is the Headquarters of Ford of Britain, as well as the owner-occupier, Ford of Europe), to the Directors' Offices on the sixth floor and the Penthouse and Gymnasium above.

Ford Central Office conveys an immediate impression of strength and restraint: the aesthetically acceptable face of multinational capitalism. Perched high up on the windy ridge above Childerditch Common, the Warley building commands a panoramic view across the featureless plain of alluvial Essex: from the green fields and leafy lanes which surround Central Office, right down to the smudgy outline of industrial development along the River Thames at Dagenham, some 12 miles to the south. On a clear day, with the wind in the north, the Directors of Ford of Britain enjoy a magnificent view of the Company's largest manufacturing site in Europe — the Dagenham square mile — of which the twin gas holders, blast furnace and coke ovens,[1] iron foundry and forge, machine shops, body stamping and paint, trim and assembly buildings are all visible on the distant skyline. They offer Ford of Britain's Directors a constant reminder — if any were needed — that from Ford Central Office they control and manage over £1,000 million of capital investment, spread over 24 separate British plants, which in 1978 employed over 57,000 people, producing over half a million cars, vans, trucks and tractors each year at a pre-tax profit in 1978 of over £240 million.

Since 1961, Ford Motor Company Limited has been a wholly owned subsidiary of the Ford Motor Company of Dearborn, Detroit, Michigan. Before 1966, the Chairman, Managing Director and Directors of Ford in Britain reported direct to the parent Company in Detroit. Since 1966, the Board of Ford of Britain, as the Company is more usually known, report to the President and Chairman of the Board of Ford of Europe — in organisational theory, a separate legal entity responsible for the co-ordination of Ford Operations throughout Europe; in practical terms, just one corridor and one dividing wall away. If walls have ears, they say the walls of Warley have ears so sharp, their secrets may be clearly heard as far away as Detroit.

Before Ford came here in 1961, the name of Warley was familiar to the people of this pleasant part of Essex for two particular landmarks: half-way up Warley Hill is the red-brick Victorian lunatic asylum, now modernised but still serving as the principal mental hospital for the area; and on the very site of Ford Central Office there stood the headquarters of an earlier multinational corporation — the English East India Company — and later the headquarters and barracks of the Essex Regiment, where generations of Essex men were drilled to march in step and obey the word of command. When the bulldozers arrived in 1961, they made short work of the barracks. But the regimental colours were laid up in the tiny Chapel of Remembrance which stands incongruously, amid its neat rosebeds, embraced in the evergreen arms of ancient cedars, in the very shadow of Ford Central Office. Apart from the hospital and the Chapel — twin sanctuaries from suffering and distress — the name of Warley is now synonymous with the multinational magnificence and the dark, satanic mills of Henry Ford.

As you reach the entrance of Central Office, double plate-glass doors swing open automatically and you find yourself crossing the chequered terrazzo of an imposing two-storey foyer, large enough to display several of Ford's latest models. Their gleaming chrome and immaculate paint-work are glimpsed through potted palms against a Sunday colour supple-ment background of black polished marble. The pressurised lift carries you imperceptibly to the sixth floor where the Directors each have their own Executive Suites: comfortable unostentatious offices furnished in the mid-sixties style — off-white carpet, vinyl-covered wall panels, the dark glow of a teak desk blending with the beige wool-upholstered armchairs, with a splash of scarlet or royal blue from an occasional chair, and legislated oases of refreshing plant displays, graduated in scale to execu-tive rank, set on the familiar low coffee table of plate glass and tubular chrome.

The sixth floor at Warley is deceptively calm. Except for the discreet chatter of electric typewriters and well-groomed secretaries, its execu-tive offices are rarely disturbed by noise. Directors confer with members of their staff, often without troubling to close their inner office doors.

A black-suited penthouse steward serves fresh coffee or afternoon tea without interrupting the ebb and flow of management meetings which fill every Warley day. An occasional voice is raised — more often in laughter than in anger. Humour is the key to executive survival in a multinational corporation. At Warley, the wit is cool, stories are economical, jokes pared to the bone. Ford's top managers are trained to maximise the return on every investment. Tough-minded disillusioned optimists, they practise cost-benefit ratios over their breakfast cereal and their non-alcoholic lunches. The Warley penthouse is dry, except for special occasions. Their days are dedicated to purposeful, profit-centred activity: attending meetings, committees, conferences; making or hearing presentations of management proposals, plans and objectives; scrutinising performance against target figures; drafting reports, dictating memoranda, reviewing staff papers and eventually concurring final versions to be signed off by Ford of Britain's Managing Director, on the advice of his fellow Directors, for review and approval by Ford of Europe.

As the River Thames flows into the sea, so information flows endlessly into Warley: schedules of production, planned and actual; statistical details on volume, cost and quality; reports on machinery, plant or equipment breakdown; production losses attributable to internal or external cause; every reported employee grievance or Shop Steward's failure to agree; each separate overtime ban, go-slow or work-to-rule; strikes threatened, strikes in progress or strikes ended, their total cost computed in man-hours lost or saleable units undelivered — all the information it is possible to assemble, in every useful dimension, about the plans and performance of each of the 24 plants of Ford of Britain, from Halewood on Merseyside in the north to Southampton on the Solent in the south, from Swansea, Treforest and Bridgend in the west to Daventry, Dunton and Dagenham in the east. Hard-centred data or soft-centred speculation — all this information is channelled into Warley through the mailing office, telephone exchange, telex centre and computer complex, to be logged, sorted and distributed to some 2,000 staff who make up the technocratic hierarchies of each functional Director: Manufacture; Production Planning and Control; Marketing; Finance; Industrial Relations; and others.

Between the computer complex on the first floor (Anglice: ground floor) and the Directors on the sixth floor, are sandwiched the successive layers of Ford's deep technostructure: phalanxes of middle management in rank profusion and multinational complexity: Analysts, Advisers, Associates, Supervisors, Co-ordinators and Specialists — subordinates and

superordinates of every rank, degree and status. For this is the latter-day
Essex Regiment, Mr Ford's New Model Army, who manage the business
as others wage war: gathering information; probing situation reports;
planning commercial sorties; undertaking careful reconnaissance raids
before launching a major attack on the market; briefing and de-briefing
Executives on market penetration, territory gained from competitors,
units sold and man-hours lost; preparing press reports and issuing
employee bulletins. This is the essential background to successful commercial warfare.

Ford of Britain's Central Staff at Warley carries a threefold responsibility: (1) to draw up the general policy lines and directions the
Company will follow — the annual production plan based on approved
annual budgets and profit targets; (2) to promulgate these over-all
targets or strategies in the form of detailed plans, policies and directives;
and (3) to monitor the subsequent performance of every profit centre,
production, sales or service unit, against those targets: by the hour, day
and shift, by the production week, month and quarter. Once profit
objectives have been set, the reasons for their non-achievement — the
'off-standard' condition, as it is known in the business — are painstak-
ingly analysed for precise cause and likely effect. Grand totals are dis-
aggregated and sub-totals combined; estimates made of the growth
potential and adverse effect on profit targets of every failure, breakdown
or shortfall, by Company, Group, Operation, Plant, Department, Shop,
Line, Machine and Component detail. It is probably not surprising that
the ranks of this army contain some of the sharpest-pencilled analysts,
the shrewdest business brains and the most experienced, hard-working
and highest-paid men and women in British industry. Ford of Britain has
long been known as Britain's first and most prestigious Business School.[2]

In May 1968, when the narrative of this chapter begins, Leslie
Blakeman, Ford of Britain's Director of Labour Relations, looked back
on twelve months of remarkable achievement in the history of Ford's
labour relations. In 1952, when he joined the Company as Labour
Relations Manager, the name of Ford was a four-letter word that drove
the good news off the front page of every newspaper.[3] By 1968,
Blakeman could speak of Ford as having the most improved industrial
relations record in the industry. After two major Courts of Inquiry,
Blakeman's faith in 'the Ford industrial creed' had been badly shaken.
The reports of the Forward Planning Team had convinced him that
Ford's traditional strategy of 'autocracy tempered by insurgence' would
not survive the sixties. They furnished the intellectual arguments needed
to persuade top management that the progressive weakening of manage-

ment control and the growing anarchy of Ford's shop-floor relations could be transformed by the adoption of a new industrial relations strategy, directed along more positive, pragmatic and pluralist lines. Without abandoning its traditional policy of 'direct control' and without embracing the 'responsible autonomy' strategy of the British 'human relations' school of personnel management,[4] Ford's new labour strategy set out to correct the fundamental weakness in the Company's industrial relations, a weakness which Allan Flanders was later to attribute to British management in general as comprising that 'mixture of realism and pretence, of being forced to yield to bargaining power on the shop floor while denying it any legitimacy'.[5] From the first Agreement of 1944, Ford had relied on the authority of National Trade Union Officials, as 'partners in control'. During the fifties and early sixties, their authority had progressively weakened to the point where they were no longer effective partners in such a power-sharing strategy. By the mid-sixties, Blakeman was prepared to acknowledge the central paradox of British industrial relations, as Flanders described it — a paradox 'whose truth managements have found so difficult to accept . . . that they can only regain control by sharing it'.[6] Blakeman now recognised that 'sharing control' meant sharing it, not with National Trade Union Officials, but with Shop Stewards in all Ford plants. He abandoned his earlier opposition to Shop Steward participation in any significant decision-making process by inviting them to play a full part, on equal terms with management, in the job evaluation programme. Encouraged by their constructive response, he again invited them, in 1967, to take a leading part in plant productivity bargaining. Blakeman later acknowledged that the Two-Year Package Deal, concluded in September, would be worthless unless the National Officials had first obtained the endorsement of the shop floor. The resulting Agreement was immediately singled out for praise by the Minister of Labour, Ray Gunter, as the industry's most positive response to the Prime Minister's warning in 1965 that it must put its industrial relations house in order or face the threat of legislative sanctions.

By 1968, Blakeman seemed confident that Ford's new industrial relations strategy was beginning to pay off. In January, the Industrial Court confirmed Blakeman's faith in the New Wage Structure by publishing its findings on the Ford Carpenters' grading arbitration — a test case brought by the Unions representing Carpenters and Joiners at Ford, in protest against the Company's new grading proposals which placed their members in Grade C. The Court's findings were expressed in the clearest and most unequivocal terms: 'Having given careful consideration to the evidence and submissions of the Parties, the Court finds that Carpenters and Joiners have been properly placed in Grade C within the Company's New Wage Structure and award accordingly.'[7]

In February, the Trade Union Side of the NJNC had attempted to re-open the Two-Year Agreement on the grounds that the devaluation of the pound in September 1967 had eroded the value of the wage award just won. These were precisely the circumstances, they argued, that were envisaged by that clause in the Agreement which provided for the re-opening of the contract if exceptional circumstances required and both parties agreed. The Company rejected the claim outright, and the Unions allowed the matter to die. In April, the NJNC's Grading Sub-Committee had expressed its satisfaction with the progress made by the Profile Review Committee (PRC), a joint body made up of three Managers and three Plant Conveners, to clear the backlog of grading grievances under the 1967 Grading Grievance Procedure.

When he sat down with his staff, to review Ford's labour relations record in the first quarter of 1968, Blakeman was delighted to learn that the number of man-hours lost through work stoppages had been almost halved — from 55,000 in the first three months of 1967 to a mere 28,000 in the same period of 1968. The New Wage Structure accounted for some 22,000 of the total man-hours lost, and for 23 of the total of 47 separate incidents (13 work stoppages and 10 overtime bans). If the Grading Grievance Procedure could be speeded up and made more effective, the prospects for industrial peace at Ford seemed brighter than Blakeman could ever remember.

Blakeman clearly felt that the pioneering work of voluntary reform in Ford's industrial relations policies, procedures and practices — which anticipated the recommendations of the Donovan Commission, whose Report was due to be published within a few weeks — was a major historical landmark. And although too modest to say so, Blakeman had been the driving force behind that voluntary reform. His conversion from 'the Ford industrial creed' to what might be called 'the Donovan creed of reforming pluralism' had been turned into a programme of energetic activity and lobbying to ensure its success. Aged 64 and within sight of retirement, Blakeman's large frame and full-moon face, with its drooping eyelids, combined with a slow, slightly mannered speech to suggest a tired man at the end of his working life — an impression of mental and physical weariness reinforced by his familiar posture, slumped in his chair, one hand supporting a heavy head, whilst the other toyed endlessly with a silver cigarette lighter. Such first impressions were deceptive, for Blakeman personified the principle of the conservation of energy. On the morning of an important negotiation, he could appear dull and listless. Once the negotiations had begun, however, he was transformed, calling on apparently inexhaustible reserves of physical stamina, emotional energy and verbal fluency.

In the early days of May 1968, standing at the window of his sixth-floor office at Warley, looking across at the distant outline of the Dagenham Estate, Blakeman viewed the industrial relations outlook at Ford with greater confidence than he had ever done before. There was, however, one cloud on Blakeman's horizon — a cloud no bigger than a Sewing Machinist's hand.

The Trigger

In 1968, Ford's total hourly-paid workforce exceeded 42,000, amongst whom were some 900 women workers — about 2 per cent of the total. Roughly half of these women were employed as Sewing Machinists in the Dagenham and Halewood Trim Shops, making up backs and cushions of car seats, door and facia pads and headlinings. This work is divided into three separate, linked operations: the preparatory stage, in which bolts of leather cloth or fabric are unrolled and cut into shapes by the male Bench Hands and Leathercutters; an intermediate stage, in which the shaped pieces are rough-stitched by one group of Sewing Machinists; and the final stage, in which the pieces are finished off by a second group of Sewing Machinists. Of the 380 Sewing Machinists employed by Ford in 1968, 187 worked in the Trim Shop of the Dagenham River Plant, and about the same number in the Assembly Plant at Halewood on Merseyside — all engaged on broadly similar work. Since the women were prevented by the protective clauses of the Factory Act from working shifts,[8] three male Sewing Machinists covered the night shift at the River Plant, mainly doing sewing repair work which could not conveniently be done during the day shift. At the Ford Research and Development Centre at Dunton, not far from Warley, there were two more Sewing Machinists who made up new prototype seats and cushion covers for use on new car models.

In April 1967, when the Company first put forward its proposals on pay and grading, a new job title of *Production Sewing Machinist* was introduced to cover both the Intermediate and Finishing Operations undertaken by the Sewing Machinists. In accordance with the job evaluation evidence, the job was allocated to Grade B of the New Wage

Structure, but the job of *Prototype Sewing Machinist* was allocated to Grade C, to reflect its greater job demand. No union objections were raised initially to these proposed new gradings — even though the Assistant General Secretary of the National Union of Vehicle Builders, which represented the majority of the Dagenham Sewing Machinists, raised a number of queries on the grading of other occupations. However, once the New Wage Structure had been agreed and the Two-Year Deal signed, the women Sewing Machinists at Dagenham in Grade B got in touch with their Union to complain that their job ought to have been allocated to Grade C alongside their sisters working as Prototype Sewing Machinists. The Union's Assistant General Secretary, Charles Gallagher, who liked to be known as Charlie, wrote to Blakeman in August 1967, transmitting the women's complaint, and asking him to explain and justify the difference between the grading of *Production* as against *Prototype* Sewing Machinists.

In October 1967, after detailed inquiries and checks, the Company confirmed that both gradings were correct: the Prototype job carried a significantly greater responsibility than the Production job and this justified the higher grading. On 20 January 1968, Blakeman, together with Ramsey, Hourly Personnel Manager, Labour Relations Staff, and Meredeen, met Gallagher at the Company's Regent Street Office, and took him through the two job profiles, explaining in detail the significant differences under each of the 28 sub-factors used to analyse every job. Gallagher reluctantly accepted the explanations given at the meeting. At least, he gave no indication that he intended to pursue the matter further by registering a failure to agree. At the meeting of the NJNC's Grading Sub-Committee, held in April 1968, there was a complete review of all outstanding grading grievances. Gallagher was present throughout that meeting but made no mention of any outstanding grievance in respect of Sewing Machinists. So far as management was concerned, the grievance had been disposed of and laid to rest.

Back at the River Plant, however, the Sewing Machinists were certainly not satisfied and refused to let the matter rest. At the River Plant Joint Works Committee meeting in December 1967, Shop Stewards from the Trim Shop took advantage of the newly instituted Grading Grievance Procedure formally to record their protest that the grading of the Intermediate Sewing Machinists did not reflect the substance of their job profiles as prepared during the job evaluation programme. The matter was again raised at JWC meetings in February, March and April, 1968, but the Convener refused to put the matter through the Grading Grievance Procedure. He contemptuously dismissed the formal reply sent from Warley that the job was correctly graded in relation to the benchmark job profile of the Sewing Machinist — Finishing Operations. The Convener insisted that the benchmark profile had been supplemented by the Divisional Review Committee's opinion on the Intermediate Sewing Machinists' job profile and that, in terms of job content, both profiles were clearly of a higher value than Grade B.

On 22 May, the Industrial Relations Officer at the River Plant reported to Warley that Trim Shop Workers had met the previous day and voted to impose an unlimited overtime ban, to be followed by a one-day strike on 29 May, if their job was not upgraded to Grade C by that date. The threatened overtime ban was subsequently lifted to allow the Industrial Relations Officer to meet the Convener to clarify the exact basis of the grievance and to attempt to persuade the women not to take unconstitutional action but to progress their grievance through Procedure. When the details of these discussions reached Warley, there was concern about the confused status of the grievance, but nobody recognised the signs of an impending major dispute. Since Sander Meredeen, who was responsible for the job evaluation programme and the new job gradings, was also Chairman of the Joint Profile Review Committee, it was decided that he should go down to the River Plant to meet the Convener and Shop Stewards in an attempt to clarify the grievance and get the one-day strike threat lifted.

On Tuesday morning, 28 May, Meredeen left the Profile Review Committee meeting in progress at Warley, and drove down to Dagenham to meet the Union Side of the River Plant JWC. It was an unprecedented event, and Meredeen was very much on his guard. Although he had never met the Trim Shop Stewards, he knew the Convener, Henry Friedman, reasonably well. In 1965, the Company had appointed Meredeen to be part-time Chairman of the Ford Sick Benefit Society, a jointly managed and jointly financed Friendly Society responsible for administering modest weekly payments to Ford hourly-paid workers who were absent from work through certified sickness. On taking over the Chairmanship, Meredeen inherited a massive financial crisis. With the help of Friedman, one of the principal elected members of the Society's Management Committee, he persuaded Ford to put more money into the Society, in return for an undertaking that the Society would strengthen its administration and reduce the high level of self-certified and avoidable sick absence. Friedman soon emerged as the elected side's leading strategist. At many acrimonious meetings of the Society's Committees, Friedman ran intellectual circles round other members, deploying actuarial statistics with a dazzling, almost professional, virtuosity.

In his handling of day-to-day labour relationships at the River Plant, Friedman combined a strongly rational approach to bargaining with a fund of tactical astuteness. Less abrasive and more subtle than other Ford Conveners, Friedman was at his best in exposing the contradictions contained in the arguments of others, and in making connections which others failed to recognise. His uncompromising style, combined with an unusual flair for debate and a powerful delivery, resulted in Friedman being distrusted, though secretly admired, by most of his fellow Stewards. Amongst Ford management, Friedman had become a legend: the *eminence rouge* behind the Ford Shop Stewards' Combine Committee. Blakeman had come to respect Friedman through many years of bitter conflict. It was Friedman's absence from work without permission in January 1957 which had led to the sacking of Johnny McLoughlin and the subsequent Cameron Inquiry.[9] It was Friedman who had backed Francis and Halpin against the Company at the Jack Inquiry of 1963.[10] And Friedman again who inspired his fellow Toolmakers in 1966 to threaten the withdrawal of their personal tool-kits, leading ultimately to the New Wage Structure in which Friedman played yet another prominent part.[11] For Friedman, whatever his limitations, was a Shop Steward of great resource. In Blakeman's own words: 'We should never underestimate him.'

Arriving at the River Plant, Meredeen realised that the problem facing him was quite different from what he had been led to expect. Friedman's argument was technically complicated but logically sound: he claimed to have *prima facie* evidence that there had been some 'manipulation' of the Intermediate Sewing Machinist job profile. The assessments under the job characteristics, agreed by his Divisional Review Committee, had apparently been marked down or simply ignored by a subsequent Review Committee. He wanted to know why. Friedman's argument was that the original job profile was good and the assessment levels correct when it had left his Committee. Why, then, had several job characteristics been altered? And why had the job been placed in Grade B when the original levels clearly justified Grade C?

The Trim Shop Stewards — Lil O'Callaghan and Rosie Boland — might not have followed every twist of Friedman's argument. But they admired his subtlety and were quite sure that the Company had deliberately 'done the girls down'. Meredeen denied this, but it was difficult to sustain the argument in general terms. There appeared to be one obvious solution to the problem: if the Stewards agreed that this grievance took precedence over all others from the River Plant, he would personally take it back to his Committee meeting at Warley and do his best to get it considered that day. At first, the Stewards refused, saying that they wanted the matter settled there and then. Later, they accepted Meredeen's proposal, provided the Committee limited its review to the five disputed characteristics and did not insist on examining the whole job. They also wanted the opportunity to meet the elected members of the Committee immediately before the review took place. The request was unorthodox but the circumstances were exceptional and Meredeen therefore agreed to meet the Stewards' conditions.

Back at Warley, the Profile Review Committee was meeting in its usual small committee room on the second floor, Meredeen recounted his morning discussion and explained why he had cut across Friedman's technical arguments by inviting the PRC to review the disputed job profile. The River Plant Stewards evidently distrusted Meredeen and had little faith in the PRC. But the Convener had persuaded them to let their grievance come before the Committee as a priority item. His conditions were transparently obvious: he wanted the original profile assessments restored and was counting on the Committee's elected members to secure that result. That was why he was on his way to talk to them. But he did not want the whole job profile reviewed, because he was not prepared to risk losing on the swings what he was confident of gaining on the roundabouts. That was why he refused to allow the Committee to re-examine the job down at the River Plant.

At this point the River Plant delegation arrived – the Convener, Friedman; the Deputy Convener, Passingham; and the two women Trim Shop Stewards, Lil O'Callaghan and Rosie Boland. It was the first recorded visit of Shop Stewards to Warley, constitutionally pursuing an industrial relations grievance. As the procedural discussion dragged on without agreement, the delegation waiting outside the committee room grew increasingly impatient. Before long, the Deputy Convener, Passingham, interrupted the meeting to announce that, unless the Committee produced a satisfactory answer that afternoon, 'the girls' would take strike action the following day. Faced with this new threat, the attitude of the Committee's members immediately hardened. This produced a deadlock which the Chairman was unwilling to break by use of his casting vote. The meeting broke up without agreement. Friedman and Passingham waited long enough to phone the River Plant and then announced that the women were about to walk out. The strike was on. But nobody present that afternoon could have foreseen the significance of that moment, or its consequences, for British industrial relations. Ford's Sewing Machinists had not merely walked out of the Dagenham River Plant: they had walked into the pages of history.

The Strike Begins

In the British system of industrial relations, any strike involving ten or more workers and lasting more than one day must be reported to the Department of Employment. In 1968, therefore, a one-day stoppage by nearly 200 workers was a serious strike by any reckoning. In the British motor industry, where strikes had come to be regarded as endemic, such a stoppage might not have been rated quite so seriously. At Ford, where 28,000 man-hours of lost production had already been recorded in the first quarter of the year, the loss of a further 1,500 man-hours was not serious enough to alert the sixth floor at Warley. The circumstances of this particular stoppage were nevertheless unusual: it centred upon an unprecedented grading grievance which had taken the Chairman of the Profile Review Committee down to Dagenham and brought the Convener and Shop Stewards back to Warley; the cause of the strike was obscure and its circumstances bizarre. Before going home that night Meredeen reported the day's events to his boss, Bob Ramsey. They concluded there was nothing to be done until the women returned to work on Thursday 30 May. There was only one possible response the Company could make: to stand firm, to take the strike and the overtime ban, if necessary; to make it clear beyond possible doubt that, so far as the Company was concerned, the women's jobs were correctly graded. If they felt they had a genuine grievance, they must submit it through the agreed Grading Grievance Procedure.

On Thursday morning, 30 May, on their return to work, the women strikers were each given a copy of a standard Company letter, suitably modified, warning them that, by taking unconstitutional action, they were in breach of their individual contracts of employment; that such action would do nothing to help their case, but might have serious consequences for their continued employment if it were repeated. This letter was part of the Company's standard drill – the minimum response to such wildcat strike action. In any similar situation, a group of Ford male workers presented with such a letter would have forgotten about it. The women's reaction was quite different. They refused to accept the letter and handed it back to their Supervisor. Then, they held an immediate meeting at which they resolved not only to continue their overtime ban, but to take further strike action on Monday 10 June, if their upgrading claim had not been met by then.

It now became clear to Blakeman, Ramsey and Meredeen that a protracted and potentially damaging dispute was in prospect amongst a group of normally well-disciplined women workers, whose previous record of employment was good, but whose future action nobody was prepared to predict – not least because they were all women. As Blakeman told Meredeen: 'With women, you never can tell.'

Throughout the following week, Blakeman's staff arranged a series of meetings with the River Plant Shop Stewards and then with Union District Officials in an attempt to get the overtime ban lifted, to clarify the issue and to direct the women's grievance into constitutional channels. River Plant management continued to report only one clear message from these meetings: nobody – except perhaps Henry Friedman – was quite certain where the heart of the dispute lay. In view of the imminent one-day strike on Monday 10 June, Ramsey decided on Thursday 6 June to go down to the River Plant himself to meet the Stewards and their District Officials, to find out exactly which group of women the grievance concerned, and to decide how best to progress the matter through Procedure.

As things turned out, the meeting only increased the confusion: one District Official said the claim for upgrading concerned only the Intermediate Sewing Machinists; another said it referred to all Sewing Machinists. Friedman persisted with his argument that the benchmark profile for the Sewing Machinist – Finishing Operations was wrong and should be replaced by that of the Intermediate Sewing Machinist. Ramsey saw Friedman's argument as a attack on the fundamental basis of the job evaluation and wage structure. The benchmarks had been established with great care in order to serve as dependable reference points for the whole job evaluation programme. Friedman's attack, said Ramsey, could be dealt with only through the NJNC, which had given its blessing to the scheme as a whole. The tone of the meeting deteriorated at this point and the exchanges became quite emotional: Ramsey refused to do a special deal with the Stewards. He confirmed that the PRC had acted correctly in rejecting the restrictions which the Stewards had attempted to place on their review of the disputed profile. Any departure from the agreed Grievance Procedure could bring the whole New Wage Structure into disrepute. He was not prepared to allow this to happen. The District Officials registered a failure to agree and undertook to refer the problem to their respective National Officials.

By the time he left the meeting late that evening, Ramsey was clear that a major dispute was now likely: the women seemed to have taken the 'bit' firmly between their teeth and there was no way of holding them back. It came as no surprise, therefore, when River Plant management reported on the following morning, Friday 7 June, that the women had unanimously supported the Stewards' recommendation of an all-out strike. They had walked out of the River Plant to the last woman — saying that they would not return until their jobs had been upgraded to Grade C.

In this confused situation, Ford's normal industrial relations drill for securing an early return to work seemed unlikely to succeed — but it had to be given a chance. The usual questions were posed. How many workers were on strike? How many were likely to be laid off in consequence? What were the strikers' latest reported plans? When did they next intend to meet? Which Unions did they belong to? Were they likely to receive support or be joined by others? What pressure could be brought to bear on them to secure a quick return to work? How long could the Assembly Plant go on building cars without car seats and cushions? Since the District Officials had already registered a failure to agree, the best chance of containing the dispute seemed to lie with the women's National Officials. However, when Ramsey eventually tracked Gallagher down in Scotland and spoke to him by phone, his position was characteristically perverse: he confirmed Friedman's claim that the Union supported the women's strike, but agreed that he would attempt to secure a resumption of work so that the issue could be progressed without duress.

On Monday 10 June, the newspapers carried varying accounts of the weekend events at Dagenham, but several agreed in their reports that the women intended to meet again later that day. To the astonishment of Blakeman's staff at Warley, the women were reported to be taking militant action not simply on account of their grading grievance, but on the basis that the Company had deliberately discriminated against women in the New Wage Structure. These reports were initially greeted with incredulity at Warley. Managers stood around in their offices, comparing news items culled from the daily press cuttings. The fact of the strike was bad enough: the charge of deliberate sex discrimination was much more serious because it struck at the very principles of evaluation and the New Wage Structure. So far as management at Warley was concerned, there was simply no foundation in the allegation. But how was that to be demonstrated or proved?

Under the old wage structure, women workers at Ford had undoubtedly suffered a fivefold discrimination:

1. They were all recruited into a limited range of jobs, mainly in the Trim Shop and on some Assembly lines — although women had carried out some of the heavier and more exacting production jobs during and immediately after the Second World War.[12]

2. They were all employed in one discriminatory pay grade, Grade IV, regardless of the type of work or the demands of the job they carried out.

3. Their rate of pay in Grade IV was always lower than that of the three male grades — although the differential had narrowed from 45 per cent of the average male production worker's Grade II rate in 1935, to 80 per cent of the equivalent rate in 1965 (or 92 per cent of the lowest male rate in Grade III).

4. They were prevented by the protective clauses of the Factory Act from working shifts and so did not enjoy the benefit of enhanced rates of pay for nightwork or weekend overtime working.

5. They received less merit money than their male counterparts because their basic rates at Ford were already higher than they could obtain in any other industrial employment close to their homes and domestic responsibilities.

The New Wage Structure, based on job evaluation, had changed all that. To begin with, job evaluation was concerned with the different levels and varying demands of work tasks. It was no more concerned with a worker's sex than it was with her age, nationality, colour or creed. In short, it was the jobs which were graded under job evaluation, not the men and women doing them. In framing their new grading and pay proposals, the Company's Grading Committee relied on the results of the evaluation to determine the job gradings. As Blakeman was later to explain:

> When the jobs were submitted to evaluation, no discrimination entered into it. Jobs were evaluated on the basis of their actual content, irrespective of whether they were performed by men or women. It was therefore illogical to continue a discriminatory grade for women.[13]

When the question of equal pay for women was raised by the Trade Unions during the course of the protracted negotiations on the Two-Year Deal, the Company had offered to pay the women 85 per cent of the equivalent male rate in each of the grades:

> The Company had previously decided of its own volition to improve the relativity between men's and women's rates by abolishing the discriminatory grade which existed in the old wage structure. [However] a study of women employees' contribution to the Company's activi-

ties revealed that not only do they retire earlier, but on average there is a difference of approximately 4 per cent absence levels which constitutes a reduction in efficiency of approximately 1 per cent and that personal relief allowances – incorporated in the work standards – amount to a reduction of a further 1 per cent. A more significant difference, however, is that caused by the legislation of the Factories Act, restricting the hours of work of female employees. This results in a reduction of their effective contribution to the Company's utilisation of labour of approximately 4 per cent due to restrictions on overtime and approximately 6 per cent due to their inability to work the rotating day and night shifts which are worked by 73 per cent of the Company's male employees. In view of these factors, the prevailing practice in the rest of the industry, Government policy in controlling national labour costs, and in order not to discriminate unfairly against male employees, it was decided that a differential would continue to apply.[14]

Les Kealey, National Organiser, TGWU, the leading spokesman for production workers, recognised the force of the Company's case. He agreed that it was probably unrealistic to expect equal pay immediately but wanted the Company to improve its offer of 85 per cent of the men's rate and to agree in principle to move towards equal pay over a specified period. But the Company had stood firm, refusing to increase its offer for the reasons stated. The offer of 85 per cent of the men's rate was finally accepted on the clear understanding that whenever the Trade Unions were ready for a joint approach to the Ministry of Labour, which would enable the Company to operate on continuous shifts, women workers would be paid the equivalent rates to the men.

When the Company's new job grading and pay proposals were published on 10 April 1967, many groups of employees expressed strong opposition. But the Sewing Machinists were not amongst them. In the process of converting rates from the old to the new structure, Ford had announced that no employee would lose money because a minimum increase was guaranteed. The application of this formula to all 42,000 hourly-paid workers showed an average increase of 11 per cent for male workers and 20 per cent for female workers, due to the abolition of the separate discriminatory female grade. In July 1967, when the implementation of the New Wage Structure was held up by the failure of certain plants to complete their productivity bargaining, a demonstration took place in some departments against the delay. The River Plant Sewing Machinists clocked out one hour early in protest against the delay in receiving their new Grade B pay rates. That protest hardly suggested that they felt aggrieved at having been singled out for discriminatory treatment.

What had induced those women to walk out defiantly on 7 June? Or to publish their extravagant allegation that they were the victims of sex discrimination? Ramsey and Meredeen were in no doubt that Friedman had exploited a genuine grievance amongst the women and had converted the grading issue into a more general attack upon the Company with the claim for equal pay. That explanation was confirmed by reports reaching Warley on 10 June that the River Plant Shop Stewards' Committee had addressed an urgent letter to the Secretaries of all the NJNC Unions, asking for massive support for the strikers. It denied that the strike was over the simple issue of grading and pay: the basic cause was discrimination against women workers, as blatant and crude as colour or race discrimination. For management, the letter confirmed the political character of the strike and suggested some far-reaching implications.

Even an unsubstantiated charge of discrimination against women was bound to carry a strong emotional appeal and prove difficult for management to oppose with reasoned argument. But Ford was bound to oppose it for four reasons. First, discrimination of any kind was in direct conflict with explicit published Company policy. It was undeniably true that Ford *had* been notorious for its discriminatory policies[15] and, in particular, for its anti-Semitic employment policies in the United States in the 1930s. But there was now a world-wide corporate policy of equal opportunity, regardless of sex, colour, race or creed. Second, Ford of Britain's New Wage Structure was based on the evaluation of work, not workers, which ruled out the possibility of inherent sex discrimination. Third, the Company had made it clear when negotiating the New Wage Structure that it was in no way opposed to equal pay in principle and that, as soon as women began to do jobs in the higher grades, they would receive the appropriate rate of pay for the job. Fourth, if and when the protective provisions of the Factory Act were removed, and women agreed to work shifts, accepting all the obligations that men accepted, their rates of pay would be raised to full equality with those of the men.

The Company was clearly in no position to use these sophisticated arguments against a group of women strikers whose emotions were running predictably high in the early days of their first-ever strike. At a mass meeting later that day, the women not only endorsed the Strike Committee's recommendation to continue the strike until their claim had been met in full; they also decided not to meet again for another two weeks — by which time attitudes would have hardened and the task of resolving the conflict made much more difficult. To get the strike called off, management had no alternative but to seek the support of Gallagher and Kealey, the National Officials of the two principal Unions involved. It is an axiom amongst negotiators that management will not meet strikers or discuss the merits of their case without first securing a full return to normal working. When Ramsey's secretary, Chris Steele, succeeded in contacting Kealey and Gallagher, the meeting she arranged in London for the following day was for the sole purpose of discussing ways of securing a return to work.

On Tuesday morning, 11 June, before that meeting began, Blakeman and Ramsey were informed that a delegation of Sewing Machinists, led by Friedman, had lobbied their Executive Council members at the AEF Headquarters in Peckham Road, South London, and persuaded them to get their Executive to make the strike official. This news confirmed what management had suspected: an unholy alliance between Friedman, the strategist of the Dagenham Shop Stewards' Movement, and Reg Birch, the renegade Communist leader of the North London Engineers, recently elected an Executive Councilman of the AEF and now that Union's representative on the Ford NJNC. His attacks on the Company at NJNC were expressed in a rhetorical style which sometimes left his listeners amused but totally bewildered. One thing, however, Birch made abundantly clear: his implacable hostility to capitalism and all its works. With Friedman and Birch in league against the Company, the strike took on a new and more serious dimension.

At their meeting with Kealey and Gallagher, the Company represent-atives suggested alternative ways of dealing with the women's grading grievance, once the strike was called off. Kealey promised to do his best but said he had few members in the Dagenham Trim Shop. When Gallagher emerged as the man on whom the Company must rely to end the strike, any hopes of a speedy outcome soon faded. Gallagher was Assistant General Secretary of the National Union of Vehicle Builders (NUVB), a small, ambitious but ineffective Union whose fortunes had declined with its membership through weak leadership and bad manage-ment. Gallagher, whose home and Head Office were in Manchester, now spent his life stomping round the strike-prone motor industry, in a vain attempt to maintain his personal credibility and his Union's membership by a display of tetchy militancy. At his meeting with Ford management that Tuesday morning, Gallagher was both weak and truculent. He was chain-smoking and wheezing badly. Despite the early hour, he also appeared to have been drinking, which made it more difficult for Ramsey to be sure that his points had been registered. Gallagher turned down every suggestion Ramsey offered for directing the issue into procedural channels. He accused the Company of showing favours to some Unions, whilst persistently discriminating against its women workers who formed the bulk of his Union's membership on the Dagenham Estate. He would not recommend a return to work until the Company had conceded Grade C to the Production Machinists and Grade D to the Prototype Machinists at Dunton. When Ramsey protested that this was the first he had heard of the second grievance, Gallagher simply shrugged his shoulders and said he would be recommending his Executive to make the strike official on behalf of both groups of women.

Within two working days of an unconstitutional walk-out, this small and previously obscure group of women workers had gained the official support of the two principal Unions involved in the strike. If the NUVB Executive made the strike by the Dagenham women official, the women in the Halewood Trim Shop would certainly come out in support of their Dagenham sisters, and Kealey would be powerless to stop them. Their action would cut off the supply of seat covers to both Assembly Plants which, in turn, meant the Company would be forced to lay off thousands of men and eventually stop production. At the end of their abortive meeting with Gallagher and Kealey, Blakeman and Ramsey decided to call an emergency meeting of the NJNC in the hope of mobilising the combined strength of the other Union to isolate the AEF and the NUVB and so bring pressure to bear on them to end the strike. Blakeman discovered that some of the Union's Officials he needed for the NJNC were already on their way to York for a meeting of the Confederation of Shipbuilding and Engineering Unions. He dispatched an urgent letter to Jim Conway, Trade Union Side Secretary of the NJNC, asking for an emergency meeting of the NJNC's Grading Sub-Committee at York on Thursday 13 June.

On their journey to York, Blakeman and Ramsey decided on their tactics for ending the strike. The NJNC must assert its authority over a handful of militant Stewards who had defied the 1955 Procedure Agreement, and the 1967 New Wage Structure Agreement, and who were now officially supported by two Unions whose signatures were on both of those Agreements. The atmosphere at York, however, was not conducive to constructive peace moves. The Union Officials had already been through a hard day's bargaining and were in no mood to be co-operative either with the Company or with one another. Blakeman insisted that, whatever the strength of the women's case might be, the

NJNC was there as the final stage of Procedure. The strike could only bring the NJNC into disrepute and must be ended quickly. Gallagher simply confirmed that his Union had made the strike official on the grounds of discrimination in the grading of his women members. The matter was no longer in his hands. Birch dismissed Gallagher's procedural niceties: for him and for the AEF the issue at stake was not grading, but equal pay for women. He didn't give a 'fig' for the Procedure Agreement, or the job evaluation, or the grading. A matter of great principle was involved – and if he was 'ratting' on the Two-Year Agreement, that was just too bad. Birch drew a parallel between the strike at Ford and the 'revolutionary' events then taking place in France. It was just unfortunate that Ford happened to be selected as the first target of a national equal pay campaign in Britain.

On Friday 14 June Blakeman reported the failure of his York mission to top management and to Conrad Heron, Assistant Under-Secretary of State at the Department of Employment and Productivity. Heron was an old friend and an enthusiastic admirer of Blakeman's efforts to pioneer industrial relations reform in the motor industry. The implication of Blakeman's report was serious: if Birch was determined to secure equal pay through strike action, this constituted a direct threat to the Two-Year Agreement. If the Ford Agreement could be breached, so could many others. Heron agreed to brief his Minister and to seek to persuade her to make an official intervention.

Anticipating that possibility, Blakeman's team devised a three-point plan. First, Ramsey would contact Young and Conway to call an emergency meeting of the full NJNC for the following Monday, 17 June. Second, Blakeman would ask for Gillen's support in applying pressure on the Department of Employment, to ask the Secretary of State to intervene directly in the dispute and, if necessary, to be ready to appoint an official Court of Inquiry. Third, Ford of Britain's Managing Director, Sir William Batty, would be asked to issue a Press Statement saying that the women's strike action now threatened continuity of production throughout the Company and that, unless there was an immediate return to work, massive lay-offs would follow, with the complete closure of the Dagenham Body and Assembly Plants by the following Tuesday, 18 June. All three points were speedily implemented. The Press Statement was put out by Batty in time to catch the London evening papers. In addition to this Press Statement, the five-o'clock editions carried the Stop Press news that Barbara Castle had decided to intervene and had called the parties to meet her at St James's Square the following morning.

Management morale — which slumped badly after the York meeting — began immediately to recover. The essence of Ford's industrial relations strategy was that it must manage its own industrial relations without recourse to outside agencies, if at all possible. At best it must manage with the active support or, at worst, the acquiescence of the Unions at national level. If that minimum acquiescence was not forthcoming, the Company might, however reluctantly, have to call upon the state to support its own efforts to manage its affairs domestically.

On arriving at St James's Square on Saturday morning, 15 June, Blakeman and Ramsey found Gallagher besieged by a delegation of women strikers, led by Passingham. They had heard about the meeting and suspected a sell-out by Gallagher and Young. Joint discussion with separate adjournment meetings went on all morning under Conrad Heron's Chairmanship. Blakeman was eventually able to tell Heron that he and Young both favoured the NJNC, already called for Monday, as the best means of settling the issue. If they failed at NJNC, they would come back to Heron and invoke the Minister's help through more direct intervention.

It is against this background that the NJNC of Monday 17 June must be considered. The NJNC was the final stage of Procedure at which the recurrent conflicts between the Company and its disaffected workers must be worked through and resolved, using the machinery of freely negotiated collective bargaining rather than the remote mechanism of a Court of Inquiry or, worse still, a Court of Law.

Because of the short notice, the meeting could not take place in the usual NJNC conference room at Ford's Regent Street Offices, and was held instead in the unfamiliar atmosphere of the Co-operative Society's New Ambassadors Hotel in Bloomsbury. Young opened for the Union Side by proposing a Joint NJNC Committee of Inquiry — two members from each side with an independent outside Chairman.

Blakeman's response was initially cool but he was prepared to agree to an Inquiry, subject to two stipulations. First, it must be internal to the Company and report to the NJNC, which would alone jointly decide what could be released externally. Second, 'nothing in this Inquiry or anything else, must interfere with the basic wage structure . . . the fundamental principle on which it is based could not be altered.'

Conway wanted the Grading Grievance Procedure simplified so that employees got 'all the information necessary, which will allow the decision to be properly understood'. Blakeman interpreted this as an attempt to reopen the vexed question of the confidential weighting factors[16] used by the Consultants during the job evaluation programme:

This has been argued for across the table and has been rejected across the table, with reasons given, the main reason being that of objectivity, and it does not matter how many Inquiries we have, or what status they are, we cannot destroy that objectivity, otherwise it would tend to destroy the basis of the scheme altogether. Therefore, I want to make it quite clear, so that there is no dubiety about it later on as to what I mean.[17]

Blakeman finally agreed that the Inquiry could go ahead. But, he added,

Nothing we do is going to undermine the Agreement made last year and our New Wage Structure because we have got 40,000 people's wages depending on it. Destroy that and you destroy the whole thing, and we shall be in chaos again.[18]

Immediately following the NJNC, Blakeman faced the television cameras, set up in the crowded foyer of the New Ambassadors Hotel. A genuinely shy man, he was embarassed to find himself under the glare of the television arc lights, but expressed his delight at the outcome of the NJNC. He urged all those workers who had expected to be laid off to report for work as usual the following morning and was reasonably confident that the strike would now end. That appeal might well have succeeded, had he not been immediately followed on television by Rosie Boland, the leading Trim Shop Steward. She left nobody in doubt where the Machinists stood: there had been no agreement as far as *they* were concerned. The strike would continue until the Company conceded Grade C.

On the morning of Tuesday 18 June, management's worst fears were confirmed. The women not only failed to report for work, but formed a modest picket line outside the River Plant, carrying placards which proclaimed that the struggle would continue. Not one of the Sewing Machinists attempted to cross the line. The strike was 100 per cent solid. Fred Blake, the NUVB District Official, took his place alongside his members outside the gates. Whatever the NJNC had agreed the previous evening, so far as he and his members were concerned, the strike was still official.

Back at Warley, management morale slumped to its lowest level. It was always uncertain how far the Company would succeed with the NJNC formula, but it was at least expected to be helpful in getting the women back to work. Instead, they had not simply defied management:

they had now defied their own Officials and, by throwing in the allegation of sex discrimination, had divided the Union Side into two hostile
camps — those who supported and those who opposed the women's
grievance. Over the next few weeks, this small group of defiant and
publicity-hungry women dominated the headlines. By capturing the
limelight and the public's imagination, the women distracted attention
from the serious character of the dispute. The popular press had got
hold of the human angle and would not let it go. It was the price to be
paid for a free press and a free trade union movement. But it was a high
price: for every day that Dagenham stood still, some millions of pounds
of profitable export orders were lost and some thousands of pounds of
wages. But, even at that price, there was no question on Tuesday 18
June of management giving way to the strikers' demands. The NJNC's
authority had already been undermined; for management to give way to
strike pressure in those circumstances was tantamount to the unilateral
dissolution of the NJNC.

There were sharp differences amongst management on what to do
next. Gillen and Batty were incensed by the women's defiance of
authority and were determined that they should now be left to 'sweat it
out'. Blakeman and his staff took the opposite view. For every day the
women stayed out, the more difficult it would be to get them back and
the more determined they would be to get what they wanted at any
price. The women were revelling in their new-found publicity. Rosie
Boland and Lil O'Callaghan, the two most prominent Trim Shop
Stewards, were two Cockney characters who seemed destined for
television stardom. When it came to competition of that kind, Ford
management was not in the same league. Its tactics at NJNC had failed.
From this point on, the dispute was no longer within management's
control and a new phase was due to begin.

The Scamp Court of Inquiry

On Wednesday 19 June, Conrad Heron called Blakeman, Ramsey, Young
and Conway to St James's Square and informed them of the First
Secretary's decision to set up an immediate Court of Inquiry. At the
same time, he passed on the Minister's appeal to the Union leaders that
they should do their best to get the strike called off. Two points of
interest emerged from that meeting: first, the Terms of Reference
drafted by Heron for the Court of Inquiry were later to become the
source of some confusion and contention as to the exact nature of the

dispute; second, although Young and Conway undertook to do their best, they were quite unconvinced that their efforts would produce the desired result. In that, they were fully justified: the First Secretary's announcement was given the widest publicity and her appeal for a return to work was carried throughout the media. But the women refused to move one inch.

On Friday 21 June, Barbara Castle[19] announced that she had appointed Jack Scamp to chair the Ford Court of Inquiry. The news sent a shudder down the spines of Gillen and Blakeman. They at once determined that there would be no repeat of the Paint Sprayers' Inquiry and no further irresponsible meddling in the Company's internal affairs. The appointment increased their determination to use the Court as a public platform from which to expose the unprincipled behaviour of the AEF and the NUVB. Above all, Scamp must not be allowed to interfere with, or set aside, the New Wage Structure and the job-evaluated gradings. With these thoughts uppermost in his mind, Blakeman was amused to learn, over drinks that night, that Scamp was himself retained as an independent Consultant by Urwick, Orr and Partners — and that he sometimes advised them on industrial relations matters — though not, of course, on the Ford job evaluation programme!

Since the women had again refused to return to work, Barbara Castle stepped up her pressure by calling the senior representatives of the four principal Unions involved to see her at St James's Square on Saturday morning, 22 June. She told them of the damaging effect of the strike, not simply on Ford's export performance but on the country's balance of payments, and urged them to bring their influence to bear on the women to get them back to work. Without their return, the Court of Inquiry was really in no position to go ahead. They assured the First Secretary that they would do their best and in return she gave them an assurance that, if the women went back to work, they should have *all* the information they wanted, including the confidential weighting factors.

Ford management had meanwhile laid their own plans. By chance, Blakeman had noted that the Confederation of Shipbuilding and Engineering Unions was meeting at Weymouth from Saturday 22 to Tuesday 25 June and he saw this as an opportunity to talk through the fresh situation with Union Side members of the NJNC. He would not attempt to put pressure on them but simply appeal to their good sense and self-interest. After all, they each already had several hundred of their own members laid off and others would soon follow.

On Monday morning, 24 June, Blakeman called his staff together and

asked them to start work on the Company's draft evidence to the
Scamp Inquiry. For Blakeman and Ramsey, the preparation of such a
Company submission was a familiar experience. For Gillen it presented
a new opportunity that must not be missed. Gillen joined Blakeman and
his team to hear their ideas on how the submission should be structured.
He listened carefully, then added his personal contribution. For Gillen,
this was no superficial matter − a fact that should be made clear from
the outset. It was not something which involved just the Sewing
Machinists at Dagenham but was an absolutely fundamental issue. The
Company had tried to establish a new wage structure which would treat
all its employees on an equal basis. It had used every bit of modern
know-how and experience in carrying out the job evaluation. Its objective had been to eliminate the injustices inherent in the old wage structure. The Sewing Machinists were now trying to upset the New Wage
Structure, by applying pressure. The Company had leaned over back-
wards to be fair, had listened to every grievance and considered each on
its merits. Now it was faced with two Unions, each arguing a different
case, both of which had made the strike official despite the explicit provisions of a freely negotiated Agreement, which laid down a clear procedure for dealing with any such disputes.

Gillen stood up and paced about the room. What were the Unions
driving at? Somebody suggested that their real target was not simply the
Ford Agreement but the government's prices and incomes policy. If
they could leapfrog the Ford settlement, they had out-flanked the
National Board for Prices and Incomes. Gillen recalled that the DEP
had emphasised the exceptional character of the Ford Agreement in
1967, in allowing it to by-pass the incomes policy guidelines. The only
reason the Board had agreed that Ford could pay its workers an average
11 per cent increase over two years was the fact that it had a closer
control over wage drift and had produced evidence of a self-financing
productivity deal. Blakeman respectfully corrected Gillen: it was not the
Board which 'allowed' the exceptional increase but the Ministry of
Labour which had vetted the proposed settlement and 'raised no objection' to its implementation. Ray Gunter, the Minister, had been at pains
to point out that the deal had to last for two years.[20] That was why he
had 'raised no objection'. Right, said Gillen: why not call Ray Gunter as
a Company witness? It was certainly an original, if impracticable, suggestion. At this point, Blakeman left for the meeting with NJNC
Officials at Weymouth, whilst Gillen went off to have dinner with Sir
Denis Barnes, Permanent Secretary at the DEP.

On Tuesday afternoon, 25 June, Gillen met Blakeman and his staff again, to compare notes on their respective missions. Gillen had got on well with Barnes, who had been sympathetic and receptive to the Company's ideas. He was fully aware of the economic cost of the strike, both to Ford and to the country. He, too, had originally favoured an NJNC Inquiry but had come to realise that an Official Inquiry was now inevitable. Gillen had stressed that he wanted the inquiry to be public so that the press would report it fully. He had been absolutely frank with Barnes, telling him of the Company's concern about how Scamp might conduct the Inquiry and its fear that he might come up with some un-realistic compromise which would fail to respect the integrity of the job evaluation. With characteristic transatlantic directness, Gillen had told Barnes: 'I don't want a single criticism of this wage structure!' Blakeman's staff were delighted by this account of the American Chairman of a multinational corporation lecturing Barnes, the Department's top civil servant, on how to run a Court of Inquiry. 'After all', added Gillen wryly, 'he instructs Scamp. And there were only two of us present!'

Blakeman's account of his overnight trip to Weymouth was equally amusing and instructive. He had found the Union Side members pretty bloody minded – all, that is, except Conway. He and Blakeman had sat together alone on the verandah of the Royal Hotel, sipping iced gin and tonic, watching the sun go down over Portland Bill: two fellow Lancastrians, unburdening themselves of their respective disappoint-ments in the unexpected intimacy of a warm summer evening by the sea – Blakeman, an essentially shy man, quietly spoken with the slow emphatic gestures of an aristocrat, and Conway, hard-bitten, silver-haired survivor of a thousand union battles, more fiercely fought against his own left wing than against the British ruling class. Jim had confided closely in Leslie: he was scathing in his denunciation of the Unions and their disarray over the abortive NJNC Inquiry. He and Mark had done their best but Birch had fouled things up as usual. Jim hadn't minced his words: Birch was a bastard; what's more, he'd told him so to his face.

The Blakemans had joined the Union Side over dinner that evening. Blakeman's wife, Joan Woodward, sat next to Birch and the conversa-tion turned, naturally enough, to recent events in France. According to Blakeman, his wife had expressed warm sympathy with the revolution-ary approach of French students and workers who, at the time, were occupying parts of the Sorbonne and the Renault Works – equivalent, in British terms, perhaps, to an occupation of the London School of Economics and the Ford Works at Dagenham. The exchanges which followed were as piquant as the juxtaposition of the two personalities:

Joan Woodward, Reader in Industrial Sociology at London University's Imperial College of Science and Technology – normally the cool, almost matter-of-fact academic – alongside Birch, a widely read, dedicated Maoist, with the wrinkled face of some Chinese revolutionary, speaking with a Cockney accent. Mrs Blakeman had warmed to her subject: she understood what the students of Paris were trying to do. There was much to be done in putting right the world's wrongs. But human nature being what it was, we must reconcile ourselves never to achieve our utopias. Birch would have none of it: that was a determinist heresy. He'd been to China and Albania. He'd seen the socialist future – and it worked!

Blakeman's account of the dinner party was interrupted by Walter Hayes, reporting the latest news from Halewood. After their Sewing Machinists had come out in sympathy with the women from Dagenham, Halewood management had proposed that Supervisors should take their place, to make headlinings and so keep Halewood going. Warley had been consulted and agreed: if Halewood was going to be shut down, it must be as a result of management decision to lay the men off – not because of their sympathetic action in support of the women. Hayes was now reporting that the two Plant Conveners, Donnelly and Bradley, had been 'got at' by Friedman and were refusing to accept Supervisors working.

Management's tactics for containing the dispute were obviously not succeeding. Gillen was furious. It was time management stopped pussyfooting. The First Secretary must appeal to the women herself, if necessary. Somebody should get on to Barnes and tell him so. He was willing to speak to Barbara himself, if they thought that would help. He intended to sit down at once with Walter Hayes and prepare a new Press Statement. Something *had* to be done to end this ridiculous situation! He'd got Stephenson and Knudsen, two of Henry Ford's principal aides, coming to review European Automotive Operations next week. What the hell would they report to Mr Ford if this strike was still on?

On Wednesday morning, 26 June, Blakeman and his staff met the four senior Urwick Orr Consultants involved in the job evaluation programme, in preparation for the Scamp Inquiry: Gerry Wood, one of the firm's Directors; Don Fraser, Senior Consultant on the Ford assignment; Nancy Taylor, the brains behind the profile method of job evaluation used at Ford; and Edwin Singer, UOP's training specialist, who had put the one hundred or so members of the Ford Assessing Teams and Review Committees through their paces during their initial training at Warley in June 1966 and who later played a crucial role in the adjudication of the disputed profile.

Blakeman was determined to ensure that there would be no significant discrepancy between the Company's evidence and the Consultants' evidence to Scamp. Gallagher would make great play with the Company's refusal to disclose the weighting factors. It was therefore essential for the Company to bring out the fact that the Consultants had advised against disclosure. Don Fraser wondered whether the Court had the right to require disclosure. Blakeman replied that the Court might not have the legal right but the Company must not be seen to be hiding behind that fact in refusing to disclose anything. Meredeen asked whether this might not be the right occasion for voluntary disclosure. Ramsey was against disclosure; so were the Consultants. Their line was consistent with the Company's evidence to the Industrial Court's arbitration on the grading of Ford Carpenters and Joiners:

> The Society were objecting that the weighting factors had not been divulged to them, but the Consultants had recommended that in order to ensure objectivity they should not be disclosed to anybody who was in any way associated with the review of the wage structure . . . [21]

Ramsey had his own questions in which he wanted the Consultants rehearsed. The Company intended to say that, in determining job grades, it went by the results of the job evaluation, down to the last point. Did UOP still claim that degree of accuracy for its profile method? Yes, replied Taylor, you must stick by the rules of allocating jobs in accordance with their points value. The Company intended to say that it still considered the results of the evaluation were a sound basis for its New Wage Structure. Did UOP agree with that? Certainly, replied Fraser. Did you, as Consultants, play any part in developing the grades and wages? That was more complicated, said Fraser; the one shaded off into the other. How would Singer reply if asked in Court: Why did you alter the markings on the disputed job profile? Because he favoured the Assessors' markings as against those of the Divisional Review Committee. After all, added Singer, they had gathered more experience of different jobs, as they moved from plant to plant. What if the question of equal pay came up explicitly in Court? How would they handle that? Taylor said she had strong views on that subject. Why? asked Meredeen frivolously. Don't *you* receive equal pay? That, interrupted Fraser, like the weightings, was a confidential matter he preferred *not* to discuss.

After lunch, a formal letter arrived from Conrad Heron, advising the

Company of the setting up of the Court of Inquiry, and spelling out its proposed Terms of Reference. Blakeman passed the letter to Ramsey, who took one look at it — and said they had fallen for the three-card trick. Blakeman didn't understand. Ramsey pointed out that the letter referred to a dispute 'between the Ford Motor Company and the Trade Unions represented on the Trade Union Side of the NJNC'. But there *was* no dispute between the Company and the NJNC. They had, after all, agreed on an NJNC Inquiry. The dispute was between the Company and those of its employees on strike. Blakeman now saw the implication. The NJNC — the agreed locus of conflict resolution at Ford — had *not* given its support to the strike — even if certain Unions had done so. Ramsey was told to get in touch immediately with Ken Atkinson, the civil servant appointed as Secretary to the Court, to see whether there was still time to alter the Terms of Reference.

Meanwhile, Blakeman and the remainder of his team continued their preparation of the Company case. Scamp himself was known to favour a private hearing of evidence — as he normally heard it in the Motor Industry Joint Labour Council's investigations. The Unions, for their part, preferred a public hearing. They had to speak for the record and to satisfy their members that they had publicly attacked the Company. The Company, too, wanted the hearing to be public — but for quite different reasons. Gillen insisted that, since the Company had absolutely nothing to hide, and the irresponsibility of the strikers and their Unions must be exposed, the hearing should be given the maximum possible publicity. Quite apart from the imminent arrival of the Ford US Senior Managers, Gillen considered that the press had virtually ignored the Company's case. The favourable publicity which the women had attracted had cast the Company in a bad light, but the fact was that the women were in breach of their contracts of employment and the Procedure Agreement. The dispute was a graphic illustration of the chaotic state of industrial relations in Britain. Since it touched on important issues of public policy, it deserved to be fully ventilated in public.

On the morning of Thursday 27 June, an eight-man team representing Ford management, the Ford Sewing Machinists' Strike Committee and their National Officials, and the UOP contingent, assembled in separate rooms at the DEP's Headquarters in St James's Square. Atkinson invited Blakeman to confirm that the revised Terms of Reference were now acceptable: 'To enquire into the causes and circumstances of the dispute between the Ford Motor Company Limited and certain of their employees employed as Sewing Machinists, and to report'.[22]

The syntax was clumsy but the offending error had been removed.

Blakeman agreed. Atkinson then explained that the first day's hearing would be in private and deal only with procedural matters. The Unions had seen the First Secretary last Saturday and obtained an assurance. Provided they secured a return to work, they would have all the information they required — weighting factors and job profile values.

At 11 o'clock the proceedings began with a few moments of pure English farce. With the Court almost full and awaiting the arrival of the Chairman and his team, the Usher called on all present to be upstanding. As they rose, in trudged Reg Birch, bowed down by the weight of an over-stuffed briefcase. Laughter in Court. Then Sir Jack arrived and introduced the members of his Court. But there was another Courtier still to come: His Royal Highness, Prince Charles, was spending the day with the DEP and would like to meet the parties in Court. Nobody demurred. The Terms of Reference were read aloud, the Court's procedure agreed. On the question whether the hearings should be held in private, Sir Jack was the soul of discretion. He wanted to hear the parties' views before deciding. Gallagher mumbled something about the public interest. Blakeman strongly urged that the hearing should be in public, not only in the Court's interest but also in the country's interest. Birch, with studied indifference, noted that Sir Jack had already established a precedent by allowing Royalty to be present!

Scamp then offered to make a personal appeal to the women to return to work and suggested that they should be invited into Court. He did not mind whether that be done or not, said Birch with mock solemnity but, if it was, the hearing would then be in public. However, he wanted to pose a more serious question: Did Sir Jack permit smoking in his Court? Not normally, replied Sir Jack, but he did have some Spangle mints he was willing to share with Mr Birch!

The laughter had hardly died away before the Court rose again to receive its Royal visitor. The Prince entered the Court with well-brushed hair, a well-cut tweed suit and hands firmly clasped behind his back, quarterdeck fashion. Sir Jack led him down either side of the Court, introducing him to the principal witnesses. Birch accepted the Royal hand and bowed slightly from the waist: 'Look', he said, 'You might get him to let us smoke in Court . . . ' 'Why's that?' flashed the Prince. 'Are things getting sticky for you, Mr Birch?'

The exchanges between the parties in Court were never to be as bright as that. Gallagher insisted that the Company should provide all the information relevant to the job evaluation, the points values for each job and an explanation of the weightings. He also wanted the women to be present in Court. Blakeman declined to give any categorical assurance about the information Gallagher requested. But he assured the Court that, in setting out to establish its New Wage Structure, the Company had decided to be much more open and forthcoming with information than it had been in the past. He recognised the value of good communications in removing employees' suspicion, but said that the disclosure of the weighting factors would mean sacrificing the objectivity of the job evaluation. Gallagher appreciated the Court must be free from duress, but stressed that the immediate problem was getting the women back to work. He wanted an atmosphere of confidence amongst the women, so it would be most helpful if the Company said that such information as the Court required would be made available. Blakeman gave that assurance, but Birch was not impressed. His Executive was certainly not seeking a return to work. So far as the evidence was concerned, there was more than the Company involved. The Consultants might have certain information and it was by no means clear that they were a neutral party.

Scamp said it was for the Court to determine what evidence it required and whether witnesses should be called. The Court would do its job properly and it was already armed with the necessary powers. He was not prepared, at this stage, to say what information might be needed. That gave Blakeman his chance. He said he was perplexed as to what the dispute was about. At first, he thought it was about pay and grading. Then, it seemed to be about equal pay. But now it seemed to be about disclosure of information. Gallagher said he was quite clear. For the NUVB, the dispute was about the grading of the Sewing Machinists. Birch, however, would not be drawn. He thought it was up to the Court to find out what the dispute was about.

Scamp eventually decided that the full hearings would be held in private. The issues were already sufficiently complicated; having the press in Court would not help to get a solution. Members of the Court wanted to visit the plant next week, but that seemed pointless unless 'the ladies' were back at work. Gallagher then received a report: the women had just met and decided not to return to work and would not be meeting until the following Thursday. Scamp deplored their decision and urged Gallagher to do his best to convene a meeting of the strikers to plead for a return to work. But Gallagher declined: his terms of reference were to seek certain assurances from the Company. Those assurances had not been forthcoming. In these circumstances, he could do no more than report back to his Union Executive. Scamp said he was available to meet 'the ladies' if that would be helpful to both sides. The Court would proceed whether they returned to work or not – but it would be 'quite terrible' if they did not.

Blakeman expressed his extreme disappointment at this outcome. Ford was losing £1 million of sales revenue each day the strike continued. The matter was, therefore, of the greatest significance, not just for Ford but for the nation. Before the Court adjourned, he again urged that everything possible be done to end the strike.

After lunch Blakeman called the Management Side of the NJNC together to review the alternative courses now open to management for ending the dispute. He had already reported the morning's events to Gillen, who was furious with Scamp for refusing to hold the Inquiry in public. Gillen intended to phone Barnes, Permanent Secretary at the DEP, to protest strongly against the decision. Blakeman confessed his own sense of frustration and impotence: this was the most serious situation he had faced in his 15 years with the Company — and they were doing nothing to end it. What could be done to change the situation? Should they sack the women? Ramsey urged caution, recalling what had happened when Ford had tried to sack its 70 'trouble makers' in October 1962. He wanted to wait 24 hours until the NUVB Executive had met. Management would then be free to act.

Rees reported two informal conversations he'd had that morning outside the Court. Birch had admitted to Rees that the Union had 'made a bollocks of it' by confusing the grading and equal pay issues in Court. Blake, the NUVB's District Official, had told Rees he was deeply suspicious of Courts of Inquiry because they were always prejudiced in favour of management. He was still bitter about Ford's refusal to settle the issue with him locally. Why not make a direct appeal to Blake? He was the only man the women would listen to, and the only man who could get them back to work. Blakeman disagreed.

Rees was becoming impatient: Okay — what *would* persuade the women to go back? Blakeman inhaled deeply from his cigarette, looked Rees straight in the eye and said simply: 92 per cent of the men's rate. But that's chicken feed, said Rees. Why don't we go ahead and do it? Because, said Blakeman, there was a Two-Year Agreement which the Company dare not break. He then admitted what some of those present already suspected: that, on the previous Monday evening at Weymouth, he'd given Birch a broad hint that the Company was willing to reconsider the women's work contribution with a view to reducing the differential between men's and women's rates. Birch had been noncommittal but sympathetic. Kealey and others had opposed the idea, first because it had never been raised through Procedure at NJNC and second, because of the problems it would cause amongst Ford men. In any case, explained Blakeman, the offer could not be made public yet. There was NJNC protocol involved.

But Rees insisted something must be done immediately. Unfinished vehicles were piling up in the Dagenham car compounds. They were almost full. Why not call a meeting of all JWCs throughout the Company tomorrow, and ask the men to put pressure on the women to end the strike? He knew the Engine Plant JWC would co-operate. It might prove very effective. Ramsey went one better: why not call in all the Shop Stewards of the 9,000 men already laid off? They were as fed up with this continuous disruption as were management. They ought to respond to a Company initiative.

Blakeman preferred the idea of Company-wide JWCs plus a personal letter delivered by hand on Friday evening to each of the women strikers, inviting them to a special meeting with management. He decided to phone Atkinson at the DEP to report his intentions. Atkinson told him that Gallagher had not gone to meet his Executive Committee at Weymouth, but was on his way home to Manchester. In that case, said Blakeman, there was no prospect of the Company opening its plants for production for another three weeks. That was intolerable. Blakeman urged Atkinson to contact Kealey or Moss Evans, the senior officials of the TGWU, at once — or Frank Cousins, the General Secretary, if necessary. Tell them we're committed to equal pay and are ready for negotiations on shift work. The Company had got no help from anybody, said Blakeman. It had decided to take action because it had a responsibility to do something. 'And do it we shall — for better or worse!'

It was now 5 o'clock. Blakeman called Gillen to report the afternoon's events:

1. The NUVB Executive would meet on Monday and probably widen the strike.
2. Atkinson was trying to contact National Officials of the TGWU but they were unlikely to prevent a shut-down at Halewood.
3. JWCs had been called at all Company locations on Friday, to inform Shop Stewards of the critical position regarding lay-off.
4. Further lay-offs would take place in the Dagenham Press Shop on Monday.
5. Personal letters were being sent to all the women strikers on Friday, urging them to think again about their continued participation in the strike and inviting them to a meeting.
6. Urgent steps should now be taken to get a meeting with the Minister

of Technology, Wedgwood Benn, with Barbara Castle and with the
Prime Minister himself, if possible. Blakeman suggested that Bill
Batty should send an immediate telegram to Harold Wilson, asking for
his personal intervention to end the strike.

Gillen approved Blakeman's plans. He instructed Blakeman to tell
Atkinson that the Company would not participate any further in the
Court's hearing unless the women were back at work; that had been
implicit in the Terms of Reference. Blakeman should draft the telegram
to the Prime Minister. Gillen would talk to Batty about signing it.

By 10 o'clock that Thursday evening, the situation was transformed.
The BBC's 'World Tonight' programme reported the telegram to Harold
Wilson. Mrs Castle was calling on Gallagher and the Sewing Machinists to
see her at the DEP on Friday; the Scamp Inquiry would be held in
public, after all, at Mrs Castle's request.

At 10 o'clock on Friday morning, 28 June, the management team
which had assembled at Regent Street were joined by Gillen, Batty,
Rees, Hayes, Waddell and Collard. Blakeman reviewed the overnight
situation. At last, the tide had turned in management's favour. Mrs
Castle had not only called in the women to see her: she had asked
management to stand by, too. Batty's telegram had broken the negotiating deadlock. What concerned him now was the possibility that the girls
would refuse to respond to Barbara's appeal, or the advice of their
Union. What could be done then? Gillen was in no doubt: management
was free to act because public sympathy would then go against the
women. Tough action would be called for. Should they fire all the
women at once, or only some, by way of example?

Blakeman said they couldn't fire the women for fear of sympathetic
action by the men. The women must be got back to work somehow.
Unfortunately, any promise of a move towards equal pay would alienate
the men. The Unions could say the Company was discriminating against
the men by refusing to increase the men's rates at the same time. Gillen
recognised that management was trapped — but he was certainly not
prepared to compromise the integrity of the New Wage Structure by upgrading the women in response to the pressure of the strike. Gillen
spelt out the implications in transatlantic monosyllables: So help me
God — if we let this one go, we're dead! We'll end up with just one
grade — every worker in Grade F!

Rees was sceptical: We've already altered some 30 per cent of the
original gradings. Good! said Gillen. That shows we're willing to make
changes where the evidence justifies it. Blakeman agreed: the present

grading must stand. We must find an alternative route to adjusting the women's differentials. Perhaps by altering the men and women's relief times. Ramsey warned against that: the question of relief times had never been negotiated with the Union. Gillen found that incredible. It was the discovery of custom and practice deals of that kind which made him wish himself back in Detroit.

Rees returned to the women's attitude to ending the strike. Blakeman had described them as 'anarchic and irresponsible' which, Blake had told Rees, had really upset them. Blakeman shrugged his shoulders. Hayes suggested he should fix up an interview with his former *Daily Mail* colleague, Bill Hardcastle, on 'The World at One' in which Batty could explain the Company's position. Gillen liked the idea: You could explain how much the strike was costing Ford and the country. But Batty wasn't keen: he preferred to wait and see whether Barbara did her stuff. Gillen, by this time, seemed ready to explode: If you don't feel that you can handle it, Bill, *I'll* do it! If we take no action now, we could be here for months. We've kept putting this thing off too long. Now we've taken the initiative, I say we should maintain it. Okay? If you don't agree, Bill, what else should we do? Should we withdraw from the Court of Inquiry?

John Maguire, Industrial Relations Manager, Power Train Operations, asked why they didn't do a deal with the women? The Dagenham Stewards knew the grading structure was already 'bent'. Blakeman became angry: *Who* had said that? Did management support them? No, said Maguire, but some managers thought certain factors had been undervalued in the job evaulation. How could they know *that* without knowing the weightings? asked Gillen. Well, said Maguire, we think the Conveners have already got the weightings . . . Now there was some talk of equal pay . . . Power Train Management didn't favour a solution which left the impression we still had something to hide on the women's grading. Blakeman tried to reassure him: The Conveners did *not* have the weightings . . . Neither did he . . . People were jumping to conclusions . . . We were *not* going for a solution which compromised the grading structure.

All this was too much for Gillen: Didn't Maguire accept that the grading scheme was fair? He looked round the room: You fellers have fallen on your face if you're not convinced this structure's fair! If this Inquiry doesn't say this wage structure is right, we're set back 20 years! It'll take that long for anyone to try again. Our position at the Inquiry must be: No compromise on the gradings. Blakeman was absolutely sure that was right. He'd heard from Barnes that the Department was solid in its support for the structure. The gradings must be kept watertight. If there *was* to be a concession by the Company, Barnes would prefer it to come on equal pay. Ford should play on the fact that the women no longer required the protection of the Factory Act. Gillen agreed: That was just the line Blakeman should take.

At 12.30 p.m. the Department called Blakeman to say that the First Secretary would like to see him at St James's Square after lunch. The account which follows of the crucial events at the Department of Employment that day was provided by Ramsey, who later related the detail with considerable relish.

At around 3.45 p.m. on Friday 28 June, Barbara Castle adjourned her meeting with the Sewing Machinists and called Blakeman and Ramsey into her suite at St James's Square. She told them that the girls felt they had been 'cheated' over their grading and would not go back to work unless they got something out of their strike. Ramsey and Blakeman had spent the next hour taking Barbara Castle and Conrad Heron through the history of the wage structure and the Grading Grievance Procedure. They quickly grasped the essentials: You've got to convince them the grading system works, said Barbara. But they won't go back without some concession. What's it worth to you to get them back? What about the women's differential? After all, the girls had been down to Vauxhall to compare rates and found the women there got 93 per cent of the men's rates. Blakeman pointed out the difficulty of increasing rates during the period of the Two-Year Agreement. He had already offered to discuss the question of the women's differentials when he met the Unions at York. But not under the duress of the strike. Barbara said that discussions alone would not get them back to work. What was the Company prepared to offer in terms of hard cash? The only way round the Two-Year Agreement, said Blakeman, was for the government to remove the restrictions of the Factory Act which prevented women from working shifts.

Shortly afterwards, they were joined by the women, together with Gallagher, Blake and Friedman. Blakeman tried to take them through the job profiles but got nowhere. Blake tried once more to draw a distinction between the Intermediate Machinists and the Finishing Machinists, but the girls wouldn't hear of it. They'd all been 'trade-tested' and, in effect, had served a five-year apprenticeship. Barbara could see they were getting nowhere. She decided to adopt a different approach and let her hair down. She kicked off her shoes and tucked her legs under her, on the settee. She was brilliant! said Ramsey. She told the girls they must understand that the Company had got this scheme of job evaluation and grading, so they themselves couldn't do just what they liked. They were just as much the prisoners of that scheme as were the Unions. Right, girls? There were nods all round. But that wouldn't get the girls back to work, said Rosie. Barbara agreed: Of course not! Now, didn't they think it was time for some change in the differentials? She had talked to the Company about this and knew that their offer to re-examine the women's differentials was serious. They hadn't yet been formally asked about differentials. But if they were allowed to discuss the problem, she was sure it would come out alright. She trusted the Company and the girls must trust her. But the Company would not talk under duress. So, first, you've got to go back to work. Then, the Unions must seek a meeting with the Company to present their claim. Finally, you must use the grading grievance machinery and the Court of Inquiry to solve your grading claim. It's as simple as that!

After an adjournment of about one hour, the girls came back and said they would hold a meeting on Sunday and recommend a return to work on Monday. Barbara was thrilled: I *knew* you would! I've always admired your common sense! Now, what about the Grading Grievance Procedure? No, they said: they'd await the Court of Inquiry. Fine! said Barbara. Let's drink to it! A bottle and glasses were produced and Barbara insisted the toast should be 'To the victory of common sense'. Blakeman was just adding his word of thanks, when in walked Young and Birch, just in time for the drinks! They raised their glasses and hoped they would get the girls another 5 per cent. Barbara reacted sharply: You realise, she said, we can't go behind the backs of the NJNC? She'd told the Commons on Wednesday that she was going to introduce an Equal Pay Bill. It would phase in equal pay over a period of the next few years. What? said the girls. We'll be old ladies by then! No, no, said Barbara. It would take seven years at the most . . . So they all thanked Barbara again, shook hands and went down to meet the press.

Blakeman emerged smiling from his meeting with Barbara Castle. Clutching a copy of an Official Statement, he told news reporters and cameramen that the women were satisfied by the assurances obtained by Mrs Castle. The Stewards would be recommending a return to work on Monday, and the NJNC would be meeting the same day to approve the settlement. Blakeman was exhausted but happy. It had been one of the longest days of his life. But it was not yet over. As he drove back to his farmhouse home in Kent, Blakeman must have wondered how he could explain all this to his weekend house-guest, Bob Copp, the Ford US Overseas Liaison Manager, who had flown in to be briefed on the whole affair.

Ramsey and his staff were back at work on Sunday. They met in Ramsey's office at Warley and first heard his account of the events of Friday before turning to the preparation of the Company case for the Inquiry. It was one of the hottest days of the year. The air-conditioning had been turned off and the windows would not open. Outside, on the car park, a competition was in progress for 'The Lorry Driver of the Year', sponsored by Ford. The noise was deafening. At 11 o'clock, as prearranged, Ramsey put through a call to Blakeman's home to get his first reaction to the material already passed to him for vetting. It was a bad line, and the continuous crackling tried everybody's patience. At one end sat Blakeman, frantically turning the pages of an unbound typescript, trying to find his place, whilst at the other end, gathered round the telephone 'buzz-box' in Ramsey's office, were three of Ramsey's staff: Keith Court, Paul Roots and Sander Meredeen, each trying to make points where appropriate, each noting what Blakeman had said about the changes he wanted made in the draft. It was a conversation worthy of Harold Pinter: overlapping speeches; strands of dialogue left floating in the air; sentences hanging by a thread; personal asides mixed up with substantive amendments to the text.

At 11.30, the conversation was interrupted by a message from Ron Webster, the Dagenham Operations Industrial Relations Manager, to say that the women's meeting was over. They would be going back to work tomorrow — provided the NJNC gave them the increase they had been promised and provided the Court of Inquiry gave them the answer they expected on their grading. Blakeman was disturbed to hear of these conditions. When they'd been with Barbara Castle, the only condition the women had expressed was a desire to receive information on the weightings. Now they were threatening that, if there was no satisfactory settlement at Monday's NJNC, they would stop work again. This time, Barbara Castle would be on *their* side! Everything now turned on the Unions' willingness to reduce the women's differential. So the Inquiry was merely a formality? asked Meredeen. Oh no, said Blakeman. The Inquiry would deal with the grading and the NJNC would deal with the equal pay issue. Meredeen said the NJNC would never accept such a complicated formula to resolve the dispute. What's more, if the women's job was subjected to a completely fresh evaluation, the Company might then find itself reducing the differential in Grade C and not in Grade B!

Ramsey wanted to clear up other points with Blakeman. The women had repeatedly stated that they were skilled workers. How should we deal with that? Blakeman was clear: The Company had deliberately set out to challenge the traditional concept of what constituted 'skilled work'. The submission must bring that out quite clearly. What about the Two-Year Agreement? asked Ramsey. We may have broken it by the time we get into Court! Blakeman was not worried about that: These were precisely the 'special circumstances' envisaged in the reopening clause of the Two-Year Agreement . . .

Monday 1 July began with news of a political bombshell which reverberated through the Ford dispute. Ray Gunter, the former Minister of Labour, who had risen from his 'Bed of Nails' at the Department of Employment to make way for Barbara Castle, announced his resignation from Harold Wilson's Government. It was Gunter who had put pressure on Wilson to call both sides of the motor industry to Downing Street in September 1965, threatening them with some form of restrictive legislation if they did not succeed in putting their own house in order. It was Gunter who had 'raised no objection' to Ford's 1967 Agreement because it was to last for two years. Now Gunter had resigned on the very day that Blakeman was on his way to reopen that Agreement. As a professional negotiator, Blakeman had schooled himself not to display his emotions. But he was clearly distressed by Gunter's resignation. He thought he might have been influenced by Barbara Castle's handling of the women's claim. But there was also the government's intervention in the current rail dispute; and a strong possibility that he'd disagreed with the findings of the Donovan Report, published during the previous week.

The joint meeting of the NJNC, fixed for 11 o'clock that morning, had still not begun when Walter Hayes looked into Blakeman's office at 12.15, asking for news. Blakeman reported all he knew. Tempers were short on the Union Side. They were complaining about the lack of adequate notice for the meeting and weren't at all happy to discuss the issue. If they could not muster half their members, they were threatening to go home.

Hayes was concerned at the delay. As Vice-President, Public Affairs, Ford of Europe, he acted as Gillen's Chief of Staff. He was worried about getting the top brass — Gillen, Batty and Rees — back to Dagenham after the NJNC in time for another meeting. He'd got the Company launch waiting at Westminster Pier, with its engines running, to beat the traffic congestion through the City and East London.

At 12.30 Stan Cross, the Halewood Operations Manager, reported that the Halewood Foremen had all come out on strike — the first strike by Foremen in the Company's history. Blakeman passed the bad news to Gillen. Should we stand up to them? Gillen asked. Where will this chain reaction stop, for God's sake? Blakeman advised Gillen that the Company should 'roll over'. The chances of winning were nil. We would have another costly strike on our hands and then lose. It would be the Sewing Machinists all over again. We'd better give way before the strike becomes solid. Gillen reluctantly agreed: They should settle it quietly.

At 12.45 the NJNC got under way. The Union Side had mustered eleven of its twenty-one members. Young and Conway were there and so was Gallagher. But neither Kealey nor Birch nor Baker was present. All three had sent deputies. In the whole history of the Ford NJNC, there had never been — and would never again be — a meeting like this one. Blakeman began by announcing the purpose of the meeting: To report back to the NJNC on the events of the latter part of last week. Young said he understood from Gallagher that the Company would be 'making some proposals' as a result of last Friday's meeting with the Secretary of State. Blakeman then gave a brief account of what had transpired since their last meeting, just two weeks before. He noted that the women had decided to continue their strike, despite the setting up of the Court of Inquiry:

> It was in that state of affairs that the First Secretary called in all the parties concerned . . . and after discussion it was decided, on the basis that the pay and grading dispute would be placed before the Inquiry, that this Committee would meet today to discuss other aspects, and that on that basis a resumption of work would take place . . . This morning, both at Dagenham and at Halewood, the women Sewing Machinists returned and recommenced work, so that we are now in production again, trying to catch up with the considerable disruption that has taken place.[23]

The Court of Inquiry would be looking at the pay and grading dispute, said Blakeman. On the matter of the relative difference between men's and women's rates, he had already made it clear that, provided the issue was dealt with through the Procedure, the Company was ready to sit down with the Unions and discuss the question. Having secured agreement to proceed, he went on to elaborate the Company's proposals on the question of equal pay:

> **Mr Blakeman** Our general policy is that we are generally amicable to accepting the principle provided there is an equal contribution of work, but at the same time we are prevented from obtaining an equal contribution because of one or two facets concerning the employment of women, and the two very obvious ones are the question of overtime and shiftwork, both of which are restricted by the legisla-

tion of the country.

Nevertheless, we are prepared to move towards a better relativity between men's and women's rates, as and when the limitations on the Company are removed, and I have indicated that we could make progress towards this on the basis of 85 per cent when we had our negotiations, and it is on this general formula that the rates are built up in our wage structure at the moment.

But I have indicated also that we would be prepared to take this up to 90 per cent. We said this in our negotiations last year. We said, at that time, that this would be our offer if we could get the shift-work operated. The offer I am prepared to make now is that provided we can jointly evaluate the contribution that women make to our production, we would be prepared to increase the 85 per cent to 90 per cent.[24]

After an adjournment lasting one hour and five minutes – during which the normal beer and buffet lunch provided by the Company was *not* served – the Trade Union Side announced that, if the Company would increase its offer to 92 per cent they would recommend acceptance.

Blakeman's relief at that moment was almost tangible. He urged Conway to obtain the assent of the other members of the Trade Union Side as quickly as possible so that the necessary adjustments could be made in the women's pay rates. At the very last moment, Blakeman remembered to leave a trailer for their next meeting:

Mr Blakeman I think the dilemma that you and we have found ourselves in this morning points to the need for a very cool and calm look at the whole constitution, the Terms of Reference and Procedure of this body. I think that at some time, when we are not fettered with extraneous problems, we should sit down together and work something out that will give us a little more confidence; or by which we can regain some of the confidence that is fast disappearing from this body.

Mr Conway I can give you every assurance that this Trade Union Side has pledged itself at the very earliest possible moment to look at the whole question of what has happened in this case.[25]

But the NJNC, as a Joint Body, never did honour its pledge to look at the whole question. In fact, it was not until after the three-week strike on 'penalty clauses' in 1969, and after both Young and Conway had resigned from the NJNC, that the whole question of the NJNC's Constitution, Terms of Reference and Procedure were examined in detail.

The NJNC finished at 2.15. By 2.45, the Company launch left Westminster Pier for Dagenham Jetty. On board were Gillen, Batty, Rees, Hayes, Blakeman and Meredeen — together with the skipper and the bar steward. For some reason, Ramsey had missed the boat and Gillen decided not to wait for him.

Having given a quick resumé of the NJNC, Blakeman produced a typescript from his briefcase, raised his voice in competition with the launch's powerful engine and began reading aloud from the latest draft of the Company submission to the Court of Inquiry, in order that Gillen and Batty could give their comments and approval. For Blakeman, the journey was no pleasure cruise. The breeze tore at the pages of his type-script — and he needed one hand to steady himself as the launch pitched and tossed through the choppy water. He had to strain his voice to make himself heard, refreshing his throat with gin and tonic, thoughtfully provided by the steward:

> We are gratified that this Court of Inquiry has been set up to make a thorough and comprehensive investigation into the causes and circum-stances of the dispute. We welcome the fullest exposure of the circum-stances which have led to the dishonouring of our National Agreements by certain sectors of the Trade Unions. We believe that this Court of Inquiry needs to find specific answers why the Agreements were disregarded and the well-established jointly agreed machinery for dealing with grading grievances was ignored.[26]

Blakeman's words were followed intently by Gillen and Batty, who turned the pages of their own copies, interjecting here a note of encour-agement, there a suggestion to clarify the meaning or sharpen the emphasis.

Gillen liked what he had heard. But he wanted to see the conclusions sharpened up: We should enquire directly of the people concerned — Blake, Gallagher, Friedman — why they didn't abide by the Procedure Agreement. As Blakeman acknowledged Gillen's points, Meredeen noted them for incorporation into the final version. Right at the outset, there had been a reference to 'the greatest catastrophe to befall the Company'. Gillen felt they should omit that — even if it *were* true! It was too melo-dramatic coming right at the start. Better to build up to it in the conclu-sion. Why not say: I'm glad to be able to give evidence under oath because it's vital to find the truth and so *prevent* a catastrophe which would set us back 20 years in the development of our labour relations, etc.

It was now 4.15, and the launch had tied up at the Dagenham Jetty. Back in Rees' office, the text was completely reviewed for a second time, line by line: a phrase deleted, a new phrase added, the argument tightened up, the sequence re-arranged and improved. At the end, Gillen summed up. Blakeman needed to strengthen his conclusions: first, what Britain needed above everything else to improve its labour relations was clear, equitable and easily administered wage structures. Unless we find out why this dispute occurred over this New Wage Structure, we're not going to have modern industrial relations in Britain. Second, have we reached the point where Unions are no longer prepared to stand by the Agreements they've entered into in good faith? Perhaps we should say that we don't believe in legal sanctions against strikers. And that our recent experience has been that the Unions have genuinely tried to make the Agreements work. So the question was, why had they behaved this way this time?

On Tuesday 2 July, the finishing touches were put to the Company's written evidence to the Court and arrangements made for its distribution. During the morning, Jack Langston, the Industrial Relations Manager from the Dagenham Body Plant, phoned a plaintive report to Warley: the Sewing Machinists had returned to work elated by their victory but the Supervisors were deeply depressed. One was reported to be in tears, complaining bitterly that the Company had 'sold its Supervision down the river'. For years, management had told its workers they would get nothing by taking strike action. How would you suggest we explain to them why management has done this deal? asked Langston. Nobody at Warley had any suggestions to offer.

For most members of Ford management who took part in it, the Scamp Court of Inquiry was something between a modern tragedy and a conventional farce. It was tragic, after five years of sustained effort to restructure and strengthen its industrial relations with both union and shop-floor representatives, that Ford management was caught up, for the third time in ten years, in another Official Inquiry. For Blakeman, the experience was deeply distressing. He had been through it all, not once, but twice before — the allegations, the refutations, the confusions, the recriminations and the publicity. He could hardly believe it was all really happening again. The most successful multinational Company operating in Britain had been brought to a standstill and forced into a Court of Inquiry to persuade a handful of discontented women to return to their jobs. Alongside this tragic waste of energy, of wages, of products and of profits, there was the farcical element of the whole thing. Here was Blakeman, the man of principle, architect of Ford's New Wage Structure and the Two-Year Productivity Deal, upholder of the sanctity of Procedure Agreements, chief advocate of their legal enforceability, who only 48 hours before had made the biggest wage offer in his whole career – to a group of women who had not even submitted their claim for equal pay through Procedure. It was Blakeman who would shortly stand up in Court to denounce the Unions for dishonouring their national Agreements and for bringing into disrepute the voluntary system of collective bargaining in Britain.

The second day's hearing of evidence took place on Wednesday 3 July, at the Civil Service Commission building in Burlington Street, off Piccadilly. Scamp began by inviting Young to give the Union Side's account of the dispute and its causes. Young was down-to-earth, fluent and brief: the Trade Union Side of the Ford NJNC had not been in dispute with the Company at all over this particular problem. They were in considerable difficulty because they had no information on what the causes of the dispute were. He was extremely disappointed that the procedures set up jointly with the Company had failed so abysmally to settle the dispute within the Company, particularly after the improving relationships of the past two years. The Unions found it regrettable, at the end of that period, that, on an incident like this, both sides of the NJNC found themselves helpless.

Young was followed by Gallagher. On the substance of the dispute, he said his Union acknowledged the need for a rational wage structure based on job evaluation. But the grading proposals of 1967 had revealed serious anomalies that could not be dealt with through the grading grievance machinery in a manner satisfactory to the Unions, unless the Company were prepared to make known the weightings applied to each characteristic and the points value of each job. His Union's action in officially recognising the dispute had been criticised because it might have done the national economy harm and caused hardship to thousands of Ford workers. However, having regard to the history of the Sewing Machinists' case and the need to create confidence in job evaluation as a technique for rationalising out-dated wage structures, it was necessary to expose the shortcomings of the Company in applying the scheme that was agreed with the Unions in 1967.

In Birch's absence, his deputy, Kirkip, spoke for the AEF. His Union made no apologies for the statement that the dispute was about equal pay. Since that question had been resolved, he would not say much about it. The New Wage Structure was supposed to abolish this form of discrimination between males and females by evaluating jobs and not persons. Therefore, it had been welcomed with open arms by his Union's female members. It was a great disappointment to the Sewing Machinists that their skill at the trade did not find the recognition it surely deserved. The women's expectations of equality and the removal of discrimination had unfortunately not been fulfilled. He noted, from the Company's statistics, that one man in four was in a Grade C job, but only one woman in 400! He concluded that the job profile had been deliberately made to fit the Company's ideas on grading rather than reflecting the profile itself. On the evidence before him, he did not see how any other conclusion could be reached.

Kirkip was followed by Jack Mitchell, the AEF District Official. He pointed out that his office was only five miles from Dagenham, so he could hardly be said to be remote from the dispute or its origin. The sole cause of the dispute was sex discrimination. Women in the Sewing Machine Shop worked for unequal pay for identical work, despite being required to achieve the same work standards as their male counterparts. Unlike any other production worker, a Sewing Machinist had to pass a trade test and prove knowledge and recognised skills before being hired by Ford. That in itself substantiated the case made by his Union. All their attempts to deal with the matter through Procedure were completely frustrated by the absolutely unyielding attitude of the Company.

Horne, deputising for Kealey of the TGWU, made a brief pointed Statement: his Union had confined its efforts to securing a resumption of work. The issue seemed to range between the question of equal pay and the question of grading. His Union had only five members involved at Dagenham but many more at Halewood. He found it surprising that consultations had taken place at the Ministry without involving his Union and others concerned. The TGWU would not seek to do anything adversely to affect the claim of women in respect of equal pay or up-grading. But they were still in some difficulty to understand exactly what the issue was which the Court was discussing.

Members of the management team present in Court listened with a mixture of irritation and amusement to what had been said successively by the five union spokesmen. They were in complete disarray, each Union arguing its own position, adding to the confusion and the complexity of the evidence. In the question period which followed, Scamp reverted to the question of the disclosure of weightings, made so much of by Gallagher. Had Young not said that the Trade Union Side of the NJNC had voted by 12 votes to 2 *not* to ask the Company for the weightings? Young admitted it had been a bone of contention. When the Company first proposed its new gradings, he had made a Statement on behalf of the Unions that it was necessary not only to have justice, but to see justice being done, and it was argued that the fullest information should be made available. But, Young added, it was a point of some significance that no union in September of last year made this a point of principle on whether or not they would accept the Agreement. Apart from the NUVB, there had been no real depth of feeling on the Union Side about the weightings.

Scamp then turned his attention to Gallagher in a series of relentless questions: Had the Sewing Machinists' claim been referred to the Profile Review Committee? No — the women had no confidence that they would have justice done to their case. In that case, why did you not refer it to the NJNC? Because the workers at Ford had no confidence in the NJNC's Grading Sub-Committee. In that case, asked Scamp, had the normal procedure been exhausted in Gallagher's opinion? No, because we were caught up by events. We are castigated by the Court for taking unconstitutional action. But to us there was a moral issue here. It was a more important question than the niceties of constitutional action. In any case, the women would not have gone back to work. It had taken Barbara Castle seven hours of persuasion to get them back. Scamp remarked acidly that he had offered to see the ladies himself the previous day. Yes, muttered Gallagher, and you didn't have any more luck than me!

Finally, on the Union Side, came Friedman. He concentrated on the technical aspects of the vital Intermediate Sewing Machinists' job profile. It was 'the best profile of any production worker', yet it was placed in Grade B, whereas profiles of much lower value were placed in Grade C. There was nothing wrong with the profile — merely that somebody had slipped up and put it in the wrong grade. It was not until 28 May 1968, when the Profile Review Committee was asked to review the profile, that he had learnt for the first time that this profile had not been dealt with in the normal manner. It had never been accepted by the Central Review Committee, but referred to the Consultants for adjudication.

Following the lunch break and a number of detailed questions to Union Officials by Scamp, and a brief Statement by Lil O'Callaghan, Scamp invited Blakeman to open the case for the Company. He began in measured tones:

of the New Wage Structure, we have given assurances on many occasions to different groups of people that we have, at no time, done anything to vary the evidence from the Profile Review Committee. We have heard the allegation that the Company have manipulated the requirements: and whenever that allegation has been made our reply — which must be well known by now — has been a categorical denial. And yet I hear the allegation again made this morning . . .

I would like to say that I, personally, am prepared to go on oath and to assure the Court, and anybody else who cares to listen, that we have at no time discriminated in our profile work between male and female employees; and secondly, at no time have we manipulated a profile in order to achieve a pre-conceived grading . . .

With due respect, I would ask the Court to keep in mind, throughout this hearing, two fundamental points. *First,* the Ford Motor Company has a collective bargaining system such as has been advocated by the Donovan Commission on the general premise that a system of Company bargaining is to be preferred to industry-wide bargaining, and that a move in this direction would lead to greater harmony in our national industrial relationships. My Company shares that view provided there is some integrity on both sides, in the application of the system. *Secondly,* the contentious point of this issue would never have arisen if we, as a Company, had not embarked two years ago upon an exercise to change our wages structure so that it would meet the demands of modern, progressive and competitive industry. The need for just such modernising plans, resulting in up-to-date wages structures, is evident throughout industry in this country today and is one of the root causes behind the malaise in the present British economy. In pleading with the Court to bear these two points in mind, I have explained our sole reason for urging that the hearing of these proceedings should be in public.[27]

Blakeman went on to describe the progress made in improving labour relationships at Ford over the last few years. It was much too valuable to the Company to be swept away by this present dispute and all the emotions that had arisen around it. He urged the Court, when dealing with the narrower issues, to be mindful of the dangerous consequences that might easily arise should the much wider and far-reaching implications be neglected.

He then presented background information about the Company's organisation structure and about the major operation of changing the wage structure, before turning to the dispute itself. Having outlined the reasons for changing the old wage structure, he described in great detail the method of job evaluation adopted, then the fact-finding stage, followed by the Company's formulation of proposals for changing the old structure and, finally, the negotiation of the proposed changes through the NJNC. There had been no discrimination against women workers in the new structure. Jobs were evaluated on the basis of their actual job content, irrespective of whether they were performed by men or by women. It was illogical, therefore, to continue with a discriminatory grade for women, as in the old wage structure, but a differential had been established between men's and women's rates to cover the women's reduced work contribution.[28]

Blakeman declared that the cause of the dispute was the claim by the Union on behalf of the Sewing Machinists that they were incorrectly graded. It had not been put through the Grievance Procedure agreed as being necessary for dealing with grievances on grading. The Company's case was that the claim *should* be put through the agreed Procedure. Failure to do so constituted a fundamental breach of agreement by the Unions. If the matter was not dealt with by that Procedure, the whole of the wage structure and the good relations built up since 1962 would be in peril. All of the Unions and employees were interested in the operation of the agreed Procedure, and in seeing that the New Wage Structure was fairly operated and not irresponsibly undermined. The Sewing Machinists' grading was plainly correct. If they were upgraded to Grade C without justification, other employees in Grade C would press for upgrading to Grade D and consequently many of those in D Grade would press for upgrading to E Grade. In other words, the wage structure would collapse in chaos and the negotiating machinery with it.

By the time he reached his peroration, Blakeman had been speaking without a break for more than an hour and a quarter — not a bad performance by a man of 64, at the end of a long, hot and tiring day. None of his colleagues in Court that day could fail to be impressed by the energy of a man who so often conveyed the impression of physical and mental weariness. It was the measure of the man, of his training and his character, that he could rise to the occasion and conclude his Statement in this challenging way:

The Ford Motor Company, we believe, possesses a competent management which has not only applied its expertise to creating an efficient organisation making a major contribution to the country's balance of payments problems, but in so doing, has paid due regard to the human element. Constantly drawing lessons from its own and other Companies' experience, it has, over the years, developed progressive personnel policies, planned, negotiated and implemented by trained and experienced Managers, who have tried to provide for the new role that the Trade Unions play in our industrial life.

Although we do not claim that the wages structure we negotiated and introduced was perfect – if it was perfect there would be no need for Procedures to resolve grievances – we do believe that the Sewing Machinists are correctly graded because of the evidence established by the job evaluation exercise, and we believe that the position of women employees in our wages structure represents a considerable step forward. We do, however, find it difficult to understand why we have become involved in a Court of Inquiry on a matter which both we and the Trade Unions have agreed should be settled by our joint negotiating machinery. Even more difficult to understand – and this is probably unique in the history of industrial relations – is how we came to be the target of two official strikes, one we are told on an issue on which the Company has never even received a claim.

The Ford Motor Company has faced a number of strikes and two of these have also resulted in Courts of Inquiry. On each occasion the management has studied the causes to see what fault, if any, lay on the Company side . . . For the last six years the Company has steadily progressed until we justifiably felt we had reached a stage of good labour relationships. This position was achieved not by recrimination, but by the steps I have just referred to and a considerable amount of hard work by the Management and the Trade Unions.

The complexity of the details and technicalities that make up the whole sorry story of this dispute must not be allowed to cloud this simple issue. If the Company had to concede to pressure by groups resorting to unconstitutional action, it would make it impossible to apply a fair and consistent wages structure and would destroy the whole fabric of collective bargaining.

The dilemma which faces the Company and, we believe, the whole of British industry is that having taken a stand on the side of law and order in industrial relationships, what can be done to prevent the disruption of its operation by the irresponsibility of people who choose to ignore Agreements entered into in good faith?

We are pleased to co-operate with this Inquiry which we hope might help us to find some of the answers so that we can continue to move forward with our employees and the Trade Unions which represent them.

I would ask the Court to address itself to the following questions:

(1)   Why did not Mr Gallagher pursue the claim at the NJNC?

(2)   Why did his Executive declare official a dispute that had not been pursued through the Procedure?

(3)   Why did the AEF Executive declare official a dispute that had not even been registered with the Company?

(4)   Why did these two Unions' Executives fail to support the Agreement made by their representatives on the Company's Negotiating Committee?

(5)   Why did the NUVB District Official continue to support the strike to the extent of picketing, knowing that his National Officer had reached this Agreement the previous day?

(6)   Why would not the River Plant Convener allow the Profile Review Committee, which included three Union representatives, to look at the job and examine his claim?

(7)   And finally – and this is a question which must be answered, not only for the Ford Motor Company, but for every Company in Britain struggling to make itself competitive in 1968 – what can be done to ensure that Agreements entered into in good faith are not broken at will, with what may be disastrous effects on the Company's operations?[29]

Although Blakeman's Statement came towards the end of the first full day's hearing of evidence, nothing said throughout the rest of the Inquiry came anywhere near it in terms of clarity, conciseness or sincerity. For three more days, Scamp posed persistent questions. But for management, the dispute was virtually over. The women were back at work. The Court had heard evidence from all the parties. They must now await the Court's findings and then deal with the consequences.

At the end of the third day, Scamp gathered up his voluminous notes and thanked those present for their co-operation. The Inquiry was now over. As they prepared to depart, a few of the principal witnesses met face to face for the first time on the floor of the Courtroom. The atmosphere was reminiscent of those awkward moments which follow the funeral of a close friend. Everything there was to be said, had been said. The lamentations were over but it was still too soon to start rejoicing. Blakeman and Young, Ramsey and Blake, O'Callaghan and Boland, Friedman and Meredeen – all stood chatting and putting on a brave smile. Finally, in what might have been a gesture of reconciliation, Lil O'Callaghan, smartly but soberly dressed, in dark glasses and high-heeled shoes, befitting the occasion, came across to Blakeman to say goodbye. Her words could not have been more simple – or more poignant. As

they shook hands, she offered him the mourner's traditional farewell:
May we meet again — on happier occasions!

Notes

1. The blast furnace and coke ovens were finally demolished in 1978, the gas holders in 1979.

2. See Robert Heller, 'Ford Motor's Managing Machine', *Management Today* (London, February 1968).

3. In the fifties, two old pennies — the price of a phone call from Dagenham to Fleet Street — earned the caller a couple of pounds for each stoppage reported and provided the evening paper's editor with the familiar headline: 'Fords: All out again'. The advent of subscriber trunk dialling in the sixties helped to put British Leyland and Chrysler into the same news league as Ford.

4. For a comprehensive evaluation of these strategies, see Andrew Friedman, *Industry and Labour* (Macmillan, London, 1977).

5. Allan Flanders, *Management and Unions* (Faber, London, 1970), p. 172,

6. Ibid. Flanders, Blakeman and his wife, Joan Woodward, were close friends.

7. Industrial Court, *Report No. 3167: Grading of Carpenters and Joiners* (HMSO, London, 1968).

8. See note 14, p. 88 below.

9. Cf. Ch. 1, pp. 27-8 above.

10. Cf. Ch. 1, pp. 32-5 above.

11. Cf. Ch. 1, p. 43 above.

12. Factual data on the earliest employment of women as shop-floor workers by Ford in Britain is hard to establish. It is doubtful whether Perry, the Company's first Managing Director and later Chairman, employed women on production — as distinct from office work — at Trafford Park, Manchester. According to Wilkins and Hill, the same held true for Dagenham before the outbreak of World War II: 'However, increasing production demanded more men and, since men were not easily procurable, women. Never before employed at Dagenham, they numbered 1,100 in September 1941, helping to swell a workforce that had risen from less than 12,000 in 1939 and would total 34,163 in the spring of 1945.' Mira Wilkins and Frank Ernest Hill, *American Business Abroad — Ford on Six Continents,* (Wayne State University Press, Detroit, 1964), pp. 327-8. Cf. also Ch. 1, note 12, p. 22 above, for reference to women's rates of pay in the rest of the motor industry at that time, and note 17, p. 24 on the employment of women by Ford during World War II. For the position of women in Ford US plants, see note 15, p. 89 below.

13. *Record of Proceedings* (Scamp Inquiry), Second Day, 3 July 1968, p. 78.

14. Ibid.

15. Nevins explains that, when Ford introduced the $5 minimum day rate in 1914, women and salaried workers were at first left out of the plan 'except where women were the sole support of relatives . . . One reason for believing Henry Ford was the main author of the $5 minimum is the fact that it was originally planned simply for the men in the factory — the force in whom he took a direct interest. The Highland Park plant at the time had about 250 women workers. A vocal outcry in the *New York Times* in January 1941 from such feminist leaders as Helen Keller, Anna Howard Shaw and Mrs James Lees Laidlaw helped induce the Company to include them in the plan (in 1916).' Allan Nevins, *Henry Ford: the Times, the Man, the Company* (Charles Scribner's Sons, New York, 1954).

16. The subject of factor weighting — the method by which it is decided, its effect on differentials and the question of its disclosure — raises fundamental issues of fairness and equity in job evaluation. The imposition of predetermined weightings can obviously produce a manipulated ranking of jobs. The TUC warned negotiators in 1964 to 'be specially alert to discern the effects of factors and weights in any scheme with which they are concerned. In reality the choice of factors and their relative weightings is a subjective matter and . . . a highly important one.' Trades Union Congress, *Job Evaluation* (1964). The Institute of Personnel Management's 1968 *Guide to Job Evaluation* suggests that 'Selecting factors and weights is best carried out by review and comparison of existing schemes . . . but the final test is whether their employment in a scheme will produce a distribution of wage rates which is acceptable.' The National Board for Prices and Incomes, in its *Report No. 83,* concludes that 'the problem of weighting is one of striking a compromise between what is regarded as ideal and what is likely to be accepted and workable'. See also Richard Hyman and Ian Brough, *Social Values and Industrial Relations* (Blackwell, Oxford, 1975).

17. Ford NJNC, *Transcript Notes of Proceedings,* 17 June 1968, p. 7.

18. Ibid., p. 13.

19. For Barbara Castle's own account see her *Diaries* (Weidenfeld and Nicolson, London, 1980).

20. In 1967, Gunter had characterised American strikes as more predictable and therefore less damaging than British strikes because they were principally concerned with contract renewal disputes: 'When Mr Walter Reuther brings his men out on strike in the American motor car industry, they have had at least three years' peace. No one has broken a contract. When he takes them back, there is another three years in which they can plan and wait. The dilemma of British industry is continuous interruption of production lines. No one knows when it will strike next.' Quoted in *Fair Deal at Work,* Conservative Political Centre (1968), p. 28. Compare remarks by Ford's Director of Industrial Relations, R.J. Ramsey to Duffy Committee Inquiry, Ch. 6, p. 236, below.

21. Industrial Court, *Report on Grading of Carpenters and Joiners* (HMSO, London, 1968).

22. *Report of a Court of Inquiry* (The Scamp Report), Cmnd. 3749 (HMSO, London, 1968).

23. Ford NJNC, *Transcript Notes of Proceedings,* 1 July 1968, pp. 4-5.

24. Ibid., p. 7.

25. Ibid., p.10.

26. *Record of Proceedings* (Scamp Inquiry), Second Day, 3 July 1968, p. 62.

27. Ibid., pp. 61-2.

28. Ibid., p. 78.

See note 14, p. 88 above.

29. *Record of Proceedings* (Scamp Inquiry), Second Day, 3 July 1968, pp. 85-7.

4

THE DISPUTE SEEN THROUGH SHOP STEWARD'S EYES

The Sewing Machinists in the River Plant — Their Work and the Plant's Trade Union History

When the Trade Unions eventually accepted the New Wage Structure and signed the two-year deal, the Company had secured a badly needed Agreement, but appeared to have overlooked two important factors. First, there was a presupposition inherent in job evaluation, namely, that the job is being graded, and not the person doing it. This brings the concept of equal pay readily to mind. Second, if a multi-grade structure is introduced into a big enterprise against the background of large-scale participation by the workforce, nearly everyone feels, after the job values have been determined, that his or her job has been undervalued and ought to have been placed at least into the next highest grade.

This is particularly true of situations where workers accustomed to being in the same grade become separated. Those placed, or remaining, in lower grades are certainly convinced that they ought to be in this higher grade together with their previous colleagues. Even those in the top grade contend that there is a need for additional higher grades, because, for example, Toolmakers feel affronted at being placed in the same grade as Electricians, or vice versa. If, against this background, a Grading Grievance Procedure becomes operative, it is virtually certain that nearly all groups will want to utilise this machinery, the rationale being that it would be certainly worth a try to have your job upgraded and it costs nothing.

Consequently, as soon as the grading grievance machinery was brought into being and a Profile Review Committee consisting of three trade union and three Company members was established, hundreds of grading grievances from all the Ford plants in the UK were submitted. Amongst these was a grievance from the Sewing Machinists in the River Plant.

The Ford River Plant is sited on the Dagenham marshes, about one mile north of the River Thames, and about a quarter mile south of the main London-Tilbury railway line. To the east, roughly also one mile distant, is the original Ford Engine Plant, and facing the plant directly to the west is a factory belonging to the Standard Telephone Company.

The only access road runs across the main railway line at Dagenham Dock Station. This junction is controlled by level-crossing gates which are frequently closed for anything up to 15 minutes at a time. This geographical position tends to isolate the River Plant from all the other major Ford plants in the area. The access difficulty, to some extent, limits the plant's product range, and the prospect of a possible 15-minute wait at the level-crossing gate also reduces the frequency of visits by higher management.

About 2,000 workers are employed in this plant. The plant itself covers an area of about 50,000 square metres and consists of a series of separate buildings which grew in a haphazard and topsy-like fashion over the years. Some of these buildings are over eighty years old, and in the past served a quite different purpose. For example, the present administrative office block used to be a hunting lodge adjacent to a fishing lake on the Dagenham marshes. The brick buildings are rather antiquated. They were designed for the production of gunpowder and other explosive material during World War I. They now house part of the Tooling Operations, an activity which is concerned with the manufacture of press tools and jigs and fixtures. These tools are necessary for the production of car bodies and assembly line operations. Close by is a toolmaking Apprentice Training School.

The remainder of the plant consists mainly of a series of metal framed hangars, clad by a single layer of asbestos sheeting, not unlike agricultural buildings used for wheat storage. Working conditions in buildings of this kind present a constant problem. They are cold in the winter and hot and uncomfortably humid in the summer.

The Trim Shop, which makes all the seat covers for cars, is situated in two such adjoining hangars, each approximately 170 feet long, by 125 feet wide. The production cycle of seat covers begins with Eastman cutters,[1] all men, cutting layers of material prepared from rolls of cloth or plastics, into a variety of shapes and sizes. Sewing Machinists sitting behind rows and rows of sewing machines then stitch together these bewildering numbers of different pieces repetitively and with astonishing speed, and produce a variety of differently styled and coloured seat covers which suit all the Company's car model ranges. The Cortina range alone has over 250 trim variations. About 1,400 seat covers and door trims are produced daily for cars and commercial vehicles. On average, 13 metres of nylon cloth and plastic material goes into each vehicle. To stitch these together requires over 330 metres of thread per vehicle. Of necessity, a lot of foam and plastic material has to be stored in these hangars, and this makes the Trim Shop buildings the highest fire risk on the whole Dagenham Estate.

Before continuing our narrative about the Trim Shop, and in order to understand the events which led up to the Sewing Machinists' dispute, it would be useful to have a brief look at the River Plant's trade union history.

Although the River Plant is somewhat isolated and has, by comparison with the other major plants on the Dagenham Estate, a relatively small workforce, it has, nevertheless, a prominent place in Ford trade union history. Events in this plant have had a significant effect on company/union relationships. Conflicts which occurred within the confines of this plant have caused two government Courts of Inquiry to be set up within a decade. The first issue, which led to the Court of Inquiry presided over by Lord Cameron in the late 1950s, arose from the sacking of Johnny McLoughlin, the 'bell ringer', a River Plant Shop Steward, and the second Court of Inquiry, presided over by Sir Jack Scamp, arose, of course, out of the 1968 Sewing Machinists' dispute. Quite apart from this, the Plant Conveners and Shop Stewards have consistently exercised a considerable influence over general trade union policies in the last 25 years. For example, the Company's Wage Structure Review was induced by pressures which emanated from the River Plant's Toolmakers, who strove to restore their differentials and, in a sense, set into motion the causal chain which led to the Seamstresses' strike. The reason for the disproportionate influence the plant has exercised on trade union affairs can be traced back to the transfer of about 400 Toolmakers in the early 1950s. They came from the main Briggs Body Plant and amongst the men transferred, all members of the AEU, were personalities like Alf Moore, for many years South Essex AEU District President, until his death in 1962, and Alec Geddes, a stalwart of the World War I Clyde Workers' Committee, and someone who had known Lenin personally. It was these Toolmakers and their Shop Stewards who had led the unionisation struggle at Ford, and were in the forefront of the fight for union recognition in the early 1940s. In fact, the first Court of Inquiry in the Company's history, in 1941, was occasioned by a dispute in the Briggs Body Plant Toolroom, which arose from the sacking of a Shop Steward, John McDougall. To some extent, this tradition is still continued today. The present Convener of the River Plant, Bernie Passingham, is a lay member of the Transport and General Workers' Union Executive, and he is also the Secretary of the Ford National Conveners' Committee.

A rank-and-file movement and its leadership, hardened and tempered in this way through battles with one of the most ruthless employers, inevitably resisted to the utmost the Company's attempts to 'standardise' them into the Ford Agreement, which in fact meant replacing plant bargaining by national bargaining. The 'bell ringer' episode in 1957 was the climax of a five-year struggle to retain bargaining rights at the plant level. It ended in defeat for the rank-and-file movement. The sacking of Johnny McLoughlin left a legacy of bitterness and frustration which was further accentuated by the sacking of the 'seventeen trouble makers' in October 1962. The Company's 'October Revolution', or rather *coup d'état,* was an event in which leading Shop Stewards, including Conveners in the Body and Assembly Plants, were sacked and subsequently stayed sacked. Consequently, the decade following the Cameron Court of Inquiry was characterised by a repressive and restrictive Company policy towards the Shop Steward movement. Its hallmark was the denial of virtually all basic facilities to Shop Stewards and Conveners and petty personal restrictions on the freedom of movement of all Shop Stewards. For example, Shop Stewards were not allowed to leave their job unless they had written permission in the form of a signed pass by the Supervisors, stating the time of their departure, the reason for leaving their job and the time of their return. The 'pass laws' were strictly enforced, and often invoked comparisons with South African practices. These developments, interspersed by a series of minor defeats during this ten-year period, created a feeling of ineffectiveness, increasing powerlessness and growing resentment amongst the rank-and-file leadership.

Conversely, this legacy also created a subconscious desire to redress the power balance in favour of the shop floor — to even the score — at the first available opportunity. The word 'subconscious' is used advisedly because there was no deliberate strategy or any conspiracy to attain this objective, nor, as far as is known, did any individuals spend sleepless nights thinking about this problem and worrying about what action ought to be taken to resolve it. Indeed, it would be quite impossible to manufacture an issue and to manipulate the membership in order to produce this desired result. (If it can be done, why wait ten years?) Nevertheless, it is possible to spot, or fail to spot, opportunities if they happen to come along. Furthermore, such factors as resolve and ideological commitment are not dependent on any specific time scale, or on any particular issue. Be that as it may, the rank-and-file leadership clearly understood that the power balance could only be redressed by way of an out-and-out victory over the Company on a major issue. Beneath the surface, the desire to achieve this objective was ever present.

It was against this background that the Convener assisted the Trim Shop Stewards, Lil O'Callaghan and Rosie Boland, with all their shop meetings during the months of April and May 1968. The Convener's presence was motivated by two factors. First, based on the available job profiling evidence, it seemed that the Company had really 'cooked the books' in order to keep the Sewing Machinists within the confines of the 'industrial kitchen' — the womens' traditional place in industry, doing the lowest-paid jobs. Second, as an ex-member of the Divisional Review Committee, the Convener had received training and acquired specialist knowledge about job evaluation techniques and grading methods and he was therefore in a position to deal authoritatively with any matters concerning the Sewing Machinists' grading problems at any of these meetings.

Sewing car seat covers requires quite extraordinary nimbleness of fingers, speed, accuracy and a degree of hand and eye co-ordination for which females seem to have a particular aptitude, and which men just do not seem able to match. The few men who are employed on night work to do the same job can barely manage half the output. The special features of this particular job attracted a high job profile rating from the Divisional Review Committee. In fact, much too high for the job to be fitted into the Company's preconceived ranking order.

But before dealing with this aspect, it would perhaps be useful briefly to outline, in chronological order, the events which led up to the dispute.

The Grading is Contested

It was common knowledge to the workers and the Shop Stewards in the Trim Shop that the Divisional Review Committee had rated the Sewing Machinists' job highly. In consequence, Charles Gallagher, then Assistant General Secretary of the National Union of Vehicle Builders (NUVB), wrote to the Company in August 1967 querying the grading of the Sewing Machinists, and he raised the question again at a meeting with the Company in October. On both occasions the Company assured him that, based on the job profile, the Sewing Machinists had been properly graded. Because Gallagher had received no satisfaction from the Company the matter was again raised at the Joint Works Committee meeting in the River Plant in December. At this meeting the Convener requested an explanation as to how it had come about that jobs with higher profile values such as the Sewing Machinists' had been graded below jobs of lesser profile values. The Trade Unions argued ' . . . . it was illogical to have a position in the Trim Shop where Sewing Machinists obtained profiles considerably better than Leather Cutters and Eastmen Cutters, all males, and yet were in a lower grade . . . .'[2]

In January 1968, the Company again met Gallagher and discussed the Sewing Machinists' job profile with him step by step. The Company stated that by the end of the meeting he was satisfied. In February, the Company sent a further letter to him confirming the grading as correct. During February and March 1968, the River Plant Joint Works Committee discussed grievances in relation to a number of job profiles, including that of the Sewing Machinists. The Trade Union Side argued that in the particular instance of the Sewing Machinists' profile, as distinct from other job profiles, because of the Divisional Review Committee records available to them, they were quite satisfied with the assessment of all the 28 characteristics and therefore they did not want the job reviewed. What they were contesting most strongly, however, was the placement of the Sewing Machinists into Grade B, in view of the quality of their particular job profile. In reply, the Company insisted that the agreed Procedure limited queries to a review of the job and the profile itself, but that in any case the grading was correct. The reason why the Trade Union Side was apparently able to persuade the Management Side of the Joint Works Committee is contained in the AEF submission to the Court of Inquiry.

> The whole of the River Plant Joint Works Committee composed of 6 management and 6 Trade Union members, with a management-appointed chairman, dissented from this view . . . This was not a matter for the Profile Review Committee, but should be dealt with directly by the Company through the normal procedures.[3]

The AEF submitted further evidence which endeavoured to show that:

> The Company tries to project the view that in order to be fair to everybody, up-gradings can only be achieved by reference to the Profile Review Committee. This is just not so. Many more up-gradings occur by local Plant agreements and re-allocations and also by agreements at National level . . . Fitters, electricians, copper-smiths, plumbers and inspectors and others, were upgraded without any reference to the Profile Review Committee. Either by re-titling jobs or by the persuasiveness of a particular national official or through the sympathy displayed by local Plant management . . . The

Company's notion that, if you have a grading grievance you *must* go to the Profile Review Committee, is just not tenable on the evidence.[4]

In April, a national sub-committee specifically set up to deal with grading problems met. The Company claimed that Gallagher, who attended this meeting, did not mention the Sewing Machinists, nor was the Company aware that any strong feelings existed about this issue amongst the Sewing Machinists. In consequent submissions to the Scamp Court of Inquiry the Company stated that in the River Plant 'the labour relations staff were well attuned to recognise problems in their embryonic stage'.[5] None the less, the Labour Relations Staff appeared to have over-looked the extent and depth of feeling which surrounded this issue. A series of shop meetings took place in March, April and May, where the Sewing Machinists discussed all the relevant aspects of their grading grievance with the Trim Shop Stewards and the Convener.

It was Company policy to refuse permission to have report-back meetings in the plant. Nevertheless, these meetings, numbering about ten in total, took place during the lunch hour at the rear of the Trim Shop. All meetings were very well attended. Virtually all the Sewing Machinists showed up regularly. At these meetings the Convener usually stood on a bench, the best available substitute for a platform, flanked by the Trim Shop Stewards, Rosie Boland and Lil O'Callaghan. The Sewing Machinists stood closely packed around the bench in a semi-circle.

Both Rosie and Lil had many years' service with the Company. Lil O'Callaghan had been a Shop Steward for about ten years; and a Sewing Machinist for twenty; she usually took the lead in discussions and displayed a forceful manner and a forthright approach to the point, where local management tended to become subdued. Rosie Boland — who had also worked in the River Plant for many years — was a Shop Steward with less experience, and therefore more reticent, and tended to cast herself in a supporting role for Lil O'Callaghan.

The shop meetings usually lasted about half an hour. The first ten minutes or so were given over to reports on the latest developments, and the remainder of the time was taken up by questions, answers and general discussion.

From the very outset, a kind of instinctive assumption emerged, that if a job requiring similar skills had been traditionally performed by men, it would have been graded higher. One point in particular was repeatedly emphasised by the women. Sewing Machinists had to pass a trade test before being able to secure employment at Ford, and it was argued that, wherever males had to do likewise — Production Welders, for example — they were automatically placed into a higher grade for bringing job expertise, knowledge and a recognised skill to the Company. According to Rosie Boland: 'When we go into the Ford Company, we have to pass a test on three machines. If we don't pass that test, we don't get a job. So why shouldn't they recognise us as skilled workers?'[6] This feeling was articulated and summarised at these shop meetings in terms of 'They think we only come to work for pin money', or 'they think just because we are women they can get away with it'. There was an understanding that the politics of the situation — that is to say, the likely internal consequences for the Company of placing women into a higher grade than most men on production work — had overridden the basic principle enshrined in job evaluation, namely that the job and not the person doing it determines the grading.

There was more than a kernel of truth in this, because traditionally women always had been paid less than men. Prior to the introduction of the New Wage Structure, they received 80 per cent of the semi-skilled male rate, or 92 per cent of the unskilled male rate (labourers and janitors). It would, therefore, hardly have helped the Company to secure acceptance of the proposed New Wage Structure if about half of all the women production workers employed had been placed into a higher grade than the bulk of all male production workers, and also store-keepers, internal transport drivers, and men employed in similar occupations.

Women thus rightly saw themselves downgraded because of their sex. 'Women are discriminated against because the Management employ them as cheap labour.'[7] Yet, at all the meetings prior to the strike, whenever the Convener attempted to link this grievance to the much broader issues of equal pay and equal opportunity, as a means of focusing their attention on the historic discrimination women had suffered throughout the ages, and to raise their consciousness about this aspect, this was fiercely rejected as irrelevant and along the lines of: 'We don't want to confuse the issue and get mixed up in politics.' The Sewing Machinists clearly wanted to resolve their case within the framework of the grading structure, and obtain justice by utilising the Grievance Procedure, and not through embracing universal political principles such as Equal Pay or any other women's rights' causes.

The passions aroused by this issue, however, grew to such an extent that, at a shop meeting on 21 May, the Sewing Machinists decided to ban overtime immediately. This decision was later, at the Convener's request, deferred for one week, to allow time for further discussions.

The Sewing Machinists also decided to have a one-day strike on 29 May in support of their claim – to be upgraded from Grade B into Grade C – worth about 5d an hour.

Ford's Industrial Relations Alerted

This brought the Labour Relations Department into a state of 'red alert'. On the morning of 28 May, the Trim Shop Stewards, Lil O'Callaghan and Rosie Boland – the latter was destined to become a television star within two weeks – plus the Convener and the Assistant Convener, met the Company Chairman of the Profile Review Committee, Sander Meredeen, and the Plant Labour Relations Manager. Sander Meredeen, in his late 30s, was a relative newcomer to the Company's Labour Relations Staff. His approach to problems was professional and he appeared competent, but these attributes linked to newness – he had less than five years' service with the Company – made him merely all the more suspect: a 'smart Alec' who would try to pull the wool over workers' eyes whenever he could, and if you let him. At one stage during the discussion, by way of a dramatic 'Don't you trust me' gesture, he offered the Shop Stewards his wallet containing about £100 worth of holiday money as collateral: 'If I don't keep my word, you can keep it.' The Stewards present wryly told the Convener afterwards, 'You should have accepted the Meredeen wallet . . . things might have taken a different turn.' Meredeen had been wage structure overlord from the very beginning, chosen by the Company for this task because of his previous involvement in a similar exercise with British Steel at Newport.

The Company seemed very anxious to prevent a one-day strike, and Meredeen made strenuous attempts to persuade the Trade Union Side to call the whole thing off. This only served to underline for the Sewing Machinists the importance of their function. However, the Company representatives continued to present lengthy technical arguments as to why the grievance should be dealt with in the normal manner, and they further suggested that the Trade Unions should give plant priority to this problem. Provided that these two conditions were fulfilled, the Company offered to have the job reviewed on the following day.

The Company's reasoning and explanations were rejected by the Trade Union Side. The Trim Shop Stewards reiterated their view that the Company had manipulated the system and had 'doctored' the profile because of anti-female bias. In order to find a solution, however, which held out some prospect of a satisfactory conclusion, the Shop

Stewards proposed that only those job characteristics should be reviewed which had been marked down from the rating level previously established by the Divisional Review Committee.

In the end, Meredeen reluctantly agreed to this. The Convener further requested that, prior to anything being done, the Shop Stewards should have an opportunity to explain their side of the case to the three trade union members of the Profile Review Committee. The Company, with equal reluctance, agreed also to this request.

The Profile Review Committee, of which Meredeen was Chairman and also had the casting vote, always met at the Company's main offices at Warley. The three trade union members on this Committee were the Conveners of the Langley, Woolwich and Halewood Plants.

Shop Stewards go to Ford's Central Office

The Convener, Assistant Convener and two Trim Shop Stewards left the River Plant for Warley at lunch-time in a fairly optimistic mood. They had placed their hopes on the sympathy and loyalty of the three trade union members and, given their anticipated backing, there appeared to be a good chance for a satisfactory outcome. It was a warm May day and, once away from the heat and smoke of Dagenham, it turned out to be a pleasant drive through the narrow tree-lined lanes of Essex to Warley. They stopped for lunch at a country pub. Perhaps this glimpse of the 'good life' helped to reinforce their belief in a successful outcome.

After arrival at the Company's Central Office at Warley, a huge modern office complex bounded by car parks and landscaped rose gardens, they met the trade union members of the Profile Review Committee. To their surprise their reception was not altogether what they had expected. Only Les Moore, the Halewood Body Plant Convener, was helpful. The two other Conveners were positively unsympathetic, not to say hostile, not so much because of any technical matter connected with the profile, but because their normally tranquil existence and extended lunch hour seemed to have been interrupted. Furthermore, they did not altogether relish this new situation, being pressured and lobbied by a work-shop delegation, a precedent which others indeed might want to follow and which opened up the prospect of a far less comfortable lifestyle at the Company's headquarters in the future.

This incident raises the whole question of joint management/union committees, and the effect of participation on trade union representatives who sit on these committees. It would seem that trade union members on such committees can become so fascinated with the routines of management, and the attendant perks — daily good lunches and a generally comfortable existence — that their loyalty to the membership is weakened and replaced by a growing affinity to management. No doubt advocates of the co-determination system may well see this as a desirable development, and as a natural part of the assimilation and integration process. But, for others within the trade union movement, this problem of bureaucratisation is a matter of continued concern.

After discussing the Sewing Machinists' problem for about half an hour, the trade union members of the Profile Review Committee retired to their meeting place, 'the ranking room', to join their management colleagues on the Committee for a private discussion. There, Meredeen ran into trouble. The members of the Profile Review Committee considered the democracy of their Committee to be threatened. A row developed amongst them about the Chairman's right to make agreements without their prior knowledge and consent. With time running out and under two-way pressure, Meredeen backed away from the Agreement he had made in the morning:

> . . . . the Deputy Convener entered the meeting uninvited and said that the Machinists were finishing work at 4 o'clock and would not be in next day unless there was a satisfactory reply to their claim. He and the Convener were told that they could not negotiate on how the inquiry should be carried out, and the meeting broke up in some disorder.[8]

The words 'some disorder' referred to Meredeen's loss of composure under pressure, and his abrupt termination of the meeting, after unceremoniously ordering the Deputy Convener out of the 'ranking room'.

By then the time was past 4 p.m. The finishing time in the Trim Shop was, in fact, 4.15 p.m. The Stewards had no alternative but to advise the Trim Shop Committee, by telephone, that negotiations had broken down and there was now no basis or justification for calling off the intended strike action. Thus the one-day strike, which at one stage stood a good chance of being called off, took place after all and received 100 per cent support.

On 30 May, the Sewing Machinists returned to work, and were each handed a letter by the Company which stated:

Dear Employee,

On Wednesday May 29 you, together with other employees in your department, took part in a strike in violation of your Contract of Service. I understand that this action was taken because you are dissatisfied with your grade in the Wage Structure.

A procedure has been agreed between the Company and the trade unions to progress grading grievances and this system has been used effectively in recent months by many employees, who, like you, were of the opinion that the job they did was inadequately reflected by their position in the Wage Structure; I believe that your best interests would still be served in using this procedure, since strike action or restrictive practices will in no way influence any decision that has to be made on the question of grading.

The only effect of this kind of unconstitutional action, which is a direct contravention of the Procedure Agreement, is that the employees concerned lose their pay, and other people, not involved in the dispute, can be involved through consequential effects.

Unconstitutional action will do nothing to help your case and could well have serious consequences.

B F Mitchell
Superintendent
Trim Manufacture
River Plant

The Conflict Intensifies

This letter angered the Sewing Machinists; they resented its tone and content. It was their first experience of this type of communication from the management, and they were determined to show that they could not be intimidated by these methods. The Sewing Machinists therefore promptly held a shop meeting, and resolved to take another day off, on Monday 10 June, and to meet together on that morning at one of the halls in Dagenham.

The Company was clearly worried by this development, and made unsuccessful attempts to contact NUVB officials. Eventually, they tracked Gallagher down in Scotland; he said he did not know anything about the situation but would want the procedure to be used.

Between 31 May and 6 June, at a series of meetings with the Shop

Stewards, the Convener and the District Union Officials, the Company tried, unsuccessfully, to find a formula to resolve the issue and to get the overtime ban lifted. No solution emerged from these meetings, and this lack of progress caused the Sewing Machinists to hold another shop meeting on Thursday 6 June. They decided to take Friday off too, and have a long weekend before meeting together on Monday morning, as previously agreed, at Leys Hall, Dagenham.

This decision brought Bob Ramsey, Ford (UK) Labour Relations Manager, on the scene. He offered to meet the Trim Shop Stewards, the Convener and the Union District Officials that evening, provided the Sewing Machinists would agree to work normally on Friday. In view of these developments, the Sewing Machinists held another meeting late on Thursday afternoon, reversed their previous decision and agreed to report for work next day, in order to see if anything would come from the proposed meeting with Ramsey.

On Thursday afternoon Ramsey also contacted Gallagher, and the TGWU and NUVB District Officials, to prepare the ground for the evening meeting. But, according to Ramsey, the Trade Union Officials contradicted each other and did not seem to know much about the situation. According to Ramsey:

> Mr. Gallagher said he did support the action of the Sewing Machinists, but went on to say that the Company should *not* allow the matter to be pursued at Plant level, as the matter was at his level . . . . He would endeavour to obtain a resumption of normal work on Monday, 10th June.[9]

The atmosphere at the evening meeting, which took place in the Main Body Plant conference room, was tense. Ramsey was uncompromising. He outlined clearly the Company's position. There could be no departure from agreed procedures, or any deals about special job review arrangements, or the flood gates would be opened and the whole edifice of the wage structure, which had been so laboriously constructed, would be undermined. After Ramsey's opening remarks, lengthy exchanges took place about the technicalities of the situation, such as the conflicting profiling evidence, the options of how to progress the grievance through various procedural channels, and who could do what. The question of the Profile Review Committee, *in absentia,* looking at only the five disputed characteristics, was also churned over and over again. Moreover, the Trim Shop Stewards, as well as Jack Mitchell, the AEF Union District Secretary, repeatedly accused the Company of sex discrimination and of unsavoury manipulative practices on the Sewing

Machinists' job profile.

These accusations made Ramsey very angry. His face coloured up and he lost his composure and, with it, his normally unshakeable professional cool. To complicate matters further, the District Officials of the TGWU and the NUVB argued at cross-purposes, and presented conflicting claims. Harry Kendrick for the TGWU stated that the grading problem was confined to the Intermediate Sewing Machinists, whilst Fred Blake for the NUVB, the leading official union spokesman at this meeting, refuted this contention and said his Union considered this grievance concerned all the Sewing Machinists.

In the course of this wide-ranging and confusing discussion, the Convener warned Ramsey on at least two or three occasions that his refusal to make any concessions at this point in time would create an explosive situation of unknown dimensions and consequences, and furthermore that, if strike action did commence, the battleground and the issues could well be different from those facing the Company that night.

Ramsey felt he could handle this confusion on the Trade Union Side, because to him it merely typified the Unions' usual incompetence and inability to get any coherence and unity into their presentation. He was, therefore, anxious to keep the discussion on this particular pitch, and that is probably why, although a very experienced and usually perceptive and alert negotiator, he allowed the Convener's statements to slip by without comment. He obviously did not grasp the implications of the Convener's remarks because, had he done so and questioned the meaning of these statements, management would have become aware that the rank-and-file leadership had worked out a conflict strategy and were preparing for battle. The meeting was abortive and ended in disagreement.

When the result of this meeting became known in the Trim Shop next morning, there was a spontaneous reaction, and the Sewing Machinists walked out of the plant at about 10 o'clock in the morning. A historic strike, comparable with that of the 'Matchgirls', had begun.

The Strike

There were 187 Sewing Machinists involved who had no previous experience of fighting a battle of their own, let alone one of this nature. They were quite unprepared for the task ahead, which entailed taking on the might of Ford — a multinational Company — with an annual global budget which in 1968 exceeded that of India. Furthermore, there was virtually no prospect of obtaining support from any of the major unions on the narrow issue of a grading grievance. For example, Les Kealey, the National Engineering Officer of the Transport and General Workers' Union, who also sat on the NJNC, consistently argued that his Union could not support the action of one group with a grading grievance, without supporting each and every other group – a policy tantamount, he claimed, to shutting down Ford. Moreover, the Sewing Machinists stood little chance of obtaining support from any group of workers in their own plant or any other plant.

Attracting support from other departments or plants on economic issues which are craft-based or sectional in character is always difficult. Inter-union, inter-plant rivalries, as well as personality clashes, are additional factors which make solidarity action a rare event in this area of trade union activity. In the case of the Sewing Machinists' grading grievance, there were two additional complicating factors present. First, the ill feeling between plants, caused by disagreements over the introduction of the New Wage Structure, was still very much in existence. The Trade Unions in the River Plant had always keenly favoured a revision of the wage structure and, in fact, spearheaded its introduction, and the Sewing Machinists demonstrated their feelings on this issue, on one occasion, 'by clocking out one hour early to support their demand for early implementation of the new rates of pay which they knew applied to their work in Grade B'.[10] Consequently, no support could be expected by Sewing Machinists, who had decided to take industrial action against the effects of the very wage structure they themselves had only so recently welcomed.

Second, the fact that the Sewing Machinists were women made assistance from any quarter an even more remote prospect. It had to be acknowledged that, amongst their male colleagues, the prevailing view was that women going out to work for 'pin money' could not really expect consideration of active support, or any other kind of material assistance. The exceptions to this rule were, of course, the 195 Sewing Machinists at the Company's Halewood Plant in Liverpool, who had been kept informed of the developments at Dagenham. But the prevailing sentiment was that the Ford Motor Company would always win in the end and, in any case, why support somebody else's grading grievance in preference to your own?

The odds stacked against the Sewing Machinist appeared to be overwhelming, except, of course, that it is not possible for cars to be sold without seats. But, in the circumstances, this factor by itself seemed hardly weighty enough. If the strike were to succeed, it needed official

support from at least one or two of the Unions who had members
involved. The Sewing Machinists' resolve to take issue with the Company
stemmed from their conviction that sex discrimination had denied them
their rightful grade. However, to confine the dispute within these limits
precluded official support. The issue of sex discrimination somehow had
to be 'upgraded' and universalised in a manner which would make it
difficult for some Unions to deny support.

Strategy is Decided

Over the weekend, the leadership therefore once again discussed the concept of equal pay and equal opportunity. Everybody understood the
facts of the situation – the Sewing Machinists had walked out on Friday
solely because of their grading grievance, and would not be returning to
work on the following Monday. But the very act of taking strike action
had transformed the situation and brought about a qualitative change. It
was now no longer merely a dispute about grading, but a confrontation, a
triangular trial of strength, between the Sewing Machinists, the Unions
and the Company. Winning or losing in an industrial conflict, irrespective
of the issue, always matters (a factor to which the existing literature on
strikes pays little attention), but on this particular occasion the win/lose
factor acquired a more significant dimension. First, the Sewing
Machinists wanted to demonstrate to the world at large their deep feelings on the discrimination issue and, perhaps more importantly, that,
once women had decided to make a stand, it must be taken seriously.
Second, for the rank-and-file leadership the fight was now on, and the
outcome – success or failure – was of crucial importance. More important perhaps than the issue itself.

It was against this background that the discussions took place, after
the Friday morning walk-out, between the Trim Shop Stewards, the
Trim Shop Committee members – Ann East, Madge Crooks and Vi
Dawson – and the Convener and the Assistant Convener. Doubts about
making equal pay the main issue were voiced. Some said: 'But we have
never even asked for it.' However, after re-analysing the situation, any
lingering doubts were removed, because two things had emerged clearly:

1. since no support could be expected on grading, the grievance would
   have to be linked to the equal pay issue, and be subordinated to it;
2. it was essential to gain time in order to mobilise outside support for
   the equal pay cause, not only from the Unions at national level, but

also from women's organisations, Members of Parliament and other civil rights fighters.

So in the end the choice became clear and simple: 'Face certain defeat by confining the issue to grading, or fight with some prospect of success under the Equal Pay banner — a noble cause — and make history.' It was therefore agreed to recommend to the mass meeting on Monday — primarily as a tactic — to fight the grading issue under the equal pay banner.

The mass meeting on Monday was held at the Leys Hall at Dagenham; virtually all the Sewing Machinists were there. Also present were the Union District Officials with members concerned in the dispute. Harry Kendrick, the TGWU Official, recommended to the Seamstresses a return to work, exhorted them to await the outcome of the forthcoming Thursday meeting which had, in the meantime, been arranged at York, and where top Company and National Union Officials would once again meet and discuss the Sewing Machinists' grading grievance. This suggestion was rejected out of hand with a cry: 'We are not going back with nothing!' After lengthy and exhaustive debate, the mass meeting agreed to adopt the proposed strategy.

Later that day, an appeal from the River Plant Shop Stewards' Committee was circulated to the various Trade Union Executives. This appeal began as follows:

> At the very outset it must be understood that we are not dealing with an ordinary pay and grading grievance problem, the basic cause of this dispute which commenced today, is discrimination on pay and grading against our female members. We feel discrimination on grounds of sex is as indefensible as discrimination on grounds of colour and race. These are special circumstances and because of the principles involved immediate and massive support for our members from our Union is essential . . .

The Sewing Machinists made one other far-reaching decision, namely not to meet again for another two weeks in order to convey to the Company, as well as to the Trade Unions, that they really meant business. This decision, of course, also had the merit of denying a platform and repeated opportunities to all those Trade Union Officials who wanted to recommend a return to work. Furthermore, this decision also bought the necessary time for the mobilisation of outside support, including that of the Halewood Sewing Machinists. Last, but not least, hopefully the mounting economic damage would increasingly weaken the Company and their resolve, and eventually secure concessions. Finally, the meeting elected the two Trim Shop Stewards, together with their three Shop Committee members plus three volunteers, as a Strike Committee, and these eight women acted in that capacity throughout the dispute.

The four Unions with members involved were the Amalgamated Union of Engineering and Foundry Workers, AEF (now AUEW), the Transport and General Workers' Union, TGWU, the National Union of Vehicle Builders, NUVB, and the General and Municipal Workers' Union, GMWU. The NUVB, a small Union and virtually broke, had the largest membership amongst the Machinists at Dagenham; about 145 out of the 187 Sewing Machinists belonged to that particular Union.

The AEF District Secretary, Jack Mitchell, was Briggs Motor Body Plant Convener for eight years prior to his election to full-time Union Office in 1962. During his seventeen years of employment with Briggs and Ford, Jack Mitchell was in the forefront of all the main battles and, in his role as chief negotiator for the rank-and-file movement, bore the main strain of the conflict situations during this particular period. His experiences at Ford, allied to deeply held socialist convictions, reinforced his dislike for the Company as an institution. Of medium height, slim build with sunken cheeks, he was viewed by the 'gutter press' in the mid-fifties as one of the main agents of a left-wing conspiracy to wreck British industry. He therefore became one of their favourite targets. The *News of the World* engaged in a particularly lengthy and distasteful personal witch-hunt.

Due to his background, Jack Mitchell grasped the significance of the Sewing Machinists' walk-out and the potential of the situation immediately. He dispatched a special letter on Monday evening, 10 June, to the AEF Executive Council which contained an urgent request by the Unions' South Essex District Committee for immediate official backing to be given to the Sewing Machinists now in dispute.

Unions Declare Their Position

The Executive Council was due to hold its regular weekly meeting next day, Tuesday 11 June, at the Peckham Road Head Offices. A delegation of strikers, therefore, led by the Convener, went to the AEF Headquarters in South London early next morning.

Their first call was on Reg Birch in his room on the first floor at the

Union Head Office. It was 9.00 a.m., one hour before the Executive
Council was due to meet in formal session. Reg stood behind his large
desk when the delegation entered the room and received them with a
quizzical expression on his face. He had only fairly recently been elected
Executive Councilman for the Union's No. 7 Division. He had resigned
from the Communist Party over the party's decision to support Hugh
Scanlon for the Union Presidency in preference to himself. Finding himself in a political wilderness, he moved ideologically to the left into the
Maoist camp and was, therefore, more than ever disposed to support all
forms of rank-and-file struggle.

Consequently, when the delegation conveyed to him the purpose of
their visit, he responded sympathetically. The delegation handed him
Mitchell's letter and explained the facts of their case and the urgency of
the situation. Finally they exhorted him to exercise his influence and
power — 'No use sitting on the E.C. unless you are prepared to use the
authority of your office' — to secure an immediate declaration of support for the Sewing Machinists. This he promised to do, and, to the
intense delight of the delegation, the Union Executive announced their
decision at midday: 'We declare the strike official, but purely and solely
in support of the principle of Equal Pay.' It was indeed fortuitous for
the Sewing Machinists that the AEF Executive had some time previously
appointed Reg Birch as Chief Union Negotiator for all Ford UK plants,
and also that the Dagenham area came within the geographical bound-
aries of Division 7. Furthermore, Hugh Scanlon had not long before
been elected Union President, and this was also an important factor
which helped to secure a favourable decision. For the newly elected
'progressive element' on the Executive Council, the equal pay issue
provided an ideal platform for their debut on the trade union stage.

Thus, less than 24 hours after the Sewing Machinists had formally declared an unofficial strike against the Ford Motor Company, a major
Union, the second largest in the country, had announced support and
declared their strike official — an event unprecedented in the history of
trade unionism at Ford as well as in the history of the engineering
industry.

The position the NUVB adopted was more ambivalent. To a small
Union in financial straits, with a membership totalling 77,000 nationally
and confined to the motor industry, new members to replace lapsed
members and a rising total of members represented the life blood of
existence. Consequently union officialdom — from union dues collec-
tors to full-time officers — were always out to recruit new members, and
were not exactly averse to the practice of poaching. Therefore, in a sit-

uation where the majority of the strikers at Dagenham belonged to the NUVB and with the strike already declared official by the AEF, for the NUVB not to do likewise meant risking not only a loss of members but, more important, a greatly diminished prospect of recruiting new ones in the future. In a recent interview Fred Blake said:

> Now that I am a TGWU official, I see things in a quite different light. To be quite frank about it, in the old NUVB if you lost half a dozen members it was a crisis. I can lose a couple of thousand now and it doesn't mean a thing.[11]

On the other hand, unequivocal backing for a strike in support of the principle of equal pay opened the door to a financial commitment of unknown dimension and duration throughout the industry. The NUVB therefore decided to give support and declared the strike official on Thursday 13 June, but at the same time the decision confined official backing to the grading issue.

The other Unions with members involved, the TGWU and the GMWU, recoiled from giving any support on equal pay because of the national and political implications, as well as for the reasons previously outlined relative to grading issues. Additionally, they had an ideological loyalty to the right-wing-orientated trade union bureaucracy at NJNC level, and it is worth remembering that Jack Jones did not take over as General Secretary of the TGWU until December 1968.

Equal pay, however, was the crucial issue. This can be gauged from a letter which Lord Cooper, then General Secretary of the GMWU, sent to his officials on 18 June. The letter began:

> A special meeting of the NJNC was held on Monday, 17th June . . . at this meeting it was established beyond doubt irrespective of comments contained in national newspapers and television programmes, that the dispute concerns a grading grievance and is *not* linked with Equal Pay for women.

This neatly summarised the strategy which the trade union bureaucracy at NJNC level, with the exception of the AEF, attempted to pursue throughout the dispute − namely, to divest the issue of all political overtones and to reduce it to the purely economic level about grading. This also dovetailed very well with the strategy the Company had pursued from the very beginning, because, on 14 June, William Batty, then Managing Director of Ford, had a notice published on all works' notice boards which said: 'The issue was *not* Equal Pay for women, but is a dispute over grading . . .'

So there was no difficulty about establishing an alliance between the Company and the majority of the National Trade Union Officials at NJNC level, and in particular with the Chairman and Secretary of that Committee. Mark Young of the Electrical Trade Union (ETU) was Chairman of the Trade Union Side of the NJNC, and Jim Conway, who was the General Secretary of the AEF, acted as Secretary for the Trade Union Side of the National Joint Negotiating Committee. Mark Young, now General Secretary of BALPA, was one of the ETU Officials who, with Les Cannon, left the Communist Party after the 1956 uprising in Hungary. Thereafter he adopted a very right-wing political stance and was generally hostile to rank-and-file action and to any meaningful part-icipation by Conveners or Shop Stewards in the decision-making process.

However, in the early 1970s, he once again began courting the rank and file and politically veered leftwards. This change of direction was occasioned by a dispute with Frank Chapple, the General Secretary of the ETU, over the position of the Union's presidency. It was a personal power struggle, disguised as a constitutional wrangle, which eventually ended up in the High Court. Mark Young lost and was left facing a size-able bill of legal costs. In fact, he only became involved in that situation due to being Chairman of the Ford NJNC Trade Union Side. The auth-ority of his office encouraged him and others to challenge Frank Chapple's dominance and control of the Union.

Jim Conway, a victim of the 1974 air disaster near Paris, was always known for his consistently right-wing views. Endowed with more cunning than intellect, he was implacably opposed to the position his own Union had adopted in relation to the Sewing Machinists' dispute, both in his capacity as Secretary of the NJNC Trade Union Side, as well as in his personal capacity. He managed, however, to reconcile the con-tradiction of his personal position *vis-à-vis* his Union's position quite well – in fact, so well and to such an extent that he seconded two Administrative Officers on the AEF's payroll and normally employed at the AEF's Head Office at Peckham Road to the Ford National Trade Union Committee on a full-time basis. Their job was to assist with the preparation of submissions against the AEF and to arraign the Union before the Scamp Court of Inquiry.

Ford Attempts to Crush the Strike

The Company made concerted efforts during the first week of the strike to neutralise the two Unions which had declared support. The Trade Union Side of the NJNC was a ready-made vehicle for this purpose. The plan itself was quite simple — to obtain an agreement at NJNC level supported by the great majority of the Unions, who were signatories to the Ford National Agreement. These, in concert with the Company, would define the nature of the dispute, recommend a return to work on terms agreed by the NJNC and thus override the two Unions which supported the strike.

The plan was set into motion by the Company on Monday afternoon, 10 June. Ramsey once again contacted Charlie Gallagher in Scotland and arranged a formal meeting with him and Les Kealey, the National Officer of the Transport and General Workers' Union, for 2.30 p.m. on the following day.

At this meeting Ramsey recapitulated the history of the Sewing Machinists' grievance and emphasised to the two Union officials the variety of the procedural channels they could utilise in order to deal with the matter in dispute. At this meeting, Charlie Gallagher, according to the Company, made a number of allegations that the Sewing Machinists had not been fairly dealt with:

> (I) that the evaluation had been carried out properly, but that the evaluators were influenced by the fact that the Sewing Machinists were women; (II) that the correct ratings had not been applied to the profile; and (III) that in dealing with grading grievances, the Company had shown favour to some Unions and groups of employees.[12]

Ramsey absolutely refuted these allegations but Gallagher would not accept his assurances and said:

> that he would want Grade C for Sewing Machinists, Grade D for Prototype Sewing Machinists before he was prepared to ask for a return to work. He also said that he had heard that the Company was considering the question of Equal Pay, and if this was so, then it might be a compromise solution.[13]

At this meeting Kealey left the main discussion to Gallagher, but said that he had made it clear to a number of groups of his members, who felt just as strongly about their grading positions as did the Sewing

Machinists, that the matter was required to go to the NJNC Grading
Sub-committee, before procedure was completed and exhausted.

> The meeting ended with an appeal by Mr. Ramsey to Mr. Gallagher
> to reconsider his position. Mr. Gallagher promised to convey every-
> thing Mr. Ramsey had said to his colleagues, but said that he would
> be recommending that they make the strike official at their meeting
> on Thursday of that week.[14]

On 12 June, Leslie Blakeman, the Ford Director of Labour Relations,
dispatched a letter by hand to Jim Conway, outlining the seriousness of
the situation, and requested an immediate meeting of the NJNC or, if
this was not possible, the Grading Sub-Committee.

The Grading Sub-Committee consisting of Mark Young (ETU), Jim
Conway (AEF), Reg Birch (AEF), Les Kealey (TGWU), Charlie
Gallagher (NUVB) and Ken Baker (GMWU), in fact met Blakeman and
Ramsey at York on Thursday afternoon, 13 June. According to
Blakeman, at that meeting,

> Birch made an unequivocal statement that as far as his Union was
> concerned the issue was Equal Pay. He admitted, to use his own
> words, [Birch's] , that this involved 'ratting' on the agreement with
> the Company. He drew a parallel with the events in France, and said
> that it was just unfortunate that it happened to be the Ford Motor
> Company who would have to serve as the focus for the Equal Pay
> campaign.[15]

Blakeman replied that

> the situation was quite unnecessary; three agreements were being
> broken: the Company's Procedure Agreement, which provided the
> NJNC as the argument stage for discussion before official strike
> action was contemplated. Secondly, the agreement which spelt out
> the Grading Grievance Procedure, and thirdly the two-year agreement
> that the women's rate should be 85 per cent of the men's rate . . . If
> the AEF wanted to pursue the claim for Equal Pay, then their course
> was obvious, they should get their members to return to work, they
> should discuss the question of Equal Pay with their colleagues on the
> Trade Union Side of the NJNC and if the Trade Union Side decided
> to pursue that claim with the Company, then the Company could not
> refuse to receive the claim and deal with it.[16]

The meeting ended with no agreement.

Barbara Castle Intervenes

On Friday 14 June, Bill Batty, Ford's Managing Director, issued a Press Statement in the afternoon threatening massive lay-offs and the closure of the Body and Assembly Plants from Tuesday 18 June, unless there was an immediate resumption of work by the Sewing Machinists. Following this Statement, Barbara Castle, Minister of Employment and Productivity, intervened on Friday evening. She ordered Conrad Heron, Under-Secretary for Industrial Relations, to invite all sides — that is to say, the Company, the NUVB, Mark Young and Jim Conway — for talks at the Ministry next morning, Saturday 15 June. After Heron had spent over four hours in separate and joint talks with those present, it emerged that endeavours would be made to find a peace formula at a specially convened meeting of the NJNC on Monday 17 June.

The speed of these developments took the Strike Committee by surprise. None the less, they managed on Saturday morning to dispatch a delegation of five, led by Shop Steward Lil O'Callaghan, to the Ministry in St James's Square. They also managed to arrange a conference with Charlie Gallagher in a private room prior to his meeting with Conrad Heron and, according to subsequent reports, put severe pressure on him. Interviewed by the press afterwards, Gallagher said: 'I have been given my instructions. The delegation has told me, stand firm, permit nobody to confuse you. We are going to stand solid.'[17] At this juncture it may be as well to point out that, during the first week of the strike, from the walk-out on Friday 7 June until Friday 14 June, the press hardly carried a single report about this dispute. It was as if, by magic, a 'silent curtain' had been draped over the battle which was taking place at Dagenham. However, after Batty's Press Statement, this changed completely. The strike received continued and wide coverage in the press and on television, including television networks in the United States, Germany and Italy. The popular press, in particular, seized with glee upon the 'petticoat' aspect of the strike, and interlaced this publicity with dire warnings about the loss of exports, damage to the British economy and the possible loss of jobs to Ford workers.

The gyrations of the National Trade Union Officials and the Company during the first week of the strike have briefly been described in order to provide an insight about their strategy and purpose. It should, however, be emphasised that real power lay with, and was exercised by, the strikers and the rank-and-file leadership during this period and, in-deed, as we shall see, during the whole period of the dispute. It would, therefore, be appropriate to look in some detail at the activity by the rank and file during the first week of the strike.

The Strikers Develop Their Organisation

After the meeting at the Leys Hall on 10 June, the Strike Committee went to the NUVB District Office at Rainham and had a conference with Fred Blake, the NUVB District Official, who played a prominent part throughout the strike and in the subsequent equal pay campaign. He put a room at the disposal of the Strike Committee who, although quite in-experienced, had to come to grips with a number of organisational prob-lems, such as (1) maintaining contact with the women on strike, (2) pub-licity, particularly for the equal pay aspect of the strike, and (3) raising finance.

The communications problem was solved in quite a simple manner. The 187 strikers, in the main, lived in fairly close proximity to each other. Therefore, it was possible to establish a kind of 'ward system'. In each 'ward' one woman, whose home had a telephone, was designated to act as a contact. The home would also serve as a meeting place for an occasional get-together. Information and messages would be passed on by the contact to everyone else in the 'ward'. This system worked equally well in reverse, and developed into a very effective means of communication and consultation arrangement. Additionally, the Strike Committee remained in daily contact and close touch with the River Plant Shop Stewards. The Shop Stewards' Committee worked day and night for a successful outcome of the strike.

The publicity aspect developed a momentum of its own beyond the control of the Strike Committee as the political aspects of the strike began to build up and attracted increasing public interest and support. The Strike Committee also drew up a Statement and circulated this, to-gether with a financial appeal to trade union branches up and down the country. As a result, over £1,000 was collected which proved to be adequate for the needs of the strikers and the Strike Committee.

The Halewood Connection

The most crucial problem which faced the Sewing Machinists during the first week of the strike, possibly even more important than the need for early trade union recognition, was the disposition of the 195 Sewing Machinists employed at the Halewood Assembly Plant. They worked mainly on seat covers for vehicles produced at Halewood. The number of vehicles produced there was roughly half Dagenham's daily output; therefore, if the Company could continue normal production at Halewood, the prospect of achieving a satisfactory settlement was greatly reduced. From the strikers' point of view it was imperative that the Liverpool girls should come out in support and, conversely, the Company spared no effort to keep them at work. Eighty-five Sewing Machinists at Halewood were members of the TGWU, as distinct from Dagenham where this Union had only a handful of members.

Mick Donnelly, of the TGWU, was Halewood Assembly Plant Convener. In addition, he was also one of the 38 lay members of the TGWU National Executive and thus came under direct influence of Transport House. Consequently, he was closely tied to a trade union bureaucracy which from the outset had adopted a disapproving, 'stand-offish' attitude towards this particular dispute. The normal way of passing on information or discussing interrelated plant problems was for a Plant Convener to contact by telephone, or writing, his respective counterpart in another plant or plants. In this instance this practice was followed with increasing frequency and intensity, but Donnelly's response was unhelpful, to say the least.

As car production was grinding to a halt at Dagenham and the threat of massive lay-offs increased, the Company redoubled its efforts to impress upon Mick Donnelly the need for avoiding a similar situation at Halewood. Given Donnelly's own personal disposition as well as that of his Union, the requests for support either just did not get through to the Sewing Machinists or were slanted in such a manner as to make them abortive.

Les Moore, in a recent interview about the events, said of Mick Donnelly:

> He generally believed there should be no action to achieve things. If you could not get things by negotiations you should go without them. Due to his 'moderate' ideology, he was often at cross purposes with other Conveners on the Halewood estate. He also resented AEF involvement in the dispute, and in any case he didn't take the women seriously and felt they should not get anything.[18]

At Dagenham it was, therefore, decided to establish direct contact with

the Halewood Sewing Machinists. Rosie Boland, together with Bernie
Passingham, the Assistant Plant Convener, went to Liverpool.
Passingham recollects the event as follows:

> Johnson, the AEF District Secretary, met us at the station, and took
> us by car to the Plant. I endeavoured to contact Donnelly but could
> not do so, and as a last resort contacted Les Moore, the Body Plant
> Convener, and asked for his assistance. During the lunch hour, Les
> Moore went into the Assembly Plant and persuaded the women to
> attend a lunch time meeting outside the Plant. As it was a nice sunny
> day, we had a meeting on the embankment. I made our position clear,
> we were not out solely on Equal Pay, but also in dispute in relation
> to their skill. Thereafter a fair debate ensued, and I was surprised by
> their attitude towards Equal Pay. They made it quite clear to me,
> that women should not earn as much as men.[19]

Les Moore relates that, after receiving a message from the District
Secretary, according to whom Reg Birch had sent a message requesting
co-operation from the TGWU,

> I did go, or rather trespassed, into the Assembly Plant and contacted
> Donnelly and other Transport and General Workers Stewards and
> endeavoured to secure their co-operation, but I received none. I there-
> fore directly approached the AEF Sewing Machinist members in the
> department, and invited them to a lunch time meeting. I was seen by
> the Company doing this, and in consequence I received a letter of
> warning for going without permission into another Plant. After I left
> the Plant, Donnelly went round the shop afterwards and instructed
> the Transport and General Workers Sewing Machinists members *not*
> to attend the meeting, as it was none of their business, but they
> ignored him.[20]

Because there was insufficient time during the lunch hour to go into
all the aspects of the dispute, the Halewood Sewing Machinists requested
that a further meeting be held at 5.00 p.m. – their finishing time – in
order to discuss the issue more thoroughly. This was arranged and Bernie
Passingham recalls 'that without Les Moore's assistance, we could never
have succeeded in laying on the first, never mind the second, meeting'.[21]
At the second meeting, the interesting, and perhaps the most significant,
point which emerged after prolonged cross-questioning was the
Halewood Sewing Machinists' intense concern to draw a clear distinction

between the grading and equal pay issues. They repeatedly sought assurances that the central issue of the dispute was indeed grading and not equal pay. According to Rosie Boland, '. . . mention Equal Pay to the women up there and they don't want to know. They've got a different way of life up there. Up there the man is the boss.'[22] The representatives from Dagenham explained the complexity of the situation with emphasis on the grading aspect, but the Halewood girls made no decision about whether or not to stop work in support of Dagenham. They merely agreed to meet for this purpose on Monday 17 June.

The events in Liverpool, however, tend to underline the great similarity of the ideological and cultural attitudes of the Sewing Machinists and the women workers employed at Ford generally They also show to what extent inter-union rivalries and the personal ideologies of Conveners play a part in conflicts of this kind.

The 'Sell-out' is Prepared

Meanwhile, following the consultations with Conrad Heron at the Ministry, Blakeman, Young and Conway are believed to have held informal talks about (1) what kind of proposition would commend itself to the specially convened meeting of the NJNC due to be held at the New Ambassadors Hotel in Holborn on 17 June, and (2) what kind of proposition would have the merit of securing a resumption of work without substantive concessions to the rank-and-file movement. That the terms of the recommendation to be made to the forthcoming meeting of the NJNC on Monday — namely 'resumption of work pending the outcome of an internal inquiry' — were agreed, can hardly be in doubt.

Fred Blake, recollecting this specific event, makes the following comment about certain National Trade Union Officials:

> They seemed to be in league with the Company, and therefore always trying to undermine the dispute in collusion with the Company . . . I believe over the weekend, they made a deal with the Company. In those days top Trade Union Officials had home telephone numbers of top Company Officials, they did communicate, and on one occasion to my knowledge, even met at Ramsey's house.[23]

In order to prevent this development, a coachload of Seamstresses from Dagenham, led by their Shop Stewards and the Plant Conveners, also went to the New Ambassadors Hotel in order to lobby and bring pressure to bear on the National Trade Union Officials. The girls were dressed in their Sunday best and on arrival were in a noisy, boisterous, not to say aggressive, mood.

Although the hotel is owned by the Co-operative Society, it was obviously not accustomed to cope with a clientele from the Dagenham area. As the girls poured through the entrance into the hotel lobby, brushing aside American tourists and other esteemed guests, the hotel management became extremely apprehensive and embarrassed and did not know what to do. The impeccably mannered Hotel Manager in his pin-striped suit clearly was not used to this kind of situation and quite unable to respond to friendly greetings, in chorus, such as: 'How are you, darling? What can we do for you?' It was the classic 'Rag Trade scenario' which Miriam Karlin caricatured so well on television. Eventually, the hotel management decided discretion was the better part of valour and put a dining room and a lounge at the disposal of the girls. Drinks, snacks and other refreshments were supplied *à la carte,* free of charge. Perhaps this accommodating attitude was induced by the presence of a large number of press reporters and the television cameras.

After the girls had been made comfortable, the Trim Stewards went to talk with Gallagher, who seemed uneasy and very nervous. Charlie Gallagher had a gaunt look about him. His trade union record was established in his younger days and, at that time, he was well thought of in the NUVB. He undoubtedly had quite a deep attachment to the trade union movement and was ideologically committed to its objectives. He was therefore generally well intentioned towards issues which furthered the attainment of these objectives. For example, he showed off with pride to any visitor his quite extensive collection of historic trade union banners, badges and other mementoes which were displayed in his room at the NUVB's Head Office in Manchester. However, in his latter years he had become a chain-smoker and very partial to whisky, and he sometimes slipped out of meetings to fortify himself with a 'double'.

Lil O'Callaghan said of him: 'We always had to threaten him to stop him from collapsing, and we felt he was weak and unreliable.'[24] Be that as it may, the Shop Stewards on this particular occasion impressed upon him the need to stand firm, and also pointed out to him that the autonomy and the constitution of his Union would serve to reinforce his position at the forthcoming meeting, since only the NUVB Executive, and no other body, could call off the strike and recommend a resumption of work. Gallagher agreed with this approach and pledged himself not to depart from this fairly obvious and safe constitutional position.

Whilst the Stewards talked to Gallagher, the Convener became involved in a lengthy, intense and acrimonious debate with Jim Conway and Mark Young. Young argued that he was not prepared to give support to the Sewing Machinists or show any sympathy, because they had to be treated like everybody else and were not entitled to special privileges. The Convener pressed Conway to be more accommodating since, after all, the Union, of which he was General Secretary, had declared support and made the strike official. However, the discussion was abruptly terminated when Conway lost his temper and said heatedly to the Convener: 'Watch out, we've got our heels into you.'

The officials began the meeting amongst themselves one hour before their scheduled meeting with the Company. Reg Birch decided not to attend. Jim Conway, therefore, claimed to be acting in a dual capacity, as the representative of the AEF and as Secretary of the Trade Union Side of the NJNC. Young and Conway had little difficulty in selling 'their' recommendation to the Trade Union Side, although it took them nearly three hours to do so. Charlie Gallagher did not say a single word throughout the entire proceedings. When later questioned about this at the Court of Inquiry, he was engaged in the following exchange with the Chairman.

> **Mr Gallagher** . . . but I made it quite clear to the Trade Unions of the NJNC – I do not think I spoke, I was so disgusted with the . . .
> (Chairman interrupts)
> **Chairman, Sir Jack Scamp** But that is not making it absolutely clear if you say nothing.[25]

Whilst the Trade Union Side was in session, Sammy Rees, the Company's Director of Manufacture, who believed in 'the personal touch' and in his own powers of persuasion, approached the Convener and suggested a brief informal chat over drinks. He expressed the view that an immediate resumption of work was in everybody's best interest, since the matter in dispute did not justify either thousands of men being laid off, or the economic damage to the Company. In response to this approach, the Convener made it absolutely clear that only an immediate and a major concession by the Company could secure a return to work.

Eventually, after coming together with the Company, the meeting opened up as follows:

> **Mark Young** May we apologise for having kept you from our original scheduled time of 3.30, but the delay has been very

necessary . . . We would like to put a proposition to you. This proposal is, that we would jointly set up a committee of inquiry . . . obviously in addition, we, as the Trade Union Side, are recommending that the members concerned in this dispute, should return to work . . .

Mr Blakeman They will return tomorrow, I presume.

Mr Young Yes, quite.[26]

A further significant exchange followed shortly afterwards.

Mr Young . . . the facts as we know them are that we have a capital problem facing us and that we have 187 machinists who are now on strike.

Mr Blakeman I'm sorry to tell you that that number has now doubled, because the Halewood girls have taken similar action.

Mr Young That was not reported to us before. We are sorry to hear it, but we're dealing with it as just 187. If they have been joined by the Halewood people, that obviously makes the problem more pressing still.[27]

The transcript of this meeting is, in itself, a classic example of the kind of affinity some National Trade Union Officials develop *vis-à-vis* Companies, and it also demonstrates their lack of understanding and open disdain for the membership. No doubt this is the reason why the Company chose to submit the complete verbatim account of this meeting as evidence to the Scamp Court of Inquiry. Perhaps the following extract will serve to underline this point. The meeting had reached the stage of discussing the type of notice which should be published, setting out the formula which would recommend an immediate resumption of work, when Fraser, the National Official of the Plumbing Trade Union, interjected and said:

But you have got a strike on your hands, we are trying to make it brief, as our Chairman says, so as to make them understand it. Why the hell put all that stuff in? We can understand it, but can they, when we try to explain it to them? We are trying to get them back to work, so for God's sake let us make it brief.

Mr Blakeman Well you say, 'why put in that stuff when we can understand it'; we are not prepared to leave it in a loose way. We have got a strike on our hands and it is important.

Mr Young I do not think we want to get emotional about . . .

Mr Conway I think we would accept that if you are not in the situation that we are in now. What we want is something that can go out for public consumption, that is sharp, short and brief. That, quite frankly Leslie, is the workings of it, isn't it? which we can agree to once we have got rid of this major problem.

Mr Blakeman This is what we feel should be the agreement between us.

Mr Conway We feel we cannot agree to the detail until we have had sufficient time to study it. That is what I mean.

Mr Blakeman But it must be based on this.

Mr Conway Quite, but what Mark is really saying is that in this emotional time and in this emotional stress that we are all under, we would not like to commit ourselves to something which we had not had time to study. The basic principles we accept, we know what we are trying to do. I think both sides can accept this, *because there is no basic disagreement between the two sides,* is there? *It is just something that has happened externally to us* which we are trying to resolve.

Mr Blakeman Yes

Mr Conway So once we have got rid of that public thing, we can sit back and have a quick meeting and we can go into all the points of this, and decide who is going to be the Chairman of the Committee and everything else.[28]

After further exchanges, mainly concerning technicalities, the peace formula was agreed upon and the following notice, setting out the Agreement, was signed and posted on all works' notice boards.

NOTICE

NATIONAL JOINT NEGOTIATING COMMITTEE (FACT FINDING COMMITTEE)

At a special meeting of the NJNC held in London today the following was agreed:—

CONSTITUTION AND TERMS OF REFERENCE

1. To establish immediately a Ford NJNC Fact Finding Committee.

2. The constitution of the Committee shall be — two members of the NJNC nominated by the Trade Union Side and two members nominated by the Management Side.

3. That an impartial person, agreed by mutual consent, shall be invited to conduct the affairs of the Fact Finding Committee.

4. a) The Fact Finding Committee shall be required to consider whether the Sewing Machinists are properly evaluated according to established principles.

   b) To ascertain whether the application of the new Wage Structure has been conducted in accordance with the agreements of 27th July and 8th September 1967 without discrimination.

   c) To consider to what extent the agreed procedure has been observed by both parties.

5. To enable the Committee to determine the required facts they shall have facilities to question and take evidence from such members of Management as are directly concerned with the implementation of the new Wage Structure as well as Officials and members of the Trade Unions concerned in the dispute.

   They may also extend an invitation to the Consultants, Messrs. Urwick, Orr & Partners, to give evidence if this is deemed necessary. They may question other persons mutually agreed as being appropriate by the Chairman of the Company Side and the Chairman of the Trade Union Side.

6. The facts ascertained by the Committee shall only be communicated to a full meeting of the NJNC and shall not otherwise be made the subject of comment, discussion or publicity elsewhere.

This proposition has been agreed on the understanding that the full Trade Union Side of the NJNC recommend to its members, now withholding their labour that they should resume normal working tomorrow, Tuesday 18th June 1968.

Signed on behalf of the Company side	Signed on behalf of the Trade Union Side
L T Blakeman	Mark Young

17 June 1968.

The 'Sell-out' Is Frustrated

The meeting finished about 7.00 p.m.; the rank-and-file members who had stayed on to await the outcome of the meeting viewed the result with dismay and consternation. Although a sell-out of some sort had been expected, particularly in view of the opinions Conway and Young expressed prior to the meeting with the Company, none the less the nature of the decision and the speed of its implementation took everybody by surprise. Gallagher clearly had collapsed. The Stewards berated Gallagher for letting them down and selling out. He seemed quite upset and mumbled something about: 'I voted against it, but I have to abide by majority decision.' Birch had been inexplicably absent and had not even bothered to send someone to deputise for him. For example, he could have asked Jack Mitchell to stand in for him, and this, possibly, might have made a significant difference to the outcome of the meeting.

Birch later explained his absence as a 'tactic': 'Through not being present, we could not become party to any agreement reached.' However, Birch's absence may in part have been attributable to a belief in the universal truths of Mao Tse-tung's thoughts. He was fascinated by the events in China, particularly by the long guerrilla struggle which preceded the Chinese revolution. In an endeavour to apply these lessons and stratagems to the British situation, he perhaps initially saw the Sewing Machinists' strike just as another foray into the enemy's camp — advancing a general principle, but with no prospect of immediate success. Thus a resumption of work would not have been a great tragedy because, according to Birch,

> Mobile struggle is primary . . . We must fight to win, and moreover retreat at times to win. The first duty is the preservation of one's troops. Retreat is no heresy, for we never cease to struggle and can most effectively do so at the place of work.[29]

Quite an extraordinary situation. Here we had the second largest Union in the country, the AEF, descendants of the ASE, the founders of the New Model Unionism based on the constitution devised by Tom Mann in 1918, fighting for a principle cherished by the TUC for over a hundred years, giving support to a strike — a struggle for equal pay — not represented, and the General Secretary of that very Union, Conway, doing his level best to undermine the strike and to secure a resumption of work without any concessions by the Company. Additionally, we had Charlie Gallagher, the National Trade Union Official with the largest number of members involved in the dispute, sitting silently throughout five hours of actual meeting time, three hours with his trade union colleagues and two hours with the Company, and not uttering a single word in defence of his Union's position.

Another odd feature of this meeting is the total absence of any reference in the written record about the disposition of the two Unions in official dispute with the Company. Other Unions, who on other occasions were only too keen to emphasise their autonomy and independence and the need to respect their Unions' constitutions, were quite blatantly endeavouring to call off an official strike by two other Trade Unions, signatories to the Ford Agreement, without reference to the actual two Unions concerned.

Experiences of this kind tend to stimulate discussion about industrial unionism: whether this kind of structure would, in the long term, be in the best interest of the trade union members, or whether, in fact, the very multiplicity, loosenesss and resultant complexity of the trade union structure in Britain give the movement its basic strength and its resilience.

In view of these developments, the rank-and-file leadership felt quite isolated, alone and out-manoeuvred. The Company, which apparently could call on the assistance from the media at short notice, had arranged to broadcast an appeal on the radio and television for an immediate resumption of work the following morning. This was to be broadcast at 8.00 p.m. Thus, Blakeman was due to speak on television in a few minutes about the Agreement he had reached with the Trade Unions. There was no time available for calling properly constituted meetings to enable the strikers to determine their attitude. Those present had to act on the spot. Whilst the television crews were preparing the lights and setting up the cameras for the interview with Blakeman, the producer was persuaded to allow Rosie Boland to appear immediately after Blakeman in order to express the Sewing Machinists' view about the Agreement.

Blakeman, smiling broadly, went on television to announce the end of the dispute and the terms of the settlement. In conclusion, he requested that everybody should report for normal work next morning, including the 5,000 Dagenham Body and Assembly Plant workers who had previously been told not to report for work on Tuesday.

Rosie Boland, as arranged, followed Blakeman and gave an accomplished performance. She very effectively put across a simple message: 'The agreement is rejected, we are *not* going back, the strike goes on.' Rosie Boland's performance, her composure and increasing confidence, offered a prime example of how the working class has the capability to throw up a leadership which can rise to the occasion in a specific crisis. It can, indeed, be said, that the Trim Shop Stewards and the Strike Committee grew in stature day by day as the dispute progressed. They developed the necessary degree of expertise, self-assurance, and self-confidence in the shortest space of time, thus enabling them to deal with all the varied aspects of the dispute competently and effectively.

After Rosie Boland's statement on television, 'the ward system' went into operation and the telephone wires to Halewood were burning. It worked very well. The strike picket which assembled at the Dagenham gates early next morning was purely symbolic; only two or three girls, who could not be contacted on the previous evening, turned up to find out what was happening. The picket that morning consisted of the River Plant Shop Stewards and Fred Blake.

It was Fred Blake's first involvement in an official dispute since becoming a full-time Union Official. Prior to that, he had, in fact, worked in the Body Plant Trim Shop and had served as a Works Committee member and a Ford Shop Steward for many years. He says:

> The decision of the Monday meeting made me react all the more intensely, when I went down to the River Plant picket line that morning, I was more determined than ever to see that thing through. I could not have cared less if they had fired me and said, you are not fit to be a Trade Union official . . . My old Ford background helped, it gave me extra motivation, the Trim Shop was my old battleground, and it made my commitment more intense because of these past battles . . . [30]

When the 7.30 a.m. hooter blew, all the River Plant Shop Stewards not involved in the dispute left the picket line and clocked on to start work, leaving Rosie Boland and Fred Blake, as the two solitary pickets holding placards aloft which proclaimed: 'The Official Strike Continues.'

It was one of the paradoxical features of this dispute that the Company, as a matter of 'progressive' industrial relations policy, had only recently provided all Plant Conveners with office and telephone facilities, and this enabled the Shop Stewards' Committee to run the administrative side of the strike from inside the plant whilst on the Company's payroll. This proved an invaluable asset, and at that point of time simplified contacts and made the liaison problem immeasurably easier. The Company was probably aware of this, but must have thought it was a price worth paying in order to keep the channels of communications with the rank-and-file leadership open. No doubt the provision of these facilities has since served to institutionalise the conflict and perhaps made industrial relations more manageable from the Company's point of view, but it certainly did not start out that way.

The Halewood girls also met on Tuesday, and decided to stay on strike in sympathy with Dagenham, and not to meet again until the Friday of the following week. Also on Tuesday, in view of the Sewing Machinists' refusal to resume work, both the AEF and NUVB disassociated themselves from the NJNC Agreement and declared their continued support for the Ford Sewing Machinists' strike. The strike had passed its first crisis point. Leslie Blakeman, in a Press Statement on Tuesday, described the women's refusal to return to work as 'anarchic and irresponsible'.[31]

The Strike Becomes Politicised and Begins to Bite

During the second week of the strike, some interesting developments took place. On Tuesday 18 June, with Dagenham car production at a complete standstill, the Company laid off 5,100 Body and Assembly Plant workers. On the following day, 19 June, Barbara Castle asked the Unions and Company representatives to come to the Ministry once again, and she informed them of her intention to set up a Court of Inquiry. At the same time, she appealed to the trade union leaders to secure an immediate resumption of work. On Friday 21 June, Barbara Castle announced that she had appointed Sir Jack Scamp to preside over the Inquiry into 'the cause and circumstances' of the Sewing Machinists' dispute. She further increased pressure on the trade union leadership by inviting the top men of the four Unions whose members were involved in the dispute, namely Lord Cooper, Frank Cousins, Hugh Scanlon and Alf Roberts (General Secretary, NUVB), for talks at the Ministry on the following morning. At these talks, she once again urged them to use their influence to bring the women's strike to an end without delay.

During the second week, the Strike Committee was occupied largely with arrangements for sending delegates by coach to three different events. First, on 18 June, there was the Annual Conference of the NUVB at Felixstowe. Sewing Machinists from Dagenham, carrying banners inscribed with slogans such as 'No sex discrimination' and 'No surrender to Fords', were given an enthusiastic heroines' welcome by over 100 delegates – all men. The Conference passed an emergency resolution pledging the Unions' continuing support 'to our women members in their struggle to obtain the appropriate grading rate within the Ford wages structure'. Significantly, the resolution did not contain a word about equal pay.

On Thursday 20 June, a coachload of Seamstresses went to the Houses of Parliament. There, Joyce Butler, MP for Wood Green, and

Edith Summerskill arranged for a discussion between the girls and a number of 'Liberal-progressive' MPs in one of the large committee rooms upstairs, and later entertained them for tea. This was a very valuable experience. The discussion centred entirely around the underlying causes of sex discrimination and the need to make equal pay and equal rights a reality, and the possible contribution, which the legislative process could make towards achieving this end, was also discussed at length. It highlighted and brought into focus the importance of the Ford women's struggle and strengthened the strikers' resolve not to return to work empty handed. For those present this meeting added a new dimension to the struggle and gave them a degree of political understanding which was not previously there.

Another delegation went by coach to Weymouth over the weekend 22/23 June, where the Confederation of Shipbuilding and Engineering Unions was having a conference. The Union Executives of the AEF, NUVB and Les Kealey of the Transport and General Workers' Union, amongst others, were taking part.

Leslie Blakeman also went to Weymouth to see if he could capitalise on and profit from Barbara Castle's request to the four 'top men' to find a peace formula. In discussions with Birch, Blakeman for the first time gave a hint of the Company's possible willingness to make concessions. He reiterated that the Company could not give way on the grading issue since that would mean the collapse of the wage structure, but the Ford Motor Company might be prepared to 're-assess' the value of the contribution female employees were making to the Company's manufacturing activities. In other words, he was hinting at concessions on the equal pay issue.

Later in the day, Les Kealey rejected this possibility on principle, as the question of equal pay had never been placed before the NJNC by any of the signatory Unions. The remainder of the day was spent mainly in discussing technical details such as the weighting factors which the NUVB in particular wanted from the Company in order to be able to judge whether the Sewing Machinists had been correctly graded.

In separate exchanges with the Union Officials, the Sewing Machinists emphasised their determination not to return to work until a settlement satisfactory *to them* had been reached. Bernie Passingham, the Assistant Convener who led the delegation to Weymouth, recalls:

> We feared a small caucus meeting might reach a decision which could, in turn, undermine the strike . . . When I arrived with all the women and went into the hotel, nobody wanted to know. They did

not want to give us a room, but when faced with the alternative of 30 odd women blockading their hotel with placards aloft, the hotel management decided to provide us with a room, and even provided us with tea . . . We saw Reg Birch and he assured us there would be no sell out. Gallagher gave a similar assurance . . . The Company offered something on Equal Pay, but Les Kealey absolutely opposed that, his argument being, it was not an item on the agenda; by Kealey taking that stance, nothing came of it . . . It gave the women something to do, it gave them a day's outing which took them into the front of the battle where they could see their officials at work. It was a satisfying day, because nothing materialised in an out of the way place like Weymouth to undermine the dispute . . . [32]

State Intervention Increases

The first event of significance during the third week of the strike occurred on Tuesday 25 June, when the Company was forced to lay off 4,000 production workers at the Halewood Body and Assembly Plants. This, in fact, meant that most, if not all, Ford car production in the United Kingdom had been brought to a standstill.

In consequence, on Thursday 27 June, Jack Scamp hastily assembled his Court of Inquiry, in order to make an appeal for an immediate resumption of work to the Sewing Machinists. He said: 'It will make our task much easier if work is proceeding while we investigate.'[33] The Court then adjourned for a week to allow evidence to be prepared.

The Sewing Machinists also decided to have a mass meeting on this Thursday at the Leys Hall at Dagenham. They rejected Scamp's appeal outright, and reaffirmed their determination to stay out until the Company had agreed to pay up. They also decided not to meet again for another week. This meeting clearly showed by how much the Sewing Machinists' conviction and resolve had grown during the two and a half weeks of struggle. They were absolutely solid and much more confident and self-assured; the strike looked unbreakable. The Shop Stewards, after the meeting, reflected the prevailing mood when, in response to questions from the press about how much longer they were prepared to stay out, they replied, 'For a year if necessary'.

When the news of the result and the mood of this meeting filtered through to the Company, it reacted swiftly. Bill Batty, the Managing Director, sent a telegram on Thursday to Harold Wilson, the Prime Minister, and asked him to intervene. A copy of the telegram also went to

Wedgwood Benn, Minister of Technology. In the telegram, Bill Batty stated that the dispute, which had already brought the daily production of 2,200 cars to a complete halt, now threatened to close all Ford plants in the United Kingdom, and in consequence the jobs of over 40,000 Ford workers were at risk. Furthermore, £8 million of export orders for the Cortina had already been lost and the long-term losses in the American market, alone, might total more than £30,000,000.

Harold Wilson replied to that telegram, saying he shared Batty's concern about the effects of the dispute, but he declined to intervene personally. Instead, Barbara Castle acted. As a matter of urgency, she sent for Charlie Gallagher and Fred Blake on Thursday afternoon. She intimated to them that she would like to see the Strike Committee on the following morning. The Union Officials with some assistance from the Department of Employment and Productivity, contacted, late on Thursday evening, the eight members of the Strike Committee at their homes, and invited them to attend the proposed meeting with Barbara Castle at the Ministry. Charlie Gallagher, Fred Blake and the Convener also went to the Ministry. Reg Birch, once again inexplicably, declined the invitation to attend.

Barbara's Tea Party

On the following morning, Barbara Castle first of all requested to see the Strike Committee members alone, so that they could 'talk turkey'; Rosie Boland recalls that their first impression was one of disappointment, particularly in respect of Barbara's sartorial appearance. 'Whilst the girls had dressed up for the occasion, Barbara Castle seemed to have decided to dress in a manner which enabled her "to keep down with the Joneses".'[34]

During their heart-to-heart talk over cups of tea, Barbara Castle first of all pointed out to the Strike Committee the economic damage the dispute was causing to Britain, and emphasised that her main concern was to find a formula for the resolution of the dispute. The Strike Committee members in reply explained the details of their case and made it absolutely clear that, come what may, in the absence of an acceptable offer from the Company, nothing would induce them to return to work. The Minister went on to say that, of course, she too believed in equal pay, 'I get it myself', but it could not be introduced into industry overnight. She then also made known her intention to place legislation before Parliament which, over a period of time, would make equal pay a reality. None the less, the girls could not be persuaded to change their position. The discussion was adjourned and subsequently resumed with the Trade Union Officials present, but no further headway was made. Barbara Castle, therefore, asked for Blakeman and Ramsey to come to the Ministry in the afternoon, and she cancelled a luncheon appointment at the House of Lords in order to be present at the afternoon's discussion.

Fred Blake recalls of the morning meeting:

> ... It started off with everybody standing around, her offering drinks, always friendly, she telling us, being a woman herself, she sympathised with the idea of Equal Pay, but it was a question of legislation. Meanwhile, we had to get some resolution of this problem. It centred around that. With a meeting such as that you would think something would stand out but it doesn't. It was just chatting and generalising in the morning. Barbara said, 'I can't really negotiate, I can only listen to your points ...' Charlie went through the whole bloody caboosh as far as that was concerned ... [35]

A Historic Victory

A tough bargaining session took place in the afternoon. According to Rosie Boland:

> Barbara Castle said: 'Would you go back to work on Monday if you got 92 per cent?' I said 'That will be up to the girls whether they go back or not. I'd have to ask them first.' She said to the Ford Management 'Are you prepared?' They said 'No, 90 per cent'. I said 92 per cent or else no talk' so she said 'If you are prepared to talk then I'll see that you get 92 per cent.'[36]

Blakeman eventually offered to raise the women's rate from 85 per cent to 92 per cent of the male rate, starting from the following Monday, 1 July 1968, and he also gave a pledge that equal pay would become operative at Ford within three years or sooner, if the Trade Union Side wanted it. He further intimated that he would see to it that at the forthcoming meeting of the NJNC on Monday, this solution would be accepted.

Fred Blake recalls, 'When Blakeman eventually made the offer we looked at one another as much as to say, "Oh Christ, that's not too bad".'[37] In practice, this meant an immediate 7½-8½ (old) pence per hour increase for all women working at Ford. The Sewing Machinists grading problem was to be dealt with at the Court of Inquiry. Blakeman, however, made the offer conditional. He made one stipulation — in order not to humiliate the NJNC and to preserve the credibility of that Committee, he would formally make this offer to the Trade Union Side of the NJNC at the specially convened meeting on Monday 1 July, and no public announcement was to be made until then.

The Strike Committee rejected this stipulation out of hand, and demanded that Blakeman should sign on the 'dotted line' there and then, because they did not trust him or the National Trade Union Officials. Blakeman, greatly agitated and in a state of nervous exhaustion, refused to do this. Talks, once again, looked like breaking down. Barbara Castle suggested a further adjournment.

The Trade Union Side went to a separate conference room which had been placed at their disposal for the day. During the adjournment, the Convener pointed out to the Strike Committee that a notable victory was within their grasp. A rank-and-file committee had negotiated directly a settlement with the Minister and the Director of Labour Relations at Ford. The Company had conceded the principle of equal pay which would have widespread repercussions not only throughout the engineering industry but throughout Britain as a whole. Additionally, the Minister had pledged to introduce legislation on equal pay at the next session of Parliament. In response to a grading claim for five (old) pence per hour confined to 400 Sewing Machinists, Ford was conceding a pay increase 50 per cent higher than that, to all Ford women workers. This outright victory would also give renewed confidence to every other section of Ford workers and, finally, there was a good chance that the grading claim might be won at the forthcoming Court of Inquiry. For these reasons the substance of this great victory ought not to be jeopardised for the sake of appearances. In any case, the Company would be unlikely to renege on an Agreement which was concluded in the presence of the Minister.

The Strike Committee, in discussion, reiterated their distrust of the formal negotiating machinery, and argued: 'If it is good enough and proper for Blakeman to negotiate a settlement with us verbally, in the presence of the Secretary of State, what's wrong with him putting it on paper?'[38] After a lengthy debate, the Strike Committee eventually accepted the weight of the Convener's arguments, with the proviso that, if the Agreement was not promptly implemented on Monday, they would walk out again on Tuesday.

Thereafter the Strike Committee decided to convene a mass meeting of Sewing Machinists on Sunday morning, at Dagenham, and to recommend, at this meeting, that a resumption of work should take place on Monday 1 July. One immediate problem arose because there were no meeting places available at Dagenham on a Sunday. Informed of this, Barbara Castle gave instructions for the Dagenham Labour Exchange to be opened up and a large meeting room inside to be put at the disposal of the strikers. Fred Blake was particularly impressed by this development, and he said: 'Christ, we now have the Minister arranging meeting places. We really seem to be getting somewhere.'[39]

When Blakeman was informed of the Strike Committee's decisions, he was greatly relieved, so much so, that he made a personal donation of £5 to the Sewing Machinists' strike fund, saying: 'I too believe in Equal Pay.' Before he left the Ministry, he also paid a generous tribute to Barbara Castle: 'I have been particularly impressed with the way in which the First Secretary has handled the situation.' He believed that trade unionists and Ford should be grateful to Mrs Castle.[40]

Although Barbara Castle failed both in the morning and in the afternoon to persuade the girls to agree to a resumption of work on the grounds that they would get a fair hearing at the forthcoming Court of Inquiry, she nevertheless made a major contribution towards achieving a settlement, by stating that she intended to lay equal pay legislation before Parliament in the autumn. This gave reassurance to the Company that they would not be at a disadvantage *vis-à-vis* their competitors in the long term, and it gave the Trade Union Side a sense of historic achievement, without which, notwithstanding the pay offer, a settlement on that particular day would have been unlikely.

Rosie Boland, in a Press Statement after the conclusion of the talks at the Ministry, said, 'This is a great victory for us, we have every confidence that the Court of Inquiry will be on our side.'[41] The settlement reached at the Ministry highlighted two features. First, the Company was most anxious to have a 'No additional economic demands' clause enshrined in their 1967 Two-Year Agreement with the Trade Unions. Yet, when under severe pressure, the Company was able to forget all about the sanctity of this particular Agreement, and negotiated a settlement on a claim which had never been presented, with a Strike Committee of Sewing Machinists. To do this, the Company had to bypass and disregard all existing negotiating practices and agreed procedures. It was precisely this kind of conduct for which the Company later so indignantly criticised the Trade Unions at the Scamp Court of Inquiry. Second, the Agreement also dented the government's national economic policy. Ronald Kershaw in his article in *The Times* focused on this point. He wrote:

> How Mrs. Castle, whose talks with the employers, Union and Sewing Machinists last Friday, brought about a return to work at Fords yesterday, will fit a 7 per cent pay increase with no productivity guarantees into her Prices and Incomes Policy, is not quite clear.
>
> Basically the only situation where increases over the 3½ per cent ceiling is allowed, is on grounds of higher productivity and increased efficiency, and where there has been a major reorganisation of wages and salary structures. A 3½ per cent increase is allowable in cases of increased productivity of lower paid workers seriously out of line with those doing similar work.
>
> The Department of Employment and Productivity was unable to comment on the situation last night.[42]

Straight after their meeting with Barbara Castle at the Ministry, the Strike Committee joined a contingent of Sewing Machinists who were on their way to an 'Equal Rights in Industry' meeting at Friends House, Euston, which had been organised and sponsored by the NUVB.

Perhaps inevitably, the terms of the proposed settlement became unofficially known at this meeting and it caused Joyce Butler, MP for Wood Green, to state: 'When history comes to be written, seat covers will go down with matches, as the two items which really brought about emancipation for women.'[43] Baroness Summerskill at the same Conference praised the Seamstresses in terms of 'You're fighting a fight from which your daughters and grand-daughters will greatly benefit.'[44] It was at this meeting that the idea for a National Joint Action Campaign Committee for Women's Equal Rights (NJACCWER) was first raised. This Committee was, indeed, formed at the beginning of September 1968, and subsequently led and spearheaded the national equal pay campaign throughout the country. It did some very useful work, the details of which are described in the chapter on external consequences. Fred Blake became the National Secretary of this Committee:

> Due to the terrific publicity we got at that particular stage with the Barbara Castle tea-party and the Scamp Court if you like, I then received literally hundreds of letters from all over the country mostly from women who wanted to play an active part in the Equal Pay campaign . . . We set up a vast organisation . . . and if only I hadn't been a man but been a woman, we would still be operating this organ-

isation now . . . [45]

The Dagenham Labour Exchange was not really a suitable place for the Sunday morning meeting. The District Officials, the Conveners and Shop Stewards had to stand on top of the Employment Clerk's counters, and the Sewing Machinists were strung out in front of the interviewing cubicles. Nevertheless, the all-prevailing mood was festive. It was one of those rare occasions when everybody radiates goodwill, and becomes submerged in a kind of collective happiness. The speeches from the platform were self-congratulatory and focused on the unprecedented success of what had been achieved so far, and on the need to win the grading issue as well at the forthcoming Court of Inquiry.

The spirit of victory, which had taken hold of the rank-and-file leadership, was also reflected by the membership. The recommendation to return to work was supported unanimously, and with good heart. The Halewood girls held a similar meeting at the Adelphi Hotel in Liverpool. Their spirits were equally high, and the decision, as in Dagenham, was to return to work on Monday 1 July.

The NJNC Tries to Save Face

The hastily convened meeting of the NJNC, on Monday, took place in quite unique circumstances. The Company had assembled as many of the National Trade Union Officials as could be contacted over the weekend in order to secure their approval for the Agreement reached on the previous Friday with the Strike Committee at the Ministry. It meant a breach of the two-year 'no more additional economic demands' clause, and acceptance by the Trade Unions of a wage increase they had never asked for, and also the acceptance of the principle of equal pay, which, up to then, they had never formally supported or presented at any of their meetings with the Company.

Blakeman formally proposed that the women's pay rate should be raised with immediate effect. As soon as the meeting had opened, however, Jim Conway said to Blakeman:

I would like to make a personal statement. You have always known my attitude to the abrogation and breaking of agreements. I want to assure you that it was not within my power to change what has happened.

Mr Blakeman Thank you very much . . . [46]

David Fraser, National Official for the Plumbing Trade Union, did not like the meeting taking place at all. He said:

> I personally want to make a protest . . . I do not think that it is a properly constituted meeting to deal with such an issue. I was informed by phone very late last evening. Many of the other members of the Trade Union Side are not here . . . [47]

Blakeman became rather impatient and pressed the Trade Union Side hard to give its formal agreement to the proposed improvement in the women's rate. The following, perhaps rather amusing, exchange then took place.

> **Mr Conway** There is one thing I would like to say about this Mr Blakeman, although we would agree, we are in a rather ironical position on the Trade Union Side because we have had no application for Equal Pay . . . (Blakeman interrupts)
> **Mr Blakeman** No, neither have we.[48]

Later on at the meeting, Mark Young asked,

> What is the deadline for you to pay it in the normal circumstances? What is the deadline you want?
> **Mr Blakeman** Well, I think it is last Friday! (laughter)[49]

The Trade Union Side promised to give immediate consideration to the Company's proposal, and to let Blakeman know its formal decision without undue delay.

Conway made the last contribution for the Trade Union Side when he said to Blakeman: I can give you every assurance that this Trade Union Side has pledged itself at the very earliest possible moment to look at the whole question of what happened in this case.'[50] After the conclusion of the meeting, Jim Conway made a Press Statement in which he said: '*This is a great victory*!! We are very happy about this, the value of the NJNC has been more than justified.'[51] Notwithstanding Conway's Press Statement, the refusal by the Trade Union Side to formalise the Agreement on Monday, under the pretext that further clarification was needed from all the other Unions concerned, was in essence an expression of peevishness and a 'sour grapes' attitude about the preceding events.

The consequence, however, was that on Tuesday morning, in the absence of any formal notice being posted on the Company's notice board, the Sewing Machinists became very agitated and threatened to walk out again unless they could obtain a definite assurance that the Friday Agreement would, in fact, be implemented. The Convener advised the Company of the seriousness and the likely consequences of this situation, and in response to this approach he received a telephone call shortly afterwards from Mark Young, the Chairman of the Trade Union Side. Mark Young assured the Convener that the Trade Unions had no intention of obstructing the Agreement and that in fact payment would be made to all Ford women workers from 1 July, as agreed between the Trade Unions and the Company and the Secretary of State, on Friday of last week. This was a timely telephone call because, without doubt, the women would have resumed their strike action on that particular day.

The Confederation of British Industries was far less happy with the outcome than was Conway. A CBI spokesman expressed concern about the 7 per cent pay increase accorded to Ford women workers with no productivity strings, and CBI Officials were particularly apprehensive about the fact, '. . . that the Ford women's victory may start an Equal Pay rush and "rebound round" '.[52] Finally, the Company issued a Press Statement which said:

> The Company as a result of a revaluation of the contribution of the women employees in relation to male employees, offered to narrow the differential so that women employees will, in future, receive 92 per cent of the men's wage for a similar job.[53]

The Company, however, revealed its true feelings about the Sewing Machinists' strike two days later, when Leslie Blakeman on the first day of the hearing proper, at the Scamp Court of Inquiry, concluded a well-rehearsed presentation of the Company's case, with the following remarks:

> It would not be an exaggeration to say that the management of Ford Motor Company regard this as the gravest labour relation situation it has ever faced in its long and sometimes turbulent history. In this dispute one can see the whole weakness of the British structure of industrial relations. Here clearly and at times blatantly demonstrated is the open disregard for signed collective agreements which periodically cripples large sections of British industry, and makes planned effective use of the country's resources impossible.[54]

The Scamp Court of Inquiry

The members of the Court of Inquiry were the Chairman, Sir Jack Scamp, Miss Ann Shaw, Chairman and Managing Director of the Ann Shaw Management Consultancy Organisation, Mr Grange Moore, Deputy Managing Director of BTR Industries Limited, and Jack Peel, General Secretary of the National Union of Dyers, Bleachers and Textile Workers.

Jack Peel was later rewarded by Ted Heath for the 'responsible' attitude which he displayed, not only at this Court of Inquiry, but also subsequently towards the 1971 Tory Government's Industrial Relations Act, with a well-paid job in Brussels — namely, EEC Director for Industrial Relations.

The members of the Court visited the Trim Shop on Tuesday 2 July. It was a public relations exercise, a walk-about in order to give the impression that the members of the Court were familiarising themselves with the details and the location of the job in dispute. Nobody was really particularly impressed or deceived by this fleeting appearance on the shop floor by people who were generally unfamiliar with that kind of workshop environment.

After the Sewing Machinists' resumption of work on Monday, the rank-and-file leadership concentrated on two priorities: (1) to secure the implementation of the Equal Pay Agreement; and (2) to prepare and present a coherent, factual and technically competent case to the Court on the grading grievance problem.

The incompetent, unco-ordinated and bungling performances by the Trade Unions at the two previous Courts of Inquiry, the one presided over by Professor Jack and the other by Lord Cameron, had left indelible scars of shame and embarrassment on all those who had witnessed these proceedings. Further, by comparison with the two previous Courts of Inquiry, the outcome this time was of less importance to the rank-and-file movement, since a notable victory had already been won over the Company on equal pay. Nevertheless, based on the evidence available to the Shop Stewards, there were reasonable grounds for optimism that the Sewing Machinists could win their grading claim. It was, therefore, decided to focus attention on the details of the profiling evidence and on the general question of sex discrimination, and generally, if at all possible, not to allow the Company to dominate throughout the entire proceedings.

By contrast, and perhaps not surprisingly, the Company opted for a 'law and order' strategy. Management was obviously deeply disturbed

by the apparent breakdown of its existing internal structures, and also
by the general climate of unrest externally, i.e. the frequency of strikes
in British industry, the war in Vietnam, student unrest at British
Universities, the events of May 1968 in France, and so on. Clearly, existing
formal structures always feel themselves threatened by the emergence
and growth of informal structures, and it would therefore be useful to
quote some further extracts of Blakeman's concluding remarks to the
Court of Inquiry. They give us a rare insight into the Ford Motor
Company's thinking about its relationship with trade unions, with the
government and the establishment in general, which is still valid today.
   Blakeman said:

> ... It would be foolish to claim that management is always right, or
> to forget that in years gone by the Company's labour relations were
> *deliberately* undermined by a politically inspired group of trouble-
> makers. However, we had hoped that that was in the past ... We just-
> ifiably felt we had reached the stage of good labour relationships ...
> The end result of all these efforts, the study, the training, the nego-
> tiations, consultations, communications, establishing agreed proce-
> dures, the end result of all that is that the operations of one of the
> country's biggest exporters have been brought to a near standstill be-
> cause three agreements have been deliberately ignored. 1) A wages
> agreement signed only last September; 2) a procedure agreement
> which has been in existence for 13 years, and 3) an agreement to
> process grading grievances signed only 6 months ago ... If the
> Company had to concede to pressure by groups resorting to uncon-
> stitutional action ... it would destroy the whole fabric of collective
> bargaining.
>   The dilemma which faces the Company, and we believe the whole
> of British industry, is that having taken a stand on the side of law and
> order in industrial relationships, what can be done to prevent disrup-
> tion of its operations by the irresponsibility of people who choose to
> ignore agreements entered into in good faith? ... This we believe to
> be the primary purpose of this Court ... and finally, and this is a
> question which must be answered, not only for the Ford Motor
> Company, but for every Company in Britain struggling to make itself
> competitive, what can be done to ensure that agreements entered into
> in good faith, are not broken at will with what may be disastrous
> effects on the Company's operation?[55]

This peroration clearly identified the Ford Motor Company's central concern. The forum of the Court was used in order to make a plea and also send a message to the government of the day, namely to introduce labour laws which would curb the power and the activities of the rank-and-file movement.

In fact, the Company's philosophy — its belief in labour laws — was amply demonstrated nine months later when Ford took out an injunction against the Unions and endeavoured to demonstrate in the High Court that collective agreements were enforceable in law. Undoubtedly, the Company's primary industrial relations objective during this period was to contain and to subdue the rank-and-file movement, to restore the authority of the NJNC and, notwithstanding Donovan, to pressurise the government to introduce laws which would curb trade union power.

But perhaps the most important and fascinating aspect of the Court of Inquiry lay in the intense divisions within the trade union movement which for the first time were displayed publicly and were subject to public scrutiny. It showed that the internal conflict between the Unions was deeper and more significant than the immediate dispute with the Company, which largely revolved around technical details about job evaluation, such as ranking techniques, disclosure of weighting factors and other matters connected with the various job characteristics.

The open conflict in Court between the representatives of the AEF and Mark Young and Jim Conway representing the Trade Union Side of the NJNC was really a clash of ideology, in part induced by the temporary leftward shift amongst the trade union leadership of the AEF which shortly afterwards spread to the TGWU when Jack Jones took over as General Secretary in December 1968. These division, according to Fred Blake, to some extent remain:

> The wounds created by the Sewing Machinists' dispute, even ten years later, have never really healed . . . Yes, there was a lot of bitter feeling . . . There was a lot of people actually on the NJNC who didn't want to see us get anything at all. Because as far as they were concerned they had taken the decision, as I say, arising from these private meetings, and I don't know how many were involved in that incidentally, but having taken that decision they were fighting along all the lines, and I suppose it busted their ego if you like, insofar as here they had come to some private arrangement with the Company, and that had now been defeated. It was a defeat . . . [56]

These divisions accentuated and were also symptomatic of the general struggle for a greater measure of shop-floor democracy, which was gathering momentum at that time, and which grew to such an extent that the Labour Government sought to contain this development in the following year by means of legislation. It produced, in January 1969, a White Paper *In Place of Strife,* which in essence was not all that different from the Tory Government's subsequent Industrial Relations Act. The Labour Government's proposed legislation was, however, defeated by the trade union movement and to this end the Sewing Machinists indirectly, and the Ford workers much more directly, made a decisive contribution.[57]

But the Court's refusal to pronounce on the central issue before it — whether the Sewing Machinists should be in Grade B or C — merely adds another unique feature to the many other unique features of this particular dispute. The reason for this was that the Seamstresses were still very much 'on the boil', and would have reacted against any unfavourable decision by staging another immediate walk-out. On the other hand, if the Court had found in favour of the Sewing Machinists, there could have been an unpredictable reaction by the men. Male production workers might well have argued and insisted that they too should be reclassified and receive additional payment for their particular work. Bernie Passingham says;

> ... I think it was unique in the way that Jack Scamp didn't give a decision, *after all basically the dispute was about grading* and who should have gone where, and the Court avoided to make that decision, all they did was apportion blame ... I think the Court 'funked' it ... Some of us had an idea they would ... If they had come out against the Machinists there would have been uproar not only from the women Machinists, but in general from women. If they had made a decision for it, the Ford Motor Company was going to be well in trouble with the troops on the lines ... In my own mind, if the women had got C grade then I could see an immediate dispute in relation to the main bulk of production lads ... the Court did 'funk' it because they weighed their two positions up ... Even today, in 1978, they would not have made a decision. *I believe the circumstances are still identical in that sense.*[58]

Thus the Court declared itself as not 'competent' to make a judgement on the issue, and recommended instead that a 'mini' Court of Inquiry be set up consisting of three trade union members and three Company members under an independent Chairman, to review the job and to pronounce on the issue. The established Profile Review

Committee was excused from this task because of 'emotional strain' and, in fact, was never to meet again. The Sewing Machinists reacted to this outcome unfavourably. They regarded an inconclusive outcome as an insult, and imposed an immediate overtime ban which was to last for over six months.

Rosie Boland said:

> We are very upset with the Scamp Report, we consider its suggestion of an *ad hoc* committee to look into our regrading claim is laughable. It was a waste of taxpayers' money to publish the report. Since our recent holiday, we have been working 12 hours overtime, but the Company must be made to see that we deserve to be in a higher grade.[59]

Lil O'Callaghan, too, thought the Court of Inquiry had 'funked' the issue; she says:

> I thought we ought to have done better because the Company really mucked it up particularly Meredeen, he really mucked it up, especially when I shouted, 'Lies' to him. He got flustered. He also told lies when we went to Warley, you know.[60]

One effect of the ideological divide on the Trade Union Side was that, at the personal level, no fraternisation took place throughout the whole four days of the Court proceedings.

By contrast, Blakeman called the Convener to one side during the lunch break on the first day of the Court sittings proper. He asked the Convener to forget the two-sided ritualistic conflict which was being publicly acted out in the Court, and to use his good offices to get the overtime ban in the Trim Shop lifted, so that the Company could fulfil a multi-million pound contract to the United States which otherwise might be lost, if shipment was not made on time. The Convener responded by relaying the request and the Company's sentiments and its reasons to the Trim Shop Stewards over the telephone; this, in turn led to the overtime ban being temporarily suspended for the required period in order to enable the Company to meet its deadlines on the shipping dates. This incident raises the interesting point — to what extent a community of interests exists at the instrumental level within the parameters of the basic conflict between capital and labour?

The Court's eventual findings were not altogether surprising and, to some extent, predictable. They amounted to the following:

1. that the dispute was about job grading and not about equal pay, since not a single Union, including the AEF, had submitted a formal claim for equal pay either before or during the strike period;
2. that by giving official support, both the AEF and NUVB were in serious breach of their obligations under their Agreement with the Company:
3. that there was no evidence of sex discrimination against the Sewing Machinists;
4. that the Company was to be criticised for faulty communications and lack of information with regard to its employees.

This last criticism appears to be standard requirement for all Courts of Inquiry — it really signifies a reproach to employers for failing to secure the consent or acquiescence of their workforce to a particular work situation at a given point in time.

Notwithstanding this pronouncement, the Trade Union Side, and the rank-and-file leadership on the whole, did not feel too disheartened by the outcome. It was a 'No decision — No verdict' situation and, with everything still in the balance, there were still reasonable grounds for optimism that, given the right 'staffing' of the 'Mini-Court', the grading could yet be won, but it really would, in the end, all depend on who was sitting on that particular committee.

The 'Mini-Court'

A wrangle lasting over six weeks developed about the composition of this *ad hoc* committee. The Trade Union Side in the River Plant insisted that the original Body Plant Divisional Review Committee members should be the ones to re-assess the profile, or that at the very least it should be the three Trade Union members of that now disbanded Committee who would look after the interests of the Sewing Machinists' case. This proposition, however, was rejected out of hand, both by the Company and by the Chairman of the Court. There were deep divisions on the Trade Union Side as to whether to participate in the proposed profile review, or whether, not being able to choose freely their preferred nominees to the Committee, no further sittings should take place. At one stage the debate reached such intensity that Mark Young came to Dagenham to address a meeting of the Sewing Machinists at the Central Hall on this topic. He explained to them that he could not vary the Company's view or the Court Chairman's opinion and, therefore, they had a choice of no committee and no resolution to their case, or placing their trust in alternative members who might well, based on the evidence, succeed in arguing a case which could produce a favourable outcome.

After an interval of about six weeks, largely at the Convener's behest, it was agreed to nominate three Conveners from other plants, the ones most likely to be able to argue a convincing case consistently and persuasively for the Sewing Machinists.

The Committee eventually met under the Chairmanship of J. Grange Moore at a location about 15 miles from the River Plant. They sat all day studying the profiling evidence, and, after viewing the job, discussed each individual characteristic at length. Voting on each of the 28 job characteristics went strictly along partisan lines – 3:3 – the three lay trade union members always in conflict with the three Company appointed members. Grange Moore, the 'independent' Chairman, used his vote more often in support of the Company members' preference for lower ratings and therefore, at the end of the day, the Sewing Machinists lost out on the grading issue and remained in Grade B.

It should, however, be stressed that, notwithstanding the Company's subsequent undisguised relief and joy at this particular outcome, on the day when the Committee sat, the Company members who had direct responsibility for this issue were very nervous and apprehensive and quite unsure about the eventual outcome. In conversation with trade union members and the Conveners, afterwards, they expressed the view that 'It was a cliff-hanger and it might have gone either way.'

When the outcome became known, the Sewing Machinists were intensely upset. They reinforced the overtime ban and the Trim Shop Stewards severely criticised the Convener for misjudging the capabilities of the trade union members to argue their case successfully. Even ten years later this remains their most severe criticism. Lil O'Callaghan says: 'We mucked it up. We should have left it open to fight another battle on another day.'[61] Bernie Passingham supports this view: 'Yes, that's where we made our mistake. I think if we had left it, the women would have continued the overtime ban in good heart, and this would have affected the Company and they might have won out eventually.'[62] Even with hindsight, it is difficult to pronounce on these speculative assumptions. What, however, can be said with certainty, is that the Sewing Machinists and the Trim Shop Stewards still feel deeply aggrieved about their low grading. This has, in no way, been alleviated by the fact that they have managed to get a small number of Machinists upgraded through a 'back door' method. The introduction of new fitments to the existing sewing machines has enabled the Stewards to argue a case for a job re-appraisal — particularly on repair work — on the grounds that their tasks now require more comprehensive and demanding work effort. The Company has acknowledged this argument and conceded the strength of their case by upgrading about twelve Machinists during the last three or four years to Grade C in order to be available to do this more extensive work.

The Leading Participants Analyse the Outcome

None the less, it has to be said that in general terms the Ford women have not succeeded in improving their position within the grading structure during the last ten years. The latest Company statistics show that, out of 1,715 hourly-rated women employees, only 58 are in Grade C, and none in Grade D or E.[63] Compared to the situation in 1968, this means that in percentage terms the situation has remained virtually unchanged and is today as unsatisfactory as it was then.

These statistics once again draw attention to the distinction between the success achieved on equal pay and the failure on grading. Clearly the failure on grading and the static position of the Ford women within the wage structure over the last ten years point to the inability, not to say, unwillingness, of the Trade Unions to expand the achievement on equal pay to the area of equal opportunity. The women's lack of advancement is further highlighted when we examine comparable figures for their male colleagues over the same period. The ratio of males in Grade C relative to the numbers in Grade B has increased by 50 per cent, and similarly the ratio between those in Grade E relative to Grade D has, in fact, doubled.

This is paralleled by the Sewing Machinists' continued passionate commitment and belief in the grading issue and their lukewarm and somewhat disinterested attitude towards equal pay. This marked difference in attitude and commitment emerged during interviews with the Trim Shop Stewards and some Shop Committee members in the autumn of 1974, and was reconfirmed, and virtually remained unchanged, during a series of similar interviews in the spring of 1978.

Lil O'Callaghan says:

The girls felt they were in B Grade because of sex discrimination . . . it wasn't the money, it was the principle involved — our skill was not recognised, and we are skilled . . . Today, we still say it isn't fair. As regards Equal Pay, some women even today think they shouldn't earn as much or more than their husbands, but they should realise they are working for what they can get, and Fords are making a big profit out of them . . . they are not working for their husbands, they are working for Fords, and the car is the same price whether it is men or women doing the job.[64]

Rosie Boland seems to have retained an even more intense commitment to grading, when she says:

Money was not the only reason for this dispute, although we did get more money, we did not gain the point, we won a battle, but lost the war. Women feel they were used to propagate the Equal Pay principle, and the partial Equal Pay settlement was only accepted under pressure in order to enable us to resume work. I am sure, now, that the Company never did have any intention of conceding the higher grade.[65]

Jane Morton, writing in *New Society,* 29 August 1968, expressed somewhat similar sentiments, when she said:

The women emerged as pawns in the game, and nobody else gets much credit from the report of Sir Jack Scamp's Inquiry into the dispute within the Ford Motor Company and its women machinists. The Vehicle Builders Union is rapped first for failing to take the up-grading claim seriously, and then for its intransigence. The Engineering Union is in trouble for declaring the strike official in defiance of agreed negotiating procedures, and the Company is chided for its autocratic behaviour . . . refusing to consider the women's case . . . and then suddenly softening up and offering them a higher percentage of the men's rate quite irrelevantly, with no greater regard for established procedures than the Unions had shown. In all a sordid and unnecessary mess which makes nonsense of the Engineering Union's pretence that the strike was a noble battle in the struggle for Equal Pay.

Notwithstanding these comments, the rank-and-file leadership seem to have chosen the political priorities between equal pay and equal opportunity correctly. These objectives are obviously not mutually exclusive in terms of progression and achievement; however, the political realities at that particular time made equal pay the only sensible and viable option. If the fight had been confined to grading, and even if successfully concluded, the impact would merely have been local, transient and forgotten. Furthermore, now that the principle of equal pay, however nominally, has been established, it should make it a little easier to climb and conquer the next peak — equal opportunity.

Lil O'Callaghan and Rosie Boland's comments, however, give us an insight into the difference of feeling and the different level of consciousness amongst the Sewing Machinists which has persisted for the last ten years. They point out that the Seamstresses see the grading issue in the field of craft consciousness, a concern for occupational status and dignity of labour, and the equal pay issue in terms of more or less getting the same money for the same, or similar, job, which to them is a much more impersonal and therefore more remote concept. Indeed, it would seem from their statements that fighting for the concept of equal pay requires a high degree of political and social awareness, which the Ford women, subjected to the socialisation process in a male-dominated world, certainly did not possess in 1968, nor yet seem to have acquired.

British labour history shows that craft consciousness, on the whole, tends to have precedence over class and social consciousness. Concern with lines of demarcation and differentials are thus one of the main enduring threads of British trade union history. Furthermore, the 'size effect' was an additional contributory factor which caused the Sewing Machinists to concentrate on the grading issue. Moving from Grade B to Grade C looked to them like a manageable localised internal problem. Equal pay, on the other hand, seemed to have universal ramifications. In other words, equal pay was perceived as an age-old problem, requiring a national movement to secure a national solution which, no doubt, in their opinion, would be forthcoming at some future date — but not yet. Certainly, 187 Sewing Machinists in the River Plant could not be expected to fight Ford, the state and society at large, for a principle which had eluded the women's movement and the labour movement for the past hundred years.

The last stage of the 'Social Contract' in 1977 is perhaps another illustration of this 'size effect' factor. Moss Evans, in a later discussion with the author, said: 'We were conned, but we just had no experience of acting on behalf of 25 million against "our Government". It was just too big and complex an issue.'[66] Indeed, no union at official or rank-and-file level acted, until the Leyland Toolmakers and the Heathrow Airport maintenance men came along with their differential problems. These two examples, linked to the general experience of British trade union development, reinforce the view that craft consciousness frequently intensifies conflict, and also tend to refute theories about craft consciousness inevitably leading to accommodation.

Quite apart from these brief and general comments, how did the Trade Unions react to the dispute and its outcome? As previously re-counted, most of the National Trade Union Officials concerned reacted sourly. To them, it appeared a regrettable event which should never have happened and is best forgotten. It did not arise from any policy advo-cated by the Trade Union Side of the NJNC, nor was the struggle led by it. Strange as it may appear, these two factors — absence of policy initia-tion on equal pay, and only peripheral involvement in the struggle by the two Unions supporting the Sewing Machinists, namely the AEF and NUVB — have also made these two Unions reluctant to highlight this dis-pute and to tell its story. Bernie Passingham says:

> I don't think a lot of Union Officials want to recognise it as such, you don't see too much written about it, but its a fact of life because of the way it was done. It didn't come out as a policy, and if one was to think that we were battling practically all the Unions on the NJNC bar two, well, this does explain it. [67]

Fred Blake, in different words, appears to express similar sentiments. He says:

> I was proud to have been associated with the dispute . . . I am a bit concerned that I wasn't able to do more . . . I think right from the word 'go' when the actual Sewing Machinists' grievance started we should have got hold of that thing, we should have been much more politically motivated to bring about a settlement. In the past, parti-cularly at that stage, when we used to get a problem we used to go in head first, feet first, bang, that's it, without looking at the deeper implications. I believe we really learned from the Sewing Machinists' dispute to look into the wider political implications of issues. [68]

The reaction of the Conveners to the conclusion of the dispute was as muted as it was during the dispute itself. Apart from two locations, the Body Plants at Dagenham and Halewood, no positive support or expres-sions of support had been forthcoming throughout the period of the dis-pute. According to Les Moore, the Conveners' reluctance to support positively was due to:

> a fear in people's mind, in the leaders' minds, in other words in the

men's minds that women getting Equal Pay would mean women doing men's jobs, taking men's jobs off them, and that men would resent not just working alongside women, but they would be taking their jobs.[69]

But the over-all sentiment which emerged at the end of the dispute can best be described as grudging admiration from the Conveners. At the Conveners' level, without exception, everybody perceived the outcome as an outright victory over the Ford Motor Company, and Les Moore perhaps summarises their sentiments and the prevailing view, when he says:

> The fact that a victory had been won even greater than was thought of in the first place, was terrific . . . Everybody understood that the Company had made a concession. In order *not* to make a concession in one way, they made a *greater concession* in *another way,* one of far more importance anyway. Also the whole thing exposed the NJNC Trade Union Side as a remote and bureaucratic body not really in touch with things . . . [70]

As regards trade union reaction in general terms to the immediate outcome, perhaps Lil O'Callaghan should have the last word. She says,

> It was a good experience . . . most of the women throughout the Company gained by it, and I don't think it will be forgotten. I am proud to have been part of the leadership and proud we all stuck together throughout. It was very well organised. All the Stewards worked very hard. It was all worth while.[71]

As regards the Company's strategy and tactics in relation to the dispute, Fred Blake believes management misjudged the issue because:

1. the dispute commenced in one of the smallest of the six plants on the Dagenham Estate;
2. the bulk of the membership involved belonged to one of the smallest Unions (NUVB) 'I think that was their bloody mistake, and it was also our mistake because we didn't grab hold of it too quickly';[72] and
3. the most important factor was that only women were involved. Fred Blake says:

When women get the bit between their teeth, once they get going, the Company should have realised (remembered) that the women were responsible during the war for a number of improvements, tea breaks for example . . . A lot of the movement in the factory for better conditions and better wages were brought about by women. Purely on the basis that they knew once the war was over they would be moving out at any rate so they had nothing to lose. I can recall a situation which is, in fact, a bit laughable, but you can see the strength of them. When I was in Briggs Bodies, I had 300 women and 200 men, at that particular stage . . . because these women used to sit down and do their sewing and the men used to stand up and do the pulling and that kind of thing, the situation was that the men wanted to have the roof lights open and the women wanted to have them shut because it was causing a draught, so I had to see the supervisor, Ron Coates. He was at his wits' end because every time he opened them, all the women stopped work, and they stopped just like that, and when they were closed of course, the men stopped, so it was on that basis that he had to accept for 48 hours windows being shut for one hour and open for another hour and so it went on. But you see, once the women had made up their bloody mind, this is what they were going to do. Another instance was, we always used to get a position where the Company used to come round at Christmas and say, 'Right you can pack up after dinner', the women used to say, 'Not on your "Nellie"'. When we come in we'll just clock in and then we'll start drinks and getting everything prepared, the men wouldn't do that sort of thing.

Even today, everybody was saying, 'Well, if you're going to have Equal Pay, you should accept nightwork', and the women said 'No, that's not right', and now they have got it, although a number of people are murmuring, national people, Shop Stewards' Conveners, murmuring, 'Well, it's right they should do night work, they get the same pay as all the rest of us'. Those women are still standing out and saying, 'No, not on your "Nellie".' Which is another example, and this is where the Company has learnt its lesson, because they haven't taken them on have they? They won't take them on again I guarantee . . . [73]

Fred Blake's analysis seems to place too much emphasis on the less important factors. In fact, the Company's strategy throughout was shaped by its central concern to contain the rank-and-file movement, to preserve the foundations of the wage structure, and above all to maintain the power and dominance of the existing NJNC in the field of the decision- and agreement-making process. But this the Company precisely failed to do, for reasons which are outlined in Part IV.

More importantly, perhaps, the Company failed to take sufficient account of the historical experience of the rank-and-file leadership. Ford workers had been in the forefront of the industrial struggle since the war. Four government Courts of Inquiry, three in the space of ten years, bear witness to this — a fact which Henry Ford II bitterly complained about when he met Ted Heath in Downing Street in 1971.[74] He said the Ford Motor Company had become the battleground for industrial relations, over which such issues as government economic policy, equal pay, workers' control and shop-floor democracy were being fought out, and in consequence, he threatened to discontinue investments in Britain and to run the plants down. Therefore, any dispute at Dagenham, and especially one that included Halewood, was assured of a degree of publicity which no other Company, or industry, could attract at that time — an attraction Blakeman frequently and ruefully complained about to the press.

Due to this environment and background, the rank-and-file leaders at Dagenham were not merely 'good' industrial militants, but had also mastered the art of strategy and tactics and built up a rank-and-file organisation with a level of political consciousness which, at that time, was second to none. Consequently, the Sewing Machinists had three vital elements at their command: (1) organisation, (2) leadership and (3) news value, without which, even given the will, they could not have succeeded. It requires social action to universalise principles and for principles to be translated into practice. To this end the crucial factor was that the Sewing Machinists were employed at the Ford Motor Company — and not elsewhere.

There can be little doubt that, without the Sewing Machinists' strike, Barbara Castle would have continued to drag her feet and failed to have the Bill ready when she did. A couple of months after the Equal Pay Bill had become law, the Labour Government lost office. When the Tories were in power, they certainly would not have legislated for equal pay; and, in the economic climate of 1974/75, the Labour Government would not have rushed in and done so, either. Therefore, notwithstanding all its weaknesses, the Act was a timely piece of legislation which strengthened the cause of equal pay, and helped to accelerate its application.

Notes

1. The cutters derive their name from the machines they use – 'Eastman Cutters'.

2. Joint Works Committee Minutes, reference 1838/8, 194th special meeting, 12 December 1967.

3. AEF submission to the Scamp Court of Inquiry, p.3.

4. Ibid., p.6.

5. Company submission to the Scamp Court of Inquiry, p.5.

6. Rosie Boland interview, *Socialist Worker*, 21 September 1968.

7. Ibid.

8. Company submission to the Scamp Court of Inquiry, p. 7.

9. Ibid., p. 9.

10. Ibid., section 6, p.l.

11. Interview with author, February 1978.

12. Company submission to the Scamp Court of Inquiry, p. 10.

13. Ibid., p. 10.

14. Ibid., p.11.

15. Ibid., p.11.

16. Ibid., p.11.

17. *Evening Standard,* 15 June 1968.

18. Interview with author, February 1978.

19. Ibid.

20. Ibid.

21. Ibid.

22. *Socialist Worker,* 21 September 1968.

23. Interview with author, February 1978.

24. Interview with author, March 1978.

25. Transcript of Scamp Court of Inquiry, p. 145.

26. Transcript of NJNC meeting, 17 June, pp. 3 and 4.

27. Ibid., p. 4.

28. Ibid., pp. 8 and 9. Author's emphasis.

29. Reg Birch, *Guerrilla Struggle and the Working Class* (Communist Party of Britain Marxist-Leninist, 1973), pp. 4, 5 and 15.

30. Interview with author, February 1978.

31. *The Times,* 19 June 1968.

32. Interview with author, February 1978.

33. *The Times,* 27 June 1969.

34. Interview with author, March 1978.

35. Interview with author, February 1978.

36. *Socialist Worker,* 21 September 1968.

37. Interview with author, February 1978.

38. Author's recollections.

39. Ibid.

40. *Daily Telegraph,* 29 July 1968.

41. Ibid.

42. *The Times,* 2 July 1968.

43. *The Times,* 29 June 1968.

44. *Daily Telegraph,* 29 June 1968.

45. Interview with author, February 1978.

46. Transcript of NJNC meeting, 1 July 1968, p. 3.

47. Ibid., p.5.

48. Ibid., p.5.

49. Ibid., p.9.

50. Ibid., p.10.

51. *The Times,* 2 July 1968. Author's emphasis.

52. Ibid.

53. Ibid.

54. Transcript of Scamp Court of Inquiry, p. 85.

55. Ibid., p. 86.

56. Interview with author, February 1978.

57. This will be described in some detail, together with the Company's High Court action, in Part IV.

58. Interview with author, February 1978.

59. *Daily Telegraph,* 28 August 1968.

60. Interview with author, March 1978.

61. Ibid.

62. Interview with author, February 1978.

63. Company Statistics on Grading, April 1978.

64. Interview with author, February 1978.

65. Ibid.

66. Interview with author, August 1977.

67. Interview with author, February 1978.

68. Ibid.

69. Ibid.

70. Ibid.

71. Interview with author, March 1978.

72. Interview with author, February 1978.

73. Ibid.

74. See Chapter 7, p. 265, below.

Part III

FIRST DIALOGUE

5 THE DISPUTE ANALYSED

SM When I sat down with my notebooks, Henry, to read what I'd written about the dispute at the time, I found that I was able to recall a mass of additional detail about the whole period. So the dispute became almost real again in my mind. How about you?

HF Yes, I felt the same. But when I read your account, I thought you recalled events more vividly, in a less detached way than me. I detected rumbles of the battle lingering on — as if you were still not completely detached from the events of 1968.

SM Yes, perhaps you're right; I still feel very close to those events.

HF I think that enhances your account. If you're too cool and clinical, you lose out on the other side. My over-all impression is that you were — and to some extent still are — more personally involved in the dispute than me.

SM Do you mean emotionally or ideologically?

HF Both, I think. Certainly at an ideological level. But I think that's all to the good.

SM There's one question I'd like to put before we turn to the details of the dispute. At the time you lived through the events, did you realise at any particular moment that you were making history?

HF Yes, I think I did, on the second day of the dispute. The fact that the strike was made official so quickly meant there was a commitment to the issue by a major Union and by certain individuals. That was my first realisation that perhaps history was about to be made. What about you?

SM Well, I kept a running notebook throughout the dispute, which was unusual and suggests that the dispute had some special quality for me at the time. For example, if a group of men returned from a one-day strike and were handed the usual letter, telling them they had acted in breach of their contracts of employment, I think they'd have said: Another one of those bloody letters! Stick it on the lavatory wall! . . . The women wouldn't accept the letters but handed them back to the Supervisor, as if to say: We're not accepting that — it's as good as admitting we're in the wrong.

HF More than that. The women were girding themselves to do battle — to get social justice as well as economic justice. They saw the letter as a form of printed intimidation and wanted to show they had the character to stand up to Company pressure. The letter was seen by them as one of the standard methods which the Company employed to try to compel workers to stay within the Procedure.

SM The point I was trying to make was the women behaved in a distinctive way. It was as if they had learned some of the lessons of earlier disputes and were determined to act differently. If the women were going to lose their industrial virginity, so to speak, they felt they had to be more militant than a similar group of men might have been. It's noticeable, I think, that when any group of workers become involved in an industrial conflict for the first time, their adrenalin levels run abnormally high, as if they were intoxicated by their own audacity. There's a kind of Bank Holiday mood. In fact, the women treated their one-day strike like a cockney Bank Holiday by going off to the races!

HF That's one of the factors. But we should beware of over-simplifying the issues. The underlying social causes in this dispute were a subconscious feeling amongst the women that they had always been industrially disadvantaged. They'd never played a significant part before in wage negotiations and had never had their demands properly considered. I think there are comparable instances where coloured workers might react in a more determined way than indigenous workers.

SM I accept that. But I believe the women went on strike for *economic* justice — for more pay — and that it is only your hindsight, ten years later, that leads you to stress the element of *social* justice. I've no doubt the women felt some sense of sex discrimination in a predominantly male workforce. They wanted to be in Grade C but they would never have come out on strike for equal pay in the first place . . .

HF Your last point is right, but not the others. The predominant feeling *was* resentment about discrimination.

SM But then, as often happens, a strike takes on a life of its own and changes its character; the reasons that workers come out on strike are not always the same reasons that keep them out — and the reasons they go back to work are not always connected with their reasons for coming out in the first place. This dispute is a classic case in which the issue changes substantially during the course of the strike.

HF I don't think so . . . Let me reiterate, since I was a key witness to the events: for six weeks prior to the dispute, at every shop meeting, there was one central theme and one absolute conviction amongst the women — that they were not in the right grade *because* they were women. Now, let me ask you this: What's the difference in principle between a passionate feeling of being discriminated against in terms of job grading and a passionate feeling of being discriminated against in terms of pay, relative to men? Is there any difference?

SM Yes, I think there is. For years these women had suffered discrimination on grounds of sex — I noted five separate forms of discrimination under the old wage structure. But I don't know of a single case in which these women, either formally or informally, through official or unconstitutional action, raised the issue of discrimination — either in pay, or access to higher-graded jobs, or to training or promotion. In fact, it was the *Company,* not the Unions, which took the initiative under the new wage structure, by offering to put right the historic anomaly by which women were graded by their sex and not by the work they undertook.

HF Maybe so, but silence does not always imply assent.

SM So, if there had been a keen sense of social injustice amongst the women, as you claim, *there* was the opportunity for the Unions to have said: No, it's not enough to grade the women according to their work; they must be paid the full equivalent of the men's rates for the same grade. In return, we'll undertake to go along with you to the Department of Employment and ensure that the women accept the same conditions of employment as the men, including overtime, shift work and weekend work . . . The Unions and the women let that opportunity go by — and that's what detracts from your contention that the dispute was essentially about the struggle for social justice. I believe it began as a straightforward economic issue about grading. It was *your* opportunism that turned it into a social and political issue.

HF Well, let me offer you an alternative explanation. There were two factors at work: one was the Company's own propaganda about the wage structure review, which stressed the depersonalisation and objectivity of the exercise. That raised expectations amongst the women that, for once, previous occupational grading would be disregarded, that the exercise would be based on what your job was worth, measured by a set of common standards. That background indoctrination lasted for over six months. So you must face the fact that, if you fail to meet the expectations which you've raised, you run into serious trouble.

SM Yes, I agree with that.

HF Having been led to believe that the evaluation would not be concerned with the person but the job, when the grading came out as it did, the women were naturally convinced they were being discriminated against because of their sex. You can't escape that central fact, Sander. I know because I was there. All the women were shouting the same thing: Just because we're women, they think we can be left in Grade B. That's all they think of us! . . . *That* was the trigger of the dispute.

That brings us to the second point. You see, equal pay wasn't the great issue of principle which started the strike — it was a tactic — employed not only to secure attention to the grading but, above all, to ensure a successful outcome once battle had been joined.

SM Just a minute! You first said the dispute wasn't about grading but about equal pay and social justice. Now you're saying that equal pay wasn't an issue, it was merely a tactic?

HF No. I'm talking about the feeling of generally being discriminated against because of sex, rather than the feeling in favour of equal pay, as such.

SM Look, Henry: I accept your account of how the women felt and thought and reacted. What I'm saying, with equal sincerity, is that if *discrimination* had been the key issue — never mind equal pay — there were many occasions on which the women themselves, or their articulate representatives, of whom you were probably the most articulate, could have presented an irresistible case to end discrimination and to obtain equality of treatment. I entirely agree with you that the fundamental explanation of the women's militancy is what we might call 'the glimpse of freedom' — that is, that people are most revolutionary and most militant not when they are most oppressed but when they first become conscious of the possibility of freedom. It was when their heightened expectations were dashed that the women first experienced an 'explosion of consciousness'. For decades, British women had found no opportunity to achieve equal pay in industry. By 1968, there was a change in the social climate: it was a special year — a year of revolutions, when everything seemed possible — the culminating year in a decade of unprecedented material prosperity and technological change. It was the year of the Prague Spring; the year when students occupied their universities from Berkeley to the Sorbonne; there were barricades on the streets of Paris as well as Prague. The dispute has to be seen against that background of social and political ferment. For me, 1968 was an historical watershed — the year in which the rank-and-file everywhere stood up to be counted. It's surely not merely coincidence, with the advent of the Pill and the psychological confidence it conferred, that this was the time the Women's Consciousness Movement began to take off? It was a unique historical conjuncture — and at that particular moment, in 1968, this group of Ford women stood up to be counted, too. But it was on the simple issue of grading to start with, not equal pay.

HF Well, let me make a couple of points before we lose them. I accept what you say about the historical context and the glimpse of freedom. I'm saying the Ford women experienced a similar feeling about their disadvantaged position. I accept they had done nothing about it before then; that no champions had emerged to put these things right. They had heard about the suffragettes, of course, and the Matchgirls. We should remember that these historical events do become absorbed and internalised and it doesn't take a lot to revive the feelings which surround them. So, the first factor is expectations, which we've dealt with.

The second factor is that the women's representatives have a job profile in their hands which shows, on paper, that these jobs ought not to be in Grade B. Here's the profile; it's a good one, with markings higher than many others you can see. You go to a meeting and compare them and say: We don't understand the grading of these jobs. The only explanation we can offer is the inherently obvious one: the grading reflects the fact these jobs are done exclusively by women . . . Nobody comes along and says: Just a minute, that's the wrong job profile. Nobody offers any countervailing evidence . . . Now, combine these two factors — the raised expectations and the profile evidence — and you can easily understand the feeling of discrimination the women felt.

On your other point — Why hadn't the Unions raised the question before? Quite honestly, in terms of practical politics, of formulating union demands, it was unthinkable that any Ford Convener, including myself, could have championed the women's cause and set out to get them an increase worth half as much again as the men's. Today, that might sound horrific; in 1968, if you put forward such ideas, you wouldn't have lasted one day as Convener! No union could go against the cultural conservatism which prevailed at the time. I remember raising the women's question with my own Shop Stewards' Committee and they went berserk, howled with pains of anguish and outrage: What the hell do you think you're up to? Become the Joan of Arc for the women? You're not on! Forget it! . . . Except for individual cases, there was no way of acting effectively on behalf of the female membership collectively.

SM That's a substantial concession: you've acknowledged that the women's failure to achieve equal pay earlier was due *not* to Company intransigeance but to the Unions' failure to generate the necessary ideological fervour at rank-and-file level. But even in 1967, when the Company offered equal pay for an equal work contribution, and all the Unions had to do was to accept it with both hands, they refused the offer.

HF I've never claimed that the Company had any ideological objection to equal pay — only economic objections.

SM Then why did you suspect it of practising sex discrimination?

Do you mean that if the Unions had accepted the Company's offer of equal pay for the women, the men would have opposed it?

HF Possibly. I think the feeling against equal pay was there subconsciously amongst the men. But at the outset of job evaluation, when you devise the factors and the benchmarks, you control the outcome to a large extent and you can certainly guard against unexpected results.

SM No. You're giving the Company too much credit if you mean we anticipated the results of the evaluation and so rigged the results from the outset! Nothing could be further from the truth. Or do you mean that management was unconsciously biased against the women?

HF Well, I don't believe job evaluation can ever be objective because it's the standards initially chosen which determine the outcome. The Ford evaluation was intended to favour the skilled sections and, broadly speaking, not to disturb too much the existing order of run-of-the-mill production jobs.

SM Well, I agree that job evaluation is neither objective nor scientific. But I deny that it's inherently biased against women . . . If you agree, I think we might move on now to the early days of the dispute.

On management's side, the standard Warley dispute drill was put into operation to contain the conflict, and not to provoke others to come out in sympathy whilst an urgent solution was being sought. It wasn't until the Monday that the real impact of the strike was felt. The papers reported the women's allegation of discrimination and this gave some idea that this was going to be no ordinary strike . . .

By Tuesday, the AEF — with unprecedented speed — had made the strike official. So, management decided to play things cool. The women had taken the bit between their teeth. Nothing would get them back quickly. It was the height of the car-selling season and Dagenham held only limited stocks of seat covers. There was a good deal of talk about importing seat covers from elsewhere; about the risk of them being 'blacked' and of bringing out the rest of the Dagenham Estate. This was the early, phoney stage of the dispute when management's main objective was to 'snuff out' the strike. But the one question nobody could answer was: How long will the women sit it out? So we come back to the first crucial ingredient of the dispute: that the strikers were all women who had never walked out on strike before, except alongside the men. Nobody could say how they would act because there was no precedent to guide us. Would they behave like other Ford workers? Would they want to show themselves more militant than the men? Or would they capitulate before the end of the week? Did you have the same doubts about the women on your side?

HF Well, by 1968, there was a good understanding that the critical period in any dispute was the first few days. The previous 10 or 20 years had shown that most strikes tended to collapse in the first week — either through official union intervention or management intervention or the device of holding meetings every consecutive day until somebody passed a resolution to go back to work. After that, even those Union Officials who had induced the resumption of work would criticise the membership for getting cold feet. To preclude that possibility, we decided, in addition to hoisting the equal pay banner, that the women would not be meeting again for two weeks. It was the minimum period we needed to establish the necessary solidarity.

Our second perception was that once a strike lasts a couple of weeks, it begins to 'tick over' and the likelihood of a collapse is far less. People start to adjust in terms of income and of organising their domestic affairs: they start to decorate their houses, or they go down to the seaside and find it's quite pleasant, by the second week, not having to go back to the monotony of the factory . . .

SM Especially in June!

HF . . . in June, when the sun's shining and you're not starving and you've got a roof over your head. It's not a bad alternative — once you can escape the hold that work has on you. Once you break that routine of getting up at 6.30 in the morning and of feeling guilty if you're not at work when the sun's shining . . . Now, it takes a week or two to overcome the work ethic that's inculcated into us as part of the socialisation process.

The third perception was that we needed time to activate a relatively slow and cumbersome trade union machine, to gather support and get the dispute considered. Two weeks is a relatively short time to get a dispute onto the agenda at Union Executive level.

And fourth, since this dispute had obvious social and political ramifications, we needed one or two weeks to marshal the political support that was available. After all, it was about equal pay and women's rights were already a popular liberal cause. Perhaps that's the second unique ingredient in this particular dispute: that we had this segment of political support readily available, both inside and outside Parliament . . . So we needed two weeks' breathing space, without having to look over our shoulders, worrying about the possibility of a collapse. These were our initial considerations.

SM I like your phrase about the strike 'ticking over'. Just right for the motor industry! As for the two weeks' breathing space, I'd say that a short strike in a mass production industry may not cause that much economic damage, provided you've got sufficient buffer stocks. In Ford, it's possible for the Foundry, for example, to shut down for a month, I guess, without affecting the final assembly lines. Conversely, a strike in the Body or Assembly Plant causes immediate loss of saleable units, which may never be recovered, even with overtime working . . . That leads me to ask whether you considered extending the strike by sympathetic action to other workers besides the Sewing Machinists at Halewood or Southampton — for example, to men on the assembly lines.

HF We felt at the time that what we required, first of all, was union support from the AEF and possibly one other union.

SM Why the AEF? Surely the women needed the support of their own Union Executive, the NUVB?

HF No. We felt it should be the AEF because the new leadership — Birch and Scanlon — would not want to be seen to refuse us support on an issue of principle, namely equal pay. We felt that once a major union had supported us on that principle, then the NUVB could be persuaded to follow. Lil O'Callaghan, the leading NUVB steward, had quite a forceful personality and could bring considerable pressure to bear on Fred Blake and on Charlie Gallagher — including the threat of mass desertion — especially since the NUVB was already facing bankruptcy. Next, we wanted political support, which we've already discussed. As for plant-level support, we considered only Halewood to be worthwhile. But there was a very strong opinion amongst the strike leadership that to increase the numbers involved in the dispute would undermine the strike. Since they had nothing to gain from the Sewing Machinists' grievance, they would soon find some reason for wanting to return to work or to use the Procedure. So there was no inducement to increase the numbers on strike. Our efforts were concentrated on securing active union support, Halewood support, political support from outside. And on insulating the strikers from outside officials, like Young, Conway and Kealey, or from John Mills of the GMWU, who kept urging me to hold meetings to end the strike.

SM That's an important point: by introducing supporters, without an immediate interest in the outcome, you risk diluting the strength and cohesiveness of the strikers. So, in effect, in the early days of the strike, both management and strikers, for quite different reasons, were pursuing a common objective: to seal off the dispute?

HF That's right. One of the lessons we'd learned by 1968 was that you either have a *mass* strike, with everybody involved, or you have a *restricted* strike, in a key section, with nobody else involved. The worst situation is one in which other workers, who are not concerned with the issue, become involved, or, as a result of being laid off, feel entitled to a voice in determining what should happen next. So, you avoid that situation like the plague.

A second lesson we had learned was that, after a few weeks on strike, nobody wants to go back to work. That lesson was later confirmed in 1971, when Scanlon and Jones had to dragoon people to return to work. After six or eight weeks, people were really enjoying themselves — doing their gardens, going down to the seaside, finding other jobs, getting tax rebates, strike pay and social security benefits — and being none the worse for it. So they really appreciated the new lifestyle they were experiencing. I can honestly say that, at the mass meetings in 1968 and 1971, there was a genuine desire not to go back to work.

SM I think this is psychologically important: it's something which doesn't appear in the literature on strikes. Once a strike has passed a critical point — whatever that point may be — it has built up a certain momentum which keeps it going without any major refuelling. Once they've broken the rhythm of their work patterns, strikers begin to re-appraise their lives. They get up later in the morning, drink a second cup of coffee, read the newspaper, find that other people haven't gone to work either, and so on. They're concerned about the future, of course, but the world goes on. Life doesn't come to an end. In that situation a striker may well re-think his whole attitude to his life and his work for the first time in years because there's an enforced reason for doing so. Perhaps that's why management works all the harder to quench a strike in its earliest days, before it can take on a life of its own.

HF What other options were open to management in the early days of the strike?

SM Management is trained to think first in terms of Procedure: no strike should take place unless and until Procedure has been exhausted. Since the majority of British strikes are unconstitutional, your first thought is to get in touch with the appropriate District or National Official and say: Look, your people are behaving irresponsibly. Why can't we get them back to work and find out what it's all about? . . . Then comes the first problem: How do you get them back to work without talking out their grievance? To be realistic, you can't go on refusing to talk about the substantive issue so you arrange to meet in a pub or a corridor somewhere for 'talks about talks'.

In this particular dispute, management was faced with a unique set of circumstances: the women's union representative was Gallagher and, however charitably you express it, he was a weak and ineffectual

Official. But the women were led by a very experienced, articulate and aggressive Convener, working in close collusion with Birch, a totally unpredictable, libertarian socialist who was anti-procedure and anti-establishment, both Company and Union. That combination was virtually unbeatable from management's point of view. That's why Blakeman and Ramsey rushed to York to meet the Union Side of the NJNC. The strike was already beginning to bite and there was the imminent prospect of a major lay-off. In that situation, what were the options open to management? Well, it could say: To hell with the wage structure and the evaluation and the Two-Year Deal! Let's cut our losses and settle the issue by giving the women the Grade C rates they want . . . That would have been quite out of character for Ford and would have destroyed the wage structure. Or, it could have said: OK, we'll close down the Dagenham Estate and let the strikers sweat it out. But that's a weapon of last resort. Or, it could say: We'll try to break down the women's determination by issuing Press Statements and Employee Bulletins, insisting that the issue is about grading and not equal pay and so applying pressure on the women to submit their grievance through the Procedure. And, finally, of course, it could put the whole thing in the hands of the Secretary of State. The Company genuinely believed the NJNC was the appropriate body to settle this type of dispute. There had been two Courts of Inquiry in the previous decade and a third had to be avoided because it exposed the Company and the Unions as being unable jointly to manage their own affairs. It also risked putting the complex problems of Ford industrial relations into the hands of outsiders, who might leave them in a worse mess than they found them. But, after the abortive York meeting, Blakeman had to alert the Secretary of State because he realised the prospects of securing a return to work were slight. Nevertheless, he wrote urging Conway to convene the NJNC because that avenue had to be explored first. And, so far as the Company was concerned, the NJNC produced the right answer of a domestic inquiry – only to find that it couldn't be made to stick.

I suppose that was the first lesson of the strike for management: the days were gone when you could expect the membership automatically to accept an agreement reached at NJNC. Of course, there was a long tradition at Ford of defying the national leadership. But 1968 was the first year in which the rank and file successfully defied the combined strength of Ford management *and* Ford Unions – and that had many repercussions, as we shall see.

HF Well, I think it's more complicated than that. First of all, in 1968, the rank-and-file leadership saw the NJNC in terms of a set of two simple equations: (1) Company plus Union Officials *versus* rank-and-file leadership — you lose; (2) National Officials plus rank-and-file leadership *versus* the Company — you win. That's why the women went on to the New Ambassadors Hotel to lobby their Officials before the NJNC: there must be no collusion with the Company.

But there was an additional factor, not present on previous occasions: two Unions had already declared the strike official before the NJNC took place. We argued that the strike could only be called off by the Executive Committees of those Unions. They were constitutionally responsible for conducting the strike and for securing a solution. We spelled out for Gallagher before the meetings that day[1] that the only course open to his Union was to convene the lay Executive to decide whether any NJNC formula should be complied with. It still needed Rosie Boland to go on television that night to make clear that the women didn't accept the NJNC formula. And nobody was going to tell Fred Blake, who was conducting an official dispute on behalf of the NUVB, to terminate the strike, except his own Executive. He regarded the NJNC decision as a blatant interference with his Union's right and his Union's constitution. So much so that he redoubled his efforts and his determination to keep the strike going. He told me he got up extra early the following morning to make sure he was the first one outside the Ford gates with a banner, telling anyone who turned up for work that, as their Union Official, he was instructing them not to go in. Similarly with Jack Mitchell: he contacted Birch at his home that evening and confirmed that the AEF would dissociate itself from the NJNC decision.

So, it was a combination of these two factors: the machinery of the rank-and-file movement plus the constitutional autonomy of the Unions which frustrated the NJNC. This brings me to another important point: although the fragmentation of the British trade union movement may sometimes weaken its solidarity, it is also sometimes its strength. It can be used on occasions, like the Ford NJNC, to negate decisions made by a joint negotiating body over the heads of the membership.

SM Alright, Henry. I understand what you're saying. But there are aspects of that particular NJNC which can't be passed over so lightly. The NJNC was strictly concerned with the procedural question of finding a formula for a return to work. The merits of the women's claim were not mentioned. But the fact is, the Assistant General Secretary of one of the two principal Unions involved sat through the preliminary meeting of the Trade Union Side and then through the joint NJNC without saying a single word! Gallagher's silence – plus Birch's absence – meant that the two Unions most concerned said nothing. Looking back, I find it remarkable that Blakeman didn't require Gallagher to commit his Union publicly to the NJNC Inquiry. Perhaps he already knew Gallagher would refuse. Young, as Chairman of the Trade Union Side, was a constitutionalist who favoured the idea of an NJNC Inquiry. Conway was the General Secretary of the AEF but, as an office holder of the NJNC, he couldn't commit his Union. As for Gallagher, he just couldn't handle the situation: the dispute became a personal tragedy for him at that point and it eventually destroyed him. As the dispute went on, his public humiliation was seen to contribute to the disintegration of his personality and his self-respect.

HF Yes, I think that's a correct analysis of Gallagher's personality and puts the dispute in its correct setting. But, just as a multiplicity of unions is sometimes a source of strength, so, at times, a silent non-effective National Official may hand over the power of decision making to the rank-and-file leadership. We were assisted by not having to deal with a strong personality like Young or Kealey, each of whom would have wanted to assert his personality and determine the conduct of the issue. So, by an accident of history, Gallagher made the greatest *negative* contribution to the outcome of the dispute, which also marked his demise. Similarly, Birch happened to be elected to the AEF Executive less than 12 months before the dispute. So he had a vested interest in demonstrating his usefulness and virility.

SM What about his absence from the NJNC on 17 June? Did you regard it as a dereliction of duty?

HF Our view was that he should have been there, if only to assert that nobody outside the AEF could determine its policy. But I don't think Birch liked being isolated or involved in a personality clash with Mark Young.

SM How important did you regard the personalities on the management side?

HF I can honestly say we viewed them as being of secondary importance. Whether it was Blakeman or Ramsey or anybody else, we regarded them as functionaries of the Company who were simply trying to do their best, as professionals. For us, it was largely a conflict between capital and labour, a conflict of social formations. What mattered was not who represented management but the relationship of the forces brought to bear on the issue and whether we could build the intensity of the crisis to secure a favourable resolution. On lesser matters, like individual disciplinary cases, one particular Industrial Relations Manager might be more or less favourable than another, depending on how you saw that personality. But in a dispute of this dimension, the rank-and-file leadership felt the issue would be resolved by the magnitude of the forces involved.

SM I find that interesting. You seem to be saying that personality matters on the union side but not on the management side. Surely, in any formation as broad as management, there are bound to be factions and interest groups behind the facade of unity? At Ford, for example, there was the classic division between operational management, at the receiving end of the strike, concerned with its effect on schedule, cost and profit objectives, and Central IR Staff, concerned above all with the principles involved: the integrity of the grading structure, the allegation of discrimination, the effects on the Two-Year Agreement, and the need to re-establish respect for the Procedure Agreement. Are you saying that the trade union side never tried to exploit those divisions within the ranks of management? Management expects to find the trade union side divided on many issues, to a greater or lesser extent, and is always ready to exploit those divisions, as necessary. But you appear to see management as being homogeneous and united?

HF Yes, that's true. We saw all the significant decisions as having been made in Detroit or by somebody like Gillen or Batty. Blakeman or Ramsey might contribute to the formulation of policy; they might initiate policy. But, at the end of the day, they are instructed to carry out certain policies in terms of their function. They must do their best to operate a policy, even though they might themselves prefer a different policy. On the union side, where you have a rank-and-file movement like that at Ford, no one instructs anybody! Therefore, you have to pay more attention to personalities. There's an interplay between a number of fairly autonomous forces which cannot be instructed. They might listen; they might be influenced. But nobody can say: This is what we're going to do! . . . In that type of situation, you pay more attention to the way the separate entities interact in terms of personality. That inter-action is very often determined by personal likes and dislikes. You don't go out of your way to accommodate or support somebody who has 'done the dirt' on you six months or two years before. So these factors are much more important with independent and unpaid representatives than with paid functionaries, which is how the rank and file see the management side.

SM I think you exaggerate the differences. After all, if management negotiators are simply paid functionaries, where do you suppose the locus of power lies within Ford management? You surely didn't think that this dispute was being master-minded from Detroit? If day-to-day industrial relations were decided in Detroit, no dispute would ever be resolved!

HF Well, let's take this dispute as a case in point. As Conveners, we'd met Gillen and Batty face to face at Warley, when the Company was making some presentation on future prospects. We formed the view of Batty as someone who would be insensitive to the complexities and nuances of industrial relations. Similarly, we formed an impression of Gillen as a rather dapper, efficient guy, sent over by Ford US to show people in the British Company how it's really done: that it's management's right to manage; that the Unions should be kept in their place; that the existing Ford structures — wage structures, negotiating structures, management structures — were of prime importance . . . I'm not saying that with hindsight; that's how we assessed Gillen at the time . . . How did the Company assess us? Did it seek to court and accommodate particular Trade Union Officials or Shop Stewards?

SM That's a fascinating question! There was no policy, of course, but taking a broad view, I'd say that Mark Young was respected and even admired. Blakeman got on well with Young, who was intelligent and professional and good at thinking on his feet. But it was his integrity which recommended him to the Company. We saw him as a man in the mould of Les Cannon — the sort of Official the Company liked to deal with, especially one who'd turned his back on the Communist Party. So, yes, Blakeman certainly courted him.

Kealey was very acceptable because he, too, was a man whom Blakeman trusted. I recall the final stages of a major wage negotiation in the early 1960s when Blakeman told Kealey that the Company's final offer was twopence halfpenny an hour. Right, said Kealey, if you're telling me that's your final offer, Leslie, I'll accept it . . . That's how they negotiated in those days. If the two Leslies agreed, the matter was settled because Blakeman knew he could rely on Kealey to get his TGWU members to accept any deal he had made. No nonsense about report-back meetings or shop-floor endorsement! In those days, the Ford Conveners used to wait for news of the negotiations in the pub across the street from the Company's Regent Street Offices. Later, the Company invited them to wait in the Import-Export Lounge — partly to stop them parading on the pavements outside with placards and partly to prevent Kealey from pushing off without telling them the outcome!

Conway was a man Blakeman cultivated by flattery. He was limited but politically useful because he commanded the agenda, the minutes, the convening of meetings and so on. So here again, Blakeman tried to accommodate him wherever he could. I think Birch baffled Blakeman. He knew he was not to be trusted but, in another sense, he was harmless because he was so open in his opposition to the Company. If Birch didn't agree with something he'd say so, and to hell with the consequences. Ramsey used to say that Birch was a villain — 'but a likeable villain'.

The greatest threat to Ford's industrial relations in 1968, as perceived by Blakeman and Ramsey, was the combination of shop-floor militants and the newly elected left-wing National and District Officials — like Scanlon and Birch, or Mitchell and Blake, both of whom had worked for Ford and both of whom were known to be implacably opposed to the Company and ready to exploit any opportunity that came along to have a go at Ford.

As far as Conveners and Stewards were concerned, I think they were all courted to some extent because they could generally swing an issue one way or the other. I'm not surprised, for example, that Blakeman approached you directly at the Court of Inquiry to ask for your help in getting the women's overtime ban lifted. More specifically, the Company knew the Conveners in the Engine Plant and Thames Foundry were solid, middle-of-the-road, Labour Party men who could be relied on to adopt an accommodative attitude towards management. The fact that they were sometimes Irish and Roman Catholic helped, too, because they were likely to be solidaristic enough to commit their membership. The Thames Foundry stewards were always more amenable. That was partly a function of batch technology and partly of management's greater willingness to turn a blind eye to minor infringements of the Agreement or the disciplinary rules. There was more scope for 'managing around' problems at the 'top of the road'. In the Body Plant, by contrast, the militant Briggs Stewards were engaged in continuous skirmishing with plant management. But, here again, technology was an important determining factor: on moving assembly lines there's less scope for compromise solutions. The tolerances for 'managing around' are much closer.

HF What about the Conveners and Stewards at Halewood compared with those at Dagenham?

SM Management in general regarded Halewood as a separate country — a place set apart from the rest of the Company. Blakeman came from Liverpool and was initially very sympathetic to the people at Halewood. When the plants were being built in the early sixties, management tried hard to exclude the Dagenham tradition of continuous conflict and to develop a new tradition of co-operation and high productivity. But once again, there was an historical bogey in the background: Ford had attempted to impose a differential wage structure during the construction period and that was the basis of a great deal of suspicion and antagonism at Halewood in the early days. Blakeman admitted publicly in May 1968 that this had been a disastrous policy on the Company's part. It created worse labour relations than at Dagenham. Halewood was seen as a different culture, with its 'cowboys' and 'woollybacks' living in tribal hostility on either side of the Mersey. The place was regarded as an 'underdeveloped area', a part of Britain left behind in the second industrial revolution. Management saw workers at Halewood as having lower material aspirations and a much higher leisure preference than those at Dagenham — labour turnover, absenteeism and indiscipline were all much worse — and, of course, they were fanatical in their tribal loyalties, whether it was to the Beatles, or City, or Everton, or a suspended Shop Steward . . .

Can we move on now to the climax of the dispute . . . You've said the strike leadership knew they had to build the intensity of the conflict. But this was a restricted strike amongst a small, tight-knit occupational group — well led, well disciplined, one hundred per cent united, biding their time. Suppose the Company had not convened the emergency NJNC but simply laid off more workers to bring more pressure to bear on the strikers. Presumably that would have produced exactly the situation you were trying to avoid? If you wanted to increase the strike's intensity, why didn't you stop the Company by pulling out more strategic groups?

HF Because a dispute of this kind is on the whole unpopular with the workforce, you'd have got an unsympathetic response. There's no question about that. The autonomy of plants, the craft divisions, the fragmentation of interest, would never — or very rarely — permit you to call on the membership to support a sectional claim . . . Certainly not when these women came out because, rightly or wrongly, the men considered they were only at work for pin money and should really have been at home in the kitchen . . .

SM That's the first time you've admitted that the strike was unpopular with the men! Are you saying there was no feeling of solidarity between men and women workers at Ford? Or that the men had their own grading grievances in the system and felt that the women were jumping the queue?

HF No. Even if the men had had no grievances of their own, you just couldn't get a sympathetic response from them. It was a totally unrealistic proposition, so you just didn't think about it. The second best thing to do was to make sure there were no alternative sources of supply to the Company and then insulate the strikers from any undermining influences. The sensible thing to do then was to dig in and wait. The Company wouldn't consider concessions until after a certain time interval. The key question in the motor industry is: What is the time interval? Different people had different ideas about when the Company would begin to reconsider its position.

SM You mean because of losses incurred by the intensity of capital investment?

HF Capital investment and loss of markets – particularly if you can't supply spares and cars are off the road. Orders for new cars will go elsewhere; brand loyalty will be eroded; dealership problems arise . . . So there comes a time when the Company has to consider: Does it make sense to compound the economic damage? Or is it better to make some concession and find a solution? There's always some point at which the Company is prepared to review its position. Applying that principle to this dispute, we had to bring about a situation in which the Company would look for some way of making proposals for a settlement. And we had to build the dispute to that crisis.

SM Let's turn to that crisis. On Tuesday 18 June, the day after the abortive NJNC, there were pickets outside the River Plant. It was clear that the women were not going back to work and that the NJNC Inquiry would not take place. The women at Halewood had come out in sympathy with their sisters at Dagenham and 5,000 men had been laid off . . . On that same day, the Company got in touch with the Department of Employment with the result that, on Wednesday 19 June, Barbara Castle announced her intention to set up a Court of Inquiry. That must have told you the dispute had reached a point of no return and that you now faced the familiar ritual of yet another Court of Inquiry. Did you then feel you had built up the crisis to the point at which the Company had broken?

HF To answer that, we must first go back to another unique feature of this dispute: the ingredient of social justice. By the time the Court of Inquiry was announced, sufficient political support had emerged from Parliament and the women's movement to risk the unfavourable publicity normally associated with a Court of Inquiry. That was a counterbalancing feature not normally present in industrial disputes.

Secondly, since the Company had failed with the NJNC, with Barbara Castle and the General Secretaries of the Unions, and with Batty's telegram to Harold Wilson and Wedgwood Benn – that indicated to us that the Company was about to capitulate or to make proposals for terminating the dispute. So we were very confident. That's why the women immediately decided to stay out for another week, which would take them beyond the Court of Inquiry commencement date.

SM In other words, you applied the lessons learned at previous Courts of Inquiry: No return to work, even if the Chairman of the Court goes down on bended knees. Get the Court's decision first and then decide whether to go back to work?

HF That's right. It was felt that this strategy was correct. It was a matter of administering another dose of the same medicine to get a favourable conclusion. Incidentally, Arthur Scargill subsequently copied this strategy and it has since become known as 'Scargill's Law'.

SM I'd like to pursue this point of conflict resolution a bit further. Let me ask you this: At what point did it become apparent to the strikers that management was actively formulating plans or seeking a concession formula for a return to work? You see, a strike leadership doesn't normally feel any obligation to find a formula for a return to work, except having its claim met in full. But *somebody* has to find that formula – whether it's the NJNC or the Company or ACAS. The simplest formula, of course, is for the Company to concede the claim in full. More realistically, the problem is how to end the strike – though not necessarily the dispute – by getting the parties off their respective hooks. For management, that means without conceding the claim as presented in full. The need to preserve face and guard against the long-term consequences means that what you appear to concede is as important as what you in fact concede. Management may have to offer more than was first demanded. But it must not be seen to be making concessions in certain ways, through the wrong channels. Having failed to find a solution at York, at the NJNC, at Weymouth and at St James's Square, management had to find some way of getting the strikers, the Unions and itself off the hook. The Company could not allow the women to be seen to have won their up-grading claim through pressure. So it devised this two-tier solution: Use the NJNC to legitimate the re-opening of the Two-Year Agreement and the reduction in differentials as the first step towards equal pay. Use the Court of Inquiry to deal with the alleged discrimination and the grading claim . . . How did you feel about the formula at the time? Didn't you think it offered an elegant solution?

HF Well, the Company had often repeated that it couldn't give way on the grading. So it didn't require a master-mind to work out that, since the fight was about equal pay as well as grading, there was nothing to prevent the Company from making some concession under that heading. Therefore we said: OK. If the Company feels so strongly about grading, why not pay out under equal pay? And then carry on talking about grading.

SM Who said that? It certainly doesn't appear in your account of the dispute! Blakeman hinted to Birch at Weymouth, at the start of the third week of the dispute, that the Company was ready to make a move on differentials. But even then, Birch never picked it up!

HF Well, we certainly talked about it in our private conversations with Birch . . .

SM Maybe so. But nobody on the Union Side came to the Company and said: Look, why don't we get ourselves out of this mess by asking you to make a move on equal pay?

HF Because of the deep divisions on the Trade Union Side no formal suggestion was made, I agree, but eventually the Company proposed it.

SM That's right! Now, I'm asking you whether you acknowledge that, as strike solutions go, this two-tier formula was neat and effective, both in its logic and in the way it satisfied the stringent criteria at the time. You see, in your account of the dispute, you stress the solidarity of the strikers, their absolute belief in the rightness of their cause, all of which led to an inflexibility and an unwillingness to compromise. That's fine. But you say nothing about any sense of obligation on the strike leaders to find a compromise solution to the dispute. Management can't live in that world. It lives in a world of 'shabby compromises', as George Woodcock called them — a world of cutting your losses and managing around and of thinking up new ways around old and new problems. That's what management's about. Take this dispute, for example: there were four major constraints within which management had to devise an acceptable formula for a solution.

1. It could *not* compromise on the job-evaluated grading because that risked the disintegration of the whole of the new wage structure.
2. It could *not* reopen the Two-Year Agreement unilaterally without risking a major claim by the men for the restoration of their differentials.
3. It could *not* act outside the limits of incomes policy and needed the blessing of the First Secretary to any changes in the Agreement.
4. It could *not* drop the principles which guided its new industrial relations strategy, which included reasserting control by the NJNC as the joint body through which negotiated solutions must be found for all major industrial relations disputes.

The two-tier formula was designed to overcome these four constraints. And, although you may fault it in detail, I believe it was an imaginative formula for solving a complex and protracted dispute.

HF I believe you're making a virtue out of what was a necessity for the Company at the time, and are saying things with hindsight, because the Scamp Inquiry turned out the way it did! But what if it had gone in favour of the women?

SM We knew that Scamp was extremely annoyed with the Company. His Report chastised management for negotiating an important change in the wage structure, during the life of the Two-Year Agreement. But we were confident about the grading issues.

HF Of course, Scamp felt put out to some extent: the Court's work had been undermined by an Agreement which was reached even before the Court began to hear evidence! Scamp felt that if you go to the trouble of setting up a Court of Inquiry, you don't give part of the cake away before it starts. From our point of view, it looked like a good formula in the sense that the Company had already conceded more money than was thought possible when the strike began. The principle of equal pay had also been won from the Company because it said, in effect, you can have the balance of 8 per cent as soon as you want it.

SM What about the Inquiry itself? You say very little about it in your chapter on the dispute. Why is that?

HF Well, it was really an anti-climax. Although the Company had conceded equal pay, there was no certainty that the Court would find in its favour on grading. The Company might have hoped, on the basis of past experience, that it would win, but it might have gone wrong. So the women could have ended up not only with the golden egg but the goose as well! I recall my discussions with people on the Company Side at the time: they were really worried about the possible outcome. It was by no means considered certain that the Company would win the grading issue.

SM Oh, you're right! There was the gravest suspicion that Scamp might repeat his form of arbitration in the Paint Sprayers' dispute and again walk away from the problem. That's another reason why management tried to keep the two elements of the formula separate: the equal pay side to be handled by the NJNC and the grading side by the Court.

HF But, I repeat, it sounds an acceptable solution to management because of the outcome of the Inquiry: first, the Court refused to reach a decision on grading and shuffled off its responsibility to a Sub-Committee; second, it so happened that the decision of the Sub-Committee went in management's favour by the Chairman's casting vote.

But it might not have done. I remember members of management sitting there that day, biting their nails . . . There was a dread that it might go wrong and the women finish up in Grade C. Then the formula would have looked quite different and the Company would have been exposed to all sorts of criticism. If it *had* gone the other way − if the women had got Grade C as well as equal pay − would you still be saying the Company formula provided an elegant solution?

SM Certainly not! I'd criticise the Company for having misjudged the situation. As it was, the outcome completely vindicated the Company's position. If you ask me whether I had any doubts that the Court would throw out the allegation of sex discrimination, my answer is: No doubts whatsoever because there was no possible foundation for the allegation.

HF But leaving aside all conspiracy theories, I'm saying it was by no means certain the Company would win. The Court was expected to determine whether the women's grading was correct or not; but it gave the job to a Sub-Committee. And let me tell you, there was a great division of opinion on the Trade Union Side whether or not we should participate in its work. Even today, people are still critical of the fact that we did participate and so shared the responsibility for the outcome of the grading. I'm still blamed for it!

SM You mean that you should have washed your hands of it and taken no part?

HF That's right! The Sub-Committee would never have sat and the Machinists' grading would have been left in a kind of limbo, which they could have taken advantage of, as the opportunity presented itself. So, I disagree with your analysis of the formula.

SM I'm sorry but I misunderstood your point. I think you're perfectly right when you say that, when the Court was set up, nobody on the Company Side could have foreseen the outcome for certain. We did know that once a major dispute is turned over to outsiders or a government agency, anything may happen. I personally take a more charitable view of the Court's decision to recommend a Sub-Committee than you obviously do. Although the Court ducked its responsibilities, I think it highly unlikely that a decision by the Court would have been acceptable to both sides. The Court simply played for time by asking an experienced Sub-Committee to meet when the temperature had dropped somewhat.

Speaking of charity, Henry, I'd like to think that, after ten years, we can afford to take a more relaxed and open view of the dispute and acknowledge that, in a complex set of issues like those surrounding this dispute, mistakes were made by all parties. I freely admit, for my part, that I made a number of mistakes: I didn't investigate your original complaint carefully enough and failed to get to the heart of your grievance, namely that the Consultant had altered the job profile without your knowledge, so that you and I were arguing our respective cases from different profile evidence; I suppose I must also be taken to task for losing patience with you and chucking you out of the Profile Review Committee meeting, when you tried to pressurise us . . . As for my evidence in Court, which Lil O'Callaghan didn't like, I think I gave an authentic account of what took place and I would stand by it. I might use different words today but, in that unfamiliar situation, you do the best you can . . . You come through much more effectively in the transcript of evidence – but you were leading an attack whereas we were defending the status quo of the New Wage Structure . . . But I'd like to know what mistakes you think were made on your side. Had you known then what you know now, would you have played things differently?

HF The only thing I would change would be the composition of our side of the Sub-Committee. We should either not have had it at all, or only had it provided we got our own nominees representing the Trade Union Side. We wanted them to be members of our Divisional Review Committee but the Court ruled that they should not include people like myself who had been previously involved in the dispute. The worst solution was to have people on our side without the real knowledge or experience or capacity to cope with the situation.

SM I think you're doing the Court an injustice: it is simply said that members of the Sub-Committee should be people trained and experienced in the Ford evaluation, but not immediately involved in this particular dispute.

HF But the Sub-Committee *didn't* undertake an independent review: the record clearly shows how the two sides voted – three for management, three for the Unions – with the Chairman's casting vote deciding the issue for management.

SM Well, if you see it like that, then I understand why you regard the two-tier formula as a less sophisticated and elegant solution than I do!

HF It's not only that. I think the union side at the time – and perhaps still today – perceived solutions in more simplistic terms of victory and defeat. Suppose, for example, that somebody is sacked. No matter what you go through by way of appeals or tribunals, if at the end of the day he's reinstated, you've won; if he's not reinstated, you've lost. No matter how much compensation he gets for the loss of his job, you've lost. Similarly with this dispute – particularly against the background of the previous ten years – the Company tried to solve the problem at

NJNC and failed. It then raised the problem to the level of Scanlon, Jones, Batty, Gillen, Barbara Castle, Wedgwood Benn, Harold Wilson . . .

SM Only Her Majesty left out!

HF Only Her Majesty and the United Nations left out! We had telegrams from the United States; we'd been in all the newspapers; we'd been on television; we'd even been on Italian television. The dispute had reached those dimensions. Right? . . . Now, if somebody comes along in that context, when you've made a claim on behalf of 300 women, and offers you half as much again for three or four times that number of women; plus the promise of equal pay; and you've negotiated the settlement at rank-and-file level with the assistance of one or two Unions against the orchestrated disapproval of all the other Unions, of the Company and even of the government, because of incomes policy; and despite the kind of male cultural prejudice against women which prevailed at the time – if, in the face of all these odds, you've broken through, then everybody – even the people who were hostile and who are still hostile today – said clearly: *The Company was defeated.* It refused to concede on the grading issue but, in order to get out of that mess, it was forced to concede on another issue – equal pay. More money for more people plus the commitment to equal pay – a principle for which the Trade Unions had been working without success for over 100 years . . . The women came out on strike for three weeks and went back to work with more money than they originally came out for. In such circumstances, you don't look too closely to see whether the money is offered under the heading of grading, or equal pay, or dirty money or fatigue allowance or anything else . . . It's a rose by any other name! And on the Trade Union Side it's seen by friend and foe alike as an outright victory for the workers and an outright defeat for the Company. It's judged at that level, on those simple criteria, if you like.

SM All right. If you want to use military language, let's make an explicit analogy between industrial conflict and international conflict. Sovereign states rarely admit to defeats, as such: retreats become 'tactical withdrawals'; one's own losses are 'modest' whereas those inflicted on the enemy are 'crippling'. Each side claims to have made gains at the other's expense. It's all part of the psychological warfare, expressing the need of the parties to feel they have emerged from a conflict less damaged than they objectively are. We all try to preserve our own self-image, to bolster our own morale, to emerge from the conflict without too much humiliation. Right? Now let us turn back to the evaluation of this dispute. You see the outcome in terms of a zero sum game in which the Company was defeated and the strikers had an outright victory? OK.

I'm not underestimating the historic importance of the strike or its outcome for women in general. Of course, the women felt they had achieved more than they went on strike for. Who could blame them? But I'm inviting you to consider the outcome in terms of a positive sum game in which the gains of one party are not necessarily at the expense of the other. In fact, in this dispute, everybody gained something — either in material or psychological terms — though not necessarily of equal value: the women felt they had won against the Company and the rest of the Unions on the NJNC; the Company and the National Officials felt that the structure and prestige of the NJNC had been preserved; the Company felt it had avoided having to compromise the grading structure and the Two-Year Deal; the state felt it had successfully intervened by achieving a voluntary settlement through the Inquiry; women everywhere felt they had gained by the passage of the Equal Pay Act. And you and I feel we have gained, Henry, by analysing the dispute and writing this book!

HF That sounds fine until you look more closely at some of the factors you mention. I don't think the NJNC gained in strength or stature; the dispute exposed its weakness and led to its ultimate collapse. You may argue that it led to the eventual reconstitution of the NJNC along more realistic and progressive lines — and we'll be dealing with that in our following chapters. But, in terms of preserving what was there, the NJNC lost credibility. The 1 July meeting was a total humiliation and farce . . . The dispute was certainly a gain for the women's movement and the equal pay movement, as we'll show in a later chapter . . . The only losers, in fact, were the Sewing Machinists, who didn't win their C grading.

SM They didn't lose anything — they just didn't gain precisely what they set out to achieve. 'Losing' involves some cost to the party. It didn't take the women very long to recover what they'd lost in wages. So the women didn't 'lose' in material terms even if their pride was hurt by not achieving Grade C. As you say, they went back to work more than fully compensated in terms of victory over the Company.

HF That's right. What we're asking ourselves, with ten years' hindsight, is: Who won and who lost? The Company *certainly* lost. If one views the dispute in terms of a long enough time scale, then factors emerge like the increasing influence of the rank-and-file movement; the more democratic restructuring of the NJNC; the end of an era of company-union deals; and so on. The Company certainly would have preferred to continue the old tradition rather than come to terms with the new one. So, the Company clearly lost.

SM I'm afraid your assumption of a single preference on the Company Side doesn't do justice to the range of views which existed. For example, I was part of the Forward Planning Team that urged the Company to come to terms with the rank-and-file leadership. So I certainly didn't see the outcome in terms of a defeat for the Company. The women may seem to have won a 'victory' at the time but the Company's 'victory', ten years later, is that the grading structure is still intact and the women are still in Grade B. So the outcome can't be judged in simple terms of the victors and the vanquished on the day.

HF I acknowledge that the Company was successful in maintaining its position on that narrow front. I'm saying that you can't judge the outcome of the dispute in those simple terms. You have to look at what the dispute sparked off; the consequences that flowed from it — both within the Company and outside; the dimensions of those consequences in terms of the legislation they inspired; and so on. When we come to examine those consequences in social and political as well as economic terms, then I think we'll find that I'm right . . .

Note

1. Monday 17 June 1968. See Ch. 4, p. 153, above.

Part IV

INTERNAL CONSEQUENCES OF THE DISPUTE

6 A MANAGEMENT VIEW

No matter how long an industrial dispute may last, nobody can predict its outcome with certainty. But when most disputes end, each side will conduct its own private autopsy before deciding to bury the issue. Even with a major dispute, the repercussions may not have had time to fade away before they are overtaken by some fresh episode of conflict. The Sewing Machinists' dispute was different. It was the first major dispute to hit one of the national Ford companies after the establishment of Ford of Europe and the first to hit Ford of Britain following the successful negotiation of the Company's Two-Year Agreement in 1967. The origins, conduct and resolution of the dispute were without precedent in the history of Ford's industrial relations. But the decisive influence which the dispute and its outcome exerted on Ford management over the following decade is nevertheless remarkable.

The strike taught Ford management three vital lessons. First, it highlighted for the first time the acute vulnerability of Ford of Europe's integrated production system from a single source of national disruption. As a result, Study Groups were set up to review the level of intermediate stocks held at each of the critical links in the production chain and to re-assess the cost-benefit ratios of multiple sourcing as against the single sourcing of components bought outside the Company. Second, the strike demonstrated how easy it was for one small but strategically-placed group of workers successfully to breach a long-term collective agreement, no matter how carefully worded. If the potential economic benefits of such a long-term agreement were to be realised and made available in contract renewal bargaining, some new way had to be found of dissuading workers from taking unconstitutional action during the life of the agreement. Third, the strike clearly exposed the central weakness of multi-union bargaining at NJNC, as then constituted. It offered conclusive evidence of the lack of bargaining authority on the Trade Union Side of the NJNC as well as revealing the blatant opportunism and irresponsibility of two Unions, both of which had given official support to a strike on an issue which neither had raised at NJNC, let alone pursued to the exhaustion of Procedure. These were the matters to which Ford's Central Industrial Relations Staff turned their priority attention as soon as the dispute was over.

The Sewing Machinists themselves returned to work in exuberant spirits. Although their claim for higher grading had still to be decided by the Court of Inquiry Report, they had already gained a major psychological victory. By contrast, Ford management greeted the end of the strike with a mixture of relief and apprehension that the Scamp Report might still compromise the integrity of the New Wage Structure. Gillen and Blakeman were determined to defend the new structure against either internal or external attack. Having spent so much time, effort and money in re-establishing its payment system on a more equitable basis by joint participative evaluation and having succeeded in negotiating an agreed set of job gradings and differentials in a single, comprehensive agreement, Ford was bound to resist every attempt to undermine its foundations.

The publication of the Scamp Court of Inquiry Report in August brought immediate relief on that score but it also added to management's anxieties about the long-term future of the structure. The Scamp Report first identified the principal underlying causes of the dispute, then attributed responsibility for the dispute between the parties in roughly equal shares before finally leaving the resolution of the major issue at stake — in this case, the correct grading of the Sewing Machinists — to the parties themselves. The Report found that:

> this dispute is about the grading of the Sewing Machinists' job, not about equal pay . . . The AEF considered that the issue in dispute was equal pay, but they did not make a claim at any time during the dispute. The action in nevertheless giving official support to the strike was, in our view, a serious breach of their obligations under the agreed procedure. In our view it is open to question whether the Company's judgement was right in negotiating, concurrently with a return to work, an important change in the wage structure, which had been decided on nine months earlier on the basis that it should, save for exceptional circumstances, stand for two years . . .[1]

Having administered that balanced rebuke, the Report turned its attention to the allegation of sex discrimination by the Company:

> The Machinists think that in the job evaluation studies their 'job profile' was singled out for discriminatory treatment. We have considered their criticisms in detail and we are satisfied that nothing of this sort happened . . . We accept that the same set of weightings was applied to all profiles without discrimination . . . But full acceptance [of the grading] can only come with full knowledge [of the weight-

ings].

On the evidence given to us we are entirely satisfied that the
Machinists' present grading is not at variance with the job evaluation
results or the principles followed in grading other jobs. But the
Machinists feel that on five characteristics the markings on their job
profile are too low . . . The Machinists' job profile should therefore
be reviewed, like other disputed profiles, by persons experienced in
the methods used at Fords . . . The NJNC should consider whether
criticisms of its effectiveness are justified and if necessary improve
the arrangements.[2]

The Report's recommendation that the Company should now consider
with the Union the disclosure of the weightings applied to the job
evaluation factors was completely unacceptable to the Company.[3] A
large number of grading grievances still remained to be considered and
the outcome of the Sewing Machinists' strike had served only to increase
the dissatisfaction of two groups in particular, whose members now
threatened further severe disruption.

Under the old wage structure, time-served maintenance craftsmen
were all treated as one homogeneous group in Grade I and paid the same
rate for the job. Under the New Wage Structure, the majority of these
craftsmen – such as Fitters, Millwrights and Plumbers – found themselves in Grade D, alongside higher-graded production workers, and
separated from the new aristocracy of Grade E 'super-craftsmen' – such
as Experimental Mechanics and Experimental Electricians. Grade D
craftsmen bitterly opposed the grade distinction and stepped up the
pressure for upgrading. They not only refused to honour their 1967
productivity bargains, which promised more flexible working arrangements, but introduced new and more imaginative restrictions. Faced with
the threat of these damaging sanctions and the need to avoid a further
costly strike, the Company immediately devised a programme of
accelerated training, designed to increase the versatility of Grade D
craftsmen. A new set of job profiles was prepared to cover these
'amalgamated' jobs, taking into account a much wider range of duties
and a fresh commitment to regular interchangeability. A limited number
of these Grade D craftsmen succeeded in their claim for upgrading and
further immediate conflict was thereby averted.

The same scope for upgrading did not exist, however, for the very
much larger group of Grade B workers on moving assembly lines, who
were now expressing deep resentment at the outcome of the evaluation
which placed most of their jobs in the lowest grade but one – just above

the unskilled Labourer and the Toilet Janitor. Behind their grading grievance lay the long history of smouldering discontent which centres on the
degradation of work in the twentieth century and the subordination of
the worker to the machine. It is this subordination which makes the
track worker in the motor industry the most discontented and alienated
of all production workers: alienated from the end-product of his labour
by the fragmentation of the production process; alienated from his
fellow workers by the 'mechanical jungle' of large-scale production; and
alienated from his own nature by the mindless repetition of short-cycle
tasks which deny him the opportunity to realise even part of his full
human potentiality in his work.

Under the old wage structure, Ford's first line Supervisors were able
to placate potentially disruptive groups by the judicious distribution of
additional merit money. The New Wage Structure had not only done
away with merit money: it had introduced fresh sources of discontent
by breaking up many of the long-established groupings of production
workers. The most alienated workers in 'track jobs' emerged in Grade B.
When they learned that Grade D craftsmen had been upgraded to Grade
E, they immediately 'flooded' the Grading Grievance Procedure with
their own claims. Throughout the summer of 1968, Ford management
faced the daily threat of a walk-out by thousands of disaffected Grade B
production workers over their grading. In the event, what finally brought
matters to a head that summer was not the grading issue but repeated
lay-offs in the Dagenham Body and Assembly Plants.

1968 was probably the most critical year in Britain's post-war
industrial relations. The Donovan Commission, whose Report on the
subject was published during the second week of the Sewing Machinists'
strike, described the central defect in the British system of industrial
relations as 'the disorder in factory and workshop relations and pay
structures promoted by the conflict between the formal and informal
systems' of collective bargaining. Donovan's identification of 'two
systems of conflict' helped to explain the increase in unofficial and unconstitutional strikes, the overwhelming majority of which arose from –
and were settled within – the workshop and the factory. Despite this
decentralised bargaining, most companies had failed to develop comprehensive and well-ordered agreements. Many had no effective personnel
policy and perhaps no conception of one. They were content with the
informal system because it was familiar, comfortable and flexible. But
for Donovan such benefits were outweighed by the disadvantages: the
tendency of extreme decentralisation and self-government to degener-
ate into indecision and anarchy; the propensity to breed inefficiency;

and the reluctance to change.[4]

According to the Donovan Commission, the remedy for such disorder was not to be found in industry-wide agreements because the essential issues were domestic in character. What was needed was 'effective and orderly collective bargaining' and the basis for reform was to be sought in factory agreements or in company agreements for multi-plant companies. Responsibility for reform rested with the boards of companies since they alone were in a position to effect it. Having identified the key areas of policy requiring attention, the Donovan Commission again sought 'to impress upon the boards of companies and upon the public that the primary responsibility for the conduct of industrial relations within a concern, and for the framework of collective agreements within which those relations are conducted, lies with the board'.[5]

Ford's new industrial relations strategy, recommended by the Forward Planning Team in 1964, effectively anticipated the recommendations of the Donovan Report by some four years. That strategy aimed to turn the Company away from its exclusive reliance on National Officials in negotiating and enforcing collective agreements. It had persuaded the Company to invite Shop Stewards to play an active role in the job evaluation programme and productivity bargaining of 1966/67. Ford's resultant Two-Year Agreement had been widely cited as a model of successful voluntary industrial relations reform along participative lines.

As the industrial relations climate deteriorated during that long summer of industrial discontent, the new Secretary of State, Barbara Castle, had reason to be grateful to Ford for producing this pioneering model. Shortly after the Sewing Machinists resumed work, a major strike began at the Lucas-Girling Group, the principal supplier of brakes to the British motor industry. By the end of August, the strike had virtually halted the entire motor industry. The new Secretary of State was plagued by serious trouble on other fronts: Jack Scamp, 'Mrs Castle's troubleshooter', resigned as Chairman of the Motor Industry Joint Labour Council because of the loss of union support for its work. Furthermore, a national stoppage was threatened throughout the entire engineering industry for October, following the breakdown in negotiations over a comprehensive long-term agreement.

On 11 September, in an outspoken leading article on the motor industry, *The Times* noted that the summer of 1968 had witnessed

an upsurge of industrial action . . . as small, strategically-placed groups of workers take the opportunity to press the companies for pay increases, following up their claims with strikes. In a sense that is fair enough: strike action is, in the end, the only real weapon that organised labour has in its dealings with management . . . [But] the damage strikes cause . . . is so great that the management may well regard, and has often regarded, the price of paying them off as small in comparison . . . This promises to be a year perhaps as bad as 1965, when the Scamp Council was set up. It could be a year when super-human efforts are needed to hold the line against wildcat strikes by workers disillusioned by the government's policies which could snow-ball out of control.[6]

The main thrust of that leading article reinforced management thinking at Ford, whose experience certainly supported *The Times'* analysis. The Sewing Machinists were a 'strategically placed group' who had clearly demonstrated their capacity to disrupt Ford's highly integrated operations. And where the women had led, the men were not slow to follow. Between them, they had contributed to a very much worse year for Ford than 1965 had been, with three times as many work stoppages and almost six times as many man-hours lost.

This dramatic increase in lost man-hours at Ford was a reflection of the intensification of labour conflict in the motor industry, part of the spiralling increase in industrial disruption throughout the British economy in the sixties. In the absence of any announcement of the government's intentions on the implementation of the Donovan Commission's recommendations for the reform of industrial relations, Ford's Industrial Relations Staff began to prepare for the Company's first American-style 'contract renewal' negotiations in the autumn of 1968.

By October, it became clear that the Company would not be able to preserve the Two-Year Agreement until its intended expiry date in the following July. It had already rejected, in April, a claim for a general wage increase, based on the devaluation of the pound in the previous autumn and the subsequent rise in the cost of living. In August, the strength of shop-floor feeling was demonstrated in a one-day stoppage of work throughout the Company in protest against the growing disparity between Ford's wage rates and the new measured daywork rates being offered by Rootes-Chrysler as part of the price it was pre-pared to pay for replacing its long-decayed piecework payment system. Amongst the strongest supporters of the new movement for 'Pay Parity at Ford' were the Company's Body and Assembly Plant workers, whose aggravated grievances over grading and pay were now further reinforced by their frustration at being repeatedly laid off without pay as a result of supplier strikes.

Unlike those motor manufacturers who were members of the Engineering Employers' Federation, Ford had no Guaranteed Week Agreement with its workforce. In place of the 'hire and fire' policies adopted by other firms in the motor industry, to accommodate seasonal fluctuations in their demand for labour, Ford relied on the 'Continuity of employment' clauses of the Blue Book, which provided that the Company would do its best to maintain employment levels throughout the year in return for workers' co-operation in meeting requests for 'reasonable overtime'.[7] The arrangement had worked fairly well for 20 years. But, in 1968, the pattern of unofficial and unconstitutional strikes spread from the motor manufacturers' plants to those of their suppliers, causing widespread lay-offs. When the Ford Unions presented a claim at NJNC for some form of lay-off payment, the Company rejected the claim outright, saying that, whilst it sympathised with its employees, it refused to provide any form of income guarantee until the Company was itself protected against all forms of unconstitutional action.

It was in this context of national uncertainty over future legislation that Ford came forward at the end of 1968 with its own complex package of proposals for what amounted to a 'mutual security pact'. At the heart of the package was the concept of a comprehensive Income Security Plan. In addition to a general wage increase, it offered employees two-thirds of normal earnings during sickness or lay-offs, together with improved retirement pensions and more generous leave entitlements. In return, the Company wanted strict adherence to an improved Procedure Agreement which, for the first time, would incorporate stringent time limits at each stage of Procedure, to ensure the speedier processing of grievances as a further incentive to constitutional behaviour. In effect, therefore, any individual who took part in unconstitutional action would forfeit personal entitlement to the proposed income guarantees — a novel and controversial feature which was soon misrepresented as the introduction of 'penalty clauses' rather than the incentives for the observance of Procedure, as originally intended by Ford management. The argument which arose over Ford's penalty clauses became a focus for conflict over the following decade.

The Company's time-table for negotiating the Plan aimed at achieving a settlement by May 1969, to protect its advanced production plans for the new Capri, due to be launched that summer. After further lay-offs in December 1968, however, Shop Stewards increased the pressure on their National Officials for an early settlement and this may well have

resulted in the leakage of highly misleading information from the Joint
Working Panel, set up to examine the detailed working of the proposed
Plan. This leak purported to show the heavy price Ford would exact for
its offer of limited income guarantees. When the full details of the Plan
were released in January, Shop Stewards expressed fierce opposition —
but this was only to be expected, for the proposals were specifically designed to curb their power to instigate unconstitutional action. What the
Company had not anticipated was the simultaneous publication of the
government's White Paper, *In Place of Strife,* an ironic coincidence
which played directly into the hands of the Plan's opponents. Ford was
roundly attacked for introducing a 'Private Enterprise Industrial
Relations Act', as a forerunner to the White Paper's proposals.

Whilst it was certainly true that the two sets of proposals shared a
common concern to curb unofficial action, there were significant differences. In their evidence to Donovan, the Motor Industry Employers[8]
had favoured the legal enforceability of procedure agreements whereas
Ford's own proposals offered financial inducements to workers volun-
tarily to observe the provisions of the existing Procedure Agreement. In
this respect, Ford was again leading the way, for the White Paper pointed
out that the majority of collective agreements in Britain would be void
in law for uncertainty and were, therefore, unsuitable for legal enforcement, as urged by many employers. The government wanted to see the
urgent voluntary reform of such agreements and proposed the setting up
of a Commission on Industrial Relations to assist in that process. In the
meantime, legislation would be introduced which conferred on the
Secretary of State 'a discretionary power to secure a "conciliation pause"
in unconstitutional strikes' and

> to require the Union or Unions involved to hold a ballot on the
> question of strike action . . . where the Secretary of State believes
> that the proposed strike would involve a serious threat to the
> economy or public interest and there is doubt whether it commands
> the support of those concerned.

A new Industrial Board would also be set up, responsible for dealing with
union recognition, the conciliation pause, strike ballots and complaints
by individuals against unions, with 'the power to impose financial penalties on an employer, Union or individual striker as it found appropriate'.[9] In view of the widespread opposition which these proposals
aroused — and their direct relevance to Ford — it is not altogether surprising that the majority of Ford workers failed to note the distinction

between the two sets of proposals and demanded the outright rejection of both.

In February, following further negotiations on the Company's proposals, Ford increased its wage offer from 5 per cent to 8 per cent and agreed that the annual holiday bonus should be raised from £5 to £25, of which up to £20 was liable to be forfeited if an employee took part in unconstitutional action. In addition to offering further safeguards on the application of the 'penalty clauses', the Company offered full equal pay to its women workers, provided they accepted identical conditions of employment with men, including liability to shift work, as required by the Blue Book. In return, the Company sought to introduce a new clause, requiring the Unions to give 21 days' notice of official strike action.

Although the Ford Conveners continued to oppose the Plan in principle, calling for an all-out strike for 24 February, the Trade Union Side of the NJNC voted in favour of its acceptance by seven votes to five, with the AEF voting against and the TGWU abstaining. On 12 February, in accordance with normal practice, the Secretary of the Trade Union Side wrote to the Company, formally accepting the package for implementation on 1 March. On 16 February, however, the Conveners reaffirmed their strike call. Two days later, the Executive Council of the AEF rejected the Agreement and the TGWU Executive instructed its representative on the Ford NJNC, Les Kealey, to reverse his decision to stand by the majority vote in favour of acceptance. When he refused to do so, as a matter of principle, he was invited to resign from office or face dismissal. This squalid episode ended Kealey's union career and cleared the way for his successor, Moss Evans, to inherit the General Secretary' mantle.

Roughly half Ford's hourly-paid workforce reported for work on 24 February but, when the Company proposed a secret ballot on the acceptability of the new Agreement, this was rejected. The AEF went further by threatening that it would make the strike official unless (a) the wage offer was improved, and (b) the 'penalty clauses' were immediately dropped. Despite the AEF's position, the Trade Union Side as a whole again voted to accept the Agreement, this time by nine votes to six. The Company found itself locked in a bargaining stalemate, with the imminent prospect of the disintegration of the NJNC. It was in these unique circumstances that Ford decided to go to law to test the legal enforceability of the collective agreement, already accepted in writing and twice voted for by a majority of the Trade Union Side of the NJNC.[10]

The Company succeeded in securing an *ex parte* interlocutory injunction, restraining the AEF and the TGWU from furthering the strike. At the full hearing, Counsel for Ford made clear the Company's motives for undertaking the action:

> Ford did not want to conduct its industrial relations in the law courts, but the object was to secure respect for agreed negotiating machinery and agreement with the Unions that there should be no stoppage of work without agreed procedure being gone through. Ford also desired to keep faith with the majority of Trade Unionists who had accepted the package deal.

Despite the explicit nature of that statement, the Company's decision to go to law was widely attributed to pressure from Detroit. The Trade Unions were quick to point to Ford's action as an indication of 'the shape of things to come' if the legal penalties envisaged in the goverment's White Paper were put into effect. In fact, the decision was taken by Bill Batty, Managing Director of Ford of Britain, with the concurrence of the Chairman of Ford of Europe, Stanley Gillen. Blakeman's staff had properly advised them, following such eminent labour lawyers as Otto Kahn-Freund and K.W. (now Lord) Wedderburn, that collective agreements were regarded in British law as 'gentlemen's agreements', because of a lack of intention by the parties to enter a legally binding relationship. Batty and Gillen nevertheless took the view that collective labour agreements, like the commercial agreements with which they were more familiar, *ought* to be enforceable at law. Since the legal position had not been tested for some time, Gillen was persuaded by Counsel to seek a definitive ruling on the matter which might uphold the deadlocked Agreement.

Although the Company's main legal action failed — Mr Justice Lane could discover no intention by the parties to enter a legally binding agreement — Ford management felt its action was justified by the need to re-assert the authority of the NJNC as an effective and enduring bargaining institution. After the case, both sides were bound to acknowledge that the 'majority voting' constitution of the Trade Union Side no longer reflected the acceptability of NJNC Agreements on the shop floor. Of the 15 Unions with a seat on the NJNC, five Unions represented 96 per cent of Ford union membership, with the TGWU and the AEF having a majority between them. That position was subsequently changed by the adoption of proportional representation. The change required the closest degree of collaboration amongst the Unions themselves — a task to which Moss Evans and Reg Birch, who replaced Mark Young and Jim Conway as Chairman and Secretary of the Trade Union Side during the crisis, now turned their attention.

But the 1969 bargaining crisis was still not resolved. After an unsuccessful attempt at mediation by the new General Secretary Designate of the TUC, Victor Feather, the Secretary of State again intervened personally in the second major Ford dispute in less than a year. Her success in bringing together the three senior officials of the principal Unions involved — Jack Jones, Hugh Scanlon and Les Cannon, who spoke for the craft Unions — enabled the Company to put forward fresh proposals for ending the dispute. Individual penalties against unconstitutional strikers were replaced with collective penalties against *all* the workers employed in the plant concerned; the Company offered to guarantee a minimum holiday bonus of £15, leaving at risk only £20 of the Company's payment into the new combined Lay-Off and Holiday Bonus Fund; and the 21-day strike notice clause was withdrawn. Finally, as part of the agreed settlement, the Unions gave notice of their intention to pursue the question of parity of earnings with the Midlands motor industry, as soon as the 1969 Agreement had been finalised.

Following so hard on the heels of the Sewing Machinists' dispute, the 1969 contract renewal strike dealt a severe blow at the Company's new industrial relations strategy. Hard-liners of the old school urged the adoption of repressive measures against unconstitutional strikers: they should be warned, suspended and fired — as an indication of management's intention to re-assert its traditional right to manage its establishments. The Company's more liberally minded managers argued that Ford must come to terms with 'the challenge from below' and work with the newly-elected leaders of the Trade Union Side to develop a more business-like and trusting relationship. The preservation of the NJNC as an authoritative and joint union-management bargaining forum was regarded as the Company's top priority and Ford therefore welcomed the arrival of five Conveners onto the NJNC — a further indication of its recognition of the changed locus of power and of the need to reach agreements in future with the elected leaders of shop-floor opinion.

The 1969 strike also produced changes amongst the personalities who were to play key roles in the evolution of Ford's industrial relations over the following decade. The election of Moss Evans, as Chairman of the Trade Union Side of the NJNC, with a mandate on 'pay parity' at Ford, placed him in a dominant position within his Union and virtually ensured his succession to Jack Jones as General Secretary of the TGWU. Leslie Blakeman, who retired at the end of the dispute, was succeeded by Bob Ramsey, who immediately set about developing close personal ties with Moss Evans with the objective of producing a stronger and more dependable bargaining relationship between Ford and its Unions. Ramsey was fortunate in his first year as Director of Labour Relations. The lack of popular support for a further all-out strike during the contract renewal negotiations of 1970 gave Ramsey the opportunity to strengthen his reorganised team in Labour Relations Staff and to test the effectiveness of a new Labour Relations Committee, which he instituted and chaired. It was made up of senior executives who were required 'to consider and advise on significant operating matters which may affect labour relations, to review major labour relations programmes, and to advise on major issues of labour relations strategy'. For the first time, senior Operational Line and Central Staff Managers accepted collective responsibility for all key decisions affecting the Company's relationships with its hourly-paid workforce, a positive lesson derived from the experience of Forward Planning in 1964/5, and the Sewing Machinists' strike in 1968.

The Labour Relations Committee endorsed Ramsey's plan for handling the Unions' pay parity claim, which dominated the contract renewal negotiations in 1971 and which led to the first of Ford's two prolonged strikes in the seventies. In 1971, for the third time in four years, Ford was again the centre of a national industrial relations dispute – this time against the background of a new Conservative Government, under Edward Heath, elected – so he claimed – with a mandate to bring the Trade Unions under the control of the law. Once again, the Company's domestic industrial relations became entangled with national politics. Ford's resistance to the Unions' parity claim was widely interpreted on the shop floor as a denial of elementary justice. To the Company, it represented a principled refusal to follow the Midlands motor industry's pattern of inflationary settlements and uncontrolled labour costs which had already begun to threaten the future profitability of both Chrysler and British Leyland. Ford workers had been sheltered from that threat by the commercial strength of Ford in Europe. Their expectations of obtaining pay parity in 1971 had been raised by the closer links forged between National Officials and the shop floor. At the same time, the government's Industrial Relations Bill, already before Parliament, presented Ford workers with a powerful warning of the new powers which the government expected to possess in future for use against unconstitutional strikers.

The 'pay parity' claim of 1971 represented a radical departure in the formulation and presentation of contract renewal claims on behalf of the Trade Union Side at Ford. As part of his campaign to make Ford of Britain's industrial relations more 'business-like', Ramsey had encouraged Moss Evans and Reg Birch to present a clear and carefully documented claim, more in line with the American tradition of collective bargaining. To help him in this task, Evans called upon the combined resources of the TGWU's own Research Department and the special Trade Union Research Unit at Ruskin College, Oxford, and so produced a remarkably detailed and popularly acclaimed pamphlet, setting out the contract renewal claim in full — another 'first' for Ford in the evolution of a new style of bargaining in Britain. The Unions' pamphlet, comprising almost 50 pages of closely reasoned argument, culminated in the following Summary of the Case:

> No matter how well you argue, you will not be able to deny that your employees are paid less than those doing the same jobs at British Leyland and Chrysler in this country. Nor can you show that this underpayment does anything but contribute to the profits of the Company. You cannot disagree that this underpayment by Ford is damaging the rest of the motor industry. You cannot deny that Ford workers, when they have parity, will be just as secure (or insecure) as those employed by British Leyland and Chrysler. You have already agreed that Ford employees' productivity is higher than the rest of the motor industry . . . And whilst this is not your concern, you will understand our own desire as Trade Unionists to cease being the price-cutters on the British and European labour markets.[11]

In rejecting the claim, Ramsey argued that parity was not a policy — it was merely a slogan to justify a claim to put Ford's 50,000 workers on the highest hourly rate paid to a single small group of workers at British Leyland. But the average annual earnings at Leyland and Chrysler were less than those at Ford. It was true that Ford produced more per worker because it invested more in plant and equipment; but Ford was not highly profitable by the general standards of British industry: its return on net assets from 1965 to 1969 averaged 7.1 per cent. To concede the parity claim would add between £40 million and £60 million to Ford's annual labour costs. It was an invitation to commercial suicide.

When viewed in retrospect against the background of the highly successful 'Parity Campaign', the Company's rejection of the claim was almost bound to produce a major strike. There was little surprise amongst Ford management when the entire hourly-paid workforce stopped work on 29 January 1971. The Company responded by placing full-page advertisements in the national press, explaining why it was willing to face a long strike: the motor industry was already in difficulties and could not afford to pay 'ruinous rates'; Ford offered secure jobs with guaranteed income during lay-off; the Unions had claimed that productivity had gone up by 19 per cent between 1967 and 1969, but wage rates had gone up by 39 per cent between 1967 and 1970 . . . Ford's offer would put its workers at the 'top of the big league' of wage earners in Britain.

The 1971 dispute was eventually settled by the Company's success in again persuading Jack Jones and Hugh Scanlon, the senior officials of the two principal Unions involved, to intervene personally in the final negotiations and to recommend their members to accept the Company's revised wage offer in a secret ballot. The importance of this ballot cannot be exaggerated, for the Company not only aimed to prevent a recurrence of the 1969 bargaining stalemate but also sought to establish a new pattern of clear, popular endorsement of all future agreements reached at NJNC by the newly enlarged and restructured Trade Union Side. The Sewing Machinists' dispute in 1968 had exposed the dangerous rift which existed between the rank-and-file leadership and the National Trade Union Officials. The 1969 dispute had posed a serious threat to the NJNC itself. It was now a central objective of Company policy to heal that rift and so ensure that every major settlement would in future enjoy the fullest support of the shop floor.

The working-out of that policy is best seen in the series of fresh initiatives taken by Ford management in the seventies, resulting in a set of new collective agreements on a wide variety of subjects. Taken together, they have transformed the system of industrial relations at Ford. With each successive year, the scope of the bargaining agenda at NJNC has been widened to admit items formerly excluded from the bargaining table: the Ford Hourly-Paid Contributory Pension Fund; the Ford Sick Benefit Society; the compensation to be paid to workers severely injured at work; the training and re-training of workers; manning and work standards; health and safety provisions; the closed shop and 'check-off' arrangements; and so on. During this period, working parties were established and specialist Sub-Committees of the NJNC appointed to conduct a painstaking investigation into the most prevalent sources of employee discontent and to recommend ways of improving the operation of the Procedure Agreement.

One of the first deficiencies identified by management in the early seventies was the failure of the Company successfully to communicate its future plans, policies and intentions to all its employees, especially those on the shop floor. An intensive campaign was launched to improve the systematic downward flow of management information by means of Briefing Groups,[12] designed to ensure the existence of a regular drill for passing essential management messages through the hierarchy of managers, in a consistent format, with added local emphasis, down to the shop floor. The campaign was not intended to be anti-union or to circumvent established channels of consultation or negotiation: it was aimed, first, to overcome some of the most acute problems of communicating effectively across the interlocking units of a dispersed and internationally complex organisation; second, to increase the sensitivity of the Company's managers on the need for better communication as part of a more participative style of management; and third, to help restore the Plant Manager as a focus of employee loyalty and a credible source of local decision making. For over 20 years, Ford had operated a strongly unified and centrally controlled organisation structure, with the power of policy making concentrated at the centre and closely prescribed limits on the autonomy of local line management. In the early seventies, that traditional policy and structure began to change with important beneficial results in the field of industrial relations.

Despite its unprecedented length and cost, the 1971 strike did not produce the same fundamental changes as the 1969 dispute. The settlement terms comprised a further two-year contract, again designed to stabilise labour costs, which allowed the Company to ride out the storm over the Heath Government's Industrial Relations Act, introduced in 1971. Although Ford workers played a conspicuous role in opposing first the Bill and then the Act, there were no industrial incidents at Ford plants which brought the Company into conflict with its workpeople on this issue. After its unhappy excursion into British labour law in 1969, Ford management took special care to keep itself clear of the National Industrial Relations Court, encouraging its managers to do everything possible to find domestic solutions to domestic problems.

To bring home to its workforce the extent and cost of domestic disruption, the Company dropped its former policy of giving high visibility to the number of separate strikes, overtime bans and working hours lost through industrial action. It concentrated attention instead on the more immediately intelligible index of strike losses, expressed as a percentage of the potential output of its manufacturing plants. In 1971, for example, Ford of Britain estimated its strike losses as equivalent to 21.8 per cent of its total capacity of built-up units, most of which was attributable to internal disputes. In 1972, by contrast, Ford made much better use of its productive resources with only 4.5 per cent of productive capacity lost through strikes, an outcome which may reflect the unwillingness of either unions or management to engage in a major dispute in a year of widespread apprehension over the working of the 1971 Industrial Relations Act.

Bob Ramsey, who was appointed Director of Industrial Relations, Ford of Britain, in 1973, set himself the objective of finding fresh ways to keep Ford's strike losses below 5 per cent in the future. By 1973, however, strike losses were back to almost 20 per cent with a marked increase in disputes over work standards, manning levels, working conditions and disciplinary offences. To underline his determination to deal with these problems, Ramsey convened a conference of the Company's senior Industrial Relations Managers in September 1973 at which he spelled out his approach to the future. The Trade Unions, in his view, were as well disposed to the Company as they were ever likely to be and Ford must take advantage of this opportunity. The government had evidently made a disastrous start with its Industrial Relations Act but government intervention in industrial relations was here to stay and Ford management must learn to live with it. The Company had proved in 1972 that it could achieve a record level of output, sales and profit. The problem, therefore, was how to change direction in order to stay on top. It was clear to everybody that the Ford Procedure Agreement no longer worked and that labour could now ruin the Company. Nothing would be done by the wringing of hands. As Director of Industrial Relations, he was in the business of changing Ford's industrial relations — not by philosophical argument, but by taking practical steps after the careful use of planning.

Ramsey then invited Neil Duff, the American Vice-President, Industrial Relations, Ford of Europe, to address the Conference. A quiet-spoken lawyer, Duff began by quoting from an article by Arthur Koestler in which he had characterised the British as combining the qualities of the ostrich with those of the lion: they ignored every warning of danger yet were able to rise magnificently to any emergency. Duff hoped that Koestler was right. He confessed to having been shocked on his arrival in Britain and contrasted his own experience of industrial relations in Ford US with what he found here. In the US, where the Communist Party played no part in the labour movement, trade unions did not use the shop floor to achieve their political aims. In the US, men stayed at work whilst their representatives argued out the issues. In the whole of his six years in The Rouge, he had dealt with only one authorised strike and three wildcat strikes. In Britain, the preoccupation with unofficial strikes may well have blinded managers to the nature of the motor business. Success depended on four factors: (1) high volume production; (2) the maximum utilisation of installed capacity; (3) the quality of the products produced; and (4) the effective exercise of management control. In Duff's view, if British managers continued to operate as they had done in the past, there was nothing but disaster ahead. He ended his remarks by reference to his Scots ancestry and the Clyde shipyards where his grandfather had worked. He understood it was a good place to be — so long as there were ships to be built! Ford of Britain's future depended on its ability to manage change; to modernise and invest; to improve output and quality; to sustain timely production; to attract and retain good labour; to maintain employment and to share the benefit of good profits. Every Industrial Relations Manager had a positive contribution to make to those objectives. Like Ramsey, Duff acknowledged that workers' participation was here to stay. It was not all bad, either . . . The question was, at what point did management give away the keys to the plant?

Several managers took issue with Duff in the ensuing discussion. Differences in attitudes to work and authority relations in Britain and the US were not due simply to different institutions but to different cultural values and traditions which Duff would ignore at his peril. What suited Ford US might very well not suit Ford in Britain. What was needed were policies and practices which made sense and which worked in Britain. The pattern of industrial conflict in Ford of Britain reflected the values of British workers and the policies of Ford management. The only successful management in the foreseeable future for Britain was management by consent . . .

Ramsey concluded the discussion by admitting that the Company had probably been over-ambitious in the past by trying to negotiate an excessively complex package deal. The lessons of the past had to be learned and the mistakes corrected. He intended to invite the Unions and Shop Stewards to join with management in a careful investigation into the fundamental causes of disputes, plant by plant, as the first step towards working out jointly agreed solutions.

The evolution of Ford's industrial relations in the seventies may be traced through the influence of Ramsey's thinking on his senior Ford colleagues, beginning with his experience of negotiating the New Wage Structure Agreement in 1967, continuing through the major disputes of 1968, 1969 and 1971, and finding its clearest expression in the conclusion of a new set of Agreements in the second half of the decade. Ramsey's work, and that of his colleagues, furthered the implementation of Ford's new industrial relations strategy and so transformed the pattern of its industrial relations.

The four basic planks in the Company's policy for improving its industrial relations in the seventies were spelled out by Ramsey in his evidence to the Duffy Committee in March 1975:

1. to ensure that proper bargaining arrangements existed as a framework for constructive activity;
2. to update procedure for dealing with the principal causes of grievance during the contract;
3. to provide a vastly expanded Company information programme;
4. to analyse the basic causes of disputes through greater involvement of employees at plant level so that disputes could be avoided in the first place.

Elaborating this prescription, Ramsey contrasted the situation in Ford US, where relationships were of a 'highly predictable character', with that in Ford of Britain, where management faced 'perpetual chaos every day of the year'. According to Ramsey, the Company had finally turned its back on 'the Ford industrial creed' of paternalism and direct control by acknowledging that, in future, it must learn to manage by consent:

> We are trying to make sure that all the things we bargain, all the new procedures we set up are with the willing concurrence of our employees . . . We are absolutely convinced that the only solution to the problem is to get complete involvement . . . The besetting sin of British industrial relations is that it is firefighting. We are experts at improvisation; we never really make solid progress . . . What we are trying to do is step back a little and recognise that we will only make solid improvement if we devote resources to that improvement.[13]

When asked why it had taken the Company so long to identify 'this very real need', Ford's Managing Director, Terence Beckett, replied with disarming frankness:

> Over the years, a whole set of panaceas have been advanced on this, and we joined in the national feeling that such-and-such would solve the problem. But in the end we have come down to the basic situation that we, the Unions and our own workforce together have got to sort the thing out. Government will not do it for us and it was probably unreasonable to expect that they ever would. We have really got to sort the thing out for ourselves. Yes, we are late in the job, and if

we are to be criticised on it, then I make no apologies, we are to be criticised on it.[14]

In May 1975, shortly after the Duffy Committee's hearings, there came the first hard evidence of the Company's success in trying 'to sort the thing out'. From the time of the Cameron Inquiry in 1957, one of the most taxing problems facing the Company had been that of providing a legitimate and enduring role for Shop Stewards in bargaining at plant level without destroying the unity of Company-wide bargaining at NJNC. In 1969, the 1955 Procedure Agreement had been amended for the first time to incorporate time limits for dealing more expeditiously with grievances at each stage of Procedure. In 1975, it was further amended to provide a more effective role for Shop Stewards by requiring that, in future, most problems would be resolved at plant level, without the need to refer matters to NJNC for resolution. In effect, the new Procedure Agreement restored the authority of plant management by requiring the Procedure to be completed at plant level within ten working days from the date the grievance was first raised.

In a further attempt to reduce the risks of unconstitutional action, the new Agreement introduced for the first time in Clause 6(h) a status quo provision whereby:

> The Company agrees not to implement major alterations to conditions of employment of well-established work practices which have been disputed through this Procedure until either agreement has been reached or until the negotiating procedure has been exhausted and a further five working day period has elapsed, whichever is the sooner, subject to an overall maximum period of 15 working days from the date when the grievance was first raised.[15]

In return for this major concession by the Company, the Unions agreed to the introduction of a revised no-strike clause, as follows: 'There will be no industrial action of any kind whilst the issue in question is in Procedure and for a further five working days if the issue is unresolved and the Procedure has been exhausted at Stage 5(ii).'[16] If the matter remained unresolved following meetings at Stage 5(ii), Procedure was deemed to have been exhausted — and employees were free to take constitutional action — unless the matter involved any change to the Agreements.

Whilst these fundamental changes to the Procedure Agreement were being thrashed out by one Sub-Committee of the NJNC, another

Committee was engaged in an equally protracted series of discussions on work standards and efficiency — a subject on which the Company had long refused to engage in *quid pro quo* bargaining, except for its brief excursion into plant productivity bargaining in 1967. Immediately prior to signing the Two-Year Agreement in September 1967, the NJNC had agreed that 'the responsibility for increasing productivity rests primarily with management. However, productivity also depends on Employees working efficiently — which means full personal effort, based on the best use of employees' experience.'[17] Both sides of the NJNC pledged themselves 'to ensure that implementation of these plant productivity bargains shall be both real and effective'.

The limitations of 'real and effective' implementation became all too apparent in 1968. First, many employees became disillusioned when they discovered that those who had surrendered most in their plant productivity bargaining were not necessarily those who had gained most from the New Wage Structure. Second, dissatisfaction with the new job gradings had led to the erection of new job demarcations, some of which were more severe than those already surrendered. Third, as a leading commentator wrote at the time, the particular form of productivity bargaining favoured in the mid-sixties appeared to represent 'only a one-shot attack on inefficiency . . . Not only do workers save up pieces of inefficiency but they tend to raise the price in successive negotiations'.[18]

In the light of their experience of productivity bargaining in 1967, Ford management and Ford Unions had set their face against 'successive negotiations' on this subject. In the contract renewal negotiations of 1969, the Company carefully avoided any suggestion of a further round of productivity bargaining. Not only were the 1967 bargaining gains less than fully implemented: they also carried the risk of serving as a precedent for further productivity bargaining on a *quid pro quo* basis. Instead, the Company produced a Productivity Enabling Agreement which reaffirmed the earlier plant productivity bargains and focused attention on the perennial problem of how to sustain efficiency and increase productivity every day of the year in a highly competitive and constantly changing industry. The solution to this problem lay in the recognition of four basic principles, which Ford spelled out under these headings:

1. *Continuity of production and employment* — which stressed their interdependence and the need to avoid 'any action or situation that interrupts the continuity of supply and production'.
2. *Operating flexibility* — which highlighted the frequent and sometimes unpredictable fluctuations in customer demand which required flex-

ibility in working arrangements.
3. *Efficient utilisation* — which was concerned with making the fullest use of all available resources.
4. *Continuous improvement* — which linked higher real wages and fringe benefits with continued company prosperity.[19]

These productivity principles attracted fierce employee resistance during the 1969 strike and contract renewal negotiations because they were construed by employees as conferring on the Company the right to impose whatever unilateral changes it saw fit in order to achieve improved productivity. In fact, the Enabling Agreement laid down clear guidelines for implementing the 'policy of continuous improvement', requiring the Company 'to observe the normal consultative processes, including notification to the Joint Works Committee of any major change required'. But there was no question, in 1969, of a mutuality agreement on the achievement of efficiency of operations.

In the early seventies, as other British motor manufacturers became increasingly less competitive and their pre-tax profits began to fall drastically, Ford's 'policy of continuous improvement' began to pay off. In an attempt to justify their claim for wage parity in November 1970, the Ford Unions had produced what they called 'a simple statement of fact':

> On all key economic and financial indicators, Ford's is well out in front of the rest of the British car industry. It takes the lead in terms of efficiency and output per worker. It has secured remarkably high rates of profit even when it has not had its capacity as fully employed as it would have liked. It is undoubtedly in a very strong competitive position both in the home market and internationally, more so than any other British producer. In every single respect, Ford comes out on top with a performance above the other main British producers.[20]

In rejecting the parity claim, Ramsey drove home the point that Ford did not intend to follow the rest of the British motor industry down the road to economic ruin:

> The whole burden of your case is really that we should commit commercial suicide and place ourselves in the same position as our United Kingdom competitors . . . The right conclusion, of course, is that our competitors need the same level of efficiency and profitability from their plant and equipment as we have . . . You appeared to scold us for having a net added value £1,000 higher than the 1969 average for

the other British motor firms. But where does increased efficiency
come from? Fixed assets per man. And that is the key. Ford
employees can produce more as a result of the money that the
Company has put into its assets, that is, new machinery and plant.
That is the most important message of our whole case – the British
motor industry cannot improve its efficiency unless it builds new and
improved plants and buys new equipment. The important comparison
of performance is with the financially viable European vehicle manufacturers, who are constantly improving their position.[21]

By 1974, Ford's policy of high investment, high productivity and controlled wages was fully vindicated. The 'oil shock' of 1973 was quickly
followed by the Heath Government's second confrontation with the
miners over incomes policy and the election of the minority Labour
Government in February 1974. With the restoration of free collective
bargaining in the months before the election of the majority Labour
Government in October 1974, and immediately before the implementation of Stage 1 of the Social Contract, Ford concluded a substantial wage
settlement of 17 per cent. During the course of these negotiations, the
Company underlined the serious threat posed by the growing importa-
tion of foreign cars and called upon the Trade Unions for assistance 'in
ensuring that all Employees covered by our Agreements provide full co-
operation towards achieving efficiency of operations in the Company's
locations'. In a *Joint Statement on Efficiency,* dated October 1974, the
Unions reaffirmed the provisions of the 1969 Productivity Enabling
Agreement and further acknowledged 'that Employees have a responsibility to use the appropriate grievance procedures to deal with problems
that arise in the Plants, and called upon Employees to observe their
obligations in this respect'.[22]

Throughout 1974 and 1975, Ford management and Ford Unions
watched the slow economic destruction of British Leyland and Chrysler,
as the managements of both companies continued to warn their
employees of the crippling cost of internal disruption which threatened
their financial future and their immediate cash flow. By the end of 1974,
British Leyland was virtually bankrupt, to be followed shortly by
Chrysler. On 6 December 1974, the Secretary of State for Industry,
Tony Wedgwood Benn, announced that the government intended to
seek Parliament's support for a guarantee of the working capital
required by British Leyland and that, 'in response to the Company's
request for support for its investment programme, the Government also
intend to introduce longer-term arrangements, including a measure of

public ownership'.[23] To help frame a scheme for this purpose, the government had appointed a high-level team, led by Sir Don Ryder, to advise on the Company's situation and prospects. Ironically, one of the members of that team was Stanley Gillen who, by this time, had retired from Ford and was spending his retirement years in Britain.

Two further high-powered investigations into the motor industry were also in progress during 1975. In the same month as the Ryder Committee was appointed, the Trade and Industry Sub-Committee of the House of Commons Expenditure Committee, under Patrick Duffy MP, decided to undertake its own inquiry into the motor vehicle industry.[24] Whilst the Duffy Committee was hearing oral evidence from well over 100 witnesses in the first half of 1975, the government commissioned a further investigation, this time by the Central Policy Review Staff, under Lord Rothschild, into the future of the British car industry.

The Rothschild Report, which was published first, drew particular attention to the causes of relatively low productivity in the British motor industry: 'While all British car manufacturers have significantly lower manpower productivity than continental manufacturers . . . Ford is the British Company nearest to continental levels of productivity.'[25]

According to the CPRS study, the underlying causes of poor labour productivity in the British industry were (1) overmanning; (2) poor resource utilisation; and (3) lack of capital investment. Although labour costs per hour were lower in Britain than on the Continent, labour costs per unit assembled were higher because they were more than offset by higher continental productivity. Capital investment by itself would not solve the British industry's competitive weakness:

> Even with the same capital equipment, plant layout and working procedures, it takes almost twice as many hours to assemble a car in the UK as it does to assemble the same or a very similar car on the continent . . . British plants regularly fail to achieve their work standards by wide margins, often as much as 80 per cent. The immediate cause of the poor delivery performance of the British industry is that there is no continuity of production. Internal and external labour disputes . . . are responsible for some two-thirds of lost production.[26]

The Rothschild Report concluded that there was not the slightest prospect of the British car industry becoming viable at any level of production so long as three factors remained: (1) constant interruptions of production; (2) reluctance to accept new methods of working and equipment; and (3) toleration of sub-standard quality. Labour productivity, in particular, would not improve unless there was a willingness to accept new manning levels and work practices. These conclusions[27] endorsed Ford's analysis and prescription – in some cases almost literally – and threw into sharper relief the Company's continued emphasis on reducing the levels of internal disruption and on raising the levels of productivity in Ford's British assembly plants nearer to those of its continental plants.

Meanwhile, the Duffy Committee had been hearing, amongst others, the views of Ford workers and Ford management on the same theme. Ford of Britain's Managing Director described the Company's performance against target over the years as disappointing. Compared with Ford of Germany and Ford US, both of which achieved a 20 per cent return on capital employed, before tax, Ford of Britain averaged only 11.2 per cent over the decade 1965-74. In its two best years (1972 and 1973) Ford of Britain got 18.3 per cent and 23 per cent – which showed that, if the Company could sustain a run of good years, it could do as well as Ford US and Ford of Germany did in their average years. The most important single cause of the discrepancy – the difference between the two good years and the average over the decade – was 'the substantial falldown in the full utilisation of our capacity' – and the prime reason, of course, had been 'industrial relations'.[28]

The evidence of the Ford Conveners to the Duffy Committee offers valuable insights into their own perceptions of the Company's policy of continuous improvement. Asked why the Ford worker in Britain was less productive than his German counterpart, the Conveners were quick to deny there was overmanning in Britain and pointed instead to the higher investment per head in modern equipment in Germany. But they were perfectly realistic about this:

You can pump money into any industry and it means nothing really . . . You have to have good management . . . At plant level, the people often do not know that a policy is being put across one day and is going to be changed the following day . . . There should be more power or authority at plant level for people to solve their own problems . . . I am not one to accept that the management are to blame all the time and that we are always right. I think it is in the nature of the way in which we conduct ourselves in the British industry. We take advantage of various situations and so do the management . . . With a management which picks the time to create disputes to their own advantage, it is small wonder that we reciprocate in a like manner . . . The status quo is the only effective way of overcoming this sort of situation ... [29]

Those remarks reflect something of the 'perpetual chaos every day of the year' which Ford's Director of Industrial Relations described in his own evidence. Ford's new industrial relations strategy was based on the recognition that the Company had been engaged for too long in an industrial war which it could no longer win by conventional means. Ford's success in imposing a very tight network of management control systems — not just in terms of financial control or quality control but also of labour control — had helped produce a situation in which Ford of Britain was no longer manageable by direct centralised control and corrective steps were urgently needed. Given Ford's rationalisation of its wage structure and the elimination of merit money, its controlled overtime and its lack of incentive payments, the refusal to negotiate on work standards or manning levels, a grievance procedure which took ten days to complete and a policy of continuous productivity improvement, more and more employees were resorting to direct action — walking off the job, working to rule, banning overtime, indulging in acts of physical violence or occasional vandalism, threatening to occupy factories and offices and even, on at least one occasion, holding a manager hostage in his own office — simply in order to release the pent-up frustration created by an over-centralised, over-managed and over-controlled environment. Almost every incident of direct action brought with it a train of costly unintended consequences: an initial refusal by one operator to carry out what management regarded as reasonable instructions might produce a suspension, followed by sympathetic action by workmates, or the consequential lay-off of hundreds, sometimes thousands, of other workers not remotely involved in the initial dispute. The attempt to send home workers laid off in the middle of the night shift simply served to extend the area of conflict and to produce solidarity action where none had previously existed.

It was against this background that Ramsey decided to accelerate the policy of devolving authority to plant management in the mid-seventies and to encourage a high level of employee participation in all major decisions affecting employees on the shop floor:

It is not just a few people sitting at the national table saying, 'This is the way we will do it in future'. We are absolutely convinced that the only solution to the problem is to get complete employee involvement. So when we make a two-year deal, that deal does not operate until all our employees have been involved in ratifying it. Similarly,

in trying to set up improved procedures, we have got very heavy
employee involvement in the sub-committees that are trying to work
these things out. We want to be sure before we install them that they
have the willing acceptance of our employees because, from the evidence we have, when we do have that, we have something that works.[30]

As a further example of the Company's more realistic approach to the
reform of its industrial relations, the first Work Standards Agreement
was negotiated and brought into effect in June 1975, concurrently with
the new Procedure Agreement. The prime objective of the new Agreement was to provide clearly understood stages of Procedure through
which any difficulties on work standards, manning levels and efficiency
can be progressed and resolved whilst continuity of production is maintained. Although there is no provision for the negotiation of work standards as such, the Agreement prescribes that they 'must be fair and equitable and shall reflect normal working conditions and the effort and
quality of work expected from average experienced Employees'. The
Trade Unions recognise the right of the Company to establish and implement work standards but there are substantial restrictions on management's freedom to implement unilateral changes. The Company under-
takes 'to ensure that no employee is required to work in excess of the
work standard' and there is provision that any grievance about such a
standard may be pursued through the agreed Procedure which must be
completed within ten days.[31]

The introduction of these two Agreements in 1975 was followed by
the addition of a Union Membership Clause to the Procedure Agreement, conferring exclusive bargaining rights on the NJNC Unions, with
provision for a 100 per cent post-entry closed shop and the collection
of Union dues by deduction from wages through the payroll. For years,
the Company had maintained the view that employees should be encouraged — but not required — to join and remain in active membership
of an appropriate signatory union. With the 1976 Agreement, the
Company finally acknowledged that it was in the joint interest of the
Company and the Unions to foster sound relationships and that, since
all employees were expected to uphold the Agreements and understand-
ings reached by the Unions on their behalf, they must maintain union
membership, as a condition of their employment.[32]

The existence of these three new Agreements was not, of course,
expected to transform the quality of the Company's industrial relations
overnight. But there is little doubt that their beneficial effects fell far
short of the Company's expectations. At a joint meeting with national

and lay representatives of both salaried and hourly-paid employees, in September 1975, the Company's Managing Director, Terence Beckett, invited all Ford employees to face the facts and recognise that 'if we are going to progress and provide secure employment we have got to do things differently from the way we have been doing them in recent years'.[33] He was convinced that Ford could make a success of the future. It had got the strategy to achieve economies of scale. It had got the future products planned. The one fatal flaw was profitability. In the ten years to 1974, Ford of Britain had earned a return of only 5.8 per cent on capital employed, after tax, compared with 9.7 per cent in Ford US and 10.7 per cent in Ford Germany. In 1974, Ford of Britain had made virtually a nil return.

According to Beckett, there were two main reasons for this lack of profitability. The first reason was strike losses:

Every day, everywhere in the world, people making cars get problems. It's the nature of the business. The difference is this: elsewhere they carry on making cars while they solve the problems. They talk, not walk . . . The problems get solved in the end by the same methods — discussion and compromise. We are letting our bread and butter, and the jam, go down the drain first.

The second reason was poor productivity — the fact that it took more men to build a car in Britain than in car plants overseas, even after allowing for differences in equipment and other factors which legitimately put extra time on the job in Britain. There was a need for properly planned and implemented maintenance schedules to avoid breakdowns, which were almost as serious as disputes in interrupting production. Beckett recognised that management had a job to do in maintaining continuity by ensuring that the spare parts were always available. But the Company did not always make the most efficient use of its manpower:

We have got to systematically reduce the labour off-standard. We must cut out out-dated restrictive practices. They might have seemed sensible in the thirties but they are strangling us now . . . We have got to get an acceptance of greater flexibility of people's skills and effort . . . We must get back and use the productive time we lose through late starts and early finishes to shifts and the minutes tacked on to tea breaks . . . And we must reduce the amount of time and effort wasted on repairing jobs that should have been done right first time.[34]

This theme of British management's preoccupation with trivial disputes and the need to cope with 'chaos every day of the year' continued to be stressed in Company statements and presentations to the Ford NJNC and to official Inquiries throughout the latter half of the seventies. The most eloquent expression of the Company's philosophy emerged from its written evidence to the Bullock Committee on Industrial Democracy in March 1976.[35] Unlike the improvised replies given to the Duffy Committee, this carefully considered and closely argued document provides the deepest insight into the thinking of the Company's Industrial Relations Director and that of his staff, whose collective views it enshrines.

In essence, Ford did not believe that the principle of participation in appropriate forms needed to be argued as a fundamental requirement of greater efficiency in that part of the community which created the nation's wealth. It existed and in some instances might need to be extended. Over the years, Ford had developed an extensive and largely effective (but not perfect) system of joint management/employee/union trialogue. The system had not been static but had changed as events had dictated. It was characterised by four crucial factors. First, it had been tailored specifically to the Company's particular needs and traditions. Second, the development of employee institutions had only effectively been accomplished through the medium of those very institutions. Third, there had been greater involvement of shop-floor employees, as distinct from full-time Trade Union Officials, who could not expect to have the same local knowledge or expertise as the Company's own employees. Nor could management and full-time trade union leadership make arrangements which bound employees without the proper consent – or at least acquiescence – of the majority of those employees. Fourth, since it was at the grass roots – on the shop floor and in the office – that constructive relationships were developed or lost, the Company did not see the development of some participative superstructure as being its prime need. The principal thrust was needed in-plant to achieve better understanding and information and the development of wider involvement in formulating a joint approach to matters of plant significance in non-grievance situations.

In concluding its evidence, Ford cited its experience of building up its employee institutions, brick by brick, to argue that the achievement of increased participation required a fundamental change of attitudes all round. These attitudes – of hostility and suspicion, of lack of confidence and trust – were not confined to 'management' and 'workpeople' but applied equally on occasions to sectional groups of management and sectional groups of workpeople, whether organised or not. Such attitudes would not be changed by any group vilifying or seeking to deny the legitimate interest or function of the other. No lasting improvement in relationships could be achieved through imposed participative machinery unless the groups concerned consented in the institutions involved and had confidence in what was happening. It was a mistake to believe that the managements of large companies took decisions without taking into account their social responsibilities or without recognising the power of employees to thwart their implementation should they so choose. With management's responsibility for the business went the rights to make all the necessary decisions. But managements could only exercise their management rights unilaterally if they were prepared to do so at their peril. Workpeople had gained increasing rights of their own. With those rights went a similar power for self-destruction. Therefore, if companies and their employees were to survive and prosper, all groups must have proper regard to the interests of others.

In its evidence to Bullock, Ford management was explicitly summarising the lessons learned through thirty post-war years of turbulent industrial relations. Nowhere else is there to be found so clear and candid an exposition of its new industrial relations strategy of mutual interdependence. There is no trace of the heavy paternalism so evident in the first post-war Agreements. Instead, there is a classic statement of democratic pluralism — the belated recognition of the legitimacy of conflicting interest groups, and the conflicting priorities and aspirations to be found amongst management, as well as workpeople. The assertion of management prerogative remains — but is specifically confined to those decisions which have to be made without delay or which it would be unfair or impracticable to expect employees and trade unions to share. In short, Ford sees the development of participative institutions which are based on a proper appreciation of the different roles of management and trade unions, both now and in the future.

Finally, it may be useful to refer briefly [36] to the nine-week contract renewal strike of October-November 1978 as a practical example of the application of Ford's strategy of mutual interdependence. It is an indicator of management-union relations at Ford, at a critical point in the Labour Government's campaign to bring inflation under control, after the virtual collapse of Stage 3 of the Social Contract. Launching the government's policy for Stage 4 in July 1978, Albert Booth, Secretary of State of Employment, announced a 5 per cent voluntary guideline for increases in earnings, with the possibility of further increases where these could be justified by a self-financing productivity scheme. Ford management had succeeded in not becoming entangled in such a scheme during Stage 3 – and, indeed, for over ten years had set its face against *quid pro quo* productivity bargaining of the 1967 variety, adhering to the more rational and fruitful 'policy of continuous improvement', introduced in 1969.[37] It was against this background of a voluntary incomes policy, with the threat of government sanctions in the background, as yet untried against any major company, that Ford received the Trade Union Side's 1979 Wage Claim in mid-summer, well ahead of the existing contract's expiry date of 31 October. It should be noted, however, that Ford had successfully encouraged the Unions to present their claims each year in plenty of time, in order to avoid, if at all possible, the risk of negotiating the complex clauses of a new settlement against a fast-approaching time deadline.

The claim itself was presented in a more sophisticated form than ever before: an unequivocally clear catalogue of 13 separate detailed demands, ranging from a minimum increase of £20 per week (i.e. 25 per cent) and a 35-hour week to be phased in over a period of three years, to more basic vacation entitlement, service-related holidays and sabbatical leave; time-and-one-third payment for holidays and an increased holiday bonus; one extra hour's pay per shift for moving-line workers; full pay during sickness for workers with 12 months' service; payment for lay-off due to internal strikes; retirement at age 60, with improved pensions and more union representation in running the pension scheme; improved shift pay; and finally, the need for an Information and Communications Agreement to ensure the provision of adequate information for collective bargaining purposes.

The detailed justification for each of these demands was set out in a set of Background Papers, closely analysing the relative pay and hours of Ford workers, compared with those in the rest of the motor industry and in manufacturing industry in general. In its concluding comments, the analysis noted that

> Ford workers have experienced a significant decline in the real value of their pay over the past four years . . . The claim for a £20 increase is designed to put a halt to this situation and restore living standards to the approximate level established in October 1974.[38]

At a meeting of the Ford NJNC on 21 September – one full month before the contract was due to expire – Ford's Employee Relations Director, Paul Roots, offered the Unions an increase of 5 per cent for all manual workers and invited the Unions to join in productivity talks, without prior commitment, to see whether a self-financing scheme could be devised which would be acceptable to both sides. No prior conditions were set out and no detailed proposals were tabled. On behalf of the Company, Roots told the Unions that Ford's offer was 'socially responsible' because, at a rough estimate, conceding the Unions' claim in full would add at least 60 per cent to the Company's labour costs and that was without the vast costs involved in the claim for shorter hours. He told union representatives that they might feel incomes policy constraints were something for the Company alone to worry about, but government sanctions would have a serious impact on employees:

> We would not be sitting here talking about how to create new jobs, but desperately seeking to preserve the ones we have . . . The Company's prime social responsibility is to maintain its commercial viability, exercise sound stewardship over its resources and pursue policies which have enabled Ford to add substantially to its labour-force in a period when the rest of the industry has been declaring redundancies and closing plants.[39]

On the 35-hour week claim, Roots said the Company could not accept the 'bland assumption' that a phased introduction of the shorter working week would not result in major problems. Overmanning was already a very serious problem in the Company, and some way of improving performance within the existing pattern of hours was needed. A reduction of hours, 'in one company, in one country, in isolation', would undermine its ability to remain competitive.

Ron Todd, National Organiser, TGWU and newly elected Chairman of the Trade Union Side of the NJNC, told Ford that the Unions wanted to negotiate through free collective bargaining in an unfettered spirit on the ability of the Company to meet the claim. So far as he was concerned, the bargaining had only just begun . . . but the Company's offer was followed by an immediate walk-out by workers at Dagenham, Halewood and Southampton. Within a couple of days, the whole of the Company was at a standstill – and its plants remained closed for a further nine weeks.

In its issue dated 30 September 1978, *The Spectator* carried a leading article which invited its readers to examine the Ford dispute as evidence of 'the present stranglehold the unions have on British society':

> Let us look at this week's strike at Ford, a paradigm of all that is wrong with British industry. Ford UK is, needless to say, a thoroughly

inefficient organisation. Productivity at Dagenham and Halewood is so far behind productivity at Ford's plants in the United States and Germany as to be out of sight. Absenteeism at Ford is far above the national average. In a rational world, no pay offer at all would be made, except on a basis of increased productivity, but it suits Ford's convenience to make an offer. It also suits the company's convenience to shelter behind the Government's pay 'guidelines', itself a deplorable example of government by decree and bullying. As it happens, it suits Mr. Callaghan to 'stand firm' — a relative expression in his case. So the strike continues. The strikers will collect their instant income tax rebates and apply for supplementary benefit for their families. It is an odd thing that the nation should thus subsidise strikes, and the next Conservative Government might consider at least ending the tax rebate. The strike, though, is not a cause for despair, even if a nervous stock market shudders with alarm. Car workers, as Mr. Callaghan and Mr. Ford both know, do not enjoy the public sympathy of miners. Moreover, unlike miners they are not actually necessary to the country. Just how little necessary they are can only be seen if Ford stands firm and the Government shows the resolution it displayed, less appropriately, during the firemen's strike.[40] The Ford workers are out: let them stay out.[41]

It seems doubtful whether many Ford workers subscribe to *The Spectator* — or many Ford managers, if it comes to that. Neither group would have accepted without protest the assertion that they were 'not actually necessary to the country'. But Ford's top management was evidently in no mood to incur the risk of government sanctions — worth some 25,000 vehicles a year to the Company — or to be blamed for having breached the government's anti-inflation dyke. Ford's Chairman and Managing Director, Sir Terence Beckett, was particularly scathing in his comments about the Unions' inability to control their members and the serious breach of faith involved in dishonouring the existing contract by not allowing negotiations to continue, at least until the expiry date. For all these reasons, the Company and the Unions dug themselves in for a full-scale economic war of attrition.

After nine weeks — during which virtually no negotiations took place — union representatives recommended workers to accept the Company's revised offer of 17 per cent, over three times the original offer — which at 9.75 per cent on basic rates alone amounted to almost double the government's guideline. But the most interesting feature of the proposed settlement was not the basic pay element but a new element of supplementary pay, worth up to £4 per week, and designed to improve over-all efficiency. In its 'Final Offer' to the NJNC on 31 October 1978, Ford abandoned its former decision to stand by the 5 per cent guideline and, in addition to the new 17 per cent offer, set out its proposals for an Attendance Payments Plan. Under the original Plan, each employee would be eligible for a weekly supplement provided he attended for work, was not late, and worked normally so as to receive wages for all the standard weekly hours of his particular shift system. He would also receive the supplement when absent from work for specified periods approved by the Company. But an employee would not receive the supplement in a week in which he had been:

1. involved in a strike or stoppage of work whether official or unofficial;
2. taken off pay either individually or as a member of a group;
3. suspended for disciplinary reasons;
4. laid off where this results directly or indirectly from disruptive action within any of the Company's plants or establishments;
5. absent without permission;
6. absent with permission, for example, on personal business or extended unpaid leave;
7. late on more than one occasion, or on one occasion in excess of five minutes;
8. disqualified from payment for a public holiday;
9. on annual vacation for which qualification by service has not been earned.

On 20 November — after a further thirty hours' bargaining — the Company agreed to remove what Ron Todd described as most of the 'obnoxious features' from the Attendance Payments Plan, which had meanwhile been converted into a Supplementary Payments Plan to reflect its changed content. Although the Unions represented this change as a major concession on the Company's part — sufficient to allow them to urge their members to return to work — in fact the Company had insisted upon and succeeded in retaining all the *collective* penalties contained in points (1) to (4) of the original Plan. In other words, after a nine-week strike Ford had not merely ignored the government's 5 per cent pay guideline but had restored to the Agreement the former 'penalty clauses' for unconstitutional behaviour, originally introduced in 1969 but dropped in 1974. It had also introduced individual penalties on employees for absence without permission (Point 5 above). Most important of all, by enduring the nine-week strike, at a cost of some 117,000 vehicles worth £450 million of sales, Ford had succeeded in ensuring:

1. that the Agreement would come into force from the work resumption date and would run for 12 months (i.e. Ford's traditionally pace-setting pay negotiations would be moved back a further month into the annual negotiating round in 1979 and succeeding years);
2. that the Agreement specified no increase in labour costs during the 12 months of the Agreement and no strike action to put pressure on negotiations for the 1979 Agreement.

In a Press Statement at the end of the strike, Sir Terence Beckett told the government and the public that in 1977:

> Ford of Britain lost almost five million man-hours because people were not doing their job. The main reason was unofficial disputes . . . We believe that the Supplementary Payments Plan is capable, to-gether with our overall programme for improved industrial relations, of making real advances possible . . . It can increase output, reduce labour off-standard which is caused by interruptions, cut back excess charges when we have to airfreight components, and dramatically lower a whole host of costs resulting from crisis actions to cope with stoppages of work . . . We have today said to the Government, and we want to say it to the country as a whole, that what we have nego-tiated in this wage settlement is not inflationary.[42]

At this point, the focus of the Ford dispute was removed from the industrial to the parliamentary arena, where the government tried but failed to win the support of the House of Commons for the proposed application of sanctions against Ford for breaking the 5 per cent volunt-ary guidelines. Within a few days, the Ford 17 per cent settlement was being cited as the precedent for similar wage claims by groups of work-ers right across the country. And, despite disclaimers to the contrary by Moss Evans and Ron Todd, the Ford settlement was generally held res-ponsible for the spate of industrial disputes throughout the long winter of 1978-79, leading to the vote of no confidence in the government's handling of the economy and its subsequent defeat in the General Election of May 1979.

At the end of the 1978 strike — and at the end of this review of the internal consequences of the Sewing Machinists' dispute — no serious student of British industrial relations could any longer doubt that 'Ford leads the way' — an aggressively expansionist, commercially successful, productivity-conscious, highly profitable Company, fully determined to manage its industrial conflict and to achieve high levels of industrial co-operation by means of more forward-looking, imaginative and re-sourceful planning. Above all, Ford has acknowledged that, in the future if not in the past, all successful management means management by con-sent.[43] The fact that the British trade union movement is not always able or ready — for reasons of history, or structure, or ideology, or the experience of dealing with Ford management and other managements in Britain over the years — to respond to such initiatives, will not deter Ford from its new industrial relations strategy of mutual interdepend-ence. As Sir Terence Beckett told guests at an American Chamber of Commerce luncheon in London on 16 January 1979:

> We are trying to overcome a century of suspicion, ignorance and mutual distrust and I guess it is going to take a lot more effort before we are going to be able to agree on the economic facts of life so that we can bargain and make progress in a more constructive and realistic fashion.[44]

Notes

1. *Report of a Court of Inquiry* (The Scamp Report) Cmnd. 3749 (HMSO, London, 1968), paras 181-2.

2. Ibid., paras 187-93.

3. Ibid., paras 124-6.

4. *Report of the Royal Commission on Trade Unions etc.* (The Donovan Report) Cmnd. 3268 (HMSO, London, 1968), paras 1018-19.

5. Ibid.

6. *The Times,* 11 September 1968.

7. See *Statement on Overtime Working,* agreed at NJNC, 20 April 1964: 'The Company and the Trade Unions have had long discussions during which it was jointly recognised that the motor industry is subject to extreme seasonal fluctua-tions in demand and overtime is the only way to achieve overall production requirements. The Company plans its manufacturing and assembly facilities on the basis of the best forecasts available, but the peak requirements have to be met by working overtime and this also helps to minimise short-time working during periods of low demand.'

8. Motor Industry Employers, *Evidence to Royal Commission on Trade Unions etc.* (1965).

9. *In Place of Strife,* Cmnd. 3888 (HMSO, London, 1969) paras 93-8.

10. See Ford Motor Co. Ltd. *v.* AEF and Others (1969)2 QB 303. Also Roy Lewis, 'The Legal Enforceability of Collective Agreements', *British Journal of Industrial Relations,* vol. VIII, no. 3 (November 1970). For a recent comprehen-sive and authoritative exposition of the legal position, see Roy Lewis, 'Collective Agreements: The Kahn-Freund Legacy', *Modern Law Review* (November 1979).

11. *Ford Unions' Wage Claim* (October 1970).

12. Introduced to Ford by John Garnett, Director of the Industrial Society.

13. *14th Report of the Expenditure Committee of the House of Commons* (HMSO, London, 1975). Minutes of Evidence, para. 921, p.249.

14. Ibid., para. 926, p. 250.

15. Procedure Agreement (25 July 1969, amended 1 July 1975), Clause 6(h).

16. Ibid., Clause 6(i).

17. Supplement to Agreement of 27 July 1967 (8 September 1967), para. 2.

18. R.B. McKersie, 'A Behavioural Analysis of Productivity Bargaining', lecture given at the London School of Economics and Political Science, March 1966.

19. Conditions of Employment Agreement (25 July 1969), Clause 9.

20. *Ford Unions' Wage Claim* (October 1970).

21. Ford NJNC, *Transcript Notes of Proceedings.*

22. *Joint Statement on Efficiency* (19 October 1974).

23. *Hansard,* 6 December 1974.

24. *14th Report of the Expenditure Committee.*

25. Central Policy Review Staff, *The Future of the British Car Industry* (HMSO London, 1975), para. 82.

26. Ibid., paras 96 and 117.

27. Ibid.

28. *14th Report of the Expenditure Committee,* paras 829-93, p. 244.

29. Ibid., paras 2891-941, pp. 180-95.

30. Ibid., para. 921, p. 249.

31. Work Standards Agreement (6 June 1975).

32. Procedure Agreement (25 July 1969, amended 1 July 1976), Clauses 2 and 3.

33. *Ford News,* Supplement to September 1975 edn.

34. Ibid.

35. Ford Motor Company Limited, *Written Evidence to the Committee of Inquiry on Industrial Democracy* (March 1976).

36. The dispute is discussed in greater detail in the Second Dialogue, Ch. 9, p. 318

37. Ford US bitterly opposed Beeson's 'productivity' bargaining back in 1963.

38. Ford Wage Claim 1978, *Background Paper Two: Real Pay at Ford,* p. 4.

39. Ford NJNC, *Verbatim Notes of Proceedings* (21 September 1978).

40. During the ten-week strike by local authority firemen in early 1978, the government brought in the armed forces rather than capitulate to the firemen's claim for a 30 per cent wage increase.

41. *The Spectator,* 30 September 1978. In the same issue, Nicholas Davenport wrote perceptively: 'The government has got itself in a fix by issuing a 5 per cent pay guide and then postponing the election. The only chance it had of getting the Trade Union movement to comply with 5 per cent is by making them feel that if they refused, they would have Mrs Thatcher at No. 10. All Mrs Thatcher has to do now is to proclaim against 5 per cent and any other pay guidelines and she is surely the winner of a spring election.'

42. *Ford News,* 1 December 1978.

43. In a separate statement, issued after his meeting with the government at the end of the nine-week strike, Sir Terence Beckett spoke of the Company's two objectives throughout the negotiations: 'First, we wanted to negotiate a deal which was uncomplicated and would be felt to be fair by our employees, because it is only possible to manage effectively by consent. That consent was achieved when our employees returned to work, having accepted the wage offer. Secondly, we sought, in return, as our contribution towards controlling inflation and improving the prosperity of the country, an agreement to improve productivity. It had to be real, not cosmetic.' (*Ford News,* 1 December 1978).

44. *Financial Times,* 17 January 1979.

A SHOP-FLOOR VIEW

The Rank-and-file Movement Regenerated

The absence of any notable success, since the defeats of 1957 and 1962, created a loss of morale and confidence amongst the Ford workers and their Shop Stewards. This inhibited their actions because morale, conviction, resolve, and ultimately achievement, to a very large degree depend on confidence derived from success. The Sewing Machinists' victory supplied this vital ingredient and caused a turning of the tide in the industrial power relationships at Ford.

But merely to claim that this happened and to leave it at that would not illustrate the causal effects and how the learning process evolves and is applied in the sphere of industrial conflict. In order to understand this learning process it is necessary to demonstrate in some detail what happens in practice. It may, therefore, be useful briefly to examine the events in the twelve-month period subsequent to the Sewing Machinists' dispute.

After the 1968 summer holidays, the National Conveners' Committee — a committee comprised of Conveners from each of the Ford UK plant locations — began to operate much more purposefully. Policies were devised to consolidate and accelerate the shift of power to the shop floor. For this purpose, existing rank-and-file structures were reinforced. For example, the National Delegate Conference was instituted — that is to say, Shop Stewards from all the Ford plants in the UK would meet together, usually at the TGWU Transport Hall at Coventry, at least once annually, and decide general policy, formulate demands and determine the rank order of priorities. Policies agreed at these delegate Conferences were binding on all plants, and the National Conveners' Committee was given the task to secure the implementation of decisions reached.

The momentum of these activities generated a new will and created new visions. For the first time serious attempts were made to establish contacts with the Conveners of all the various Ford plants in Europe, in order to forge meaningful and enduring links with all the Ford workers throughout Europe. However, the full-time Trade Union Officials, who viewed this development as a potential threat to their authority, were generally opposed to the establishment of a European Ford workers' rank-and-file organisation. The Trade Union Officials in Belgium and Germany were particularly hostile and refused point blank to assist with the calling of such a conference.

Notwithstanding these difficulties, and as a result of a British initiative, the first Ford European Conveners' Conference took place at Ostend in the spring of 1969. The Ford European Conveners' Conference has now become an annual event and established practice. Because the Ford Motor Company has opened up new plants at Bordeaux and Valencia these Conferences have increased in scope and significance, particularly since representatives from France and Spain now regularly participate in these meetings. Channels of communication for the regular exchange of information are being developed. Co-operation, including solidarity action, as well as the co-ordination of activities on a European scale, are the primary policy objectives.

But the immediate practical after-effects of the Sewing Machinists' dispute were experienced by the Company in relation to grading issues. Shop Stewards and Conveners started to press grading grievance claims for various sections of workers with much greater determination. Consequently, stoppages of work by Internal and External Vehicle Drivers, Crane Drivers and others in support of their claims became more frequent and extensive. The most widespread unrest, however, occurred amongst tradesmen such as Millwrights, Pipefitters, Welders and so forth, who were in Grade D and not in the top Grade E. Among these groups working-to-rule, go-slows and overtime bans became the norm.

In order to overcome this problem, the Company was forced to devise various schemes. For example, a number of tradesmen's job profiles were 'amalgamated' to accommodate these claims and to justify about 2,000 individuals being upgraded from Grade D to Grade E. The concessions agreed to by the workers as part of this 'amalgamation' deal looked impressive on paper, but had very little substance in fact. Work tasks which they already performed as a matter of daily routine, were written up and made to look like radical agreements on increased job flexibility and labour mobility. The purity of the wages structure which the Company had so vigorously defended only a few short weeks before, was now being 'bastardised' and distorted to a previously inconceivable degree.

Company Counter-strategy

The Company's counter-strategy to the ripple effect of the Sewing

Machinists' dispute emerged towards the end of the year. It was contained in a document which was presented to the NJNC in January 1969. The essence of the Company's proposals amounted to this: in return for a 5 per cent pay increase, plus a £25 holiday bonus linked to a so-called 'incomes security plan', the Company would be entitled to impose financial penalties on any individual worker who participated in any form of unconstitutional action. The 'incomes security plan' proposed the establishment of a lay-off fund providing pay for up to five days' lay-off per annum, and limited payments for absence due to sickness. The amount of the penalties would be equal to the £25 holiday bonus, plus a proportionate deduction from the lay-off fund.

Further, and this was not revealed until a month later, the document also contained a clause which obliged the Unions to give 21 days' notice of strike action to the Company, an arrangement which some trade union leaders, for example Jack Jones, described as 'handing power on a plate' to Ford.

The outline of these proposals was formally made known to the Joint Works Committees of all plants at a specially arranged conference at the Company's headquarters at Warley during the last week in January 1969. It was a slick presentation. Blakeman, on behalf of the Company, extolled all the virtues of the proposal, or rather the 'package' as it was referred to, but he did so in low key, and thereafter left the real selling exercise to Mark Young and other trade union leaders.

After the Company members had withdrawn from the conference room, heated exchanges ensued between the rank-and-file representatives and Young, as well as with some of the other Trade Union Officials present. There was a clear divergence of views. The Trade Union Officials concentrated on the instrumental features of the package. They seemed particularly fascinated by the 'incomes security plan' aspect and not at all bothered about the principle of penalty clauses. They argued that these financial penalties were meaningless because: 'Strictly speaking, none of you should ever be involved in unconstitutional action anyway.' Unmistakably, however, all the detailed criticisms and objections which the Conveners and other Joint Works Committee members voiced about the proposed package deal were overshadowed by the loud and insistent demand that no agreement should be signed unless prior approval of the members and the rank-and-file leadership had been obtained.

The manner and intensity with which this demand was articulated was directly attributable to the new mood and the new confidence which the Sewing Machinists' victory had inspired. Certainly, the Conveners most closely associated with this struggle felt that they now had the measure, both of the Company and of the National Trade Union Officials. Clearly, they were no longer prepared to have agreements foisted upon them without their prior consent.

Following this meeting, a National Conveners' Conference on the same afternoon formally rejected these proposals on three counts: 1) the pay offer was inadequate; 2) the 'income security plan' was a 'confidence trick', i.e. it meant, in fact, that, taking into account tax deductions, the majority of members would be worse off by comparison to the benefits they were currently receiving from the Ford Sick Benefit Society;[1] and 3) the imposition by the Ford Motor Company of financial penalties on workers for taking unconstitutional action could never be accepted in principle. The Conveners, therefore, decided to hold mass meetings at all plants and to recommend that the package be rejected outright. In fact, at all the mass meetings which were held during that particular week — from Dagenham to Halewood — the members, with hardly any dissent, voted against the proposed Agreement.

Further, Jack Jones, who had just become General Secretary of the TGWU, acted in line with his frequently proclaimed commitment to workshop democracy and arranged a delegate conference of his union members. This conference took place on 30 January 1969, and it instructed Les Kealey, the TGWU National Engineering Officer, and their representative on the Ford NJNC, to reject the Agreement. The Conference further instructed Kealey to have a report-back meeting before any amended agreement was signed.

Faced with this massive opposition, the Trade Union Side of the NJNC met on February and formally rejected the Company's proposals and instructed the members of their Sub-Committee (Working Panel), which had been involved in detailed discussions since October, to re-negotiate the package. This opposition, however, was more apparent than real, because these proposals dovetailed neatly with the government's own White Paper, *In Place of Strife*, which had been published two or three weeks previously. The central objective of the government's White Paper and the Ford Agreement was to curb rank-and-file activity and shop-floor power, and to punish all those who engaged in any form of 'unofficial' industrial action.

Blakeman, throughout this period, kept in close touch with Young and Conway, and also took some soundings from Conveners with whom he came in contact through attending meetings of the Ford Pension Fund Management Committee. In the course of these informal discussions, Blakeman conveyed a sense of urgency about the need for an early agreement. He repeatedly used the phrase 'I want to clinch the deal next week'. And he did so.

As a result of these soundings, the Company came to the conclusion that a 2.5 per cent improvement on the previous wage offer would be sufficient to persuade the majority of Trade Union Officials to accept the Agreement, including the imposition of penalties for unconstitutional action. This assumption proved correct because, when the Trade Union Officials met on 11 February, they voted 7-5 in favour of the package.

In order to minimise agitation and forestall a possible rank-and-file 'rebellion', the Company made arrangements for an immediate announcement of the Agreement, and the posting of notices signed by Young and Blakeman in all plants. A well-orchestrated and sustained publicity campaign in the national press accompanied the negotiations. The media praised the Agreement and hailed it as a 'milestone in British industrial relations'; for example, John Torode, the *Guardian*'s labour correspondent, described the package as 'a revolutionary pay and discipline deal',[2] and he categorised opposition to it as 'a threat by shop floor guerrillas'.[3] Government support was publicly expressed by the DEP when it stated that 'the 7.5 per cent increase will only be allowed *if some form of disciplinary clauses are maintained'*.[4]

Against this background an AEF Delegate Conference was convened at the Union's divisional office in London. The purpose was to pronounce on the Agreement. The delegates, one from each of the Ford UK plants, rejected the Agreement unanimously. The delegates further called upon the AEF Executive Council to support strike action against the Agreement as from Monday 24 February. Reg Birch, who presided over this meeting, received these resolutions sympathetically.

This decision reinforced and gave further impetus to the rank-and-file movement. A National Conveners' Conference was held on Sunday 16 February in London at the Great Northern Hotel. It unanimously adopted the AEF's Delegate Conference resolution, and issued a formal strike call for Monday 24 February, to all members in all plants. These two conference decisions clearly reflected the change of mood and the new will which had taken hold of the rank-and-file leadership. A decision to call a national strike against a national agreement at that point in time would have been inconceivable but for the recent example of the Sewing Machinists.

The 1969 'Penalty Clause' Strike

In response to the strike call, Mark Young declared publicly that he would 'not be a party to capitulation to the unofficial Shop Stewards' Movement'[5] and that 'as Chairman of the Trade Union Side, I expect the men to be at work on Monday'.[6]

The Company's response to this challenge was one of quiet confidence. They made no overtures to the Conveners for the strike to be called off. The Company was obviously very sure that it had the Agreement signed, sealed and delivered. Ford still had sufficient faith in the well-tried formula that Company and National Trade Union Officials could always, in the end, beat off and defeat any significant challenge by the rank-and-file movement. Furthermore, since on this occasion the issue was one of penalties, i.e. sanctions against unofficial strikers, it fitted in nicely with known government policies and the prevailing climate of public opinion. Thus an agreement, which enjoyed the Wilson Government's political support and the support of the majority of the national trade union leaders, encouraged some Personnel Officers to advise various Conveners — strictly off the record, of course — that the Company positively welcomed the Conveners' foolhardy decision to call a national strike because, in their view, the proposed action was doomed to failure. It would also expose the Conveners' lack of support, and firmly restore authority to the quarters where it rightfully belonged.

The moment of truth came on Monday. The response to the strike call was mixed. Halewood came out solid. Dagenham was half and half. The Conveners were particularly concerned about the weaknesses in the Body and Assembly Plants. The actual response did not measure up to the support which had been promised and confidently expected, particularly from these plants. Crisis point at Dagenham was reached on Monday afternoon, when the morale of the rank-and-file leadership reached its lowest ebb. Throughout the remainder of the UK plants the response was also 50-50. The radio and the newspapers reported 'the state of play' hourly, in a manner reminiscent of a general election. By doing so, the media clearly identified this as a struggle of national importance — a trial of strength — the outcome of which would have great significance on the nature and future shape of industrial relations in Britain.

By Monday evening, the situation had become critical. The next two days would see the strike either collapse or reinforced. At this point, the lessons learnt from the Sewing Machinists' dispute were put into practice, and the previous winning formula was re-applied. Jack Mitchell once again sent a special letter on Monday evening, requesting support from the AEF Executive Council.[7] Once again a delegation of Conveners went to the Peckham Road AEF Head Offices early on the following morning, and discussed the situation with various Executive Council members. The AEF Executive Council, greatly encouraged by the successful outcome of the Sewing Machinists' strike and still basking in the glow of congratulations and praise for their 'principled stand' in support of the equal pay struggle, gave Reg Birch plenary powers and a free hand 'to act in the best interest of the Union' on the issue of the penalty clauses.

Reg Birch relished operating in that kind of situation. Armed with plenary powers, he went to the NJNC meeting which had been arranged for later that day. During the first adjournment, after the meeting had been formally opened, he called Blakeman to one side and presented him with an ultimatum — renegotiate the Agreement, or face an official strike! Blakeman replied that he was only prepared to renegotiate the Agreement if the majority of the Trade Union Side requested such a course of action. When the meeting resumed, the National Trade Union Officials present voted 9-6 to uphold their previous decision, and to stand by the proposed Agreement. Les Kealey, in defiance of his Union's position, was amongst those who voted in favour of implementing the Agreement. Birch then left the meeting and announced to the press that an official strike against the Ford Motor Company had been declared and union instructions were dispatched to AEF members in all the plants to withdraw their labour forthwith.

Shortly afterwards, Mark Young, in his capacity as Chairman of the NJNC Trade Union Side, issued a countervailing Press Statement reconfirming the Agreement. He urged all trade union members to remain at work and called upon those out on strike to return to work.

On the following day, Jack Jones called a meeting of the General Purpose and Finance Committee of the TGWU. This committee has the task of looking after the Union's day-to-day affairs in between the quarterly meetings of the full Union Executive. Les Kealey was present and, after giving an account of the negotiations, he was instructed to renegotiate the Agreement. When he refused to do this on the grounds that he would never renege on any agreement he had personally supported at the NJNC, he was replaced by Moss Evans. Jack Jones then made a telephone call to Scanlon and thereafter the strike was declared official on behalf of the TGWU. Jack Jones subsequently explained Kealey's removal on two counts: 1) that the TGWU Executive was opposed to penalty clauses; and 2) that when official lay delegate conferences make decisions these cannot be ignored by any TGWU Official.[8]

The Company was stunned by this unexpected turn of events. Blakeman said he felt 'just like Alice in Wonderland . . . as confused and bewildered as any industrial relations man could be'.[9]

High Court Action Against the Unions

But on the following day, the Ford industrial relations strategists had sufficiently recovered to seek a writ in the High Court in order to prevent the Unions from going back on their Agreement, and the Company was granted an *ex parte* injunction by Justice Geoffrey Lane, which placed a restraint on the Unions as regards 'attempting to procure a variation in the Agreement or procuring an unconstitutional stoppage of work'. Simultaneously, the Company issued a Press Statement which said, 'If ever a Government needed to be impressed about the urgency of making Unions honour agreements and keeping their members under control, then the time is now'.[10]

The Company's legal ploy was in part a sign of desperation – an endeavour to prevent the existing structures from disintegrating – and in part an expression of the Company's firm belief that the introduction of labour laws were imminent. It was an attempt to establish a precedent in anticipation of parliamentary legislation.

The hearings themselves were complicated. Blakeman and Gillen (Chairman, Ford of Europe) as well as Scanlon and Jones, amongst others, were in Court listening attentively to learned Counsel's arguments. A moment of light relief was provided by the look of total incomprehension on Justice Lane's face when Jim Conway attempted to explain to him how it had come about that he had sent two letters on the same day to the Ford Motor Company, one in his capacity as Secretary of the Trade Union Side of the NJNC reaffirming the Agreement, and another in his capacity as General Secretary of the AEF repudiating the Agreement.

The Unions argued successfully that collective agreements were not legally binding and, therefore, not enforceable in law. But during the three-day hearing, Scanlon and Jones displayed signs of anxiety and they appeared apprehensive about the outcome. In informal discussions with Conveners about the possible verdict, and the consequences, they adopted positions ranging from that of potential martyrs languishing in gaol, to preaching the need for trade unions to obey the law on the grounds that on the whole the trade union movement required the law's protection as much, if not more, than most other institutions in society. Had the decision gone the other way, it is anybody's guess what might have happened.

After the conclusion of the Court hearings, the June 1968 events were, to some extent, re-enacted with an enlarged cast. Vic Feather, newly appointed General Secretary of the TUC, tried to mediate and failed. Thereafter, Batty again sent a telegram to Harold Wilson, who responded this time by making a speech in his Huyton constituency, saying the Halewood strikers were making 'a mockery of all our efforts to build up employment on Merseyside'.[11] The day after Wilson's speech, 13 March, with all Ford's UK plants at a complete standstill, Barbara Castle intervened.

Once again, she invited the three parties involved in the dispute to the Ministry in St James's Square. Scanlon and Jones represented the Unions which supported the strike, Les Cannon, the ETU President, represented the Unions which were opposed to the strike and in favour of the Agreement. Blakeman and Ramsey, as usual, were there for the Ford Motor Company. The rank and file were represented by the Conveners' Committee which liaised closely with Scanlon and Jones and in fact acted as a national strike committee. The outcome after three days of bargaining at the Ministry was a settlement whereby the penalty clauses were watered down to such an extent that in practice they became meaningless. Moss Evans, addressing a mass meeting at Dagenham, described the change of the penalty clauses in terms of 'the iron chain and balls intended to shackle the workers and prevent them from taking action have been replaced by balls of cotton wool'.[12]

Les Cannon had left the Communist Party after the 1956 events in Hungary. He became violently anti-party and led the campaign against the CP-dominated ETU leadership in the early 1960s – and secured its removal after a successful High Court action on ballot-rigging charges! By 1969, Cannon had come to the conclusion that Shop Stewards were a potential threat to union discipline because they could not be rigidly controlled. He therefore categorised the settlement 'as a tragedy' and saw the collapse of the Agreement as a missed opportunity because 'the Unions could have successfully asserted their authority over unauthorised calls for an unofficial strike by Shop Stewards'.[13] For Blakeman, the Sewing Machinists' strike, followed by this dispute, was a harrowing experience. At the peak of his career and just when he was about to retire, he saw his long-cherished policies in ruins and his reputation severely tarnished. No wonder he summarised the settlement in terms of 'the sooner this nightmare is over, the better'.[14] Work was resumed on

20 March, and on 22 March *The Economist,* under the headline 'Who's afraid of Jack Jones?', commented:

> The Ford strike has been settled on disastrous terms . . . the fact that the settlement was finally agreed in the DEP was a defeat for everybody except for the militant Ford Shop Stewards and their protectors like Jones, Birch and Scanlon . . . it was a defeat for the Ford Management's attempt to ensure continuity of production . . . it was a defeat for moderate Trade Union leaders, who wished to honour properly negotiated agreements . . . it reflects a decline in the calibre of Trade Union leaderships since 1945, and finally . . . *The Economist* has long argued that the cure for the cause and the symptoms is to put industrial relations on a firm and enforceable legal footing.

The foundations of the NJNC, rent apart by the Sewing Machinists' strike, were finally shattered during the course of this dispute. As a result, the NJNC structure collapsed. Mark Young resigned the Chairmanship of that Committee on 8 March, because he had been 'unhappy for some time about the way the trend was going'.[15] Jim Conway, after his schizophrenic performance in the High Court, soon followed suit and resigned as Secretary. Over the course of the next few months the Committee was reconstructed, and new rules and a new constitution were finally put into effect in September 1969. It gave numerical dominance to the AEF and the TGWU. Moss Evans became Chairman, and Reg Birch, Secretary. Moss Evans continued to act as Chairman until he became General Secretary of the TGWU in March 1978. In an interview with the author he readily acknowledged that his succession to Jack Jones was largely due to the prominence he achieved as Chairman of the Ford Trade Union Side. He was succeeded by Ron Todd, TGWU National Officer, who used to be Works Convener at the old Ford Walthamstow Plant, before becoming District Officer for Dagenham and subsequently Secretary for the TGWU No. 1 Region. Reg Birch remained Secretary of the NJNC Trade Union Side until he retired in June 1979. Another new feature of the Committee was that five Conveners were given places on the NJNC — on a committee which previously had objected to Conveners even being seen standing on pavements ('fouling up the pavement' was the expression used by some Company and Trade Union Officials) outside the NJNC's meeting places.

The 1969 settlement accelerated the growth of confidence and resolve within the rank-and-file movement. This impetus enabled it to take effective political and industrial action against the Tory Industrial

Relations Act, and its activities reached a new height during the 10 week 'parity' pay strike in 1971.

The 1971 strike was in a sense a delayed action response to the 1970 pay deal. This deal was accepted by the workforce against the advice of the rank-and-file leadership. Because of this split, growing doubts emerged about this settlement. Subsequently, there was a widespread feeling among the workers that perhaps they had settled too easily and sold themselves short. Therefore, when in 1971 the Company's initial pay offer was well below the level of the 1970 settlement, Halewood workers, followed by others, walked off the job spontaneously. It was the beginning of a ten-week strike. After the dispute had lasted eight weeks, the Company considered its position to be so serious that Henry Ford II flew in from the United States. He conferred with Ted Heath at Downing Street. His attention was drawn to the prospect of a significant improvement in industrial relations once the government's Industrial Relations Act had been put on the Statute Book. That apart, Henry Ford II received no tangible governmental assistance towards ending the dispute. After his meeting in Downing Street, he met some Conveners, who made it clear that only a £10-a-week pay increase, in other words 'parity' with the prevailing wage rates in the Midland motor industry, would end the strike. Henry Ford II thereafter instructed Stanley Gillen to do everything possible to secure a settlement. Gillen achieved this, thanks to the enthusiastic assistance of Hugh (later Lord) Scanlon[16] and Jack Jones, with whom he made a private deal at a secret meeting which lasted two days. The deal was that, provided Scanlon and Jones were prepared to recommend acceptance, the Company would be willing to raise basic pay rates by £8 a week over a period of 18 months and thus go a long way towards establishing pay parity with the Midlands. Despite strenuous opposition by all the Conveners to the proposed deal, Scanlon and Jones — through the element of surprise and by adroit manipulation of a hurriedly called NJNC Trade Union Side meeting — managed to railroad the majority of the Trade Union Officials present into recommending to the workforce that the Company offer be accepted. A ballot, partly administered by the Company, was organised with equal haste and the workers voted by a sizeable majority to accept the offer.[17] The methods Scanlon and Jones employed to secure this settlement left a legacy of bitterness on the Trade Union Side which has not been eroded by the passage of time. Furthermore, this experience also had a significant bearing on the conduct of the 1978 Ford nine-week pay strike.

The ten-week strike was followed by a period of relative calm in labour relations. But it did not last. The level of conflict again increased, and Ford claimed that, due to 'unconstitutional' actions, over 20 per cent of potential output had been lost in 1973. Lay-offs, disputes over works standards and disciplinary issues such as suspensions and dismissals were the main causes of conflict.

The Company believed the introduction of new procedural practices and a radical reform of the existing collective bargaining institutions would make a significant contribution towards the avoidance of disputes. For the purpose of examining these problems in depth and to make recommendations, the Company promoted the establishment of Joint Company/Union Sub-Committees at NJNC level. From their endeavours emerged the 1975 Works Standards Agreement, which seeks to resolve all operator complaints about the nature and speed of prescribed work tasks within ten days. A status quo clause was also incorporated into the Procedure Agreement, whereby the Company in return for a 15-day period of 'no industrial action of any kind . . . agrees not to implement major alterations to conditions of employment or well established work practices which have been disputed . . . for a maximum period of 15 working days.'[18]

In September 1975, the Company circulated a confidential memorandum to Plant Managers and Plant Industrial Relations Managers, which outlined proposals for 'revising the framework of Representative Institutions'.[19] It envisaged enlargement of the NJNC and the JWCs, but the innovative core of the proposals concerned the establishment of Departmental Groups consisting of Superintendent, Foremen, Shop Stewards and Lay Representatives. These Groups were seen as providing the foundations for the achievement of efficiency of operations and harmonious industrial relations. Suggested topics, appropriate for Departmental Group discussion, outlined in the Memorandum, included: ' . . . Production matters, fall down and reasons for it, forward schedules, quality status, future overtime requirements, vacancies, absence levels, accident reports, new products, equipment and operations etc. . .'.[20] But, due to managerial resistance at the 'front line' level, these Groups were never established nor were the proposals ever submitted to the Unions for their consideration.

In order to reduce the high level of conflict, the Company continued to press the Unions for the reform of representational structure. At an NJNC Sub-Committee meeting in May 1977, the Company pointed out 'that the current impasse arose from the absence of unanimously agreed Trade Union proposals'[21] and went on to draw attention 'to the failure of the reconstituted NJNC of 1969 to solve basic problems, . . . and the crucial interdependence of national and local level representative arrangements'.[22]

The Unions were unable to agree on proposals to reform the NJNC and the JWCs because of the Ford Toolmakers and their allies in other craft sections. Like the Leyland Toolmakers, they demanded separate representation and negotiating rights and above all, the restoration of differentials. The Toolmakers formed a National Co-ordinating Committee and established links with Leyland. They waged a quite effective campaign for about three years, which seriously weakened the unity of the Ford Unions, and their 'unconstitutional' actions also considerably inconvenienced and embarrassed the Company. Although the Toolmakers failed to secure separate negotiating rights, they made some headway in restoring differentials and, because of this, their campaign fizzled out in 1977.

Conflict and Reform

But the most persistent causes of intense and sometimes violent conflict in the 1973-74 period were lay-offs. The Company operated a stringent policy of laying groups of workers off whenever the consequential effects of 'unconstitutional' actions prevented them from doing their jobs in the normal manner. Workers, particularly when on night shift, increasingly objected to being taken off the payroll and sent home shortly after arriving for work. These lay-offs gave rise to severe, and sometimes violent, confrontations.

In September 1973, laid-off workers at the Dagenham Body Plant locked management in their offices and staged protest marches through the plant. In the process, fire alarms were set off and windows broken. In the Paint, Trim and Assembly (PTA) Plant at Dagenham, lay-offs became the central concern for production workers. In November 1973 and again in June 1974, laid-off PTA workers physically blocked production lines and banned all overtime.

The next serious clash over lay-offs occurred in October 1974 at the Dagenham Body Plant. After being told to go home, workers held an angry meeting in the Works canteen. According to management, they broke windows and reduced the canteen to a shambles. Six months later, 'Left Wingers' employed in the Body Plant, in a 'vanguardist' type of action, tried to make a stand against lay-offs by occupying part of the plant.

As regards violence, the events of September 1976 were the most

serious. After a thousand men on night shift in the Dagenham Body
Plant were told to go home, they became very angry.

> Rioting car workers went on a rampage . . . they smashed cars,
> attacked the security gates and started fires inside the factory. When
> police arrived they were bombarded with a hail of missiles. Bottles
> and bricks were thrown through the windows . . . Hundreds of police
> surrounded the area, but the car men locked the gates and refused to
> let them or the fire brigade inside. Instead the rioters found their own
> hosepipes and turned them on the police . . . [23]

The next lay-off battle occurred in the PTA in June 1977; it led to a
prolonged strike in the course of which parts of the plant were occupied
and the entrance to other plants on the Dagenham Estate were bloc-
kaded.[24]

The Shop Stewards disassociated themselves from the 1976 riots in
the Body Plant. They expressed their disapproval of this type of violence
and did not seriously contest the subsequent dismissal of ten 'Rioters'.
At one stage, when small groups of workers caused large-scale disruption
to production, the Company suggested to the Unions that the mobility
of labour clause in the Ford Agreement should be used to replace those
unwilling to work by groups of 'volunteers'. But the Unions were not
prepared to agree to this 'Blacklegs Charter'. In 1977, the Company
made a relatively minor concession on lay-off procedure and agreed
that, once workers had clocked on, they would be paid for the remainder
of their working shift.

After the lay-off conflicts and the Toolmakers' campaign had abated,
the NJNC Trade Union Side was eventually enlarged in May 1978. All
Plant Conveners, as well as some lay members of craft unions, were given
seats. This reform meant that, for the first time, lay representatives had
secured a numerical majority on the Trade Union Side. Although gaining
this majority has taken the rank and file four years longer than Moss
Evans originally forecast in 1969, the shift of power to the shop floor
has remained an ongoing process since the Sewing Machinists' strike in
1968.

The decade subsequent to that dispute has seen the rank-and-file
movement also grow in sophistication. The Company, as well as the
National Trade Union Officials, opted for a strategy of accommodation
and integration. Conveners and Shop Stewards have been given greatly
enhanced status and recognition as well as much more extensive facilities. Rank-and-file structures such as the Combine Committee, the Plant

Shop Stewards' Committees and the Plant Joint Works Committees have, as a result, become much more closely linked to the formal trade union machine. In consequence, these Committees have been exposed to the effects of institutionalisation and to the dangers of bureaucrat-isation. The possible dangers inherent in this development were pointed out by Moss Evans as long ago as 1969 when the NJNC was restructured. He said:

> the big problem in the Trade Union movement, and in the socialist society, is bureaucracy. The old structure on the NJNC was a perfect example of this. No bugger knew, really, what went on in there . . . I think the national negotiating body should be the Conveners — with the national officers along in an advisory capacity . . . But there is a problem there as well. The Conveners themselves may become bureau-cratic. I say this because of the conversations I've had with Shop Stewards. They say that they come to work in their best suits, sit in their offices, too busy to see anyone. Or talk about what they are doing. So you need a national Shop Stewards' meeting to which the Conveners of the NJNC will be accountable. I think we' ll have all this at Fords by 1974.[25]

The preparation and presentation of claims had also become increas-ingly professional. For example, City stockbrokers Phillips and Drew were employed by the Unions to assist with the 1977 wage claim sub-missions and they managed to cast considerable doubt on Ford's accountancy methods.

The 1978 Pay Strike and its Consequences

But as regards negotiating and organisational ability, capacity for leader-ship, and the degree of democratic practices, the 1978 Ford pay claim and subsequent nine-week strike provided an early test for the newly reconstituted Trade Union Side of the NJNC and its new Chairman, Ron Todd.

What happened in the course of this dispute underlines the import-ance of the learning process in industrial relations, both in terms of the benefits which are derived from 'learning the lessons' and conversely the penalties which are incurred if the 'lessons' are insufficiently heeded. Some features of the 1978 strike situation bore a striking resemblance to the events of the 1969-71 period but, of course, there were also some significant differences. For example, the eventual disregard by the Company of the government pay policy, the degree of state intervention, and the level of national and international solidarity action by the Trade Unions, were all on an unprecedented scale.

The claim, in essence, was a demand for a £20-a-week pay rise, a 35-hour week, longer holidays and improvement of fringe benefits. Both sides employed the now customary degree of professionalism in the presentation and the refutation of the claim. In compliance with the government pay guidelines, Ford offered to raise basic pay rates by 5 per cent and, dependent on a self-financing productivity deal, an additional unspecified amount. The Company totally rejected the 35-hour week demand on the grounds that, if granted, it would entail the loss of ten hours' productive capacity a week and, since there was no move to reduce working hours in Japan, car production in Britain, the Company claimed, would suffer the same fate as had befallen motorcycles and television tubes.

Locked in the cut and thrust of these exchanges, both sides misjudged the mood of the membership. Yet the portents were there for all to see. The circumstances of the 1977 pay settlement were almost a replication of 1970. Against the advice of the trade union leadership, workers had voted to accept a 12 per cent pay offer by the Company. This was one of the first settlements in the annual pay round. Many others which followed used the level of the Ford pay settlement as a starting point, and subsequently secured pay deals well in excess of 12 per cent. Once again, a feeling of having 'sold themselves short' began to spread across the shop floor as the size of other settlements became known.

In 1977, the Ford Motor Company doubled its profits. They rose from £121.6 million in 1976 to £246.1 million. Ford workers, therefore, were unlikely to accept less than 12 per cent in 1978. Thus, when the Company met the Trade Unions on 21 September 1978, and only offered half of what they offered in the previous year, the response was a spontaneous walk-out. Halewood workers led the way. Parts of Dagenham, Swansea, Daventry and Basildon quickly followed. By Monday 25 September, the walk-out of 57,000 manual workers, spread over 23 plants, based on 16 sites, was complete. Even the Ford security men joined in. To make matters worse, the Company revealed that the salary of Ford Chairman and Managing Director, Sir Terence Beckett, would be raised from £30,457 to £54,843 per annum – the announcement of this rise of 80 per cent, which the Company justified on the grounds of increased profitability, was surely a classic example of inept timing.

Ford limited its initial offer to 5 per cent because of government pressure and the threat of sanctions, In any case, multinational companies on the whole do not like to be seen publicly to defy the policies of their host government. But 'the corporate strategies of multinational groups and the economic policies of individual Governments may, particularly in times of economic turbulence, be irreconcilable.'[26]

The strength of multinational companies is derived from the development and the integration of complex productive processes on a transnational scale. Yet this structure also presents them with dilemmas and creates weaknesses. In the Ford context, it presently means that a serious and prolonged strike in Britain halts all of Ford's European operations within a relatively short space of time. The Company and union negotiators are certainly aware of this. It is sometimes argued that multi-sourcing would enable the Company to overcome this problem. But, taking the Fiesta car as an example, which cost £500 million to launch and is produced in Britain, Germany and Spain, multi-sourcing of components would have greatly increased the cost of the final product and made it uncompetitive.

However, to the government, the outcome of the Ford pay talks was crucial. It would make or break the pay policy. That is why the Prime Minister made it clear in Parliament that the government intended to act, notwithstanding the fact that, in the past, Ford had always been allowed to circumvent pay restraints for one reason or another.

When the economic damage of the strike – amounting to £10 million per day – began significantly to outweight the cost of possible government sanctions, Ford decided to pay the political price and advised the Trade Unions, on 9 October, that the Company was prepared to ignore the government's pay guideline and bargain freely. In return, the Company asked for work to be resumed forthwith. That was rejected by the Trade Unions, and Ford thereafter complained, with increasing bitterness, that the strike was being unnecessarily prolonged for political reasons.

The importance of the challenge to the government pay policy was well understood by the labour and trade union movement. Ford workers were once again perceived to be in the forefront of industrial and political conflict – a ground occupied by the mine-workers since 1972. This perception accounts for the speedy and unprecedented degree of external support for Ford workers received from the outset, from dockers, transport drivers and others – even white-collar staff.

The 1978 Ford pay claim, like the Sewing Machinists' grading griev-

ance in 1968, and the miners' pay claims in 1972 and 1974, illustrates
the absence of a clear dividing line between economic and political
issues. Although trade unions are sometimes accused of being obsessed
with 'economism', these examples show that some of these criticisms
are theoretically misconceived and unjustified in practice.

This pay strike marked the end of a decade in industrial relations at
Ford which was characterised by a continuous shift of power to the shop
floor. It also meant that many of the old hands had become 'respected'
members of the NJNC. To them, the 1971 Scanlon/Jones intervention
at Ford, their secret deal with the Company, and the subsequent manipulation of the trade union machine, were still vivid and bitter memories.
They resolved not to allow that to happen again. Although fears were
expressed in some of the left-wing press about a possible repeat performance in the shape of a Duffy[27]/Evans intervention, this was never a real
possibility. Moss Evans — quite apart from his belief in free collective
bargaining and a measure of trade union democracy — had, as Chairman
of the NJNC Trade Union Side in 1971, personally experienced the
divisiveness, the recriminations and the loss of faith in Trade Union
Officials which the Scanlon/Jones manoeuvre had caused. He was, therefore, not disposed to allow himself to be cast in a similar role. As far as
Reg Birch was concerned, there wasn't going to be a 1971 repeat performance either. He was due to retire in June 1979, so the dispute was
his 'swansong' as Secretary of the NJNC Trade Union Side. He wanted to
be remembered as the strong man and astute tactician, who played a
leading and instrumental part in smashing the government's pay policy
and defeating the Ford Motor Company. As in 1968 and 1969, he persuaded the AUEW Executive Council to declare the strike official as
soon as it had started. Duffy, Scanlon and the remainder of the generally
right-wing Executive, agreed, first, in order to exercise some measure
of control over the conduct of the dispute, and second, because the
intense rivalry with the TGWU about union control and dominance in
the automotive industry made this tactically necessary.

Most other unions followed suit and declared the strike official within one week. This meant the abrogation of existing Agreements —
Agreements which still had one month to run. In a radio interview,
Scanlon described this breach, in view of all the circumstances, as a mere
'technicality'. The Electrical and Plumbing Trade Union Executive
(EETPU), however, subsequently disassociated themselves from this
'technicality' by announcing it would only pay strike benefit from 21
October, the expiry date of the existing Agreement, because to do otherwise would create a precedent for breaking agreements with employers,

a practice which was unacceptable to the Union.

During the third week of the strike, on 13 October, the Company improved its pay offer to 8 per cent. This was rejected outright by the union negotiators without reference to the membership. Because of the growing effects of the strike on the continental Ford plants, the International Metal Workers' Federation (IMF), following a precedent established during the 1971 strike, convened a conference in London on 19 October, which was attended by trade union representatives from all Ford European plants. IMF Executive Herbert Rebhan promised financial assistance to the British Unions, if they required it.

At workshop level, the precedents established during the 1971 dispute were reactivated and extended. For example, Bosch workers in Germany refused to produce instrument panels and other electrical components for Ford, thereby denying the Company an alternative source of supply. Ford foundry workers at Bruhl (Cologne) blacked work normally done in Britain and the IMF Conference on the whole pledged that work belonging to British factories would not be done by Ford workers on the Continent or by any of their sub-contractors. The German delegation explained that its support was not purely altruistic, but a matter of self-interest because, if the disparity of wage levels between Germany and Britain continued to increase, this would jeopardise their long-term employment and growth prospects. Carlos Pardo, leader of the Spanish Ford workers, indicated that, because of their low basic salary, the Spanish workers, in their turn, could well be asking for similar support early in 1979, the time of their annual pay negotiations and, indeed, Spanish Ford workers commenced one-day strikes in support of their pay claims in mid-January 1979.

On 31 October 1978, after 'exploratory' talks between Company officials and the Chairman and Secretary of the Trade Union Side, Ford made a further improved but 'final' pay offer worth about 16.6 per cent in total, of which 5.15 per cent would be paid in the form of a weekly flat rate Attendance Allowance. The payment of this allowance was conditional upon the observance of a code of practice which contained thirteen grounds for disqualification – ranging from lateness to participation in any form of unconstitutional action. It was a rehash of the 1969 penalty concept, which assumes more 'orderly' industrial relations can be secured by means of an inducement-cum-penalty strategy. Approximately half of the NJNC union negotiators had been personally involved in the 1969 battle against the introduction of financial penalties, and predictably they recommended rejection of the Company offer.

Although the Company's 'intelligence service' had forecast that the offer would be accepted, if employees were allowed to vote, and even confidently talked to union negotiators about a 'phased return' to work, at mass meetings which were held at all plants, the Company's proposals were overwhelmingly rejected. Only five small plants voted in favour, but these, without question, subsequently accepted the national majority decision.

Apart from the media-inspired 'Ford wives back to work campaign', at Southampton, which was quickly and effectively countered by Ford wives who supported the strike, there were no divisions on the Trade Union Side. The craft sections solidly supported the strike and racial tensions, which some had anticipated, did not materialise. Although coloured production workers constitute a majority in some plants, for example at Langley where they number over 60 per cent, there has been a remarkable absence of racial tension on the shop floor since the mid 1960s when the Shop Stewards firmly and successfully dealt with an attempt by internal transport drivers to join the London meat porters' march to Parliament in support of Enoch Powell.

Trade union opposition to penalty clauses, in 1969, was based on a three-stage strategy: 1) avoid them altogether; 2) failing that, minimise their scope — turn them into 'balls of cotton wool'; and 3) if introduced, eliminate them as soon as possible. This is precisely the strategy the Unions adopted towards the proposed Attendance Allowance. After three weeks of haggling, the Attendance Allowance was retitled 'Supplementary Payments Plan'. The original thirteen grounds of dis-qualifications were reduced to four which, in essence, amount to being penalised for taking part in strike action. Sid Harroway, Chairman of the Body Plant Shop Stewards' Committee, stated,

> on the question of the penalty clauses . . . it took us a couple of weeks to negotiate the elimination of the best part of them . . . and of course, now the workers' position within the factories is to begin to look for ways of eliminating them in the next agreement.[28]

This may, however, be an optimistic time-table, because it took the Unions over five years to eliminate the 1969 penalty clauses.

Apart from scaling down the extent of the penalty clauses, the Company also marginally improved their pay offer, and the union negotiators agreed on 20 November, by 33 votes to 12, to recommend acceptance of the Company's proposals. The opposition to acceptance was led by the Halewood Conveners. Since the early sixties Halewood

Conveners have sometimes wanted to be seen to outlast the 'softies' from Dagenham. But embourgeoisement theorists may be encouraged by the fact that the size of the majority which voted for acceptance at the Halewood mass meeting was roughly the same as at Dagenham and other plants. All plants voted to accept, and work was resumed on 24 November 1978.

The democratic process within the Trade Union Negotiating Committee, and the degree of membership involvement, was an improvement on the past. Ron Todd and Reg Birch did contact the Company informally on two separate occasions, without the knowledge and approval of the Union Negotiating Committee, to pave the way for a resumption of talks. But they justified their conduct on the grounds that, had they not done so, it might have provided an excuse for an intervention by Duffy and Co.

The trauma of 1971 was still sufficiently strong for their explanation to be accepted. Although the 'nitty gritty' negotiations about detail — the horse trading — always took place at private and informal sessions between the Chairman, Vice-Chairman and Secretary of the Trade Union Side and three Company officials, the ultimate decision-making power always remained with the 56 union representatives on the NJNC and the membership. According to Sid Harroway:

> This was just three officers meeting three people from the Company to discuss various questions. They had no powers of negotiations, they were purely in a position of attempting to establish whether there was any flexibility in any aspect of the situation . . . Obviously 56 people can't do that major negotiating with the Company . . . The settlement was obviously a satisfactory one . . . The move from the position of the original 5 per cent to ultimately the settlement of 17 per cent . . . with improvements in holiday pay to 'time and a third' meant that there was much satisfaction, and the atmosphere within the factory is one of success.[29]

But this experience has further hardened opinion amongst the Conveners on the NJNC against delegating responsibilities to smaller Committees. When, in the early part of 1979, the Chairman of the NJNC Trade Union Side proposed the establishment of a small Negotiating Committee, this was rejected. Conveners have also developed second thoughts about referring 'knotty' problems to a number of different Sub-Committees. They argue that, since the majority of trade union members on the NJNC are not involved in the deliberations of these Sub-Committees, this practice constitutes a threat to the democratic process and also exposes the main Committee to domination by a caucus of 'specialists'.

The experiences and implications of the dispute were further discussed and analysed at a Conference at Eastbourne early in December 1978. Leading Shop Stewards from Ford Germany and Ford of Britain took part. A Joint Declaration was issued which 'confirmed the need for mutual support between Ford workers of all countries . . . ' The Declaration recognised that 'unique challenge to the Trade Union movement, the integration of Ford operations in Europe presents . . .', and pledged itself 'to develop closer relationships in view of the pressing need for international contacts'.[30]

The strategy management pursued throughout this dispute was a mixture consisting of applied lessons, 'articles of faith' and tactical errors. For example, management's initial response to the claim seems to have been too inflexible and brusque. More emphasis on supplementary payment options and less on the basic 5 per cent pay limitations might just conceivably have averted the walk-out. The Company reaffirmed two articles of faith: 1) that the militants are not representative of the silent majority (because of this, management − bypassing the union machinery − communicated twice by letter with each employee but, as happened in the Sewing Machinists' dispute, these letters merely exacerbated feelings); and 2) that the imposition of financial penalties will significantly reduce the numbers of strikes and other forms of unconstitutional action. This remains to be seen, but the proposition is doubtful. Indeed, the circumstances giving rise to the imposition of penalties may cause more controversy and create additional friction points.

Henry Ford II arrived in the middle of the dispute to see for himself, and according to the *Observer*,

> Sir Terence embarrassedly explained to his boss . . . the Company in the UK had fallen victim to the government policy. 'Well then, surely Jim Callaghan will intervene to help?' Henry Ford is reported to have asked. 'No', said Beckett. 'Then you had better settle on the terms you think right', Ford is supposed to have answered.[31]

To Henry Ford II, it must have seemed a familiar scenario − 1971 all over again. He confessed to being perplexed by British industrial relations practices, said he did not want to become personally involved and left the country.

From a management perspective, the central 'lesson' of the last ten years was written into the Agreement − 'No increase in labour costs during the 12 months of the Agreement, and no strike action to put pressure on negotiations for the 1979 Agreement'.

Ford's Managing Director, Sir Terence Beckett, justified the reintroduction of penalty clauses and the 17 per cent pay rise on the grounds that, in the preceding twelve months, the Company lost five million man-hours of production, worth £83 million, because of over 1,000 unofficial disputes. He further argued that the portion of the pay settlement in excess of the 5 per cent guideline was not inflationary, but self-financing, provided the frequency of work interruptions could be substantially reduced because 'this would dramatically lower a whole host of costs resulting from crisis actions to cope with stoppages of work'.[32]

Compared to the evidence the Company submitted to the three Courts of Inquiry in the 1957-68 period, the 1977/78 strike statistics confirm the absence of any substantive improvement in Ford's labour relations. This suggests that Ford's strength and profitability as a Company, despite the failure of its industrial relations policies, has been achieved mainly as a result of timely and good product development on an international scale, sound marketing, and the existence of relatively efficient administrative and financial structures.

The government announced its intention to apply sanctions against Ford as soon as the pay deal had been concluded. If a feeling of success was the prevalent mood on the shop floor, this was certainly not true of the boardroom. After losing £450 million worth of production, the market lead in Europe, and a £12½ million Pakistan contract, amongst others, because of initial compliance with the government's pay policy, the Company felt particularly aggrieved by government sanctions. 'We have been hit below the belt by the strike, and then mugged by the referee in the form of sanctions', said Sir Terence Beckett, and then went on to state, that 'when you add the damage from this strike, to other strike losses earlier this year, we have lost the equivalent of all the Japanese industry imports into this country in 1978'.[33]

The Company's concern about industrial conflict was voiced by Bob Ramsey, Ford UK Director of Industrial Relations, in an article headed, 'British Strikes, Why Managers can't Sleep at Night'. He diagnosed the central problem as

the failure of the British Trade Union Movement to be able to sign a Procedure Agreement with a 'no strike' clause until the Procedure is exhausted, or an annual economic agreement with a 'no strike' clause and be able to guarantee absolutely that the signatures on the Agreement will be honoured.[34]

Sir Terence Beckett reinforced the attack on the Unions at an American Chamber of Commerce lunch; he said

> British Trade Unions will argue endlessly for money wages, but are just not interested in the creation of wealth for its members or for the community . . . it has that debilitating and costly tradition of leaving the honouring of agreements to the discretion of individual members rather than establishing some form of control over them. . . In short, on this issue, the Unions don't deliver . . . The result is a less predictable situation than in any other country, and it gives a greater opportunity for dissidents to ignore the interests of the majority.[35]

The effects of the strike also reduced Ford's global profits — 'It wiped £97.5 million off the parent Company's 1978 after-tax earnings.'[36] In this connection, it is interesting to note that in 1978 Ford's 'Foreign earnings of £385 million, were 9.2 per cent higher than in 1977 . . . and amounted to 48 per cent of the Company's total profit'.[37]

The sanctions policy was opposed in Parliament by the Tories as well as by some Labour MPs and perhaps more importantly, outside Parliament by the TUC and the CBI. This line-up ensured the defeat of the sanctions policy and the government was forced to abandon it. However, had the intended sanctions been applied — refusal to place government contracts for Ford vehicles for one year, and an 'invitation' to nationalised industries to do likewise — the impact on Ford would hardly have been damaging. Development grants, particularly for the new Engine Plant at Bridgend in Wales, were never in jeopardy. In fact, it was disclosed that

> Fords will receive £148 million in aid for its Bridgend Engine Plant . . . this is more than four times the amount announced by the Department of Industry a year ago. How £36 million of the Taxpayers' money ballooned without anyone knowing into a tax-free hand out of nearly £150 million, despite the Company's breach of the pay limit, provides an interesting example of closed Government.[38]

In addition, some local authorities, such as the London and the Essex County Council, announced that they would switch their fleet orders to Ford, to make good any losses arising from government sanctions.

Supporters of pluralist theory may claim that these events validate their assumptions about the distribution and the diffusion of power in

Western capitalist society. Others, on the other hand, may argue that the intense and effective lobby by the Ford Motor Company against sanctions merely proved the correctness of Karl Kautsky's maxim, 'The capitalist class rules, but does not govern.' However that may be, what is not in doubt is the fact the Ford settlement shattered the government's pay policy. Inconceivable as it might have seemed at the beginning of October 1978, a level three times higher than the original government pay guideline had become the norm by the end of December 1978. Subsequent events — the strikes by petrol tanker drivers, road haulage drivers and engine drivers, local authority and hospital workers — severely damaged the economy as well as Labour's electoral chances. They caused a Labour Prime Minister, in desperation, publicly to encourage the crossing of picket lines manned by union members on official strike, and David Steel, the Liberal leader, called for the formation of a national government in order to curb trade union power. James Prior, then Shadow Minister for Employment, complained in a television interview[39] that Britain was now being run by local strike committees — 'little Soviets'. Demands for the reintroduction of labour laws, secret ballots, the limitation of picketing, the outlawing of the closed shop and strikes in public services, accompanied by action in the High Court against pickets, finally led to a 'Concordat' being signed between the government and the TUC.[40] But the 'Concordat' was largely a public relations exercise — an attempt to make good the potential electoral damage which the industrial strife in the winter of 1979 had caused. However, the 1978 Ford pay strike triggered off a chain of events which could not be blotted out by a mere cosmetic exercise, and it proved to be one of the major causes which brought about the defeat of the Labour Government in the May 1979 General Election.

The Sewing Machinists After 1968

The Sewing Machinists and Ford women workers in general have played no significant part in any of the conflicts since 1968. Indeed, by the time the Ford Motor Company had conceded equal pay unconditionally in February 1970, the Sewing Machinists' degree of militancy had markedly declined. After being in the forefront of industrial conflict, the Sewing Machinists abandoned their 'vanguard' role fairly quickly and returned to their more placid and traditional place amongst the less militant sections of Ford workers. Since 1970, the Sewing Machinists have, on the whole, not voted in support of any form of direct action on general issues, whenever this had been proposed by the rank-and-file leadership. It can, perhaps, be said that the Sewing Machinists' militancy and level of consciousness were transplanted into larger organisational bodies, i.e. internally into the various Shop Steward Plant Committees and the National Conveners' Committee and externally into the women's equal pay movement.[41]

It would, therefore, seem that a fleeting appearance on the stage of trade union history — a once-in-a-lifetime struggle — is quite insufficient for the maintenance of a high degree of trade union or class consciousness. If correct, this then raises a number of questions, e.g. Why does consciousness recede? What motivates workers to struggle? What determines their level of involvement? Does a major conflict experience have lasting effects on the workers concerned?[42]

In this connection, particularly since women workers are the focus of attention in Part II of this book, it would be worth while to look very briefly at some factors which do have a bearing on these issues, for example, nature of employment, social role and degree of participation in union affairs.

As regards the nature of employment, the highest proportion of women workers are in industries and occupations where unions have traditionally been weak and relatively ineffective, i.e. catering, cleaning, clothing, distributive trades, clerical work, nursing and so on. In fact, in some of these occupations the concentration of women workers reaches ghetto-like dimensions. Over 90 per cent of all typists, secretaries, office machine operators, sewing machinists and nurses are women. Similarly, among shop assistants, hairdressers and waiters the proportion of women workers is between 75 per cent and 90 per cent.[43] Conversely, the lowest proportion of women work in industries which have the longest and strongest traditions of struggle, such as the docks, shipbuilding, mining, construction, mechanical engineering, transport and printing.

This situation is largely the result of the social role women have in our society, both within the family and, historically, in the labour market as a source of cheap labour. Even today, women's identity is still located in the home. Going out to work is secondary and peripheral. The weight of family responsibilities generally pulls working women back into the isolation of the home and makes it very difficult for them to take part in union affairs, particularly outside normal working hours, e.g. attending union branch meetings or weekend conferences. Lunch breaks, too, are frequently used for shopping. This lack of participation in general union affairs separates women workers from the mainstream of union activities and in consequence only a very low proportion of women activists become full-time Trade Union Officials or gain places on Union Executive Councils.

These two factors, then – uneven distribution in employment and negligible involvement in general union affairs – make it doubly difficult for women workers to acquire extensive and wide-ranging collective bargaining experiences and to develop and establish the customs and traditions which are a prerequisite for the maintenance of a high level of trade union consciousness.

Due to their limited collective bargaining experience, the Sewing Machinists had to rely on their male colleagues to steer their claim through the maze of procedures and agreements which is the veneer covering company/union power relationships, because only *they* knew how to 'play the system'. Consequently, their aspirations were filtered and progressed through a male-dominated structure – a process which not only inhibited their degree of commitment to women's rights causes but also dimmed their enthusiasm about supporting general union struggles.

One significant legacy, however, has remained. Since the end of the Sewing Machinists' strike, the women workers in the Trim Shop and their Shop Stewards have displayed a more self-assured and determined attitude in negotiations with management, relative to departmental and local plant issues such as manning levels, work methods, welfare matters and general working conditions. Management, in their turn, now treat their requests and complaints much more seriously and with more urgency. This positive gain has been consolidated and in some respects extended. Women now have a seat on the River Plant Joint Works Committee and consequently exert more influence on union affairs at the plant level.

But the effects of the Sewing Machinists' dispute were not limited to industrial relations at Ford. Externally, the equal pay movement was brought to life and the 1969 penalty clause dispute committed the two largest Unions in Britain to oppose much more resolutely the introduction of labour laws. The results of union opposition to *In Place of Strife* and the 1971 Industrial Relations Act are well known. Union policies and actions at Ford during the 1970s had an increasing impact externally – culminating finally in the 1978 Ford pay strike which not only caused the collapse of the Labour Government's pay policy but led to the fall of the government itself. Some of these events are described and discussed in Chapters 8 and 9 and in the Conclusions.

Notes

1. The Ford Sick Benefit Society is a registered Friendly Society jointly administered by an equal number of elected workers' representatives and Company-appointed officials. In accordance with the Society's rules, non-taxable sick benefit payments are made to hourly-paid workers who are absent from work due to certified illness.

2. *The Guardian,* 19 February 1969.

3. Ibid., 21 February 1969.

4. Ibid., 17 February 1969.

5. *The Times,* 18 February 1969.

6. Ibid., 22 February 1969.

7. See Ch. 4, p.142.

8. *Sunday Times,* 16 March 1969.

9. *The Guardian,* 26 February 1969.

10. *The Times,* 28 February 1969.

11. Ibid., 15 March 1969.

12. Mass meeting, Leys Bath, Dagenham, 19 March 1969.

13. *The Guardian,* 13 March 1969.

14. Ibid., 19 March 1969.

15. *Daily Telegraph,* 9 March 1969.

16. The AEUW seems to have established a tradition whereby Union Presidents, whether initially elected as the 'darlings' of the 'Right', like Bill Carron, or of the 'Left', like Hugh Scanlon, end up in the House of Lords.

17. For a more detailed account, see J. Matthews, *The 1971 Ford Strike* (Panther, 1972).

18. Ford Agreements (Blue) Book, p.14.

19. Memorandum, 1 September 1975.

20. Ibid.

21. Company Proposals to Improve Representation, 27 May 1977.

22. Ibid.

23. *Daily Mirror,* 29 September 1976.

24. For a detailed account of these conflicts see *Little Red Blue Book* (Red Notes, 1978).

25. Huw Beynon, *Working for Ford* (Penguin, 1973), p.285.

26. *The Times,* 22 November 1978.

27. Terence Duffy became AUEW President after Hugh Scanlon's retirement in 1978.

28. *Socialist Challenge,* 4 January 1979.

29. Ibid.

30. Eastbourne Declaration (December 1978).

31. *Observer,* 3 December 1978.

32. *Ford News,* 1 December 1978.

33. Ibid.

34. *Financial Times,* 10 January 1979.

35. Ibid., 17 January 1979.

36. Ibid. 16 February 1979.

37. Ibid.

38. *Observer,* 3 December 1978.

39. 25 January 1979.

40. In February 1979.

41. See Dialogue, Part III.

42. For a lucid discussion about trade union and class consciousness see Michael Mann, *Consciousness and Action among the Western Working Class* (Macmillan,

London, 1973).

43. Judith Hunt, 'Organising Women Workers', *Studies for Trade Unionists,* vol. 1, no. 3 (WEA, 1975).

Part V

EXTERNAL CONSEQUENCES OF THE DISPUTE

8 A JOINT VIEW

No system of industrial relations stands in isolation of the wider society of which it forms a part. As John Dunlop and his followers have shown,[1] the system of industrial relations within a given company is heavily influenced by the 'inputs' to that system from the economic, social, legal and political life of the wider society. Academic writers have paid less attention, however, to the reciprocal effect, the influence exerted by the industrial relations 'outputs' from a particular company on the economic, social, legal and political life of the surrounding community. It is not difficult to recognise that the 'general climate' of industrial relations in a given national system − or in a particular industry at a particular time − may lead the government to introduce legislation to secure certain major policy objectives. On the other hand, it is extremely rare for the dynamics of industrial conflict within a particular company to exert a significant influence on the development of the national system as a whole. Ford of Britain is an important exception to that general rule.

In Part IV of this study, the authors have tried to show the inter-action between Ford's attempts to reform its own domestic industrial relations and the parallel attempts made by successive governments to achieve similar objectives on a national scale. Attention has been focused on the efforts made to contain and channel unofficial and unconstitutional strikes; to improve communication both within and between management and the Unions; to achieve and sustain higher levels of productivity; and to build the new foundations of high trust relationships as the basis for future productive co-operation. The impact of Ford's industrial relations on the national scene has also been noted: the effect of particular strikes on the development of labour law, on strike ballots, and on the development and application of incomes policies, culminating in the defeat of the Labour Government in May 1979. The present chapter traces the external consequences of the dispute in one specific area of public policy − namely the effect of the strike and its outcome on the equal pay movement and its influence on legislation designed to promote equality and to remove sex discrimination in Britain.

The Coming of Equal Pay and Equal Opportunity[2]

No single article of faith more effectively unites British working men than their attachment to the principle of 'the rate for the job'[3] — an elementary principle of distributive justice which implies that all those who work at the same job should be paid at the same rate. Although the application of this principle may be traced back to the beginnings of trade unionism in Britain, it is a principle which British working men have not always seemed anxious to share with British working women. Consequently, the struggle by women to achieve economic and social equality has a long and bitter history.

The earliest recorded collective action by women to achieve equal pay in Britain goes back to 1833 when the women power-loom weavers of Scotland finally won a long battle to secure equal wages with the men alongside whom they worked. But it took another 55 years before the organised labour movement formally acknowledged the legitimate aspiration for equality amongst the working women of Britain. In 1888, the year of the famous and successful strike by the Bryant & May Matchgirls,[4] the Trades Union Congress carried a resolution, proposed by Clementina Black, that 'in the opinion of this Congress, it is desirable in the interests of both men and women that in trades where women do the same work as men, they shall receive the same payment'.[5]

For more than a quarter-century, the TUC and the labour movement continued to pay lip service to that resolution but concentrated their efforts on achieving equal pay by means of their traditional reliance on collective bargaining rather than by invoking the assistance of the state to achieve emancipatory legislation. The great upsurge of middle-class radical feminism before the First World War barely touched working-class women and appears not to have been concerned with the achievement of equal pay. In short, the fight for equal pay took second place to the fight for equal political rights, finally conceded by the wartime coalition government in 1918.

It was the mass mobilisation of women into the munitions' industry during the First World War that first drew the public's attention to the ethical claim by women for equality at work. Despite the categorical assurances of the Prime Minister, Lloyd George, that 'if the women turn out the same quantity of work they will receive exactly the same pay',[6] the government's pledges on equal pay, set out in the Treasury Agreement of 19 March 1915, were more honoured in the breach than in the observance. This failure by the government 'to honour its war pledges' outraged and politicised large numbers of women who took part in a series of protracted labour disputes which threatened vital war production. In an effort to prevent all-out conflict between the newly formed Federation of Women Workers and his own War Departments, Lloyd George appointed the War Cabinet Committee on Women in Industry, under Sir James Atkin,

> To investigate and report on the relationship which should be maintained between the wages of women and men, having regard to the interests of both, as well as the value of their work. The recommendations should have in view the necessity of output during the war, and the progress and well-being of industry in the future.

The Atkin Committee's Report,[7] which was not published until 1919, provided a comprehensive analysis of women's employment and wages before and during the war but said little about the future. It was left to Beatrice Webb, the leading woman member of the Committee, to publish a Minority Report, offering her own characteristically lucid exposition of the three separate meanings enshrined within the classic formulation – 'equal pay for equal work':

1. *equal pay for equal efforts and sacrifices* – identified with 'the rate for the job' – that is, the occupational or standard rate on a time-work basis, backed by a minimum wage;
2. *equal pay for equal product* – identified with 'the quantity and quality of the product irrespective of the effect upon the several operatives, or of the value of the service to the employer';
3. *equal pay for equal value to the employer* – identified with the fact that 'equal workshop wages may stand at very different costs in the enterprise as a whole, according to their different demands in the way of time and space, involving greater or lesser overhead charges for rent and repairs, lighting and heating, superintendence, and other expenses incidental to a factory staff, interest on cost of machinery and its annual maintenance or renewal'.[8]

Despite this subtle elucidation, Beatrice Webb was in no doubt that the reason why equal pay had not been implemented was 'not the ambiguity of the phrase but the ease with which its honest application whatever it may be taken to mean, can be evaded or dodged', as, for example, 'by the simple expedient of not allowing the women to be paid by results at all, and thus keeping them to a "women's rate" for timework'.[9] Having dismissed as ambiguous and unworkable both the Atkin Committee's

Recommendations and the International Labour Organisation's first guiding principle of 1919 that 'men and women should receive equal treatment for work of equal value', she proposed the adoption of several guiding principles, such as a national minimum wage, occupational differentials, the linking of money wages to the cost of living, etc. In her view, men and women in industry were no longer distinct classes but were 'more and more becoming merged in the armies of the skilled and the semi-skilled, each of them divided into numerous sectional grades'.[10] Future trade union struggles would centre on these sectional interests, not on the irrelevant distinctions between the sexes. But Beatrice Webb was not to have her way. British governments of the inter-war period gave little attention to the noble aspirations of the ILO or to the timid recommendations of the Atkin Committee's Report. The proportion of women in Britain's labour force gradually declined throughout the twenties and thirties with little recorded progress made in reducing the traditional differential of about 50 per cent between the rates of pay of men and women engaged in similar work.[11]

Popular interest in the subject was temporarily rekindled at the ILO Conference of 1939, when the American delegation moved a resolution declaring that 'it is in the best interests of society that women should have full opportunity to work and should receive remuneration without discrimination because of sex'.[12] But the first real breakthrough came towards the end of the Second World War, at the 26th Session of the ILO, held in Philadelphia in 1944. The Declaration of Philadelphia, as it became known, spelled out for the first time that:

> The redistribution of women workers in each national economy should be carried out on the principle of complete equality of opportunity for men and women in respect of admission to employment on the basis of individual merit, skill and experience, and steps should be taken to encourage the establishment of wage rates on the basis of job content, without regard to sex.[13]

The detailed and specific recommendations which followed, 'for the purpose of establishing precise and objective standards for determining job content, irrespective of the sex of the worker', marked a significant step forward, from pious exhortation towards specific action needed to achieve practical results.[14]

In Britain, Winston Churchill's Government, recognising the complexity of the issues raised by these recommendations, reserved judgement on their implementation pending the advice of the Royal

Commission on Equal Pay, set up in October 1944 under the Chairmanship of Sir Cyril Asquith,

> To examine the existing relationship between the remuneration of
> men and women in the public services, in industry and in other fields
> of employment; to consider the social, economic and financial impli-
> cations of the claim of equal pay for equal work; and to report.

The essentially conservative recommendations of the Asquith
Commission Report[15] should not detract from its dedicated attempt to
clarify the semantic, philosophic, ethical and practical arguments surrounding equality at work. The battle-cry of 'equal pay for equal work'
expressed a demand for simple justice – but the search for 'justice' was
anything but simple. The Asquith Commissioners concentrated their
attention on the ambiguities to be found on both sides of the 'equal pay
for equal work' equation. They finally decided that the formula meant
the same as 'the rate for the job', ignoring differential value to the
employer. The whole tendency of collective bargaining and industrial
legislation in Britain had been in the direction of establishing standard
rates of time wages. As the TUC had argued in its Memorandum of
Evidence to the Commission:

> It is an essential part of the principle of collective bargaining – now
> universally accepted in this country – that wage-rates should not be
> settled according to the various capacities of individual workmen,
> but for the whole of the workpeople employed in a particular indus-
> trial grade or occupation.[16]

The Asquith Report concluded that there was no justification for discriminatory rates of pay in the public services but carefully avoided any
clear-cut decision about industrial employment, on the grounds that the
expense involved in such a move towards equal pay precluded any
serious consideration of the problems involved in achieving it.

Despite strong opposition from employers, trade unions in the
engineering and other manufacturing industries began the process of reducing the differential between men's and women's rates by penny
increments in the immediate post-war period. By 1950, they had succeeded in pushing the women's rate up to about 60 per cent of the men's
rate for equivalent work. With the defeat of the Labour Government in
1951, the period of 'austerity economics' came to an abrupt end. Wages
began to rise more rapidly and the women's percentage of men's rates

declined as a result. This effect was reinforced by substantial 'wage drift' — that is, the widening gap between basic rates and actual earnings, with bonuses and overtime pay — which has always been a special feature of earnings in the engineering industry. Plant bargaining gains, obtained with no particular regard for equal pay, more than outweighed the importance of national wage agreements upon which the women's rate was much more dependent.

The end of this 'austerity' period also opened the door for the public-sector Unions — representing civil servants, local government officers and teachers — to launch a campaign for the implementation of the Asquith Commission's recommendations. During the years 1953 and 1954, mass action — including street demonstrations — persuaded the government to enter into an agreement with the Unions and phase the introduction of equal pay into all national and local authority government services over a period of seven years, from 1955 to 1961. By 1955, however, despite pay advances amongst some white-collar workers, women's rates as a whole had already fallen back by 2 per cent. It took a further 14 years to recover that 2 per cent. Bearing in mind the vast increases obtained in the public services, this figure must conceal a massive real decline in women's pay in most of the manufacturing sectors.

Although the general principles of equal pay had been adopted by the ILO as early as 1918, it was not formulated as a Convention until the 34th meeting of the ILO in Geneva, on 6 June 1951. The seminal Convention 100 concerning 'Equal Remuneration for Men and Women for Work of Equal Value' states that 'the term equal remuneration for men and women for work of equal value refers to rates of remuneration established without discrimination based on sex' (Article 1b). According to Article 2(2), this principle may be applied by means of (a) national laws or regulations, (b) legally established or recognised machinery for wage determination, (c) collective agreements between employers and workers, or (d) a combination of these various means.[17]

The British Government was alone amongst the advanced industrial nations in refusing to ratify ILO Convention 100 during the fifties or even the sixties. The Conservative Government, in office from 1951 to 1964, seldom referred to equal pay in industry without declaring that the country's economy could not possibly afford its implementation. In 1953, the Labour Party committed itself to implement equal pay for equal work on its return to power and to endorse the 1951 ILO Convention. By the time Labour was returned to office in 1964, the TUC had significantly changed its traditional policy. Faced with the intransigence of the employers and the inability of the Trade Unions to make significant progress through collective bargaining, and perhaps with an eye to the forthcoming General Election, the TUC passed a resolution at its 1963 Congress urging the next Labour Government to introduce legislation to make equal pay mandatory. The Labour Party responded by including pledges to introduce such legislation, based on the ILO's 1951 Convention, in both its 1964 and 1966 election manifestos. On achieving office in 1964, the first Wilson Government got off to a good start by appointing an Inter-Departmental Committee to examine the problems of implementing such legislation. By the end of 1965 the Committee duly presented its Report but it was never published. The issue became submerged amongst the more pressing and immediate problems facing the government.

On the return of the second Wilson Government in 1966, with an increased majority, the TUC met the Minister of Labour and agreed to take part in a tripartite working committee to progress the equal pay issue. Representatives of the government, the TUC and the CBI were asked to examine four major areas of equal pay policy – definition, cost, implementation and timing. But the second Report was not published either, because of a disagreement in principle between the TUC and the CBI on the fundamental matter of definition. Whereas the TUC was committed to the ILO's 1951 Convention, namely 'equal pay for work of equal value', the CBI wanted to see equal pay introduced only for the same work or work of a similar nature as that carried out by men. The distinction is manifestly crucial, as Beatrice Webb had noted almost 50 years earlier.[18] For the TUC, equality was to be dependent on the economic value of the women's work contribution, whereas for the CBI it was to be dependent on the nature and content of particular jobs. The latter definition was unacceptable to the TUC because of the loopholes it afforded for evasion. First, if there was no immediate and obvious comparator between men's and women's jobs, there would be no basis for establishing equality, regardless of the economic value of the women's work. Second, if jobs were carried out by workers of both sexes, an unscrupulous employer might seek to remove men from such jobs which would then become 'women's work' for which no male job comparator remained. Third, it might be possible for an employer simply to re-title some jobs in order to evade the requirements of legislation.

The dispute over definitions was no mere academic quibble: it raised a series of fundamental issues which were never debated in public because the Report was not published. The Trade Unions, who had been pressing for the implementation of equal pay, assumed the Labour

Government remained committed to the principles enshrined in Convention 100. They were shocked, therefore, when no less a figure than Mrs Barbara Castle announced that the government could not endorse ILO Convention 100 because it might be in conflict with the comparable regulations of the European Economic Community, to which Britain was then seeking admission. And there the matter was allowed to rest − a back-room debating matter, to be discussed from time to time in the corridors of power but with no action taken to effect implementation. In 1968, after four years in power, the Labour Government had still made no official announcement of its intentions on equal pay.

Within a few weeks, that situation was completely transformed, thanks to the action of the Ford Sewing Machinists and the impact of the strike on the newly appointed Secretary of Employment and Productivity, Mrs Barbara Castle. Although the Ford strike did not begin until the token stoppage on 29 May 1968, there is evidence in the columns of *The Times* and elsewhere of a public issue, suppressed for too many years, about to come to the boil.

On 4 May, under the provocative title 'A Feminine Elbow',*The Times* leader writer commented on Mrs Castle's appointment as follows:

> Mrs. Barbara Castle is not a patient politician . . . but industrial management is conscious that a hasty step may set back years of patient progress . . . The incursions of Mrs. Castle into industrial re-lations could be expected to have and has had a disturbing effect . . . Consciousness of the importance of moving carefully often leads to a tendency hardly to move at all . . . A feminine elbow stuck into management's ribs could stir them up but it needs to be done in the right place, at the right time.[19]

On the previous day, Margaret Allen of *The Times,* writing in the 'Money Matters' column, was more to the point:

> Many women cheered when Barbara Castle was given one of the top executive jobs in government. One thing she seems to have forgotten so far, however, is her own statement on equal pay for women made in 1964 . . . 'The only answer now is legislation' . . . This is one sub-ject on which Mrs. Castle has been strangely silent. Women's wages are rarely more than 60 per cent of men's. On Tuesday, the engineering Unions unanimously agreed to instruct their executives to press for equal pay for equal work, even to the point of industrial action . . .

How about action now, Mrs. Castle?[20]

On 6 May, the First Secretary told the Commons that the definition of equal pay being discussed with the CBI and the TUC was not that contained in Convention 100 but that laid down in Article 119 of the Rome Treaty — namely 'equal remuneration for the same work as between male and female workers'. Many Labour back-benchers protested about the delay in securing agreement and legislation. Mr English, the Labour Member for Nottingham West, asked the Prime Minister to arrange for Mrs Castle's salary to be cut by 50 per cent until she had implemented the equal pay legislation.

On 7 May, Mrs Joyce Butler was given leave by the House to introduce a Private Member's Bill which would enable a board to be set up to examine and remove sex discrimination in employment and elsewhere and to provide equal pay for work of equal value. The Bill was sponsored by eight women MPs from both sides of the House.

During that same week, the *Department of Employment Gazette* published a summary of *A Survey of Women's Employment*[21] by Audrey Hunt, the most comprehensive and up-to-date investigation into women's employment in Britain for several years. It confirmed the popular impression that women's hourly earnings averaged only 60 per cent of men's earnings for the same work. The *DEP Gazette* noted that the government fully supported the principle of equal pay 'but in the present circumstances it is not possible to take immediate steps to implement it in full'. The government, the TUC and the CBI were continuing their joint examination of the various problems.

The Times devoted a leading article to the same report under the heading 'The urgent need for granting equal pay'. It noted that the most obvious form of discrimination was in women's rates of pay. Half of all employed women earned less than five shillings an hour and only one woman in thirty earned more than ten shillings an hour. Yet the government was committed to equal pay and Mrs Castle was one of its senior Ministers, perhaps in real terms the most powerful. The US had made the change-over to equal pay in the previous year and its economy had not crumbled. It was a change that should be made here too and with all deliberate speed.[22]

In a review of Audrey Hunt's *Survey* in *New Society,* Margherita Rendel wrote that equal pay was

one of the three most important measures needed to give women the opportunity to make a full contribution to the community . . . The

Survey shows clearly that women, especially older women, are stable
workers, in spite of the many disadvantages and discriminations to
which they are subjected . . . The most severe is unequal pay . . . It
could be implemented in two years, according to a Government
estimate of the cost. If all wage increases at 3½ per cent per annum
were devoted to this purpose, therefore, the introduction of equal
pay over, say, a seven-year period is practicable.[23]

On 10 May, *The Times* published a letter from Baroness (Edith)
Summerskill headed 'Women's pay: the loud clear cry for equality'. She
wrote:

The cry for equal pay has been repeated loud and clear for so long
that it has almost ceased to register in the minds of politicians and
the public alike. Discrimination against women is more blatant and
more widespread than racial discrimination and can be legislated
against. We are continually being told that 'the time is not right'.
When is it ever right?[24]

Within one month of the publication of that letter, the Ford Sewing
Machinists had taken strike action in support of their grading claim
which, in turn, gave rise to the demand for equal pay at Ford. The
impact of the dispute, already described in Part II of this study, together with the volume of press, radio and television publicity it
received, transferred the debate from the correspondence columns of
The Times into the popular dailies, the learned weeklies and the pages of
Hansard. As part of the formula for ending the Ford strike, Mrs Castle
had committed the Labour Government to start talks with both sides
of industry on the implementation of equal pay over a period of not
more than seven years.[25]   Responding to Mrs Castle's statement to this
effect in the House of Commons on 26 June 1968, Dame Joan Vickers,
Conservative Member for Plymouth, supported the urgent need for
legislation. 'Not since the Match Girls' strike of 1888 has there been
such a strike as the one at Ford's, or have women felt so militant about
the question of equality.'[26]

Even before the settlement of the Ford strike, a campaign had begun
to maintain pressure on the government to enact appropriate legislation.
This campaign, sponsored by the London District Committee of the
NUVB, opened with a 'Women's Conference on Equal Rights in
Industry' at Friends House, Euston on 28 June 1968. Announcing the
forthcoming Conference in the Union's publication *Headlight,* the cam-

paign organisers declared that 'Whatever the outcome of the Ford dispute, it is clear that things will never be the same again, and other Trade
Unions, management and government can never relapse into the old
complacency on women's wages.'[27] The same sentiments were echoed
in the *Daily Mirror,* immediately following the successful outcome of
the Ford women's strike: 'The 8½ million women workers should raise
their teacups today in a toast to the petticoat strikers at Fords, for they
have taken a big step forward in the battle for equal pay.'[28]

At the TUC Annual Conference in September 1968, union delegates,
roused by the outcome of the Ford strike, were in militant mood on the
subject of equal pay. Despite strenuous opposition from the General
Council, they carried an amendment to the Council's Report which
'urged the TUC to call on Unions to give full support to any groups of
workers fighting to achieve equal pay'. Moving the amendment, Joan
Connell of DATA (now TASS) declared that 'This industrial apartheid
will continue unless women everywhere follow the example of those at
Ford's'. In response to Congress pressure – and to take some of the
heat out of the issue – the General Council agreed to convene a separate
TUC Women's Conference in November to provide a forum for more
thorough discussion of the problems of implementation.

Meantime, the London District Committee of the NUVB, encouraged
by the success of its Friends House meeting and heartened by the TUC
debate on equal pay, organised a mass lobby of Parliament on 22
October 1968, to be followed by an evening conference. The response
was overwhelming. The lobby was supported by the widest variety of
organisations, with 26 trade union delegations, from ASTMS to USDAW,
and five delegations from National Women's Committees representing
such diverse bodies as the National Human Rights Committee and the
National Mothers in Action Committee. The Ford Sewing Machinists
were represented by a delegation of about fifty. It was reported to be
the biggest lobby ever assembled at the Houses of Parliament in support
of women's rights.

For the evening conference, permission was obtained to use the
largest Committee Room in the House of Commons. At the end of a
long and enthusiastic meeting, attended by many sympathetic MPs, the
decision was taken to set up a National Joint Action Campaign
Committee for Women's Equal Rights (NJACCWER, hereafter referred
to as the Action Campaign Committee) with the principal objective of
achieving 'equal pay now' and of advancing the general cause of equal
rights for women. The atmosphere was one of great hope and expecta-
tion. Many delegates sensed that they were at the beginning of a new

era. The women's movement seemed at last to have been infused with working-class dynamism, the former absence of which had proved its fundamental weakness. Over 100 MPs subsequently pledged their support for the campaign's objectives and the movement spread rapidly across the country. Within a few weeks, it had established 37 groups, with a Campaign Secretary in 20 counties covering England, Scotland and Wales. Amongst a Steering Committee of 40 were several MPs, and members of the Dagenham Sewing Machinists' Strike Committee. Chris Norwood MP and Audrey Hunt were elected 'Joint Chairmen' (sic) and Fred Blake, the hero of the Dagenham Sewing Machinists, became National Secretary.

The TUC Women's Conference in November 1968 gave the equal pay campaign a further fillip. In the presence of delegates from 59 trade unions with a women's membership of almost 1¾ million, the Conference discussed the achievements of the Ford Sewing Machinists and the details of the proposed legislation. In a fiery speech, one woman delegate, Miss Connell of DATA, called for the use of industrial action because 'This is the only language which will be understood — and it's now or never!'[29] In fact, the Action Campaign Committee adopted the traditional methods of issuing campaign badges and lapel buttons, urging general support and encouragement for industrial and political action on all matters concerned with equal pay. To complement its activities on the industrial front, the Committee stepped up its political work, bringing together under one single umbrella women's organisations, Trades Councils, Union District Committees and other bodies, organising joint local and regional conferences in support of the equal pay campaign.

On International Women's Day, 8 March 1969, a resolution was sent from the Action Campaign Committee to the Prime Minister, demanding immediate ratification and implementation of the ILO's Conventions 100 and 111. Harold Walker, Under-Secretary at the DEP, replying in April on behalf of the government, said that:

> The Government fully accepted the principle of equal pay and are anxious to implement it as soon as economic circumstances permit. It has been the practice of successive British Governments to ratify ILO Conventions only when domestic law and practice are in conformity with their requirements . . . Pay in government industrial employment is, in accordance with long standing practice, determined by reference to practice in private industry and whilst collective bargaining in the private sector prolongs the existence of discriminatory rates of pay for men and women, we feel that it would not be proper

> to ratify a Convention or Conventions with terms of which we are not
> ourselves wholly complying . . . This is not a situation in which male
> workers are likely to be willing to forgo part of their expectations in
> order to promote equal pay . . . I am sure you will appreciate that it
> would be unrealistic for the Government to endorse any particular
> period of time for the implementation of equal pay either in the
> public sector or elsewhere.[30]

In essence, the letter reflected the government's anxiety to shift the
responsibility for the lack of progress on equal pay onto the shoulders
of the TUC and the CBI. The outcome of the 1968 Pay Agreement in
the engineering industry gave some justification for the government's
attitude. Unsatisfactory progress on equal pay was blamed on the
National Committee of the AEF, the Union's policy-making body, because it had refused to scale down demands on behalf of men and so
made it possible for the employers to refuse to make proportionately
higher payments to the industry's women workers.

The Action Campaign Committee refused to be put off by this reply.
It continued to concern itself with two basic issues: first, an adherence
to the concept of equal pay, as laid down in ILO Convention 100; and
second, a reduction in the proposed seven-year implementation period,
proposed by Barbara Castle. Although the Committee concentrated its
activities in the regions, the subject of equal pay and women's emancipation was rarely off the front pages of the popular newspapers or the
serious magazines throughout 1968 and 1969.

On 1 May 1969, the Action Campaign Committee organised a further
lobby of Parliament and a mass rally in Trafalgar Square later that
month. The rally – intended to mark the high point of the campaign to
date and a springboard for further mobilisation of political support –
was dampened by torrential rain. But some 1,500 supporters nevertheless marched from the Embankment to Trafalgar Square, holding aloft
their rain-soaked banners which bore such inscriptions as 'Equal Pay
Now!' and 'Vive la différence! But not in pay!' After the rally had been
addressed by a wide spectrum of speakers, including Baroness
Summerskill, Audrey Wise MP, Ernie Roberts, Assistant General
Secretary, AEF (now the AUEW) and Moss Evans, its participants
enthusiastically endorsed a five-point Working Charter of objectives to
be achieved by the following year:

1. to demand the removal of sex discrimination from employment, education, social and public life;

2. to demand the inclusion of equal pay for work of equal value in all agreements between employers and trade unions;
3. to demand that Members of Parliament enforce equal legal rights for women by means of parliamentary action in 1969;
4. to demand that the TUC should take the lead and co-ordinate a national Action Campaign for equal pay and equal opportunities in industry in fulfilment of the decisions taken at the 1968 Congress;
5. to demand immediate government ratification of ILO Convention 100.

Under the slogan 'Step up the campaign!' the Action Campaign Committee launched a national petition and intensified the drive for support by holding factory gate meetings and seeking to establish more local joint action committees. Chris Norwood MP obtained from Lord Shackleton a list of all government factories employing more than 50 women, using the list as the basis for mobilising support for equal pay in the public manufacturing sector. In response to these mounting pressures, Barbara Castle was reported to have taken 'the bit between her teeth . . . She is said to have decided that equal pay is the issue on which she must act.'[31]

With the forthcoming TUC and Labour Party Conferences as their next obvious targets, the Action Campaign Committee proclaimed 12 September 1969 as National Equal Pay Day, calling for mass action in support of the campaign up and down the country. The response was encouraging: every Trade Union Conference held that summer passed resolutions pledging support for the principle of equal pay and this fervour was reflected at the 101st TUC held in Portsmouth. When Harold Wilson sought to persuade Congress that 'equal pay for women must be based on incomes restraint and phased in over a period of years', he was rebuked in an angry response by Frank Cousins, the re-tiring General Secretary of the TGWU, who reminded Congress that 'We, in the Trade Union movement, are giving notice, we have tolerated it too long. Talks should not be about women's rights but about the rate for the job.' Bob Wright, speaking on behalf of the AEF Executive Council, pledged his Union 'to support its women members irrespective of what the Prices and Incomes Board have to say. It's time to stop talking and get into action.' Commenting on the TUC, the *Daily Mirror* told its readers that ' "Equal Pay for Women Now" was the battle-cry at their 101st Trades Union Congress at Portsmouth'. The resolution finally passed at the TUC called on the government once again to implement equal pay and to ratify ILO Convention 100. On 9 September a TUC delegation of seven members, led by its new General Secretary, Victor Feather, called on Mrs Castle to press the TUC demands on equal pay.

At the Labour Party Conference in October 1969, the Action Campaign Committee organised an Equal Pay Forum to ensure that the issue received adequate attention. The Conference, in fact, provided the last significant opportunity for the Committee to complete the drive for equal pay. At the time Barbara Castle introduced the Equal Pay Bill in the Commons at the end of January 1970, the Action Campaign Committee had achieved its goal and began to disband. By the time the Bill became law in May 1970, the Committee had virtually faded away.

Although employers, trade unions and workers were allowed over five years to prepare for the implementation of the Equal Pay Act 1970, some commentators may feel − more than ten years later − that it is still too soon to judge the effectiveness of Britain's anti-sex discrimination legislation. They would argue that since the Act has been in force only five years − and has been followed by the Sex Discrimination Act 1975 and the Employment Protection Act 1975 − much more time is needed to effect the radical changes in British society which will finally eliminate discrimination between the sexes. In sharp opposition to this view, there are the radical feminists who point to the alleged massive evasion of legislation and to the failure of women to achieve the equality of consideration for access to the prerequisite education, training and promotion opportunities which alone can provide the basis for the eventual achievement of equal opportunities for women in Britain.

The fact, nevertheless, remains that Britain has taken two bold legislative strides towards the elimination of sex discrimination − the first relating to equal pay, the second to equal opportunity. Both strides must be considered together when measuring the distance covered since the Ford Sewing Machinists walked out of the River Plant in May 1968. The remainder of this chapter is devoted to a brief review of the new legislation and its impact on some of the wider aspects of British industrial relations, together with some of the policy issues posed for both management and the Unions.

Under section 2(1) of the European Communities Act 1971, the British Parliament gave legal effect to all the rights and obligations under the Rome Treaty of 1957, Article 119 of which laid down firmly the principle of 'equal pay for equal work'. For the purposes of this Article, 'pay' means 'the ordinary basic or minimum wage or salary and any other consideration, whether in cash or in kind, which the worker receives directly and indirectly in respect of his employment from his employer'. In other words, equal pay means that pay for the same work at piece-rates is to be calculated on the basis of the same unit of measurement; and that pay for work at time-rates must be the same for the same job. It may be noted that, whereas ILO Convention 100 refers to 'equal remuneration for work of equal value', Article 119 adheres to the older formulation 'equal pay for equal work', but without defining what is meant by 'equal work' or 'the same work' or 'the same job'. The principle enshrined in Article 119 is, of course, easy to apply when men and women are consistently engaged in exactly the same work — that is, when they carry out the same bundle of tasks which make up a job — but much more difficult to apply when they differ, to a greater or lesser extent. The Community's lawyers eventually recognised the need to prevent an unscrupulous employer from introducing artificial differences between 'men's work' and 'women's work' simply in order to evade equal pay, as Beatrice Webb had noted some 60 years earlier. In its Directive of 10 February 1975,[32] the Council extended 'the principle of equal pay' to 'the principle of equal value'. That closed the loophole so far as equal pay was concerned. But, as Beatrice Webb again noted, an employer might still discriminate against women by employing only men on work which could be done equally well by women. To exclude this, the Council's Directive of 9 February 1976[33] established 'the principle of equal treatment for men and women as regards access to employment, including promotion, as to practical training and as regards working conditions'.

The problems for the student of British sex discrimination law begin at this point because its provisions are not to be found in a single consolidated Statute but distributed between three separate Acts:[34]

1. the *Equal Pay Act 1970,* as subsequently amended, which established the right of men and women to equal treatment as regards terms and conditions of employment when they are employed on the same or broadly similar work or work which, though different, has been given the same value under a job evaluation scheme;

2. the *Sex Discrimination Act 1975*, which amended the Equal Pay Act and which makes sex discrimination unlawful in full-time and part-time employment, training and related matters, as well as in various other fields; and which established the Equal Opportunities Commission with responsibility for working towards the elimination of discrimination, for promoting equality between men and women generally, and for keeping under review the working of the two Acts.

3. the *Employment Protection Act 1975,* as amended in 1976, which is principally concerned with the improvement in industrial relations and which set up the Advisory, Conciliation and Arbitration Service

(ACAS) and the Central Arbitration Council (CAC), to which ACAS may refer cases, including disputes over equal pay and sex discrimination, if the parties agree; and which confers individual employment rights, including a woman worker's right to statutory maternity leave and the right to return to her job after the birth of her child.

The first two Acts add up, in effect, to a single anti-sex discrimination code in employment and in other fields. Taken in conjunction with the Employment Protection Act, they are designed to fulfil the United Kingdom's obligations under the Treaty of Rome and the Directives following upon it. The best approach to an understanding of the legislation is probably not through the earlier Equal Pay Act but through the Sex Discrimination Act which amended it.

The Sex Discrimination Act 1975 — which is now the key Statute — defines discrimination in two ways:

1. *direct discrimination* — which occurs where a woman is treated less favourably than a man 'on the ground of her sex';[35]
2. *indirect discrimination* — which occurs where, even though the same 'requirement or condition' is or would be applied to both sexes, 'it is such that the proportion of women who can comply with it is considerably smaller than the proportion of men'; where it cannot be shown to be justifiable 'irrespective of the sex of the person to whom it is applied'; and where it is applied to a woman's detriment 'because she cannot comply with it'.[36]

These indirect discrimination provisions are clearly fundamental to the achievement of equal opportunity since, without them, an unscrupulous employer might continue to hire only men on the grounds that they alone possess the necessary qualifications and experience. An employer may offer a defence against indirect discrimination, provided he can show it to be justifiable 'irrespective of the sex of the person'. But no such defence is available against direct discrimination. The difficulties in drawing a clear line between direct and indirect discrimination soon become apparent, since the characteristics and qualities which each sex may be said to possess range from purely social conventions, such as appearance (which might give rise to indirect discrimination), to more fundamental biological differences (which might give rise to direct discrimination). As one writer has put it: 'It could be argued that sex means nothing more than the possession of male or female reproductive organs; if this is so then the plea of justification will be available in the great majority of cases.'[37]

The Equal Pay Act 1970 provides a similar framework of comparison in the more restricted field of pay discrimination. Whereas the original version of the Act was not concerned with wider aspects of discrimination beyond pay, the amended version imports an 'equality clause' into employment contracts as a means of determining whether discrimination has occurred. The effect of this is that, where a woman is employed on like work, or work rated as equivalent to that of a man in the same employment, her contract shall be deemed to include an equality clause which gives her the same terms and conditions as the man. Thus, if a woman wishes to claim equal pay with a man in the same employment, she has first to show that she is employed on 'like work' — that is, her work and that of the man with whom she wishes to establish a comparison must be 'of the same or a broadly similar nature'. This leads directly to the key notion of 'equivalence', as defined in section 1(5) of the Act:

> A woman is to be regarded as employed on work rates as equivalent with that of any men if, but only if, her job and their job have been given an equal value, in terms of the demand made on the worker under various headings (for instance effort, skill, decision) on a study undertaken with a view to evaluating in those terms the jobs to be done by all or any of the employees in an undertaking or group of undertakings, or would have been given equal value but for the evaluation being made on a system setting different values for men and women on the same demand under any heading.[38]

As noted above,[39] the Declaration of Philadelphia, some 30 years earlier, had called on management and unions to co-operate in establishing 'precise and objective standards for determining job content, irrespective of the sex of the worker as the basis for determining wage rates'. In Britain that call went largely unheeded until the Equal Pay Act prescribed that a valid job evaluation scheme was an acceptable basis for 'work rated as equivalent'. 'Job evaluation' is a generic term applied to a wide variety of schemes which aim 'to compare all jobs under review, using common criteria to define the relationship of one job to another'.[40] The standards set for determining job content may be 'precise' but they cannot be 'objective', as the Declaration of Philadelphia urged, since every scheme 'must by its nature contain subjective elements'. On the other hand, a valid scheme of job evaluation is 'impersonal in character . . . in the sense that it seeks to evaluate jobs, not persons'.[41] Such a scheme would, *prima facie,* be non-discriminatory on grounds of sex. Thus, if the value of a man's job exceeds that of a woman's job, it is lawful for the man to be paid more than the woman. But if the 'value' of their jobs is equal, they are legally entitled to receive the same 'rate for the job'.

Conversely, 'if the employer proves that the variation is genuinely due to a material difference (other than the difference of sex) between her case and his',[42] then the variation between their rates of pay is justifiable and no equality clause may be implied. Even where job evaluation shows that two jobs are of 'equal value', there may nevertheless be a genuine 'material difference', other than the difference of sex — for example, different lengths of service or the possession of some higher qualification, which may justify the variation in pay. Such a defence applies equally to 'work rated as equivalent' cases and to 'like work' cases. In the same way, a higher rate may be paid for higher output or productivity, always provided it is not based on sex — that is, on either direct or indirect discrimination.

During the first four years' operation of the two Acts, most of the cases brought by women to Industrial Tribunals have been concerned with the interpretation of these key sections. In the first year (1976), many women were apparently discouraged from bringing claims for equal pay by the unimaginative and conflicting decisions of some Tribunals. More recently, however, the Employment Appeal Tribunal, which hears appeals from the Industrial Tribunals, has done much to restore confidence in the new jurisdictions by boldly asserting their 'reforming' character. In a series of important decisions, it has developed a body of authoritative principles which encourage Tribunals to construe the Acts in a much broader manner, more sympathetic to claimants. Amongst the more significant decisions on equal pay are those concerned with the meaning of 'like work' under section 1(4) — including the validity of job evaluation schemes — and with an employer's defence of inequality based on 'material difference' under section 1(3) of the Equal Pay Act.[43]

A great deal of criticism surrounds the alleged ineffectiveness of the Equal Opportunities Commission, the principal enforcement agency of the two Acts. Established under section 53 of the Sex Discrimination Act, the Commission is charged with the duty of (a) working towards the elimination of discrimination; (b) promoting equality of opportunity between men and women generally; and (c) keeping under review the working of the Acts and submitting proposals to the Home Secretary for their amendment from time to time. In its second Annual Report, published in 1978, the Commission freely admitted that it was 'not satisfied . . .

with the pace of progress towards equality generally'.[44] Not surprisingly, it has come under fierce attack from feminists for its failure to spearhead an aggressive campaign to secure effective equality for British women. Defending itself against that charge, the Commission pointed to 'the complexity of the problems we are required to deal with, and the entrenched habits, practices and attitudes which surround them'. In its first year, the Commission's energies 'were devoted almost exclusively to responding to the volume of inquiries from members of the public'. In its second year, its main resources were deployed in executing in a systematic way the strategic role with which Parliament entrusted the Commission. Its overriding duty to the public interest was, 'so far as possible, *to change the practice* which gave rise to the isolated complaint'. The Commission concluded that Britain was

> very close to the end of the first phase in the use of the law to promote progress towards equal pay. The next phase, it seems clear, will involve widening opportunities and breaking down job segregation through the Sex Discrimination Act.[45]

In its survey of the policies and practices of Britain's 500 largest employers towards the achievement of equality at work, published in 1978, the Commission found the over-all picture 'largely disappointing'; the majority of employers had taken formal steps to ensure the avoidance of unlawful discrimination but 'the wider issues of equal opportunities have hardly been examined, indeed they may not even have been acknowledged as issues'. The continued segregation of work into jobs performed historically by men or women was still one of the major obstacles to promoting 'real equality between the sexes'. Women still found great difficulty in moving into certain jobs offering higher pay, more personal fulfilment and greater promotion chances. The consciousness amongst employers of such root issues and of the concept of indirect sex discrimination was low. A small number of companies had adopted 'positive discrimination' policies but the Commission concluded that Britain had 'clearly a long way to go before equality between the sexes is achieved in the workplace'.[46]

The pessimistic tone of much recent comment on the working of the two Acts may well derive, first, from excessive expectations of what the law alone can achieve and, second, from a lack of historical perspective amongst some commentators on the long and bitter struggle by women for equality in all aspects of British society. Feminists are understandably impatient to abolish sex discrimination but their enthusiasm sometimes appears to conceal a lack of direct experience in achieving practical results by agreement within the British system of industrial relations. Those with personal experience of working to implement the two Acts are likely to emphasise the primacy of voluntary agreements reached through collective bargaining at the workplace rather than reliance on Tribunal decisions.

The 'declaratory effect' of the two Acts has been of undoubted value in focusing attention on the persistence of intolerable discrimination against women in British society. The Acts themselves are highly legalistic and of tortuous compexlity so it is hardly surprising that only modest progress has been made in abolishing discrimination over the past four years as a result of legislation alone. Finally, it may be worth again emphasising that – as in the case of the Bryant & May Matchgirls – it was direct action by one small group of women workers – the Ford Sewing Machinists – exerting pressure on a multinational corporation, that compelled the British Parliament to legislate against that discrimination. Over the past four years, those legislative intentions have been slowly translated into an impressive body of case law which defines rigorous standards for treating 'equals as equals' at work and in society at large. But 'real equality' is not a right conferred by the law or by Tribunals, however sympathetic they may be; it is an evolving code of practice, built up by workers and managers through direct action as well as by negotiation, and requiring the continuous attention of the rank and file, the Unions, employers and the state's agencies to ensure its fulfilment.

No substantial progress can now be expected towards the objective of effective equality at work in Britain until long-cherished and often outmoded traditions – such as the present protective laws which prevent women who wish to do so from working overtime, night shifts or weekend work – are vigorously challenged and, where appropriate, brought up to date. For the majority of British working men, it is as ethically offensive to grant women equal pay and equal opportunity without requiring of them an equal work contribution as it is to deny them equality where that contribution is given. The Equal Opportunity Commission's current five-year strategy promises more emphasis on its law enforcement activities, more vigorous use of its formal investigation powers[47] and 'programmes to enable women to break out of their segregated and isolated position in the employment market'.[48] Representatives of both sides of industry may support equality at work as an abstract principle. Management and unions at local level may reach agreement on some form of words which allows equality to be written

into collective bargaining agreements. But there is little evidence –
particularly at a time of rising unemployment and recurrent inflation –
that men, who monopolise most decision making in Britain today, are
ready to support a wide-ranging campaign of positive discrimination in
favour of women, a campaign which alone can end discrimination. The
Ford Sewing Machinists may have shown the way – but there is still a
long way to go.

Notes

1. J.T. Dunlop, *Industrial Relations Systems* (Holt, New York, 1958). See
Ch. 9, p. 314 below for further discussion.

2. Some of the material in this section has been adapted from an earlier
article. See Sander Meredeen, 'Sex Discrimination in Britain: A Provisional
Evaluation', *Sociologie du Travail*, (forthcoming).

3. Sidney and Beatrice Webb, *Industrial Democracy* (Longmans, London, 1902
edn), p.173; Allan Flanders, 'Collective Bargaining: A Theoretical Analysis' in
Management and Unions (Faber, London, 1975 edn), p.216.

4. A. Stafford, *A Match to Fire the Thames* (Hodder and Stoughton, London, 1961).

5. TUC Annual Report (1888).

6. *Report of the War Cabinet Committee on Women in Industry* (the Atkin
Committee Report), Cmd. 135 (HMSO, London, 1919), Appendix IV –
Documents.

7. Ibid.

8. Mrs Sidney Webb, *Minority Report;* see Atkin Committee Report, above,
p.288.

9. Ibid., p.270.

10. Ibid., p.294.

11. See Ch. 1, note 12, p. 22 above.

12. *Conventions and Recommendations adopted by the International Labour
Organisation* (ILO, Geneva, 1960).

13. *Fighting Discrimination in Employment and Occupation* (ILO, Geneva,
1968), Appendix 1.

14. These recommendations clearly reflect US experience in the design and
application of job evaluation techniques during the Second World War, notably in
the heavy steel industry. See Jack Stieber, *The Steel Industry Wage Structure*
(Harvard University Press, 1959).

15. *Royal Commission on Equal Pay* (1944-46) (the Asquith Commission
Report), Cmd. 6937 (HMSO, London, 1946).

16. TUC, *Memorandum of Evidence* to Royal Commission on Equal Pay.

17. *Conventions and Recommendations.*

18. See note 8, p. 289, above.

19. *The Times,* 4 May 1968.

20. Ibid., 3 May 1968.

21. Audrey Hunt, *A Survey of Women's Employment* (Department of
Employment and Productivity, HMSO, London, 1968).

22. *The Times,* 6 May 1968.

23. *New Society,* 9 May 1968.

24. *The Times,* 10 May 1968.

25. *Hansard,* 26 June 1968, vol. 767, col. 506.

26. Ibid., vol. 767, col. 492.

27. *Headlight,* vol. 10, no. 5 (June 1968).

28. *Daily Mirror,* 2 July 1968.

29. *Financial Times,* 22 November 1968.

30. Department of Employment and Productivity letter, dated 14 April 1969, to the Secretary of the National Assembly of Women.

31. *Financial Times,* 21 July 1969.

32. European Economic Community, *Directive 75/117/EEC.*

33. European Economic Community, *Directive 76/207/EEC.*

34. Yet a fourth Act is involved since Schedule 4 of the Race Relations Act 1977 amends section 58 of the Sex Discrimination Act 1975.

35. Sex Discrimination Act 1975, section 1(1)(9).

36. Ibid., section 1(1)(6).

37. Judith Reid, 'Women in Employment', *Modern Law Journal,* vol. 39 (July 1977).

38. Equal Pay Act 1970, section 1(5).

39. See note 13, above.

40. National Board for Prices and Incomes, *Report No. 83: Job Evaluation,* Cmnd. 3772 (HMSO, London, 1968), p.3.

41. Ibid.

42. Equal Pay Act 1970, section 1(3).

43. For a useful summary, see *Industrial Relations Review and Report,* no. 155 and 158 (July and August 1977) and no. 185 (October 1978).

44. Equal Opportunities Commission, *Second Annual Report* (HMSO, London, 1978), p.3. Compare the findings of the London School of Economics' 'Equal Pay and Opportunities Project' in *Department of Employment Gazette* (July 1978).

45. Ibid., p.4.

46. Equal Opportunities Commission, *Equality Between the Sexes in Industry — How Far Have We Come?* (HMSO, London, 1978).

47. Amongst the strongest powers conferred on the Commission is that of conducting a formal investigation into alleged discrimination, including the power to compel information to be given. The first such investigation was initiated in February 1977 at the Luton factory in Bedfordshire of Electrolux Limited, the British subsidiary of the Swedish multinational, making vacuum cleaners, refrigerators and other domestic appliances. After two and a half years of investigation, the Commission issued its first industrial Non-Discrimination Notice to Electrolux Limited in July 1979. See Equal Opportunities Commission, *Report on Electrolux Limited* (1980).

48. Equal Opportunities Commission, *Second Annual Report* (HMSO, London, 1978), p. 4.

Part VI

SECOND DIALOGUE

9 THE LEARNING PROCESS IN INDUSTRIAL CONFLICT

SM Last time we dealt at length with the specific events of the dispute. Today, I think we should try to place them in a broader perspective and pick up some of the more theoretical points they raise. For example, what do you think we learn about the nature of industrial conflict which we didn't know before? What does the dispute tell us about the political consciousness of British working women in the late sixties?

HF OK. Let's begin with that point. Here was a group of previously deferential women who, once they had decided to enter the arena and pick up the glove, were determined to fight more resolutely, to go to any lengths to succeed. But even this was not the major factor. The major factor was their determination to show that just because they'd been acquiescent in the past — and might be so again in the future — once they decide to take up the cudgels, they have to be taken more seriously than an equivalent group of men. Now, how does one explain that 'explosion of consciousness'? It's happened elsewhere, of course, at places like Pilkington's,[1] where it's an isolated event and, perhaps more to the point, at Trico.[2] It flares up and then it subsides and nothing much is heard of it again. I think we explain it by the lack of developed customs and traditions. My theory is that the one-off battle is totally inadequate for any enduring, long-term, conscious, calculated development of a movement. It just can't happen that way. All it can do — and it did so on this occasion — is to transmit that explosion. In other words, the women's consciousness was diffused or transfused into other bodies, for example, into the equal pay movement which subsequently swept across the country. And, of course, it was this dispute which infused new confidence and determination into the rank-and-file leadership.

SM Yes, I agree with that. The 'birth of consciousness' is particularly important. But we still haven't explained under what conditions that consciousness is more likely to emerge. Why that particular group of women? Why that particular moment? You describe the women's sense of dedication to the cause. But I've never seen the dispute in terms of spontaneous action. I've seen it throughout as illustrating the key role of the intellectual — your role, in fact — the role of articulating and

313

making explicit the political dimension latent within the instrumental issue. It was *your* action, after the dispute had begun, which politicised the struggle and turned it from a mere grading issue into an equal pay and sex discrimination struggle and which − only temporarily − raised the women's level of consciousness. But, as you say, it was the outcome of that battle which resurrected the Dagenham Shop Stewards' movement.

HF Yes, that's one aspect. Another aspect we bring out is the way in which management and workers develop certain kinds of tactics about the conduct of conflict. When do you decide to turn the screw? When do you involve larger numbers? When do you start to make concessions?

SM Right. That's crucially important. I think Ford of Britain provides a unique context in which to study British industrial relations in the post-war period. The Sewing Machinists' dispute enables us to study the dynamics of industrial conflict in Ford which I take as both a microcosm and a magnifier of British industrial relations. You might describe it as one continuous 'learning process'. Ford shows the character of industrial conflict and collective bargaining at its most highly developed stage. That's why we can use it as a working model of the underlying structure and the processes of change through time.

When John Dunlop wrote *Industrial Relations Systems*[3] in 1958, he put forward a very ambitious claim: he had developed the concept of an industrial relations system as comprising a web of rules, devised by the actors within the system − that is, chiefly management and unions but also government − and he intended to show how those rules arise − i.e., the procedural and substantive rules which govern the conduct of the actors within the system − and how those rules change in response to changes in the wider society. In short, he claimed to show a *dynamic* process of rule making and rule changing. In fact, he doesn't do anything of the sort: instead of a dynamic model he presents a *static* model. Walton and McKersie[4] took up the Dunlop model and presented a behavioural theory of labour negotiations in order to dynamise the model. It seems to fit the American contract renewal type of bargaining but has had little application in Britain.

I think we show the British system of industrial relations in dynamic evolution. To use Dunlop's own terminology, we show clearly the different 'contexts' in which the actors meet and confront the issues: the context of *technology* and particularly the impact of technological change in the motor industry; the context of *product markets* and the effect of foreign competition; the context of quite distinct *labour markets,* with the emphasis on Ford's high day rates and the drive for parity with the Midlands piecework earnings; and the context of *capital markets* with the flow of international capital by multinational corporations to maximise returns on investment. And, finally, we provide an exceptionally detailed account of the shifting locus and distribution of *power* within the system.

But you remember Dunlop's last crucial variable — the existence of a *shared ideology* which is commonly accepted by the actors and which helps to bind the system together. I'd like to discuss that aspect with you because it seems to me that it's the clash of conflicting ideologies at Ford that helps to explain the character of industrial relations at Ford and the way the rules at Ford are made and applied.

In reading your account of the internal consequences of the dispute, Henry, I was struck by your extremely cavalier treatment of the Procedure Agreement and the obligation to observe the rules for managing conflict. It seems to me you believe that workers are ideologically justified in breaking the rules. I've tried to argue that the network of rules are of mutual advantage to both sides in industrial relations and that Shop Stewards have a vested interest — as part of the 'loyal opposition' — to respect and maintain the system of rule making, rule interpretation and rule changing. The dynamics of industrial conflict are concerned essentially first, with operating the rules and, second, with changing those rules.

HF Well, I think it's necessary to recognise, first, that to play any oppositional role helps the system itself to survive. The very fact that you play the role of opposition — whether parliamentary opposition or industrial opposition — presumes that you play by the rules which secure and reinforce the system itself. And, second, breaking the rules is not inconsistent with that role. It entails, if you like, an occasional disregard of the rules. The problem arises because you tend to focus on the non-observance of the rules, as opposed to their observance. Shop Stewards, like me, would observe the rules for most of the time. By and large — in the widest sense, not the strict application — the rules are in fact generally observed. Speaking as a former Convener, I can tell you that you *do* go to the Personnel Office. You *do* explain the problem. You *do* discuss it and try to get an answer. You *do* try to put forward a formula which you think might be acceptable to both sides and which will resolve the problem. And so does the other side. There is an initial willingness to seek a solution via the established channels. Notwithstanding that fact, specific occasions occur from time to time which offer the opportunity of extending the frontier of workers' control and encroaching on management prerogative. Then you feel entitled to take a short cut, to disregard the rules in order to achieve a particular objective . . . There's no question of pangs of conscience about it. If such an opportunity presents itself, the standard practice is to 'review the troops' and, if they're ready and willing to take action to bring about certain changes from next Monday, so be it. You don't say to them on the Friday: Look, I'm sorry, you can't take this action. Mr Ramsey won't be able to sleep at night because you're not observing the rules!

SM No. You misunderstood me. I wasn't making a sentimental appeal. I hope I was being realistic in saying that, if you don't even acknowledge that the rules are there and you ignore them completely, then you do so at great risk. First, because you release a force of unconstitutionality which you can't yourself control. You can't dictate when the next group of workers will follow your lead and take similar action which will throw others out of work. And so on. But, second, you alert management to the need for some fresh sanctions to ensure that Procedure is observed — either by means of the law, which we both agree is irrelevant and unhelpful, or by means of other inducements, like the penalty clauses.

HF Well, perhaps I can give you a much better analogy. The TUC or the trade union movement at large is perhaps much more willing than Shop Stewards to observe the rules and the laws prevailing at the time. But if you look at trade union history, you find that, on occasions, even they choose to disregard the law. The 1971 Industrial Relations Act was the most recent occasion when trade unions took a conscious decision to disobey the law — despite the fact that they always preach to their members that they should observe the law in general because it helps the working class to win decisions, too.

SM I have no problem with that. That's an act of conscious policy, a decision taken after the most careful consideration. It was a policy decision taken in principle to oppose the very objectives of the Industrial Relations Bill. . . . .

HF But that conflicts, if I may say so, with the ground rules that trade unions can't afford to defy the law. You can't lay down that ground rule and then choose to say, every so often: Never mind the ground rules, we're going to defy the law!

SM I'm not saying that. I'm saying that liberal democracy depends on a willingness to acknowledge that nobody has a monopoly of the truth — neither management nor the Unions — and that if, in fact, you don't acknowledge the rules and make some attempt to work the rules and to change them, then you aim a blow not simply at the substantive rules themselves, but at the very procedural rules, rule making and rule changing – in short, at the whole process of negotiation and accommodation of conflicting interests. Take the 1969 situation at Ford: the Trade Unions were urging the Company to admit Shop Stewards to the NJNC so that they themselves could have the opportunity to participate in making the rules. So Shop Stewards themselves *do* have a vested interest in rules.

HF I'm not denying that. I've acknowledged that if you want to participate actively in industrial relations, the very fact that you choose to play an opposition role implies that you have some regard for the rules of the game. But that does not imply that you've got no other choice, that you must always play the game according to those rules and that you're committed to their observance at all times. After all, one could cite many examples of management disregarding the rules and existing procedures, when temptation or opportunity presents itself. Ah, but then you say: That's only to be expected. That's capitalist mal-practice . . . Do you really believe it's a matter of virtuous angels on the Trade Union Side and wicked capitalist devils on the other? Isn't it true in politics generally that, from time to time, when the opportunity occurs, the temptation is there to take advantage of the opportunity? Never mind the rules.

SM No, I expect unions to behave within a higher code of morality than management. Trade unions in practice regularly invoke principle in support of their actions. Indeed, in this very dispute, when asked how he could justify his Union's official support for the women's strike, Birch himself said that equal pay was a matter of principle. Too bad that the Procedure had to be broken or the Agreement 'ratted on'. Principles are principles. When a principle is at stake, you don't expect to be hamstrung by the petty rules of Procedure . . . That leads me to suppose that unions are not simply pragmatic. There must be some pragmatism, of course. You can't survive without considering the situations which present themselves from day to day. But certainly I would expect trade unions to subscribe to a code of higher principles than management. Management, after all, exists to exploit the conjuncture of the market, to take advantage of the laws of supply and demand. Wherever the 'invisible hand' of competition leads, management follows. But I expect trade unions, who came into being to defend humane values, to subscribe to a higher code of behaviour, rather than follow the code which capitalists have adopted in order to enrich themselves at the expense of others.

HF But when it comes to industrial conflict, it's unrealistic to expect one side – the Trade Unions – to observe the Queensbury Rules and the other side – the Management Side – not to do so. If the importance of the issue transcends the observance of agreements and rules, then you have to make a choice. That applies generally in life.

SM Yes. I agree that rules are man-made institutions which are there to be interpreted and disregarded, where necessary – but at a price. In a democracy, you are entitled to say: No, I will not pay my taxes. I will not go to war. I will not obey the law of the land, for conscientious reasons, and I'm prepared to pay the price for that refusal. Of course, we're touching on difficult questions of political philosophy when we speak of a mass refusal to obey the law. I'm simply pleading for some acknowledgement on your part that procedural rules and agreements have a valid role in a mixed capitalist economy and in a system of industrial relations like that at Ford, where it is very often in the *Unions'* interest to invoke Procedure. Why else would you have been a member of the Joint Works Committee?

HF Because committees of that kind provide a facility for transmitting messages and articulating demands and sometimes resolve problems. They are part of a framework of rules and procedures which can be used as stepping stones for advancing workers' interests. But rules and procedures *per se* can be self-defeating articles. For example, if all the railwaymen observed all the rules all the time, no trains would run. That apart, rule observance is dependent on the power relationship at a given point in time between parties to an agreement and how useful, irksome or harmless particular rules are considered by those concerned. Employers have frequently abrogated agreements unilaterally – the Coventry Toolroom Agreement is a prime example. But reverting back to Ford, the 1968 Sewing Machinists' strike demonstrated how, under the pressure of events, both unions and management readily disregarded existing procedures and agreements. Similarly in 1978, unions felt either entitled or obliged to break the existing Agreement after the pay strike had started.

SM OK then. Let's turn to the 1978 dispute and examine it closely to see what each of the four principal actors – the rank and file, the Unions, management and the state – had learned about observing the rules or breaking the rules under what you describe as 'the pressure of events'.

HF Right. When the Company made the first offer in September, neither side seemed to be aware that a major dispute was imminent. Ron Todd, Chairman of the Trade Union Side, said: 'We've got a long way to go . . . Don't let's worry too much about the initial offer . . . It's how we end up that matters . . . There is still a lot of talking to be done.' For management, the existing Agreement had another four weeks to run — sufficient time for the normal negotiating manoeuvres to take place. Management's chief concern was how to present an offer — which at that stage was limited to 5 per cent because of the government's pay norm — and how to push the Unions as quickly as possible into discussions on productivity. So the Company was more concerned with tone, manner of presentation and appearances than with substantive issues. But the actual amount offered plus the impression that management was simply complying with a government-determined pay limit caused the spontaneous walk-out. Once the membership had taken the lead — the leadership followed.

SM You say that Ron Todd and the Conveners did nothing to discourage the walk-out, but merely adopted the line of supporting the membership after the walk-out?

HF Yes, but I'm talking about the Conveners, in particular. There were some who said the walk-out was premature and who wanted to see what the negotiations might produce and there were others who favoured some delay in order to co-ordinate action between plants, but once the walk-out had taken place, they had no choice but to give support. The power of decision had been effectively removed from the NJNC and, although, for example, neither Duffy nor Scanlon was happy about the walk-out, they recognised the reality of the situation and, therefore, the AUEW Executive repeated on Tuesday what the Conveners had done on the previous Friday. They made the strike official, no doubt in the hope of securing some measure of involvement and control, although this meant a flagrant breach of existing Agreements.

SM That put management in an extremely difficult situation because, although it would rather have an official strike, once an unofficial strike has been given official status, the breach of procedure lies at the feet of the official leadership and not just the rank-and-file leadership. That presents enormous problems for a Company that wants to encourage more sophisticated bargaining and an inevitably protracted bargaining process. Management must begin to wonder, were they right to encourage the Unions to present an early claim, and to make an early offer before the contract had expired. That's what incensed Terry Beckett and led him to condemn the Unions for a flagrant breach of the existing Agreements . . .

Let's turn from the procedural to the substantive aspects of the claim which the Unions represented as being 'socially responsible', and on which they wanted to negotiate in an atmosphere of free collective bargaining, in an unfettered spirit, and based on the Company's ability to meet the claim. By the time Ford came to reply to the claim it was clear that the Company was trapped between the pressure from the shop floor below and the pressure from government policy above. Ford knew that, if its initial offer exceeded the 5 per cent guideline, and if its proposed productivity deal were rejected, it would be subjected to untested sanctions. It was only after the nine-week strike, when the government asked for, and was refused, the support of Parliament in applying sanctions, that Ford managed to divert attention from its breach of the inflationary dyke. In my judgement, the Unions had expected Ford to meet the claim in large measure based on its profitability and Ford, for its part, was almost certainly ready to go a long way towards meeting that claim, except that it felt trapped by the 5 per cent limit.

HF I can see that, but with hindsight one can argue that the Company should have had informal talks with the Unions to prepare the ground better for a productivity deal which would have ensured that the money was paid by some other means. In practice, rather than show their hand, Ford played it by ear, and hoped for a repeat of the 1977 negotiating pattern when, after a month-long haggle, punctuated by several all-night sittings, the membership eventually accepted the Company's offer.

SM Well, yes, I think Ford expected there might be a two- or three-week strike if they took a stand on the 5 per cent limit, but not a nine-week strike. Then again, there was no support for the 5 per cent limit at the Labour Party Conference in the second week of the strike.

HF Right, I'm coming to that. On the Union Side, there was a resolve by Moss Evans and others to break away from the Social Contract and to restore free collective bargaining. That resolve was backed up by the TUC in September and by the Labour Party Conference in October. Moss Evans saw this as a political fight and not just a bargaining issue at Ford. But, as we have said before, Ford represents the most highly developed structure of capital and the Unions at Ford are amongst the most highly developed sections of organised labour in Britain, so if you decide to challenge the government's pay policy, that's one of the best industrial battlegrounds.

When I had a long interview with Moss Evans about one year before the strike, he not only made it very clear that he was opposed to the continuance of the Social Contract, but stated that his primary responsibility was to the membership, and not the government. Consequently, irrespective of anything else, the Ford Unions were determined to pursue the objective of free collective bargaining, and they were quite happy to mount the challenge to the government's incomes policy at Ford, because of the Company's undoubted ability to pay, and the TUC and Labour Party resolutions against the 5 per cent norm.

SM In effect, Moss Evans and others were willing to use Ford as the context in which to fight a political battle with the Labour Government over the future of incomes policy. Well, Moss Evans is entitled to the credit or must take much of the blame for what followed. His action at Ford was invoked as a precedent by the tanker drivers, the road haulage drivers and then by workers in the public sector to justify their own claims for increases above the 5 per cent limit. So Ford certainly does lead the way — politically as well as industrially! . . . Can we come back to the key issues in this dispute, which I think boil down to three: first, the wage claim; second, the 35-hour week claim; and, third, the claim for a more effective voice in Ford's decision-making processes. Do you believe the nine-week strike was successful in terms of those three principal claims?

HF Well, so far as the wage settlement is concerned, the 17 per cent settlement was certainly satisfactory. As far as expectations were concerned, it failed to secure any advance on the shorter working week, but I think that was always more a political demand than an economic demand. It's a 'tongue in cheek' demand because, in my experience, the Unions know the membership aren't really all that interested. It just means the same hours at overtime rates . . .

SM So the membership weren't disappointed at the rejection?

HF Well, the leadership might have been disappointed because they had hoped to achieve a political breakthrough at Ford on the work-sharing argument with an eye to future unemployment trends.[5] With the impact of micro-processors and so on, they would have liked a breakthrough, even in a limited way — a phased reduction — to open a window on a new area of bargaining. But the fact that it wasn't successful didn't really worry the membership too much and, without their support, there is not much you can do. The leadership just has to swallow hard, gnash their teeth, grin and bear it.

SM Can we move on then to what you have called 'building the climax' of the dispute. It's my impression that by the sixth week of the dispute, there was an absolute impasse in which neither side appeared to make any movement. I wonder whether you began to see that, if Ford was to escape from this dilemma of being trapped in the fight between the Ford Unions and the government, by being in the forefront of the bargaining round, then the longer the 1978 strike dragged on, the later the renewal date of the next contract would be? So that every week longer the strike lasted, the further removed Ford would be in 1979, and succeeding years, from the head of the pay round. I wonder whether we should give Bob Ramsey and his Forward Planning Team the credit for having foreseen that, by allowing the strike to drag on, Ford would off-set some of the costs in later years? That's borne out by the fact that the new Agreement is for a twelve-month economic standstill and that the contract negotiations will not begin until November 1979.

HF Well, if that was the Company's objective — and I don't deny it might have been — it would certainly fit in with the trade union objectives in this country, namely, to shift the negotiations to January, which would align the British and the German Ford Companies' contract renewal dates.

SM That's right. Now, I can't believe the Company hadn't considered the possibility that sooner or later the two contract renewal dates would coincide, which would allow trade unions, for the first time, to take concerted action to pursue their wage claim against Ford on a European basis.[6]

HF But for completely different reasons. The Company would no longer be in the forefront of the annual round, but the Unions, because of a common contract renewal date, could become more effective in a European context. That would help the Unions to achieve their long-cherished objective of joint action and largely nullify any advantage the Company might derive from discarding its role as the pace-setters in the annual pay round.

SM Right. Now let's come on to what I find the most interesting part of the 1978 dispute. The government's productivity guideline said that 'Any improvement in productivity, compared with a recent representa-tive period, must be demonstrated before payments are actually made, by a properly audited trial'. The only way the Company could demon-strate a productivity gain was to produce evidence to show that it had dealt with *all* forms of interruption to the smooth rhythm of produc-tion — whether through lateness, absenteeism, restrictive practices, extended tea-breaks and so on, but in particular through unconstitu-tional action. When we compare the final offer with the initial offer, the *Attendance Allowances Plan* has been converted into a straightforward *Supplementary Payments Plan,* but the one element which the Company refused to drop were the penalties against workers who take part in un-constitutional action. These penalty clauses, or incentives to follow Procedure, which were first introduced in 1969, and dropped after con-siderable trade union pressure in 1974/75, were written back into the bargaining package in a much more effective way. First, they provide the Company with its most effective weapon for persuading workers to think before they take strike action; and, second, they provide a new bargainable element in the contract which Unions will wish to exploit by bidding up the amount of the Supplementary Payments Plan every year.

HF Well, I think there were two productivity factors. One was the record of over 1,000 work stoppages in 1977/78, which Beckett himself said had cost the Company over £80 million and which required a *collective* penalty to deal with it effectively. The other relates to the alleged lower productivity of the British plants as compared with the German or Belgian plants making the same, or similar, units. That can be explained in terms of *individuals* not being available for work due to absenteeism, lateness and so on. Therefore, the Company's response, along the lines of an Attendance Allowance Plan, was designed to make some progress on both the individual and collective fronts. It wasn't a question of the Company asking a higher price and expecting to be beaten down. It was a genuine response to the productivity problem. So when the strike pressure was applied, it wasn't a question of the company falling back to a prepared position; it was strike pressure which forced the Company to retreat by abandoning the individual penalties.

SM I agree with that, but the fact is that it dropped the individual penalties but retained the collective penalties, which have been written into the new contract and which I believe will become more important every year. As the Unions seek to increase the amount of the Supplementary Payments, they play directly into the Company's hands. The more they squeeze out of the Company, the more successful the disincentive to strike action becomes.

HF I don't think so. Sid Harroway has already stated that the Unions will seek to eliminate the penalty clauses in the next Agreement. Apart from that, it is much more the issue, the prevailing climate of opinion and the mood the workers are in that determine whether unconstitutional action takes place — and not £3 or £4 a week, less tax. Furthermore, the very existence of these penalty clauses can increase conflict. For example, if workers feel that their working conditions are intolerable, if it's too hot or too cold to work, or if there is some chemical or fume hazard in a particular area — and the Supervisor feels it's a marginal case, and thinks that workers should have stayed at work — then once the penalties are invoked you get a further conflict over whether it was right to apply that penalty; and that, on past precedent, sometimes leads to a further stoppage and enlarges the area of conflict.

SM I'd like to move on to the point at which Birch and Todd took the initiative and wrote to the Company asking for a resumption of negotiations. I interpreted that as meaning the Company had no intention of coming forward, as it had done in earlier disputes, to get Scanlon and Jones to call off the dispute, partly because they were no longer in office, but more important because it had a genuine interest in allowing the strike to drag on, to push back the contract renewal date. Birch and Todd had their knuckles rapped by the Stewards for taking that initiative, didn't they?

HF Yes, I think Birch and Todd at one stage saw the Company prepared to go on with the strike until Christmas. But once a strike in the motor industry goes on beyond eight weeks, it begins to damage employment prospects and the Company begins to risk losing its market share. I think the union leadership decided to secure the best possible settlement rather than risk the consequences of another seven weeks of strike, but some of the Conveners disapproved. They assumed that in a war of attrition the Company would give in before they did.

SM I see that as part of the learning process. Ford was prepared to hold out, take no further steps to improve its outstanding offer, but leave the initiative to the Union side. The Company made great play with the fact that its workers had lost a great deal of money by their strike action and had gained nothing which they could not have secured by staying at work. I don't think they'd have got the full 17 per cent, but it will be interesting to see whether either side has learned any further lessons from this most damaging strike and risk a stoppage of more than nine weeks in 1979[7] or 1980.

HF Well, there were some special factors at work in 1978, as we have said. The Company had learned from the 1971 experience that, because of the right-wing leadership of the AUEW, because of the drain on union funds, and because of state pressure on the unions over the level of settlements, on this occasion it paid the Company to take a more positive stand. And by adopting that posture, by standing off and refusing to be forced into an unacceptable deal, the Company hoped that the Unions would crack and so create a climate in which the Company was at a bargaining advantage. Management had internalised those lessons.

SM I'm not sure that collectivities – the management, the rank and file – do learn as individuals learn. Collectivities don't *really* learn; certain individuals learn and are sometimes able to share their insights with a group. What about the role of individual personalities?

HF I think we've touched on this point before, and I drew attention to the fundamental difference between paid functionaries carrying out Company policy as instructed, and unpaid, annually elected office holders such as Shop Stewards. In 1969, Mark Young did not resign because he's a 'quitter', but because he could no longer deliver. You simply cannot instruct voluntary office holders. The learning process on the Trade Union Side is, therefore, much more a collective expression of past experiences which is then related to the mood and momentum of a given situation. Decisions about policies and actions, therefore, do not depend on whether a particular individual can, or cannot, get to a meeting.

SM You mean the learning process is the exchange of day-to-day experiences in the plant, from which a consensus eventually emerges?

HF Yes, priorities put forward by plants generally reflect the occupational mix of their labour force. Conflicts over priorities are mainly due to craft divisions but, on the whole, policies evolve over periods of months based on an exchange of views between Conveners and Works Committees, and are eventually formulated at such gatherings as National Conveners' meetings, or National Delegate Conferences. The nature of the demands vary, some are political and formalistic, others concern economic and control issues very close to the heart of the membership. But all of these incorporate the lessons of the past, and reflect the endeavours to make good the failures and shortcomings of successive years.

SM I'd like to relate these points about the learning process at Ford to the more general question of the learning process in industrial conflict. How far can we generalise from the Ford experience? Throughout our discussion, we have stressed the fact that the historical experience of the parties plays a crucial role in shaping the thinking and action of the actors in the Ford system of industrial relations. Does that learning process have a restricted meaning within the Ford context, or can we build on it to develop a more general theory? Because of the intense conflict in Ford's industrial relations, there was an accelerated learning process. It's not simply that trade unions at Ford are a 'school for socialism', but that Ford is also a 'school for British industrial relations', offering examples of both the positive and negative learning process. By the *positive* learning process I mean the capacity and the willingness of the parties to evaluate their experience, to extract some meaning from it and to apply the lessons of that experience — continuously to correct their course of action to achieve the objectives they've set themselves. For example, the Company's belated recognition that it must come to terms with the rank-and-file leadership and not seek to conclude deals over the heads of the membership — that's an example of positive learning on the Company's part. The *negative* learning process is best seen where one of the parties reverses its policies and regresses to an earlier habituated form of behaviour. For example, the Company's obsessional preoccupation with the honouring of agreements — as if all conflicts at work could be settled by reason and compromise. Or, to take an example from the shop floor, the idea that force is the only language that management understands and that to get action on a grievance you must take direct action.

HF Well, I made the point earlier, that the nature and complexity of the productive process in the motor industry and the complexity of the Company structure in seeking to exploit volume output on an international scale — those factors create a conflict between the most developed forms of capital and the most advanced sections of labour. Therefore, if one may draw on Ford's experience, then what you say is correct; that is, the heightened form of conflict at Ford enables us to see industrial relations operating in their most advanced and sophisticated form. As I see it, other forms of manufacturing and service industries — engineering, electronics, clerical processes and information handling — will all become increasingly complex and tend towards the Ford experience.

SM We might express that in terms of a technical lag: the more technologically advanced the industry, the more pressure there is to find and maintain some comprehensive and authoritative bargaining structures for handling the conflict which will inevitably arise. You can't rely on a nineteenth-century bargaining structure to cope with twentieth-century technology.

HF That's right. At the moment we try to manage our industrial relations with stone-age tools alongside highly sophisticated, automated production systems.

SM So we're saying that technology and the structure of capital needed to exploit the product market are the prime determinants of industrial relationships. Not in the sense of technological determinism; it's not that a given technology produces certain patterns of conflict, but that the intensity of capital utilisation dictates the priority given to the rationalisation of labour relations and collective bargaining structures themselves.

HF Well, let's start from the most basic proposition; all industrial relations are in essence a matter of technical relationships between the worker and the work process. How does management secure the worker's co-operation or acquiescence to respond willingly to the technical requirements of the machine system? The basic Taylorist concept is that you devise a human system which encourages productivity through motivation of the individual. The worker's acceptance of the technology or work process is dependent on a framework of collectively agreed rules. It assumes a rough relationship between technology and the social system. But this is not so. The problem is that the technology is far in advance of the skills required for managing human relationships, and the range of options for managing industrial relations have not advanced significantly over the past 20 or 30 years. When you read ten year-old newspapers you feel you have been there before – the same basic problems and, in the Ford context of industrial relations in general, 1977/78 is a re-run of events which occurred during the past decade.

SM Would you develop that point about the range of options?

HF OK. Forget about industrial relations for a minute and just think about the management of the technical process. Economists used to argue that if you wanted to reap the economies of scale you needed a plant of a minimum size. Now managers are recognising that there's an optimum size for management, which is smaller than the economic size. Why? Because management skills have not kept pace with technology. You sometimes have to sacrifice the economies of technical scale. And industrial relations fit into that framework.

SM I agree with that.

HF When you look at objectives, there's a constancy of objectives within society – economic growth, efficiency of production, full employment and so on. If you look back over the last generation, there has been this constancy of objectives. All we have been arguing about within this framework of objectives has been the means of obtaining them. So that when we talk about industrial relations as being based on voluntarism or coercion or a system of agreed rules, there has been a limitation of options, a time-lag in terms of management thinking.

SM Yes, I understand what you are saying, but I would argue that there has always been uneven development between technology, the scale of enterprise, management skills and work organisation. Are we saying anything more than that technology is a stimulus to change in social systems? From the industrial revolution of the eighteenth century, social structure has always lagged behind technology. In the 1950s, when automation first became technically feasible, many firms ran into trouble because their social infrastructure was unable to cope with the new technical input. So the fact that you *can* automate an assembly line does not mean you *should* do so, unless you've thought through the human implications. Industrial relations learning processes are often found at the frontier of technological development.

HF You seem to be supporting some kind of technological determinism, by saying that. I would argue that the availability of advanced technical systems – communications technology for example – ought to narrow or eliminate the gap. Education systems, learning systems, audio-visual systems like television – these were inconceivable fifty years ago –

but are now as advanced as the technology for setting up a car assembly line. The question arises, why is it still necessary for the TUC and the government to issue guidelines in the form of the 1979 Concordat to state some basic, essential but obvious facts? Given our command of the new educational and communication technology, why do we still have this gap?

SM Well, the mass media offer a powerful illustration of the unintended consequences of technological development. The fact that you can produce television or radio signals and communicate with a mass population almost instantaneously develops expectations and attitudes which may not have been anticipated. There's no question that television affects the way people think and feel about their own lives. For example, the upsurge of violence in American negro ghettos in the mid-1960s reflected the impact of televised images of conspicuous consumption on the experience of multiple deprivation — of private affluence and public squalor. So that the new mass media are potentially the most powerful catalytic agents for social change, but it depends what messages you pass through the technical system. My point is that technology arrives first and we apply it at our peril.

HF How do you see that applying in industrial relations?

SM Automation or micro-processors may give us economic advantages, but we need to consider the industrial relations implications and anticipate the human consequences of adopting a new technology. If industrial relations have a central focus it must be the institutionalisation of conflict — conflict between capital and labour, conflict between different groups of workers and between economic values and human values — conflict which cannot be resolved merely by agreement, but also by confrontation. That confrontation has to be channelled into less destructive outlets, hence the heavy preoccupation with institutionalisation. If there *is* a learning process in industrial conflict, it reflects the attempts by the actors in the system to close the gap between technical and human systems. Much of our social disruption arises because of our failure to invest sufficient resources and energy into social engineering as compared with technical engineering.

For example, one way of explaining the relatively high number of stoppages at Ford is in terms of the inherent and irreconcilable conflict between the private ownership of capital and an alienated propertyless workforce. Hence the struggle over surplus value which arises from social relations of production. Another way of explaining the same conflict is in terms of the organisation structure. Overt conflict is a function not so much of size but of the hierarchical form of organisation, with too little decision making at the lower end of the organisation. That's just one step in the learning process that's now fairly widespread in society. Namely, that the village, for all its parochialism, is still preferable to the anonymity of the big city; that the suburban semi still meets more human needs than the high-rise block of flats; that local government is still better than remote central government, and that local plant decisions are still more acceptable and workable than decisions made by faceless bureaucrats at Central Office or worse still in Detroit.

HF Small may be beautiful, but you still have to face up to the continuance of industrial conflict on an undiminished scale, notwithstanding all the new technology which has become available. The basic conflict between capitalists' constant objective of profit maximisation and labour's constant objective of higher living standards and more workers' control remains.

SM I don't accept that those objectives are necessarily constant.

HF Well, if that is so then one might expect to see change, but in fact the opposite happens. For example, take the opinion polls about the spate of industrial action during the winter of 1978/9. Ninety per cent said they were in favour of secret ballots, against a closed shop, against secondary picketing. But those involved in conflict, when it was an issue of bread and butter and victory or defeat, continued the secondary picketing. Similarly, in the case of the closed shop, the position still is: 'No card – No start'. Once you arrive at the concrete situation you revert to using the same old weapons. Furthermore, groups who have traditionally refrained from taking industrial action have now joined in. It led to the sick not being cared for and the dead not being buried.

SM Well, I think I could make out just the opposite case; that people in occupational groups who never took industrial action before are now prepared to take strike action to defend and advance their interests. Doctors, nurses, local authority workers, civil servants, have felt the pressure society has put on them to the point where they do change their habits and do take action.

HF Then how do you explain the lack of effect of the mass media which has always been trying to persuade people that striking is wrong? How does one explain the apparent contradiction between the willingness of new occupational groups to enter industrial conflict – to become proletarianised – notwithstanding the dominant ideology, and the powerful effects of the media, unless you acknowledge the constancy of conflict below the surface?

SM I would say that most of these groups were formerly rather passive in terms of social conflict, but the pressure of inflation has politicised them. Although they may feel a sense of guilt about their strike action, they feel they must defend their living standards.

HF Let me pick up two points there. First, I would argue that in a mixed capitalist economy there is an underlying belief in the basic conflict between capital and labour. It may be manageable, but it's irreconcilable. And while we have this basic conflict you will not be able to reduce the gap between technology and industrial relations. Second, if you argue that some form of advanced participation for greater involvement of workers in the decision-making process would mitigate the conflict, or help overcome some of the worst effects of the present system, then I would say that experience in this country has shown that this is not the case. The central problem which emerges when you try to give people some meaningful involvement as distinct from rubber stamping, for example by devolving power from the trade union bureaucracy to plant level, is that the cry goes up: Too much power in the hands of the workers! The lorry drivers' dispute in January 1979 was a case in point. According to Jim Callaghan, they couldn't cope with the dilemma of how to reconcile self-interest with the general interest. It caused him to say that the devolution of power to the shop floor had gone too far. And nobody, as yet, has found the answer to that problem. How do you give workers the power of decision and involvement, and yet ensure that they use that power in the general interest? How do you get people to subordinate sectional interest to the general interest without operating a system of hierarchical authority?

SM I think people who have thought about such questions polarise themselves into two camps. Those who say: We must change our objectives. We must socialise the means of production and transform capitalism either by revolutionary means or by the evolutionary changes, such as those proposed in the Majority Report of the Bullock Committee on Industrial Democracy. Or those in the other camp would say, we must go back to the free play of the market and suffer the conflict, subject to greater use of the law, in order to restore efficient wealth creation.

HF You can argue that Bullock shows one possible way forward. But Ford and the CBI, amongst others, argued very strongly that Bullock would merely have extended the conflict into the boardroom and led to a further degeneration of industrial relations and made conflict more severe and less manageable.

SM But this is an end-means argument. Given that society is now more interdependent than ever before, I don't think it's just an argument about ends. Management may have all the technological aces up its sleeve, but it can't play them unless it's converted to management by consent. Whether you call that 'participation', or 'industrial democracy', whether you start at the shop floor and work upwards, as the CBI wanted, or whether you start with the worker representatives on the boards of our major industrial companies, and work downwards, as the Bullock Committee wanted, there's general agreement that conflict must be institutionalised by one means or another. And whether we like it or not, the argument in Britain at the present time is about means, not about ends.

HF As far as we can look ahead — the next five or ten years — there's the prospect of irreconcilable conflict between capital and labour and so I come back to my argument about the constancy of objectives. Unless you can change the objectives, the goals, you can't really narrow the lag in industrial relations, or reduce the level of conflict, unless you are going to argue that society is just one big happy family with an over-riding common interest?

SM No, I don't subscribe to a unitary view of society, but a pluralist view which acknowledges the existence of competing interest groups, but does not accept that they are inherently irreconcilable. And technology will do most of the reconciling, in this sense: if management seeks to secure its constant objective — the creation of surplus or profit maximisation — it cannot use the positive power which derives from the ownership of capital and the ability to switch investment without taking into account the countervailing power of workers — that is, the negative power of workers to disrupt increasingly interdependent units of technology. Technology has put into the hands of both management and workers such a potential for profitable production — or mutual impoverishment — that technology itself will force the pace of change in social systems and industrial relations. I argue that way because there's no management control system so powerful, no state agency so strong, that could ever prevent the imagination and enterprise of workers from subverting the system, if they chose to do so. So the only way to reconcile the apparently irreconcilable forces in society is through some institutional means. Call it 'collective bargaining' or call it 'industrial democracy' — it's still an institutionalised means to a commonly agreed end.

HF I don't see how you can reconcile pluralist interdependency with continuity of constant conflict over the control of industry. In industry, today's opposition is *not* tomorrow's government. If workers get control, employers are unlikely to be recalled in a couple of years' time to take charge again. I don't see how you can argue that, on the one hand, the workers have the imagination to subvert the system . . .

SM But it's very real, it happens every day of the week. Are you denying it?

HF I'm not denying it, I merely want to solve the contradiction. On the one hand, you have this unlimited imagination of the workers to subvert the system and, on the other, workers can see that it's not in their interests to be simply negative. Why, then, are workers so negative? Is it because of an ideological commitment to a different kind of society, or is part of the sub-culture of the working class? If you look at actors who represent workers in the present system — Works Conveners like Derek Robinson[8] at Longbridge, or Danny Connor at Dagenham — underlying all their activities is a desire to bring about fundamental change in society, and to do away with the system in which Henry Ford or the ICI make all the fundamental decisions. They want workers to take charge of their own destiny and to substitute the existing system with another one, call it public ownership with all its defects, or call it socialism . . .

SM But, Henry, surely you're not denying that the distribution of power in society is changing and will continue to change?

HF Let me make my point again, Sander. Your assumption that technology will become the major determinant of industrial relations is only valid if workers or the rank-and-file leadership subscribe to a belief in a mixed economy. But my contention is that deep down *they do not*. And you can't have, on the one hand, an ardent belief in fundamental change and of transforming society and, at the same time, be devoted to operating a system of rules and procedures which preclude change and which sustain and reinforce existing society.

SM I find that provocative, but not very helpful. In the 1950s, one could talk about substantial support for Labour Party policies on the shop floor, with the CP acting as a 'ginger group' of the left. Today, we have a spectrum of views on the left ranging from central social democratic groups, right through to left Labour groups, to International Socialists and the International Marxist Group. But there is no way in which I can see these groups co-operating to achieve the transformation of society which you speak about. All I can see is competition for support in the short run.

HF I don't know why you should find that provocative, I didn't say they were all eager revolutionaries, ready to storm the barricades and to smash the system next Monday. All I'm saying is that, amongst these very diverse groups, none will subscribe to a belief in the permanence of the mixed economy. All will at least pay lip service, including the TUC and the Labour Party — Clause 4 and all — to a belief in the creation of a socialist society, if not in their lifetime, then in the lifetime of their children. So it's not just an argument about means, but an argument about ends too. Unless you can change people's objectives, you will not be able to enlarge your options in managing, or reconciling the conflict we spoke about. You will only succeed in damping it down intermittently, but it will break out more fiercely and more extensively in unexpected quarters later on.

SM But that's exactly what industrial relations are about. Industrial relations are not about *removing* conflict, they are about *managing* conflict. What I found provocative was your assertion that the system precludes the possibility of fundamental change, including the sharing of strategic decision making. So far as workers are concerned, industrial relations are about generating conflict in order to change some parts of the status quo. So far as management is concerned, industrial relations are about containing and channelling conflict within manageable limits. If we think of the learning process on both sides at Ford, it's surely this: the *workforce* has learned no lesson more important than the need for self-help and self-reliance and direct action to get results. Workers don't want a seat in the boardroom of the Ford Motor Company. They prefer to achieve their aims by using their industrial strength — a good old-fashioned, craft-conscious self-reliance. They use that strength, not as a means of helping them fulfil their vision of the transformed society, but to achieve their instrumental, their economic objectives, of improved pay and conditions.

HF I can only accept that argument provided it's confined to short-term aims. There is a significant difference between short- and long-term aims.

SM *Management,* for its part, has learned no lesson more important than the fact that you cannot force people to work on the assembly line; you must manage by consent every day of the year.

HF But where's the learning process at Ford over the last years? In 1978, Ford had 1,000 stoppages of work by workers who have internalised the strike lesson. If you want to get something done, don't talk, walk . . . If you relate those 1,000 stoppages with the numbers employed, that's a depressing picture from the industrial relations point of view. If anything, Ford workers were more ready to walk than talk than ever before, and they did so more deliberately, more consciously on the short-term issues. And, since they have not changed, we should ask why not?

SM Well, to begin with we must get those 1,000 stoppages into perspective. If you relate them to the 60,000 workers employed in 24 separate plants for over 200 working days a year, that's 1,000 stoppages spread over 12 million man-days worked. I'd like to know the average size and duration of those 1,000 stoppages before I could assess their significance in economic terms. So I would argue, first, that Ford management uses the number of short-term disruptive stoppages as a weapon in its rhetorical armoury. Second, those 1,000 stoppages may seem too many, but there might have been 5,000 and, despite its 1,000 stoppages in 1978, Ford is by far the most profitable company in the British motor industry. And, third, those stoppages are the price Ford pays for the freedom it enjoys to run the Company in the way it chooses. It may concern those Ford managers who would like to legislate conflict out of the system because they think all conflict is pathological. But if we look at the facts with any kind of sociological imagination, then 1,000 stoppages in Ford terms is a fairly small price to pay for almost £250 million profit in the same year.

HF This is a perverse argument. If there had been 5,000 stoppages, then they can be rationalised on the basis it could have been 10,000. Ford made that profit despite its relative failure in industrial relations, and not because of it. The profit comes from good product development, good international marketing, good integration between the various national companies. Terry Beckett's argument was that if Ford had only managed to reduce that large number of stoppages — in fact five million man-hours were lost in 1978 — before the start of the pay strike, it would have produced another 180,000 vehicles worth over £80 million and so have contributed more to the bargaining fund.

SM But in 1978 Ford was not able to bargain freely, anyway!

HF But, Sander, my point is that, before the 1978 bargaining began, there had been a continuous interruption of work which led both the Chairman and the Director of Industrial Relations at Ford to say that no other Company in the world had to cope with this level of conflict. My point is, why has there been this failure to achieve any significant progress at Ford in dealing with unconstitutional stoppages? If there *has* been a learning process on the management side, as you argue, then by implication there ought to have been a significant reduction in the level of stoppages.

SM You are looking for simple explanations for highly complex phenomena. You can't sum up the total learning experience in a few lines. What you will find, however, if you look at the record of the past ten years, is that Ford management has learned the value of a new short Procedure Agreement which terminates at plant level for most grievances, which incorporates time limits for each stage of the Procedure, which gives Conveners a more responsible role in bargaining at national level, which greatly widens the scope of bargaining and which provides for a much greater willingness to disclose information. Maybe these changes don't go far enough, but I cite them as evidence of Ford's positive learning about the management of conflict and co-operation. I'm not denying the significance of the 1,000 stoppages in the short run; I'm just saying they should be seen in their proper perspective against the background of Ford's rising productivity and profitability in the long run.

HF I understand your argument. Ford had a lot of problems about sacking workers, so it instituted a disciplinary procedure with an appeals mechanism. Ford has a lot of problems with lay-offs, so workers are no longer sent home in the middle of the night shift — to save its canteens from being wrecked, or its Plant Managers from being locked into their offices all night. But when they have done all that, at the end of the road, Ford is still faced with the same mountain of conflict — whether for reasons of workers' unthinking behaviour or anything else — there is still apparently an irreducible mountain of conflict. The Company argues that it is reducible and the whole object of its industrial relations strategy is to reduce it, but the simple facts are that its strategy has failed. So far it has not persuaded people to talk and not walk.

SM Correct and, incidentally, the same message was contained in the TUC-Labour Government Concordat in 1979.

HF Absolutely, so we must recognise the limitations of the available options. Perhaps we ought to restructure our systems more along German or Swedish lines?

SM I'm not advocating that. I was pointing to an institutional lag and distinguishing between the advances in technology and the relative backwardness of industrial relations thinking. In other words, you can't go on pumping technological change into the system at one end, and expect the people to keep calm and conduct orderly discussion at the other end when they perceive that their interests are threatened. I'm not looking for a German or Swedish system, but a more effective British system for handling inevitable conflict. I begin with the idea that conflict is inevitable, but I conclude that it is neither irreducible, nor irreconcilable.

HF Let me point out the contradiction, then. If you avoid the national label and just call it some new tripartite arrangement, some new broad consensus about economic policy and expectations between the TUC, the CBI and the government, then it's this central bureaucratic organisation that makes the key decisions or establishes the consensus. Right? But how does that involve workers in the decision-making process? That's not really enlarging the options, is it? So you say, that's only the start, we involve workers through regional conferences or industrial conferences or national conferences. And, as a result, we can expect more responsible behaviour at workshop-floor level, because workshop representatives will be directly involved in formulating the consensus.

SM Provided it isn't some kind of 'con' trick, provided it isn't just a wage freeze to persuade people to hold back — after which the lion's share goes to the lions. If some new authoritative body is going to formulate norms and exceptions and deal with a wider range of comparative wealth and income distribution — if it's also going to deal with the lower paid, with pensioners, with housing subsidies — in short, if it's concerned with social justice as well as efficiency and productivity, if it's concerned with wider political and social as well as economic issues, then I think it will command support and persuade workers to moderate their wage claims or accept a flat-rate increase or even a wage freeze, for a limited period.

HF I think I agree with you there. It represents an attempt to enlarge the range of options. Whether it will significantly reduce the level of conflict over low pay or differentials, however, remains doubtful. People, including trade union members, are generally reluctant to subordinate their sectional interests to the general interest. And my reasons for saying that are based on my experiences as a Convener. The more information you provide, the more you encourage members to participate in discussion on details and policy making — the more democracy you try to operate, the more insoluble problems sometimes tend to become. I have certainly found that, in trying to operate a more democratic system in a meaningful way, the harder it often became to manage affairs. Once you involve people meaningfully, they want to be further involved and that sometimes intensifies the conflict between different sectional interests. It can lead to a situation which makes it harder in the short run to find a common denominator. Incomes policy has proved this point many times over. How do you solve the problem of low pay whilst maintaining differentials? No significant work group has, as yet, volunteered to take less, so that others can have more. Similarly, devolving power to the shop floor conflicts with the maintenance of centralised and effective control by National Trade Union Officials, national negotiating bodies, Wages Councils and so on.

SM So you are proposing to abandon consultation and democratic processes just because they are difficult to operate?

HF No, I'm merely trying to explain that, in our type of society, at the end of the day people believe that 'charity begins at home' and they will protect their own interest frequently at the expense of others. Any consensus you are trying to establish will break down at that point, because no mechanism exists whereby Ford workers settling for less ensures that nurses get more. Therefore, large-scale shop-floor involvement tends to intensify and heighten conflict. Where, compared to Britain, you have much less industrial conflict, the way it does work is by *not* .nvolving the shop floor, by taking decision and bargaining power away from the workplace. Germany, Sweden, and the US are prime examples, where bargaining about significant issues is done exclusively outside the workplace. Even in Yugoslavia there has been a significant trend towards more centralised control in recent years. Although not strictly comparable. Italy comes nearest to the British model of shop-floor power and involvement. And there, certainly since the 'hot autumn' of Turin 1969, industrial conflict has greatly intensified and become much more extensive.

SM You mean we should revert to the system of the 1950s, when trade union leaders did deals over the heads of the workforce?

HF No, I'm simply pointing out that, in the 1958-68 period, the amount of conflict and the degree of shop-floor power at Ford was very much less than in the 1968-78 period.

SM What you are really arguing is that, if you want to reduce the level of conflict, then industry-wide bargaining is better than plant bargaining, and centralised bargaining along Swedish lines is better than industry-wide bargaining and, finally, if you have a central planning office in the Kremlin, you have no conflict at all! But the trick of course is how to produce a truly participative industrial democracy in which everyone has a voice, but where the owners of capital, who exercise great power, can only operate successfully by taking careful account of the potentially much greater power which organised workers have, which they have rarely used in this country, and which frankly they are only just beginning to realise. The dilemma facing all advanced interdependent mixed economies of the liberal democratic variety, is how to persuade groups of workers to give up some measure of their short-term selfish interests in favour of the longer-term and wider interest.

HF I accept that.

SM In that sense, the learning process in the search for a more effective incomes policy is a good example of the lag between advanced technology, which can generate unprecedented wealth, and the failure to develop adequate social systems for deciding what share of that increased wealth different sections of the community shall enjoy. It offers almost an exact parallel at the national level to the dynamics of conflict between management and workers and between different groups of workers at plant level. That's why I'm optimistic that technology will force the pace of the learning process and that some further institu-tionalisation of conflict is the only answer.

HF I accept your argument that, if you follow the Kremlin analogy, the less involvement, the less the work conflict. But then, of course, you have other problems of greater magnitude such as repression and ineffi-ciency. Ideally, I would like to share your optimism and conclude our dialogue on a cheerful note. But I'm afraid the outlook for a significant improvement in British industrial relations in the next few years is not very encouraging. Quite apart from the reasons I have outlined, factors such as the economic and industrial relations policies of the present Conservative Government, the energy crisis, the inflation rate, new technology, rising unemployment, and union attempts to defend jobs and living standards will make solutions to industrial relations problems more intractable in the early 1980s.

SM With that, I certainly agree!

Notes

1. A seven-week strike took place at Pilkington Glass in the spring of 1970. See Tony Lane and Kenneth Roberts, *Strike at Pilkingtons* (Fontana, London, 1971).

2. A strike for equal pay at Trico-Folberth Ltd lasted 21 weeks from May to September 1976.

3. J.T. Dunlop, *Industrial Relations Systems* (Holt, New York, 1958).

4. R.E. Walton and R.B. McKersie, *A Behavioural Theory of Labor Negotiations* (McGraw Hill, New York, 1965).

5. The breakthrough on shorter working time did not come at Ford but in the federated establishments of the engineering industry. See Postscript, pp.355-7 below.

6. In a comprehensive review of research into the impact of multinational enterprise on industrial relations, B.C. Roberts notes that 'One of the main objec-tives of the International Metalworkers' Federation is to try to bring about a common date for the termination of agreements between the unions and the managements of automobile manufacturers in advanced industrial societies.' Roberts concludes that 'Some progress has been made towards the achievement of this goal, more by accident than design, in the negotiations with the Ford Motor Company in Europe but no serious attempt has been made to co-ordinate union demands and bargaining tactics.' B.C. Roberts, 'Multinational Enterprise and Labor' in P. Doeringer (ed.), *Industrial Relations Research in International Perspective* (Harvard University Press, forthcoming).

7. The 1979/80 Agreement at Ford was reached without a strike. See Postscript.

8. Robinson was dismissed by BL in November 1979 for alleged anti-company activities. For a discussion of the Robinson sacking, its consequences and similar-ities with earlier sackings of Shop Stewards by Ford, see relevant chapter in Henry Friedman and Sander Meredeen, *Industrial Relations in the Eighties,* British Sociological Association Series, *Sociology in Practice* (Croom Helm, London, forthcoming).

CONCLUSIONS

When they embarked on this study of industrial conflict, the authors set themselves a limited objective: to provide a documentary account and retrospective analysis of one important dispute in the British motor industry. They selected the Ford Sewing Machinists' 1968 strike for three main reasons:

First, the dispute marked a decisive turning-point in Ford's industrial relations and exerted a powerful influence on the subsequent shaping of both union and management strategies. Seen in retrospect, the dispute clearly emerges as the culmination of twenty years' failure on the part of management to meet the mounting challenge by the shop floor to Ford's managerial prerogative. After this dispute, industrial relations at Ford were never the same again.

Second, although the dispute began as a modest protest over a domestic grading grievance by a small group of women, it soon developed into a major strike on an issue of national — and even international — significance: the demand for equal pay as the first step towards the emancipation of women at work. The Ford Sewing Machinists, like the Bryant & May Matchgirls before them, taught the working women of Britain to stand up and fight for their rights. Their example inspired thousands of other women to support the emerging women's movement of the late sixties. The strike itself led directly to the passage of the Equal Pay Act 1970 and helped indirectly to secure the enactment of comprehensive legislation designed to eliminate sex discrimination in Britain.

Third, by an exquisite irony of history, the climax of the dispute coincided exactly with the publication in June 1968 of the *Donovan Report on Trade Unions and Employers' Associations* — the most influential document on British industrial relations to be published this century. 1968 was thus a critical year in the history of industrial relations, not only for Ford but also for Britain. As the Ford strike grew and began to make an impact on the economy, it assumed the dimensions of a national political issue. It was not just another strike which halted all the production at Ford: it required the personal intervention of several Cabinet Ministers; it affected the national balance of payments; it led to an Official Court of Inquiry; and it triggered new major high-priority legislation. For all these reasons, the Ford Sewing Machinists' strike helped to shape the climate of public and political opinion and to focus the issues in the crucial policy debate on the reform of the British system of industrial relations in the seventies.

There was, however, a *fourth* and more personal reason for choosing to write about this particular dispute. When they sat down to review the existing literature on industrial conflict, the authors were struck by the fact that most of the available texts on the subject are extremely general in character. A handful of detailed case studies of particular disputes has been compiled by investigative journalists or academic research teams. But these have relied heavily on newspaper reports or the second-hand evidence of carefully selected participants in the relevant disputes. Since the present authors were two of the principal protagonists in the Sewing Machinists' dispute, they felt they must offer something more ambitious than a second-hand case study. By drawing on their own direct experience and combining their personal insights, they hoped to provide a detailed reconstruction of the origins, conduct and resolution of the Sewing Machinists' dispute and to convey something of its dramatic tension — that intoxicating mixture of anxiety and exuberance experienced by the leading actors in a major industrial conflict. The authors set out to confront their subjective perceptions and their divergent experience of the dispute, in order to deepen their understanding with the wisdom of hindsight.

By the time they had completed their separate accounts of the dispute, the authors were convinced that the significance of the Sewing Machinists' dispute — or of any other dispute — could only be properly understood by placing it in its historical perspective: a unique series of events, standing at a unique conjuncture in a unique system of industrial relations. Every system of industrial relations is a dynamic system in a state of continuous evolution. Whether we analyse it at the level of the nation, the industry, the district or the organisation, we discover in every system a rich and distinctive pattern and texture of relationships, brought into being by the interaction of the most powerful forces in the wider society — history and economics, politics and law, technology and ideology — and shaped by the personality and idiosyncratic behaviour of the leading actors within the system. The inimitable character of a particular industrial relations system is determined by a series of crucial, and generally concealed, decisions taken by the key actors in specific historical contexts. Whilst the full significance of those decisions may not be recognised at the time, their consequences — both intended and unintended — leave an indelible mark on the character of the system and affect the quality of its relationships for a long time to come — perhaps for ever. It is the actors' experience of that conflict and the lessons they derive from it which largely determine the way they operate the system and set about reshaping it.

The authors therefore decided to extend their original study and to draw on their inside knowledge of the system of industrial relations in Ford of Britain. What began as a study of the Ford Sewing Machinists' dispute — a study of the passion for equality in the workplace, analysed in the tranquillity of academic detachment, some ten years after the event — broadened into a much wider study of a neglected aspect of industrial relations — the experiential learning process in the management of industrial conflict. In the preparation and writing of this material, the authors have deliberately gone far beyond their original objective in the hope of throwing more light on the general character of industrial conflict in the British system of industrial relations.

Although the study does not seek to deal with the complex and contrasted patterns of industrial relations in the British motor industry, the fact that it is set in that industry is no mere coincidence. For the authors, the motor industry is *the prime example* of a twentieth-century industry — the prototype of all the modern manufacturing industries of our time. If there *were*, as some still believe, an 'invisible hand' of history leading all the industrialised and industrialising countries towards some more or less common pattern of economic development — as propounded in Clark Kerr's influential theory of technological and social convergence[1] — then the motor industry would stand out as the index finger of that hand, clearly pointing the future direction of change.

If history is bunk, as Henry Ford claimed — if the only lesson to be learned from history is that there *are* no lessons to be learned from history — there would be no Ford Motor Company today. But since Ford himself was talking bunk, his Company has grown from small beginnings to become one of the largest and most successful multinational enterprises in the world. Those who are employed by Ford — both workers and managers — have turned their hard-won experience to good account by learning to cope with the trauma of industrial conflict. Where better, then, to study the learning process in the management of industrial conflict than at Ford?

It was never intended, however, that this study should provide a definitive history of industrial relations at Ford, however desirable such a project might be. The analysis presented here is inevitably selective. It says little, for example, about staff relations at Ford and the spectacular growth of union membership and political consciousness amongst the Company's 15,000 or so white-collar staff — one of the most far-reaching developments in Ford's industrial relations over the past decade. Instead, the authors have chosen to focus on particular aspects of the Company's *labour* relations: to identify the sources of recurrent conflict; to examine its structure and character; and to make explicit the underlying assumptions which determine the actions of both sides in the struggle for ascendancy at the point of production. By picking out these aspects, the authors have tried to get below the surface and reveal the inner workings of conflict and co-operation at Ford.

The principal strands identified in this study may now be conveniently summarised as follows:

1. the persistent tension which exists between the official and the unofficial wings of the highly fragmented British trade union movement;

2. the interdependence of sectional opportunism and concerted action by workers who seek to advance their general interest without neglecting the differential claims of particular groups;

3. the unremitting search by management for greater stability and predictability in every aspect of industrial relations, from control over labour costs to the maintenance of an effective set of bargaining institutions;

4. the elevation by management of the observance of Procedure into an article of faith in the service of the uninterrupted creation of wealth through continuous production;

5. the ambivalent role of the state, looming ever larger in the background, acting now as final custodian of industrial peace and impartial arbiter of industrial conflict, now as pro-active interventionist manager of the national economy, enforcing its policies, where necessary, by a variety of economic and political weapons — from incomes policies and trade sanctions to tax concessions and investment subsidies;

6. the pervasive influence of the past on the conduct of current industrial relations, which makes both sides determined to maintain the initiative, to make good past losses, and permanently to redress the perceived imbalance in power relations;

7. the continuously shifting locus of power within the area of interaction between the four principal actors in the system — the two wings of the trade union movement, management and the state;

8. the cumulative learning process which takes place amongst the actors in the system, based on the experience of past conflict and sustained by the necessity for present co-operation. As a result of this experience, all four actors in the system attempt to embody their

own ideological assumptions and values in customs, rules, procedures and agreements which maintain the system, to legitimate their own actions whilst denouncing the actions of others for attempting to change the system;

9. the special problems of particular disadvantaged socio-economic groups – in this case, women workers – which are highlighted by industrial conflict. For the authors, the Ford Sewing Machinists are representative of most of the women working in the British engineering and automotive industries. As earlier chapters have shown, the Sewing Machinists' priorities in the 1968 grading dispute were 'rearranged' for them. Another example is provided by the 1978 Ford pay settlement, which took no account of the Ford women's clearly expressed preference for a shorter working week rather than more money. The problem of how women – who lack effective representation – can achieve recognition for their *own* priorities is likely to become more acute if the percentage of women in the total labour force continues to rise.

As well as highlighting these principal features of the Ford system of industrial relations, the study has also identified those features which have more general relevance and wider application within the British system of industrial relations. Whether or not Marxists are right in their contention that fundamental and irreconcilable conflict is the inevitable corollary of a capitalist system of production, the fact remains that, in an advanced industrial society characterised by scarce resources – both natural and man-made – and by unlimited if over-stimulated appetites, social conflict is inevitable. Industrial conflict is simply one manifestation of that inevitable conflict. The central task facing management in such a society is to persuade workers with real or imagined grievances to abide by the rules of Procedure so that their grievances may be speedily investigated and disputes resolved without interrupting the rhythm of mass production and wealth creation. In such a society, ruled by the managerial logic of industrial efficiency, it is hardly surprising that workers utilise such opportunities as may occur to pursue their own divergent objectives. By its repeated insistence that 'The production track never stops' and that 'Procedure is the only vehicle for resolving grievances', top management has not only tied the hands of line managers and Supervisors; it has freely conferred on shop-floor workers their most effective weapon – the ability to stop the track instantly in order to dramatise a grievance and so fetch management running. The higher the level of capital concentration, the greater the degree of technical integration, the faster they run.

The Learning Process in Industrial Conflict

The skilful management of industrial conflict and co-operation — knowing when to advance, when to concede and when to stand firm against the pressures exerted by the other side — is the essence of good industrial relations. A system of 'good industrial relations' is not one in which there is an absence of overt conflict or in which management or unions enjoy a preponderant power which ensures compliance. It is a system in which both sides have learned from experience how to exercise their limited power with restraint — but to good effect; in short, a system in which the actors have developed a measure of mutual respect by recognising their mutual interdependence. There are certainly no universally applicable rules: the expertise can only be acquired by the painful experience of learning how to manage industrial conflict. For a small minority on the trade union side, who believe our society is basically unjust and in need of radical transformation, industrial relations are not just about bread and butter issues but have the more fundamental purpose of promoting social change. This minority measures good industrial relations by the extent of trade union encroachment on managerial prerogatives and the shift of power to the shop floor.

When the authors speak of 'the learning process' in the management of industrial conflict, they refer to a desire and capacity amongst the principal actors in a system of industrial relations to reflect upon their experience, to extract some significant meaning from it and to apply some of the lessons which experience and reflection have taught. As in other complex social systems, the individuals and groups which make up an industrial relations system vary considerably in their capacity to learn from their own experience or to profit vicariously from the experience of others. Although unions and management will from time to time accuse the other side of behaving like Bourbons — who have learned nothing and forgotten nothing — there is nevertheless a cumulative 'learning process' amongst the principal actors who engage in the habitual exchanges of a mature industrial relations system. And there is abundant evidence, as this study has shown, of the actors' desire and capacity to profit by that experience.

At first sight, it may appear that Ford management has been more successful than the Unions in establishing the institutional framework required by any large organisation which sets out to master the 'learning process'. But the differences should not be exaggerated. In the post-war period, Ford persistently failed to deal with its relatively poor performance in the management of a greatly expanded and widely dispersed labour force. It was only after the economic losses of a rising trend of internal disruption and the public humiliation of two official Courts of Inquiry in the space of six years that top management came to grips with its failures. It professionalised its industrial relations; appointed its first Industrial Relations Director; set up a Forward Planning Team to develop a new and more appropriate industrial relations strategy. The results of adopting that strategy may be seen in the series of structural reforms and bargaining initiatives taken by management in the late sixties and early seventies which have contributed significantly to the development of more mature industrial relationships in the late seventies.

It would be over-simplistic, of course, to attribute Ford's return to economic profitability in the late seventies merely to a superior capacity to learn from the past. Ford management has nevertheless demonstrated its determination systematically to evaluate its own mistakes and to learn from its past experience. Above all, there has been no attempt to turn back the clock or return to the crude application of 'the Ford industrial creed'.

By contrast, the British trade union movement – of which the Ford Unions are a representative, if advanced, example – frequently appear to manage their affairs 'by the seat of their pants'. By comparison with some unions in Europe and the US, British unions operate on a shoe-string budget, with inadequate ratio of staff to membership. Judged by these criteria, National and District Officials are over-worked, under-paid and inadequately provided with essential back-up services, as compared with their management counterparts. More important, however, are differences in the structure, style and character of the two sets of actors in the system. Management, by definition, is concerned to improve performance, to increase its professional skills in managing complexity and uncertainty. To offset the handicap of inadequate resources, trade unions delight in the tradition of inspired opportunism and excel in the virtues of improvisation. Trade Union Officials have learned to make a virtue of necessity: conscious of the inadequacies of their own forward planning, they have been largely content to allow management to take the initiative, reserving for themselves an essentially reactive role.

In the case of Ford, for example, the Trade Unions at both national and shop-floor level never seem to find the time for a systematic analysis of a major dispute. One reason for this is the 'grass-hopper' life-style of the typical Trade Union Official, burdened with too many pressing engagements – a characteristic feature of multiple unionism in Britain which wastes resources through duplication of effort but still fails to offer the membership an adequate service. Another reason is that the membership at plant level is represented by elected but unpaid officials. It requires a high level of commitment to give up leisure time for the systematic analysis of industrial conflict. Trade union analysis is therefore often conducted during breaks in other meetings or over a drink at a local pub. As a result, meetings of the Trade Union Side of the NJNC or the National Ford Conveners' Committee tend to concentrate either on the formulation of priority demands for the next bargaining round or on deciding the minimum acceptable conditions for the resolution of a current problem. The 'tactics of the day' may be born out of past experience but they seldom extend to the formulation of specific long-term objectives which translate easily into definitive strategies.

So far, the authors are agreed on the differential learning process amongst the actors within the Ford system of industrial relations. Their views begin to diverge when it comes to an evaluation of the benefits derived by the actors.

Sander Meredeen believes that Ford management has crossed two historic watersheds in the recent development of its industrial relations. The first came in 1963 with the decision to set up a Forward Planning Team, which has remained in existence in modified form ever since. By its advocacy of a strongly pro-active management strategy, backed up by well-informed and timely analysis, Forward Planning successfully weaned the Company away from the dogmatic assertion of 'the Ford industrial creed'. The new industrial relations strategy pointed the direction of future change.

In carrying out the first important element in that change programme, Ford was carried much closer to the second watershed: a more equal sharing of power with the rank-and-file leadership in place of the traditional reliance on 'responsible' National Trade Union Officials as 'partners in control' of the Ford workforce. The Wage Structure Review and the productivity bargaining of 1967 demonstrated the virtues of responsible power-sharing. The widening gap between National Officials and shop-floor leadership revealed by the Sewing Machinists' dispute finally persuaded management that it was better to deal directly with accountable shop-floor leaders, who could be held responsible for their side of a negotiated agreement, rather than rely on National Officials alone. It prepared management for the fundamental break with the past represented by the 1969 Agreement, which admitted Shop Stewards to the NJNC, the highest bargaining forum in the Company.

Despite the publicity given to the major strikes of 1968, 1969, 1971 and 1978, Ford's new industrial relations strategy of responsible power-sharing and mutual interdependence has made a major contribution towards the Company's sustained profitability and economic recovery in recent years. Nobody who has read the evidence given to the 1975 Duffy Committee could be left in any doubt that Ford, unlike its competitors in the British motor industry, has taken the measure of its domestic labour problems. The admission of all 23 Ford Conveners to the Trade Union Side of the NJNC in 1978 was more than a symbol of the transformation in Ford's industrial relations: it reinforced the authority of the NJNC and demonstrated how far the Company has been prepared to go to seal the new relationship of mutual interdependence. In its efforts to build that relationship, Ford has continued to stress the paramount importance of respect for Procedure – but it is a very different Procedure Agreement from that which the National Officials were expected to enforce in the fifties and sixties. The realities of the new distribution of power have led to the shortening of Procedure, so that most grievances are now capable of resolution at plant level. The NJNC is left free to deal with the more complex and aggravated matters which threaten to become serious disputes. A Disciplinary Code has been introduced which incorporates a quasi-judicial procedure for hearing evidence and appeals before penalties are confirmed. Work standards have become the subject of a separate agreement which incorporates an important status quo clause. Working Parties have been set up to consider new and important issues never before dealt with under collective bargaining. Exclusive bargaining rights have been conferred on the Ford Unions by means of the 100 per cent post-entry closed shop Agreement of June 1976, with deduction of union dues through the payroll.

One of the Company's principal methods of arriving at more dependable bargains with its workforce has been its willingness to adopt a more open programme of communication. Coveners and Deputy Conveners meet top management at regular intervals to hear advance production plans and proposals for new investment and modernisation. At plant level, management has been authorised to stop the track, where necessary, in order to convey urgent management information which directly affects people at work. This does not mean that the Unions are satisfied that they possess all the information they would like for bargaining purposes; at NJNC, the Unions continue to press Ford to release more of what they consider to be relevant information on such subjects as internal pricing policies and the transfer of production across national frontiers – and Ford continues to resist demands for what it considers to be irrelevant information. The fact that Ford negotiations have become more protracted and acrimonious of late is due less to the withholding of information by Ford and more to direct government intervention in collective bargaining through the application of incomes policies and the threat of economic sanctions. Looking back to the major Ford strike in the autumn of 1978, one thing is perfectly clear: that only Ford amongst the British motor manufacturers could have faced a nine-week strike — followed by the threat of government sanctions — and still produced a pre-tax profit in excess of £240 million in 1978. Chrysler, Vauxhall and British Leyland would have been commercially annihilated by such a dispute.

From his reading of Ford's handling of its recent industrial conflict, *Sander Meredeen* believes that Ford is capable of sustaining its profitable performance over the next decade. Just as Ford leads the British motor industry in terms of investment and profitability, so it will continue to maintain its lead in industrial relations. Since there can be no reversal of the trend towards more complete technical and economic integration at Ford, management will continue to adapt its policies to meet the demands of new technology and growing international competition. Ford's contract renewal strikes will continue to dominate the news headlines. Small-scale internal disruption seems likely to persist, despite the Company's latest attempt to 'buy off' trouble by the offer of more lucrative incentives for adherence to Procedure. But the scale of this disruption will diminish in proportion to the increase in the incentives, until they finally become transformed into some form of profit-sharing arrangement. An irreducible level of unconstitutional action will remain. But Ford managers, who are past masters at cost-benefit analysis, know that this is a relatively small price for the Company to pay for the freedom it enjoys to manage the business in the way it chooses.

The success of Ford's industrial relations strategy depends on its ability progressively to involve shop-floor leaders in the further institutionalisation of conflict. By sitting alongside management at all relevant levels in the organisation — from Joint Works Committees to Consultative Committees and Joint Working Parties at Operation and Group level, and finally as members of the Trade Union Side of the NJNC — Shop Stewards will inevitably become 'partners in control' of the workforce they represent — a logical and more acceptable form of 'industrial democracy' at Ford than that advocated in the Bullock Report. The Company will gladly extend the bargaining area and willingly meet the substantially greater settlement costs of annual contract negotiations, provided its shop-floor leaders take a more active part in persuading their members to remain at work and *talk out* their grievances rather than *walk out* without allowing Procedure to operate. Finally, although disputes will continue to preoccupy management's attention — and Ford will cling to its sacred prerogative of deciding what products to make, in what volumes, in which locations, with no voice for trade unions in product design, quality, quantity or price — the long-term trend at Ford seems to point in the direction of more mature and dependable bargaining relationships with mutual advantages for both workers and management.

Henry Friedman believes that, when judged by the criterion of recent levels of conflict, Ford's new industrial relations strategy has not been particularly successful. The Company's rebuke to the Unions for the failure of the NJNC to solve basic problems[2] and Beckett's condemnation of the loss of five million man-hours in 1978 due to unofficial strikes[3] tend to confirm this assessment. In his view, the Company has not convincingly demonstrated that its command of superior resources to conduct research and analysis has enabled it to outwit or outmanoeuvre the Trade Unions. This suggests that a great deal of management's activity in the strategic planning of its industrial relations is more cosmetic than substantial. This comparative lack of success in eliminating conflict is due in part to the limited and rather antiquated range of options available for the resolution of industrial conflict and, more importantly perhaps, to the irreconcilable nature of the conflict between capital and labour in advanced industrial societies, which reaches its most developed form in multinational companies like Ford. Neither coercive tactics — such as the mass sacking of militants in 1947, 1957 and 1962, or the introduction of penalty clauses in 1969 and again in 1978 — nor the more accommodative management practices of the seventies seem to have reduced the amount of conflict on the shop floor at Ford. In view of the basic conflict over long-term and ultimate objectives, and frequently over short-term objectives too, this is not altogether surprising. Indeed, there appears to be no reason, in principle, why the amount of actual conflict should have abated, as long as the present system seeks to preserve the inequalities of status, power and reward, condemns the bulk of its manual workers — the wealth creators — to soul-destroying labour and ultimately denies them control over their destiny.

Finding new ways to manage and contain industrial conflict is nevertheless the continuing and dominant concern not only of management and unions but also of government. Increasing state intervention in industrial relations over the last ten years furnishes abundant evidence of concern at government level. Conversely, the non-implementation of Donovan and the legislation proposed by *In Place of Strife,* the collapse of the Industrial Relations Act and of Income Policies in 1972, 1974 and 1978, the demise of the Social Contract, the shelving of the Bullock Committee's proposals and the ill-fated 1979 Concordat all confirm that no new options containing promising solutions have yet emerged from either of the main political parties.

Attempts to establish Worker Co-operatives have so far failed and the 1976 Industrial Common Ownership Act is in itself a prime example of 'tokenism'. The renewed vogue for Comparability Commissions (e.g. the Clegg Commission) a less overt form of state intervention, are at best short-term palliatives, not intended to produce long-term results. Even if partly successful, they would probably frustrate rather than facilitate meaningful participation in decision making at grass-roots level. Since January 1979, an establishment consensus has emerged to oppose the apparent increase in shop-floor power. James Callaghan and Margaret Thatcher have each expressed their concern at this development with equal conviction. The TUC widely circulated a Code of Practice which, in essence, exhorts the membership to refrain from action. The media as a whole have enthusiastically supported demands to curb trade union power at grass-roots level and the Conservative Government, elected in May 1979, is pledged to secure this objective. Such a climate is hardly conducive to the meaningful extension of industrial democracy.

The desirability and extent of state intervention through the legislative process into the area of industrial relations — mainly intended to curb shop-floor power — is the subject matter of a protracted debate which has been conducted over the past decade. Suggestions are frequently made that British industrial relations should be remodelled to conform more closely to the German and Swedish pattern. But for historical reasons — mainly to do with the sheer size and the deep-rooted independent traditions of the British Shop Steward movement — this is not a viable option for the foreseeable future.

For these reasons alone *Henry Friedman* holds the rather unfashionable view amongst trade unionists that an extension of industrial democracy, within the restricted meaning of the current debate, is not a realistic option at Ford. Since most companies employing over 100 people are multi-plant enterprises, the concentration of capital in the private sector and the increasing reliance on state funds for technical and scientific research and for investment in ailing firms, such as those in the aerospace and shipbuilding industries, makes centralised planning and decision making inevitable. However well entrenched they may be, shop-floor organisations are essentially defensive bodies, set up to protect and, where possible, to advance sectional interests. Their frequently conflicting priorities override their allegiance to any central organisation, whether it be their employers, the state or even their own institutions, such as the TUC or Labour Party. They frequently assert their 'sectional interests' against the 'common good' — as, for example, when Ford workers oppose the Labour Government's pay policy or when British Leyland craftsmen oppose the Company's centralised bargaining structure. These actions tend to invoke authoritarian responses — government sanctions in the case of Ford and threatened plant closures at British Leyland. The difficulty which confronts those concerned, of course, is the question of who defines and determines the 'common good'?

From his own experience, *Henry Friedman* believes that, quite apart from the historical development of British rank-and-file organisations, the size effect of multi-plant structures and the emergence of multinational companies, coupled with the multiplicity of British unions, present formidable obstacles to the extension of industrial democracy — as distinct from attempts to coerce, cajole and manipulate the rank and file for the purpose of endorsing major policy decisions in which they themselves have not been meaningfully involved. For example, in the Ford context, an extension of industrial democracy would not mean that trade unions would share the decisions on plant closures or where to locate new plants, or on Company finance, marketing, pricing or product development, or on the appropriate differential between, say, the Managing Director and the man on the assembly line. The way in which Ford, in the early part of 1979, induced the Governments of Austria, France, Portugal and Spain to engage in competitive bidding in an effort to attract Ford's proposed investment in a new assembly plant, offers an example of the difficulty likely to face trade unionists in Europe who seek a voice in the fundamental decision-making process of multinational companies. The acquisition of all the Chrysler UK car plants by Peugeot-Citroen in the latter part of 1978 and the total exclusion of trade unions from these take-over negotiations further serve to underline the extent of this problem.

But grappling with problems of this magnitude, including the closing of ranks by the establishment against shop-floor organisations, is a familiar experience to those active in the rank-and-file movement at Ford since the end of the war. Ford workers and their representatives have learned to cope with this situation and others will learn by their example. The central lessons which have emerged from the sum total of these experiences and which are of relevance to other rank-and-file organisations are the need (1) for increased self-reliance and (2) for a more thoughtful and systematic exercise of shop-floor power. At Ford, the shop floor has learned to create more effective rank-and-file organisations, such as Combine Committees, and the rank-and-file leaders have developed and strengthened the links between such organisations at local, regional, national and international level.

If *Henry Friedman* takes a more pessimistic view than *Sander Meredeen* on the likely achievement of more co-operative relationships in Ford of Britain, their views are less divergent on the future of the British system of industrial relations in general. From their experience of industrial conflict and the lessons learned at Ford, they are led to conclude that no lasting benefits can be derived from the introduction of further major legislative measures, intended to bring about the fundamental changes required in the British system of industrial relations. The Thatcher Government's proposals[4] for introducing fresh legislation to deal with the closed shop, secondary picketing, secret ballots and the withholding of social security benefits and tax rebates from strikers and their families will do nothing to improve the quality of industrial relations at the workplace. Good industrial relations — the anticipation, avoidance and resolution of industrial conflict — are too important to be entrusted to the law courts. They must be achieved from within, as in the case of Ford of Britain. What's good for Ford is not necessarily good for the rest of Britain. But where 'Ford leads the way', others may choose to follow and to learn some of the lessons from Ford's experience in the management of industrial conflict and co-operation.

Although the authors do not advance specific solutions for particular problems, they are convinced that the actors in the British system of industrial relations must evolve their own solutions along the lines already indicated. For there can be no doubt of the critical importance of industrial relations in maintaining political stability and in furthering economic and social development. The advent of a new Conservative Government in May 1979 opened a new chapter in the history of Britain's post-war industrial relations. There is no lack of problems to be solved: the application of new technology based on micro-processors; the need for long-term policies to deal with the secular decline in employment; the search for greater equity in the distribution of wealth and incomes; the need to bring inflation under greater control and to restore Britain's flagging economy against the background of rising world commodity prices; and the international energy crisis. Such problems, amongst others, will ensure that industrial relations remain the central concern of governments, employers, trade unions, producers and consumers in the 1980s.

Notes

1. Clark Kerr *et al., Industrialism and Industrial Man* (Harvard University Press, Cambridge, 1960).
2. See Ch. 7, pp. 266-7.
3. *Ford News,* 1 December 1978.
4. See Employment Act 1980, forthcoming. For a critical analysis of the Bill and the likely consequences of the Act, see Roy Lewis, Paul Davies and K.W. Wedderburn, *Industrial Relations Law and the Conservative Government* (NCLC Publishing Society, October 1979).

POSTSCRIPT

The 1979 Pay Claim and the 1979/80 Agreement

Ford's 1978/79 Agreement, discussed at length in Chapter 9, ran for a 12-month period and was due to expire at midnight on 23 November 1979. A settlement was reached on the 1979/80 Agreement just a few hours before the old contract expired.

On 16 November 1979, the Trade Unions had submitted a three-part claim for: (1) increases in the basic rates of pay; (2) shorter working time; (3) better pensions. The claim for increased pay consisted of four elements: (i) £30 per week flat increase in basic rates; (ii) consolidation of the Supplementary Payments introduced in 1978; (iii) a threshold agreement linking additional payments with increases in the retail price index or a re-opener clause entitling the Unions to apply for more money before the expiry of the new 12-month Agreement; and (iv) the introduction of a special production line workers' allowance to compensate them for the severity of assembly track work. The claim for shorter working time took the unusual form of (a) reduction in annual working hours, with no loss of earnings, equivalent to a 35-hour week; (b) an increase in annual holiday entitlement by length of service; (c) the introduction of a sabbatical leave scheme. In addition, the Unions wanted to see major improvements in the Company's occupational pension scheme for hourly-paid workers: (i) optional retirement on full pension at age 60; and (ii) full pension rights after 30 years completed service, regardless of age.

In response to this claim – which the Company alleged would increase its labour costs by a 'suicidal' 65 per cent if met in full – Ford initially offered to raise pay levels by an average of about 16 per cent – an offer which was immediately rejected by the Unions. When negotiations resumed on 23 November, the Company improved its offer, first to 18.25 per cent and finally to 21.5 per cent. In addition, Ford offered: (1) a negotiated reduction in working time to become effective from November 1980; (2) an average increase of £1.50 in the weekly Supplementary Payments; (3) increased weekly per capita lay-off credits; (4) pay-related improvements in the annual holiday bonus, ranging from £25 to £40 per worker, dependent on grade and service. The Company rejected the Union claim for (i) a line workers' allowance; (ii) threshold payments; (iii) consolidation of Supplementary Payments; and (iv) substantial pension improvements. The Company made its final offer conditional upon the Unions' acceptance of a new agreement for 1979/80 containing clauses providing for (a) no further economic demands and a 'freeze' on occupational up-gradings during the life of the Agreement; and (b) Union agreement to a Joint Statement on the achievement of manufacturing efficiency and the introduction of new technology.

The Trade Unions recommended the Company's final offer to their members for acceptance and all 24 Ford plants returned an overwhelming vote in favour shortly afterwards. There was no reported unofficial action at any of the plants in favour of rejecting the offer. Consequently, the new hourly pay rates — ranging from £2.23 for Grade B production workers to £2.60 for Grade E craftsmen — became effective on 24 November 1979, giving the biggest single group of Ford workers — some 25,000 in Grade B — increases of £15 per week (i.e. from £74.52 to £89.52) plus a further £5 Supplementary Payment for every week they were not on strike. For those Grade B workers on fortnightly alternating day and night shifts — the commonest pattern of working amongst Ford production workers — the increases amounted to just over £19 per week (i.e. from £90.42 to £109.44) including Supplementary Payment but excluding overtime.

How is this new Agreement to be interpreted? First, the settlement was reached fairly quickly because both sides were evidently anxious to avoid another damaging strike on the lines of the 9-week stoppage of 1978. Second, although Ford's Chairman and Managing Director, Sir Terence Beckett, attributed the improvement in Ford's 1978/79 performance to what he described as 'a sharp reduction in the number of stoppages' (*Financial Times,* 20 December 1979) the Company failed to publish the figures to substantiate this claim. Whilst Ford is entitled to some credit for the fact that, in the 12 months following the 1978 strike, it captured no less than 28 per cent of a record UK car market, its record sales of 485,559 units for the year must be put into some perspective: for no less than 237,000 of these vehicles — roughly half of all newly-registered Ford cars — were assembled at Ford plants *outside* the UK and so contributed to the 54 per cent 'foreign-made' penetration of the UK car market in 1979. Third, there is no evidence of complacency on either side of the bargaining table: the Unions achieved what their chief negotiator, Ron Todd, described as 'a considerable measure of success in terms of basic wages . . . and a considerable milestone in terms of shorter working time' (*The Times,* 24 November 1979). There is little doubt that the Unions will continue to press their claim for a special allowance for line workers and the consolidation of the Supplementary Payments. Conversely, Ford implicitly demonstrated its belief that these Supplementary Payments had played a valuable part in reducing the incidence of work stoppages by increasing their value in 1979/80. Furthermore, it has insisted on obtaining — and has secured — Union acceptance of a further Joint Statement (which invites comparison with earlier Joint Statements on the Achievement of Efficiency, q.v.) pledging moral commitment to sustaining efficiency and accepting the new technology.

Finally, it is interesting to note that, although Ford had strenuously resisted Union demands for a shorter working week for many years — despite the fact that it introduced a 40-hour week of its own volition as long ago as 1926! — the determination of the Ford Unions to achieve a breakthrough at Ford in 1979/80 was greatly strengthened by the Engineering Employers' Federation's concession in October 1979 of a 39-hour week for 1.25 million workers in federated engineering establishments in September 1981. By insisting that the new Agreement on 'shorter working time' becomes effective at Ford from *November 1980,* the Unions have once again demonstrated that 'Ford leads the way'.

Following the Ford Agreement, the CBI came forward with the 'novel suggestion' that working hours might be calculated on an 'annual time basis', instead of on a weekly basis. This suggestion was one of six proposals on employment and productivity, tabled by the CBI for discussion with the government and the TUC in an attempt to generate 2.5 million new jobs in the 1980s and to make industry more profitable. Taking its lead again from Ford, the CBI also wanted agreements on increasing productivity, improving the work of the labour market, a more flexible retirement age and improved employee communications (Confederation of British Industry, 'Jobs — Facing the Future', January 1980).

HF/SM
28 January 1980

WHO'S WHO
An Alphabetical Listing of Principal Names
Appearing in the Text

Atkinson, Ken	Secretary, Scamp Court of Inquiry
Baker, Ken	National Officer, GMWU
	Chairman, CSEU, 1979-
Barnes (Sir) Denis	Permanent Secretary, Dept of Employment, 1968-73
	Chairman, Manpower Services Commission, 1974/6
Barber, John	Director of Finance, FMC Ltd, 1962-5
	Deputy Chairman and Managing Director, British Leyland, 1973-5
Batty (Sir) William	Managing Director, FMC Ltd, 1968-73
	Chairman, FMC Ltd, 1972-5
Beckett (Sir) Terence	Managing Director, FMC Ltd, 1974-
	Chairman, FMC Ltd, 1976-
Benn, Tony	Labour MP Bristol, (South East)
	Secretary of State for Trade and Industry, 1964-70
Birch, Reg	Executive Councilman, AUEW, Division 7
	Secretary, Trade Union Side, NJNC, 1969-79
	Chairman, Communist Party of Gt Britain (Marxist-Leninist)
Blake, Fred	District Officer, NUVB
	District Officer, TGWU
	National Secretary, NJACCWER
Blakeman, Leslie	Labour Relations Manager, FMC Ltd, 1953-66
	Director, Labour Relations, FMC Ltd, 1966-9
	Member, CIR, 1970-1
Boland, Rosie	Trim Shop Steward, River Plant, Dagenham
Booth, Albert	Labour MP Barrow-in-Furness, 1966-
	Secretary of State for Employment, 1976-9
Boyd (Sir) John	General Secretary, AUEW, 1975-
Butler, Joyce	Labour MP Wood Green, 1955-74
Callaghan, James	Labour MP Cardiff, 1945-
	Prime Minister, 1975-9
Cameron (Lord) John	Judge of the Court of Session (Scotland)
	Chairman, Court of Inquiry, 1957
Cannon (Sir) Leslie	President, ETU, 1963-70
Carron (Lord) William	President AEU, 1956-67
Castle, Barbara	Labour MP Blackburn, 1955-79
	First Secretary of State and Secretary of State for Employment and Productivity, 1968-70
	Leader, Labour Representatives European Assembly, 1979-
Chapple, Frank	General Secretary, EETPU
Charles, HRH Prince	Heir to the Throne
Citrine (Lord) Walter	General Secretary, TUC, 1926-46
Collard, Bill	Dagenham Operations Manager, FMC Ltd, 1967-
	Member, Company Side, NJNC

Connell, Joan	DATA Delegate to TUC Equal Pay Conference, 1969
Connor, Danny	Dagenham Body Plant Convener
Conway, Jim	General Secretary, AUEW, 1960-74
	Secretary, Trade Union Side, NJNC, 1960-9
Cooper (Lord) Jack	General Secretary, GMWU, 1962-73
Copp, Robert	Overseas Liaison Manager, Labor Relations Staff, Ford US
Cornwell, Doug	National Officer, AUEW (Foundry Section)
Cousins, Frank	General Secretary, TGWU, 1956-68
Cross, Stan	Halewood Operations Manager, FMC Ltd, 1966-70
	Member, Company Side, NJNC
Davies (Sir) John	Director General, CBI, 1965-9
	Conservative MP Knutsford, 1970-8
Donnelly, Mick	Convener, Halewood Paint Trim and Assembly Plant
Donovan (Lord) Terence	Lord of Appeal in Ordinary
	Chairman, Royal Commission on Trade Unions and Employers' Assocns. 1965-8
Doughty (Sir) Charles	Chairman, Court of Inquiry, 1941
Duff, Neil	Vice-President, Industrial Relations, FOE, 1972-4
Duffy, Patrick	Labour MP Sheffield, 1970-
	Chairman, Trade and Industry Sub-Committee, House of Commons Expenditure Committee, Session 1974-5
Duffy, Terence	President, AUEW, 1978-
East, Ann	Member, Trimshop Committee, River Plant, Dagenham
Evans, Moss	National Officer, TGWU (Automotive) 1969-78
	Chairman, Trade Union Side, NJNC, 1969-78
	General Secretary, TGWU, 1978-
Feather (Lord) Victor	General Secretary, TUC, 1968-73
Ford, Henry (I)	Founder, Ford Motor Company
Ford, Henry (II)	President, Ford Motor Company
Friedman, Henry	Convener, River Plant, Dagenham, 1962-72
Francis, Bill	Shop Steward, Dagenham Paint Trim and Assembly Plant
	Dismissed 1962
Fraser, Dave	National Officer, PTU, 1963-
	Member, Trade Union Side, NJNC
Fraser, Don	Management Consultant, Urwick, Orr and Partners
Gallagher, Charlie	Asst General Secretary, NUVB, 1965-70
	Member, Trade Union Side, NJNC
Gillen, Stan	Managing Director, FMC Ltd, 1965-8
	Chairman, FOE, 1969-71
Grange Moore, J.	Member, Scamp Court of Inquiry, 1968
	Chairman, Special Grading Committee, 1968
Halpin, Kevin	Convener, Dagenham Paint Trim and Assembly Plant
	Dismissed 1962
Harraway, Sid	Assistant Convener, Dagenham Body Plant, 1962-
Hayes, Walter	Director, Public Affairs, FMC Ltd, 1962-6

	Vice-President, Public Affairs, FOE, 1966-79
	Vice-President, Public Affairs, Ford US, 1980-
Heath, Edward	Conservative MP Bexley, 1950-
	Prime Minister, 1970-4
Hennessy (Sir) Patrick	Chairman, FMC Ltd, 1956-68
Heron, Conrad	Deputy Under Secretary of State, Dept of Employment, 1968-71
	Permanent Secretary, Dept of Employment 1973-6
Hunt, Audrey	Joint Chairman, NJACCWER
Jack (Professor) D.T.	Chairman, Court of Inquiry, 1963
Jones, Jack	General Secretary, TGWU, 1968-78
Kealey, Les	National Officer, TGWU (Automotive) 195ɔ-69
	Member, Trade Union Side, NJNC
Kendrick, Harry	District Officer, TGWU, Dagenham, 1955-70
Kirkip, Bill	National Officer, AUEW
Langston, Jack	Industrial Relations Manager, Dagenham Body Plant, 1950-78
Maguire, John	Industrial Relations Manager, Power Train Group 1966-70
Mayhew, Phil	Manager, Personnel & Organisation, FMC Ltd, 1960-9
McDougall, John	Shop Steward, Toolroom, Briggs Motor Bodies Ltd Dismissed 1941
McLoughlin, Johnny	Shop Steward, Jig and Fixtures Dept, River Plant, Dagenham
	Dismissed 1957
Meredeen, Sander	Industrial Relations Manager, Central Industrial Relations Staff FMC Ltd. 1964-75
	Member, Company Side, NJNC
Mitchell, Jack	Convener, (Briggs) Body Plant, 1953-63
	District Secretary, AUEW, South Essex District, 1963-
Moore, Les	Convener, Halewood Body Plant
Nolan, Daisy	Member, NJACCWER
Norwood, Chris	Labour MP Norwich South, 1964-70
	Joint Chairman, NJACCWER
O'Callaghan, Lil	Trim Shop Steward, River Plant, Dagenham
Passingham, Bernard	Assistant Convener, River Plant, Dagenham, 1962-72
	Convener, River Plant, Dagenham, 1972-
	Secretary, Ford National Conveners' Committee
	Member, TGWU Executive Committee
	Member, Trade Union Side, NJNC
Peel, Jack	General Secretary, National Union of Dyers, Bleachers and Textile Workers, 1960-73
	Member, Scamp Court of Inquiry, 1968
	Director, Industrial Relations, EEC, 1970-
Perry (Sir) Percival	First Chairman and Managing Director FMC Ltd, 1928-41

Prior, James
    Conservative MP Lowestoft, 1959-
        PPS to Edward Heath, 1965-70
        Leader of Commons, 1972-4
        Opposition Spokesman on employment, 1974-9
        Secretary of State for Employment, 1979-

Ramsey, Bob
    Industrial Relations Manager, FMC Ltd, 1958-69
        Director, Labour Relations, FMC Ltd, 1969-73
        Director, Industrial Relations, FMC Ltd, 1973-

Rees, Sam
    Director, Manufacture, FMC Ltd
        Vice-President, Manufacture, FOE
        Member, Company Side, NJNC

Roberts, Alf
    General Secretary, NUVB, 1960-70

Roots, Paul
    Employee Relations Director, FMC Ltd, 1975-

Ryder (Lord) Don
    Chairman, Committee of Inquiry into British
        Leyland, 1975

Scamp (Sir) Jack
    Director, Industrial Relations, General Electric Co.
        Ltd, 1960-70
        Chairman, Motor Industry Joint Labour Council,
        1965-70
        Chairman, Court of Inquiry, 1968

Scanlon (Lord) Hugh
    President, AUEW, 1968-78

Shaw, Anne
    Managing Director, Anne Shaw Associates, Manage-
        ment Consultants
        Member, Scamp Court of Inquiry, 1968

Singer, Edwin
    Management Consultant, Urwick, Orr and Partners

Smith (Sir) Rowland
    Joint Managing Director FMC Ltd, 1941-50

Summerskill (Baroness) E.
    Labour MP, Halifax
        Labour Life Peer

Taylor, Nancy
    Management Consultant, Urwick, Orr and Partners

Todd, Ron
    District Officer TGWU, Dagenham District Secretary
        National Organiser, TGWU
        Chairman, Trade Union Side, NJNC, 1978-

Walker, Harold
    Labour MP Doncaster 1964-
        Parliamentary Under Secretary of State, Dept of
        Employment, 1968-70; 1974-6
        Minister of State, Dept of Employment, 1976-9

Wilson (Sir) Harold
    Labour MP Huyton, 1945-
        Prime Minister, 1964-70; 1974-6

Wood, Gerry
    Management Consultant, Urwick, Orr and Partners

Woodward, Joan
    Professor of Industrial Sociology, Imperial College,
        London (Wife of Leslie Blakeman, q.v.)

CHRONOLOGY OF KEY EVENTS IN FORD'S INDUSTRIAL RELATIONS, 1900-1980

Year	Events Within Ford in Britain	Events Outside Ford in Britain
1903	First Detroit-built Model A's imported into Britain.	
1911	Ford Motor Company (England) registered. First Model T's assembled at Trafford Park Works, Manchester.	
1914-18		First World War.
1926	Ford introduced 5-day 40-hour week.	
1928	Ford Motor Company Limited registered.	
1931	Production began at Dagenham Works, Essex. Manchester Works phased out.	
1939		Second World War began.
1940	Ford opened 'shadow factory' near Manchester to produce Rolls Royce Merlin aircraft engines.	
1941	Doughty Court of Inquiry at Briggs Motor Bodies Ltd. Unions secured limited recognition.	United Auto Workers secured recognition from Ford US after National Labor Relations Board ballot. First Union-Management Agreement signed at Ford.
1944	Unions secured recognition from Ford in Britain. First Procedure Agreement signed. National Joint Negotiating Committee established.	
1945		Second World War ended. Labour Government elected.
1947	National fuel crisis. Mass redundancies at Dagenham.	
1951		Conservative Government elected.
1953	Ford acquired Briggs Motor Bodies Ltd. 3-week strike over wage claim.	
1955	Revised Procedure Agreement signed.	
1956	Suez crisis. Mass redundancies at Dagenham.	
1957	Major dispute following dismissal of Shop Steward. (McLoughlin.) Cameron Court of Inquiry.	
1958	Standardisation Agreement signed covering all Ford plants in Britain,	

Year	Events Within Ford in Britain	Events Outside Ford in Britain
	including Briggs.	
1961	Ford Motor Company Ltd became wholly-owned subsidiary of Ford US.	Special talks convened by Minister of Labour to discuss reforms of motor industry's labour relations. Joint Statement signed by employers and unions.
1962	Ford's first Director of Industrial Relations appointed. Major dispute following dismissal of Shop Steward at former Briggs Body Plant, Dagenham.(Francis.)	National Economic Development Council established.
1963	Jack Court of Inquiry. Forward Planning, Industrial Relations, established. Hourly-paid charge-hands discontinued. Production began at Halewood (Liverpool) Plants.	Contracts of Employment Act. Motor Industry Joint Labour Council established.
1964	First Agreement regulating Redundancy Procedures and Compensation signed.	Industrial Training Act. Labour Government elected. Statement of Intent on Productivity, Prices and Incomes.
1965	Motor Industry Joint Labour Council investigation of Dagenham Paint Sprayers' dispute.	Royal Commission(Donovan) appointed on Trade Unions and Employers' Associations. Prime Minister convened motor industry talks at Downing Street on reform of industry's labour relations. National Board for Prices and Incomes established.
1966	Crisis over Toolmakers' allowance claim. NJNC agreed to review of hourly-paid wage structure by jointly-conducted job evaluation. Ford of Europe established.	
1967	First Two-year Agreement signed, following plant productivity bargaining. Agreement incorporated new 5-grade wage structure.	
1968	Industrial Court arbitration award confirmed Company's grading of Carpenters and Joiners. Sewing Machinists' strike over pay and grading. (See separate *Strike Diary*.) Scamp Court of Inquiry.	Donovan Commission Report on Trade Unions and Employers' Associations published. Chrysler changed from piecework to measured day work.
1969	3-week strike over 'Penalty Clauses' during negotiations on	White Paper, *In Place of Strife*. Labour Relations Bill introduced

Year	Events Within Ford in Britain	Events Outside Ford in Britain
	annual wage agreement. High Court action: Ford *v.* AEF and TGWU	in Parliament, but not enacted.
1970	Ford women granted full equal pay.	Equal Pay Act on Statute Book, to take effect end-1975. Conservative Government elected.
1971	10-week strike over wage parity claim during negotiations of 2-year wage agreement.	Industrial Relations Act. TUC-Labour Party Liaison Committee formed.
1972		Government financial rescue of Rolls Royce. First miners' strike. Chequers and Downing Street Talks.
1974	Major disputes over lay-offs.	Second miners' strike. Labour (minority) Government elected. Social Contract – Stage I Industrial Relations Act 1971 repealed. Trade Union and Labour Relations Act. Labour (majority) Government elected.
1975	Further major disputes over lay-offs.	Employment Protection Act. Trade Union and Labour Relations (Amendment) Act. Health and Safety at Work Act. Equal Pay Act took effect. Sex Discrimination Act. Government financial rescue of Chrysler UK. Duffy Report on British Motor Industry. Central Policy Review Staff Report on Motor Industry. Ryder Report on British Leyland. Social Contract – Stage II.
1976	New Agreement signed on exclusive bargaining rights, 100 per cent post-entry closed shop and check-off.	White Paper, *The British Motor Vehicle Industry.*
1977	First Ford recognition of Conveners' National Committee.	Bullock Committee Report on Industrial Democracy. Social Contract – Stage III.
1978	National Joint Negotiating Committee reconstituted. All Ford Conveners admitted to NJNC.	

Year	Events Within Ford in Britain	Events Outside Ford in Britain
	9-week strike during negotiations over annual wage agreement.	
1979		Government attempt to apply sanctions against Ford for breaking unofficial 5 per cent pay guidelines. Major industrial disputes (lorry, tanker drivers, public sector workers). TUC-Labour Government 'Concordat'. Conservative Government elected. Government's Working Documents on reform of industrial relations law. Employment Bill published.
	Annual wage and shorter working time agreement signed without a strike.	TUC launched Campaign for Economic and Social Advance. EEF-CSEU agree 39-hour week by 1981. Robinson sacked by BL.

STRIKE DIARY

1968	May		June					July
Saturday	18	25	1	8	15	22	29	
Sunday	19	26	2	9	16	23	30	
Monday	20	27	3	10	17	24		1
Tuesday	21	28	4	11	18	25		2
Wednesday	22	29	5	12	19	26		3
Thursday	23	30	6	13	20	27		4
Friday	24	31	7	14	21	28		5

21 May   Sewing Machinists impose overtime ban and threaten strike on 29 May.

28 May   River Plant meeting of Shop Stewards and the Company Officials followed by further meeting at Central Office.

29 May   Sewing Machinists one-day token strike.

30 May   Company issues warning letter to strikers.
Strikers vote for further strike action on 10 June.

31 May-
4 June   Union District Officials meet Company Officials to prevent strike.

6 June   Senior Company management meets District Officials at River Plant.

7 June   Sewing Machinists begin all-out strike at Dagenham.

10 June   Strikers decide not to meet again for 2 weeks.

11 June   AEF declares strike official.

13 June   Company and Union Officials meet at York to discuss ways to end strike.

14 June   Company calls emergency meeting of NJNC for 17 June.
Company and Union Officials meet at Dept of Employment.

17 June   NJNC agrees to conduct its own Inquiry into dispute.
Halewood Sewing Machinists come out in sympathy with Dagenham strikers.

18 June   NUVB Annual Conference at Felixstowe officially supports strike.

	AEF confirms official support for strike.
	Pickets out at River Plant.
	5,000 workers laid off at Dagenham.
19 June	Secretary of State decides to appoint Court of Inquiry.
20 June	NUVB and AEF re-affirm support for strike.
22 June	Secretary of State calls Company and Union Officials to Dept of Employment to urge ending of strike.
24 June	Director of Labour Relations meets Union Official at Weymouth.
27 June	First (procedural) meeting of Court of Inquiry.
	Chairman of Inquiry urges strikers to return to work.
	Strikers vote to continue strike.
	Ford Managing Director sends telegram to Prime Minister.
28 June	Secretary of State calls in strikers, then Company and Union Officials for talks at Dept of Employment.
	Settlement formula agreed.
1 July	Strikers return to work.
	NJNC meets to ratify settlement.
3 July	Second day of Court of Inquiry.
4 July	Third day of Court of Inquiry.
21 August	Court of Inquiry Report published.
	Sewing Machinists impose overtime ban.
4 September	Special Grading Committee meets to consider Sewing Machinists' grading and confirm grading.

BIBLIOGRAPHY

In addition tb the material cited below, there is a wealth of valuable information to be found in the *Ford Blue Book* (Book of Collective Agreements and Joint Statements, issued periodically by the Ford National Joint Negotiating Committee), *Verbatim Transcripts* of the Ford National Joint Negotiating Committee, Full Transcripts of Courts of Inquiries, *Ford News* (formerly *Ford Bulletin,* both Company newspapers), Ford Motor Company Limited *Annual Reports,* Ford National Joint Negotiating Committee (Trade Union Side) *Wage Claims, Voice of the Ford Worker* (a rank-and-file news-sheet) and various left-wing pamphlets which appear during wage contract negotiations and major strikes.

Asquith (Sir) Cyril, *Report of the Royal Commission on Equal Pay (1944-46)* (the Asquith Commission Report), Cmd. 6937 (HMSO, London, 1946)

Atkin (Sir) James, *Report of the War Cabinet Committee on Women in Industry* (the Atkin Committee Report), Cmd. 135 (HMSO, London, 1919)

Beynon, Huw, *Working for Ford* (Penguin, Harmondsworth, 1973)

Birch, Reg, *Guerrilla Struggle and the Working Class* (Communist Party of Britain (Marxist-Leninist), London, 1973)

Braverman, Harry, *Labor and Monopoly Capital* (Monthly Review Press, New York, 1974)

Cameron (Lord), *Report of a Court of Inquiry* (the Cameron Report), Cmnd. 131 (HMSO, London, 1957)

Castle, Barbara, *Diaries* (Weidenfeld and Nicolson, London, 1980)

Central Policy Review Staff, *The Future of the British Car Industry* (HMSO, London, 1975)

Clegg, Hugh (Chairman), *Standing Committee on Pay Comparability Reports,* Cmnd. 7640/7641 (HMSO, London, 1979)

———, *Pay Comparability Commission Reports* (HMSO, London, 1979/80)

Cole, G.D.H. and Postgate, Raymond, *The Common People* (Methuen, London, 1938)

Copp, Robert C., *Locus of Management Decisions in Industrial Relations in Multinationals,* Conference Papers on Industrial Relations Problems raised by Multinationals in Advanced Industrial Societies (Michigan State University, November 1974)

—— 'The Labor Affairs Function in a Multinational Firm', Proceedings of the 1973 Annual Spring Meeting of the Industrial Relations Research Association, *Labor Law Journal* (August 1973)

Department of Economic Affairs, *Statement on Productivity, Prices and Incomes* (HMSO, London, 1964)

Donovan (Lord), *Report of Royal Commission on Trade Unions and Employers' Associations* (the Donovan Commission Report), Cmnd. 6323 (HMSO, London, 1968)

Doughty (Sir) George, *Report of a Court of Inquiry* (the Doughty Report), Cmd. 6284 (HMSO, London, 1941)

Duffy, Patrick, *Report (14th) from the Expenditure Committee of the House of Commons (Industry and Trade Sub-Committee)* (the Duffy Committee Report), House of Commons Paper 617 (Session 1974/75)

Dunlop, John T., *Industrial Relations Systems* (Holt, New York, 1958)

Equal Opportunities Commission, *Annual Reports* (1976 – to date)

——, *Equality Between the Sexes in Industry – How Far Have We Come?* (HMSO, London, 1978)

——, Report on Electrolux Limited (HMSO, London, 1980)

Flanders, Allan, *Management and Unions* (Faber, London, 1970)

Ford, Henry, *My Life and Works* (New York, 1922)

Ford Motor Company Limited, *A Study in Practical Sociology* (Dagenham, 1937)

——, *Evidence to the Committee of Inquiry on Industrial Democracy* (the Bullock Committee) (3 March 1976)

Ford National Joint Negotiating Committee (Trade Union Side), *Wage Claims* (1970 – to date)

Fox, Alan, *Beyond Contract: Work, Power and Trust Relations* (Faber, London, 1973)

Friedman, Andrew L., *Industry and Labour* (Macmillan, London, 1977)

Friedman, Henry, 'Multi-Plant Working and Trade Union Organisation', *Studies for Trade Unionists,* vol. II, no. 8 (Workers' Education Association, London, 1976)

Gramsci, Antonio, 'Americanism and Fordism', *Prison Notebooks* (Lawrence and Wishart, London, 1971)

Heller, Robert, 'Ford Motor's Managing Machine', *Management Today* (London, February 1968)

Hennessy (Sir) Patrick, *Paper No. 159,* Seminar in Industrial Administration, London School of Economics and Political Science (30

November 1954)

Hobsbawm, E.J., 'Custom, Wages and Work-Load in Nineteenth Century Industry' in Asa Briggs and John Saville (eds.) *Essays in Labour History* (Macmillan, London, 1960)

Hunt, Audrey, *A Survey on Women's Employment,* Department of Employment and Productivity (HMSO, London, 1968)

Hunt, Judith, 'Organising Women Workers', *Studies for Trade Unionists,* vol. I, No. 3 (Workers' Education Association, London, 1975)

Hyman, Richard and Brough, Ian, *Social Values and Industrial Relations: A Study of Fairness and Inequality* (Blackwell, Oxford, 1975)

Industrial Court, *Report No. 3167: Grading of (Ford) Carpenters and Joiners* (HMSO, London, 1968)

Institute of Personnel Management, *Guide to Job Evaluation* (London, 1968)

International Labour Organisation, *Conventions and Recommendations adopted by the ILO* (Geneva, 1960)

——, *Fighting Discrimination in Employment and Occupations* (Geneva, 1968)

Jack, D.T., *Report of a Court of Inquiry* (the Jack Report), Cmnd. 1999 (HMSO, London, 1963).

Kerr, Clark *et al.*, *Industrialism and Industrial Man* (Harvard University Press, Cambridge, 1960)

Kujawa, Duane, *International Labor Relations Management in the Automotive Industry* (Praeger Publications, New York, 1971)

Lane, Tony and Roberts, Kenneth, *Strike at Pilkingtons* (Fontana, London, 1971)

Lewis, Roy, 'The Legal Enforceability of Collective Agreements', *British Journal of Industrial Relations,* vol. III, no. 3 (November 1970)

——, 'Collective Agreements: The Kahn-Freund Legacy', *Modern Law Review* (November 1979)

——, Davies, Paul and Wedderburn, K.W., *Industrial Relations Law and the Conservative Government* (NCLC Publishing Society, October 1979)

Livy, Brian, *Job Evaluation* (Allen and Unwin, London, 1975)

McKersie, R.B., 'A Behavioural Analysis of Productivity Bargaining', Public lecture, *London* School of Economics and Political Science, 8 March 1966

Mann, Michael, *Consciousness and Action among the Western Working Class* (Macmillan, London, 1973)

Matthews, J., *The 1971 Ford Strike* (Panther Books, London, 1972)

Meredeen, Sander, 'Sex Discrimination in Britain: A Provisional Evaluation', *Sociologie du Travail* (forthcoming)

Motor Industry Employers, *Evidence to Royal Commission on Trade Unions etc.* (London, 1965)

Motor Industry Joint Labour Council, *Report on First Year's Activities* (HMSO, London, 1966)

——, *Report of an Inquiry into Paint Sprayers' Dispute* (HMSO, London, 1966)

National Board for Prices and Incomes, *Report No. 83: Job Evaluation*, Cmnd. 3722 (HMSO, London, 1965)

National Economic Development Council, *Management Training in Industrial Relations* (HMSO, London, 1975)

National Incomes Commission, *Report No. 4 (Final)*, Cmnd. 2583 (HMSO, London, 1965)

Nevins, Allan, *Henry Ford: the Times, the Man, the Company* (Charles Scribner's Sons, New York, 1954)

——, and Hill, Frank Ernest, *Ford – Decline and Rebirth, 1933-1962* (Charles Scribner's Sons, New York, 1964)

O'Leary J.G., *The Book of Dagenham* (Borough of Dagenham, 1963)

Passingham, Bernie and Connor, Danny, *Ford Shop Stewards on Industrial Democracy* (Institute for Workers' Control, 1977)

Red Notes, *Little Red Blue Book* (Red Notes Publications, London 1978)

Reid, Judith, 'Women in Employment', *Modern Law Journal*, vol. 39 (July 1977)

Roberts, B.C. 'Multinational Enterprise and Labor' in P. Doeringer (ed.), *Industrial Relations Research in International Perspective* (Harvard University Press, forthcoming)

Ryder (Lord), *British Leyland – The Next Decade* (the Ryder Report) (HMSO, London, 1975)

Scamp (Sir) Jack, *Paper No. 376*, Seminar on Problems in Industrial Administration, London School of Economics and Political Science (26 November 1966)

——, *Report of a Court of Inquiry* (the Scamp Report), Cmnd. 3749 (HMSO, London, 1968)

Sloan, Alfred P., *My Years with General Motors* (Sidgwick and Jackson, London, 1963)

Solidarity, *What Happened at Ford?* Pamphlet no. 26 (Solidarity Publications, London, 1967)

Stafford, A., *A Match to Fire the Thames* (Hodder and Stoughton, London, 1961)

Stieber, Jack, *The Steel Industry Wage Structure* (Harvard University Press, 1959)

Taylor, A.L.T. (ed.), *Job Evaluation* (British Institute of Management, London, 1970)

Trades Union Congress, *Job Evaluation* (1964)

——, *The Government, the Economy and Trade Union Responsibilities* (the *Concordat*), 1979

Turner, H.A., Clack, G. and Roberts, G., *Labour Relations in the Motor Industry* (Allen and Unwin, London, 1967)

Walton, R.E. and McKersie, R.B., *A Behavioural Theory of Labor Negotiations* (McGraw Hill, New York, 1965)

Webb, Sidney and Beatrice, *Industrial Democracy* (Longman, London, 1902)

White Paper, *In Place of Strife,* Cmnd. 3888 (HMSO, London, 1969)

——, *The British Motor Vehicle Industry,* Cmnd. 6377 (HMSO, London, 1976)

Wilkins, Mira and Hill, Frank Ernest, *American Business Abroad – Ford on Six Continents* (Wayne State University Press, Detroit, 1967)

Young, T., *Becontree and Dagenham,* Report to the Pilgrims Trust (London, 1934)